The Zohar

TRANSLATED BY HARRY SPERLING AND MAURICE SIMON

FIVE VOLUMES

I

WITH AN INTRODUCTION BY
DR. J. ABELSON

All rights are reserved. No portion of this work may be reproduced, stored in a retrieval system, or transmitted in any form or by any means, electronic, mechanical, photocopying, recording, or otherwise, without the prior written permission of the copyright holder.

© Copyright 1962 by Soncino Press.

Published by Parker Publishing Company

www.parkerpub.co

Contact us: info@parkerpub.co

CONTENTS

Introduction   *page* ix

Translators' Preface   xxix

Prologue   3

Bereshith   63

Noah   192

Lech Lecha   260

Vayera   321

Appendices
   I. On the Zoharic Exposition of the
      First Chapter of Genesis   379
   II. Hebrew Alphabet   386

Glossary
   Hebrew and Technical Terms in Vol. I   387

INTRODUCTION

If the world's literature holds any book which might truly be described as being sealed with seven seals, that book is the *Zohar*. What with the difficulties and obscurities clustering round its origin and authorship, what with the baffling obscurities of its language, style, and contents, and what with the problems that must inevitably be presented by a book which is not a homogeneous work but a compilation pieced together at times and under circumstances which are by no means clear, the task of bringing out, for the first time, a complete English translation needs not only learning but much moral courage as well.

No one will deny that an English rendering of such a pivotal Hebrew work as the *Zohar* is long overdue. For the *Zohar* is the fundamental book of Jewish Cabbalism. It is the premier text-book of medieval Jewish mysticism. If, as Professor Rufus Jones has so finely said, 'mysticism is religion in its most acute, intense, and living stage', then it follows that Jewish mysticism as enshrined and taught in the *Zohar* represents Judaism in its 'most acute, intense, and living stage'. This is no small prerogative. But how are both Jews and Christians to get to know these quintessential characteristics of the Jewish religion if they are locked up and secreted in a book whose language, style, and contents no one but a deeply accomplished Hebraist can comprehend? As a matter of fact, Jews are not infrequently blamed for what is regarded on their part as some mysterious desire to keep their spiritual and literary treasures all to themselves, stored away in the trappings of a strange language like Rabbinic Hebrew or Aramaic, and hence inaccessible to the average honest seeker after knowledge. This translation will, it is to be hoped, serve to remedy the defect as well as to roll away the implied reproach.

The *Zohar* is in form a Commentary on the Pentateuch, and its language is partly Aramaic and partly Hebrew. It purports to be a record of discourses carried on between Rabbi Simeon ben Yohai, who lived in the second century of the common era, and certain contemporary Jewish mystical exegetes. There is a story in the Talmud that Simeon and his son, in order to escape the fury of the Roman persecution, hid themselves in a cave for thirteen years, during which they gave themselves up to those mystical speculations on God, Torah, and the universe which compose the *Zohar*. Simeon came thus to be regarded as the author of the *Zohar*. But scholarship and research have forced us to dismiss this supposition as nothing more than legend. Even the most superficial perusal of any section of the *Zohar* will convince the reader of the absurdity of this view of its high antiquity. The merest tyro in Rabbinic literature will find in the *Zohar* a great many Rabbinic comments and observations which belong without question to a period (and periods) later than that in which Simeon ben Yohai lived. A legend of a more elaborate type, and one which modern critics have been much more ready to accept, attributes the *Zohar* to a thirteenth-century Cabbalistic writer, Moses de Leon, of Granada in Spain, who certainly was the first to make it known to the general public. Moses de Leon published the *Zohar* as the work of Simeon ben Yohai, professing to have transcribed the copies which he issued from an ancient manuscript which had come into his possession. After his death, however, his widow confessed that her husband possessed no such manuscript, and that he wrote the work himself. When asked why he did not publish the book in his own name but chose that of Simeon ben Yohai, she replied that her husband always said that a book by a miracle-working Rabbi like Simeon ben Yohai would prove more lucrative than a book bearing his own name.

Though the widow's story bristles with contradictions and absurdities, many Jewish writers and scholars have maintained that de Leon was the sole author of the *Zohar*. On the other hand, many books have been written, mainly in Hebrew, to show that the *Zohar* is a work of great antiquity and that its authorship can very properly and suitably be attributed to the ancient Sage, Simeon ben Yohai. But neither of these views can hold water in the light of all the facts as we know them. No student of the *Zohar*, indeed no competent assessor of literature generally, can believe that it ever could have emanated from the brain of one man. To call it a book is to misname it. It is a literature—a literature of immense variety and compass. It embraces so many diverse themes, it holds within its folds such a number of views and doctrines which are often mutually irreconcilable, that it cannot possibly be the production of one individual, however gifted. And to credit a Rabbi of the second century with the authorship of a book which describes the sayings and doings of men who lived long after his time, is to adopt a standpoint which no one in these times will seriously countenance.

The *Zohar* is a congeries of treatises, texts, extracts or fragments of texts, belonging to different periods, but all resembling one another in their method of mystical interpretation of the Torah as well as in the baffling anonymity in which they are shrouded. The ways in which these component parts are pieced together strikes one as arbitrary in the extreme. They often appear to bear little or no relation to that which precedes or follows. The arrangement is all so destitute of design that it might have been done by the printers and publishers of the first edition whenever they felt that it suited their convenience or whenever they happened to come across some anonymous fragments which, in their unlearned opinion, could be suitably interpolated at a certain point in the main text.

From a survey of the whole subject, one is drawn irresistibly to the conclusion that the *Zohar*, so far from being a homogeneous work, is a compilation of a mass of material drawn from many strata of Jewish and non-Jewish mystical thought and covering numerous centuries. Many of both its fundamental and subsidiary teachings are to be found in the oldest portions of the Babylonian and Palestinian Talmuds, as well as in that large mass of Jewish Apocalyptic literature which was produced in the centuries immediately before and after the destruction of the second Temple. Discussions on Jewish law and Biblical interpretations (which are often almost verbal repetitions of passages to be found in the two recensions of the Talmud), speculations on theology, theosophy, and cosmogony which have their counterpart in Hellenistic literature and which sometimes show resemblances to certain ideas contained in the Zend Avesta—a fact which has induced some scholars to find a good deal of the background of the *Zohar* in the religion of ancient Zoroastrianism—the allegorical type of exegesis of which Philo is the leading exponent, Gnostic theories concerning the relation between the human and the divine, echoes of medieval beliefs regarding astrology, physiognomy, necromancy, magic, and metempsychosis which are alien to the Jewish spirit, all these elements jostle one another at random in the pages of the *Zohar*. A veritable storehouse of anachronisms, incongruities and surprises!

And yet, with all its faults, the *Zohar* appeals to many Jews in a way that makes them regard it as the most sacred of sacred books! For it mirrors Judaism as an intensely vital religion of the spirit. More overpoweringly than any other book or code, more even than the Bible, does it give to the Jew the conviction of an inner, unseen, spiritual universe—an eternal moral order.

The constituent parts of the *Zohar* are as follows: There is (i) the main portion which bears the general title of '*Sefer Ha-Zohar*'. To this are attached (ii) the '*Sifra-di-Tseniuta*' ('The Book of the Veiled Mystery'), consisting of five chapters inserted in the Book of Exodus and dealing with the mysteries of creation, the human soul and the relation between spirit and matter. (iii) '*Sitré Torah*' ('Secrets of the Torah'), treating largely of Cabbalistic angelology and the mysteries clustering round the Divine Name and the Divine Unity. (iv) '*Ra'ya Mehemna*' ('The True Shepherd', *Pastor Fidelis*), which, besides dealing with topics similar to the foregoing, lays down definite precepts and rules of conduct, the exegesis being usually introduced with the words 'The true shepherd saith'—the true shepherd being Moses. (v) '*Midrash Ha-ne'lam*' ('Recondite Exposition'), which contains a great deal of Scriptural exposition by the method of 'Gematria', i.e. the permutations and combinations of the letters of the Hebrew alphabet and the Hebrew numerals. It also contains some allegorical exegesis of Scripture reminding one of the methods of Philo. (vi) '*Tosefta*' ('Additions'), some stray fragmentary supplements to the main exegesis of the *Zohar* in which are contained references to the *Sefiroth*.

(vii) *'Hekaloth'* ('halls' or 'palaces'), wherein are pictured with a dazzling literality the abodes of paradise and hell, the dwelling-places of the varying grades of the angelic hosts and their dealings with the souls of men. There are also in this section several recondite allusions to astrology and magic. (viii) The *Idra Rabba* ('Greater Synod') and *Idra Zuta* ('Lesser Synod'), which are amplifications of (ii). Speaking generally, none of these sections can be said to differ very greatly from any other or from the main body of the *Zohar*, either in style or contents. There is considerable overlapping. There is also a frequent repetition of the same theme, the same treatment, even the same words.

The first printed edition of the *Zohar* appeared almost simultaneously in two different places, viz. Mantua and Cremona, in 1588–90. Later editions are those of Lublin, 1623; Amsterdam, 1714 and 1805; Constantinople, 1736; and Venice. The Mantua edition, with a long and elaborate Introduction by Isaac de Lattes, has always had the greatest vogue, nearly all subsequent editions being based upon the Mantua text. An interesting fact is that almost simultaneously with the publication of the first Mantua edition—but to all appearance quite independently of it—there was issued from the same press the *Tikkuné Ha-Zohar* ('Emendations to the Zohar'), a book written in Aramaic and with the same kind of subject-matter as the *Zohar*. Another similar work which has always enjoyed great popularity, and which first saw the light at Salonika in 1597, is the *Zohar Hadash* ('The New Zohar'), which is an independent mystical commentary on the same lines as the *Zohar*, but embracing, in addition to the Pentateuch, the 'Five *Megilloth*' (Scrolls), viz. the Song of Songs, Ruth, Lamentations, Ecclesiastes, and Esther.

The *Zohar* humbly professes to be no more than a Commentary on the Pentateuch; and it might hence be interesting to hear its own expressed views on the correct method of Biblical exegesis. It says: 'Woe unto those who see in the Law nothing but simple narratives and ordinary words! Were this really the case, then could we, even to-day, compose a Law equally worthy of admiration. But it is all quite otherwise.... Every word of the Law contains an elevated sense and a sublime mystery. . . . The narratives of the Law are but the raiment in which it is swathed. Woe unto him who mistakes the raiment for the Law itself! It was to avert such a calamity that David prayed, "Open mine eyes that I might behold wondrous things out of thy Law".' Another passage states similarly, but even more strikingly: 'If the Law merely consisted of ordinary words and narratives like the stories of Esau, Hagar, and Laban, or like the words which were spoken by Balaam's ass or by Balaam himself, why should it have been called the Law of Truth, the perfect Law, the faithful testimony of God?'

These statements may well be regarded as a sort of rationale of the aim and purpose of the Zoharic exegesis; and they summarise the basic characteristics of all schools of Cabbalistic interpretation, both before and after the *Zohar*. Indeed, herein may be said to lie the undying service which Cabbalism has rendered to Judaism, whether as creed or as life. A too literal interpretation of the words of Scripture giving Judaism the appearance of being nothing more than an ordered legalism, an apotheosis of the 'letter which killeth', a formal and petrified system of external commands bereft of all spirit and denying all freedom to the individual—these have been, and are still in some quarters, the blemishes and shortcomings cast in the teeth of Rabbinic Judaism. The supreme rebutter of such taunts and objections is Cabbalah. The arid field of Rabbinism was always kept well watered and fresh by the living streams of Cabbalistic lore. Mystic schools and mystic circles flourished at nearly every important epoch of Jewish history, and the object of their studies was to penetrate to the true meaning hidden beneath the letter of Scripture. Some of the foremost Jewish legalists were also pronounced Cabbalists. And this esoteric study of the Law which is the quintessence of Cabbalah gave to its devotees not a shackled creed comprehended in formulæ, but a religion of intense spiritual possibilities, rendering the Jew capable of a vivid sense of the nearness of God and filling him with a constant longing for communion with Him.

Illustrations of the way in which the *Zohar* penetrates the outer shell of Scripture in order to extract the esoteric kernel within could be quoted, did not space forbid, in great abundance. I will only refer here to some specimens of Zoharic exegesis on the Psalms which are frequently interspersed in the exegesis on the Pentateuchal books. Thus, Psalm XXXIII, 6, says: 'By the word of the Lord were the heavens made; and all the hosts of them by the breath of his mouth.' This verse gives the impetus to a whole series of mystic axioms proving that the world rests on Divine spirit. The 'upper universe' resembles the 'lower universe', and both find their unity in God. Earth is a copy of Heaven. Heaven is a copy of earth. They are no duality but an absolute unity. Any other view of the universe is irreligious because it makes an *alma de peruda* (a world of division), an idea which, by the way, is paralleled by Blake's argument that the universe as we know it, i.e. the sheer material unspiritual universe, is the result of the fall of the one life from unity into division. Again, Psalm CXLV, 18, declares: 'The Lord is near unto all them that call upon him, to all that call upon him in truth.' What is the meaning of the phrase 'in truth', asks the *Zohar*? And the reply is 'a knowledge of how to declare the Divine Unity in prayer. For in this knowledge consists the service of the Holy King; and whosoever knows how to declare the Divine Unity is a helper in establishing that one unique nation of whom it is said, "And who is like thy people Israel, one unique nation in the earth?" And when all those who know how to declare the Divine Unity do so in the right way, then are all the walls of darkness cleft in twain. The face of the Heavenly King is revealed. There is light unto all. The "realms above" as well as the "realms below" draw unto themselves blessings without end.' In these quaintly original remarks on the effects wrought by prayer, there are many points which are of fundamental importance in Jewish mystical teaching of all ages. The declaration of the Divine Unity in prayer does not mean merely the clear and unequivocal pronouncement of the word *Echad* (One). It goes much deeper. It implies the conviction that all things should be regarded as so many manifestations of the Divine whose vivifying power is never for an instant withdrawn from the world which it animates. To pray is thus, in the last resort, to become absorbed in God; and only in the enjoyment of such an experience does man find light, truth, and bliss, both for himself and for others. This type of theological doctrine comes to the front more particularly in the later Cabbalists, i.e. the Hassidic literature, starting with Israel Baalshem.

The fundamental note in the *Zohar's* treatment of the Divine nature is the attempt to combine the transcendent and immanent aspects of the Deity in a single concept. Not that it does this with a strictly scientific consistency. Far from it. God, in the *Zohar*, is the great Unknowable, the Supreme Incomprehensible. God is exalted above human understanding; the depths of the Divine wisdom are beyond human penetration. To quote the words of the *Idra Rabba*, God is 'the most ancient of the ancient, the mystery of mysteries, the unknown of the unknown'. Here we have the doctrine of the Divine Transcendency *par excellence*. Nevertheless, God in the *Zohar* is very knowable, very fathomable. The universe as well as man's heart reveal His infinite power and infinite love. Nay, even the human organs and limbs reflect certain static and dynamic characteristics of Deity. The world is an image of the Divine. There is a constant and conscious interaction between 'the above' (the celestial kingdom) and 'the below' (the mundane kingdom). Here we have the doctrine of the Divine immanence *par excellence*. It is the ceaseless interweaving of these two doctrines in the pages of the *Zohar* that supplies the book with its uncompromisingly spiritual atmosphere. Without this combination, the *Zohar* would be a false presentation of Judaism. Had it emphasized exclusively a 'mysterious' and 'unknowable' Deity, it would but have supplied one more weapon to the armoury of the Pauline critics of a 'legalistic' Judaism. On the other hand, an unbalanced insistence on the doctrine that the world is but a manifestation or mirror of a Divine life pulsating everywhere would lead men away to a Spinozistic pantheism—a creed which is at out-and-out variance with the postulates of Jewish theism.

The transcendent God of the Cabbalah, called the *En Sof* (the limitless one), becomes immanent in the cosmos by a species of 'flowings forth' or emanations, which in their turn give rise to 'four universes', viz. (*a*) *Atsiluth*; (*b*) *Beriah*; (*c*) *Yetsirah*; (*d*) *Asiah*, i.e. Emanation, Creation, Formation, and Action, respectively. These 'four universes' are apportioned among 'Ten *Sefiroth*', which are named as follows: (*a*) *Kether* (The Crown); (*b*) *Ḥokmah* (Wisdom); (*c*) *Binah* (Understanding); (*d*) *Ḥesed* (Mercy); (*e*) *Geburah* (Force or Severity); (*f*) *Tifereth* (Beauty); (*g*) *Neẓaḥ* (Victory); (*h*) *Hod* (Glory); (*i*) *Yesod* (Foundation); (*j*) *Malkuth* (Kingdom); These names are, on the surface, largely arbitrary and conventional; and as for the way in which these 'Ten *Sefiroth*' are allocated to the worlds of Cabbalism—this is an extremely complicated theme into the consideration of which it is not possible to enter in the limited space of an Introduction such as this.

The feature in the Jewish Cabbalistic literature which is calculated to recommend it for all time to the admiration of scholars and thinkers is the high place which it accords to the human soul. The *Zohar* is replete with references to the dominating part played by man's soul in the furtherance of his own good, as well as in the development of all these 'universes' with whose workings man is so intensely and inevitably bound up. Man is man only because of his soul. On this point the *Zohar* is far more definite and uncompromising than the Bible and the Talmud. A statement like 'For dust thou art and unto dust shalt thou return' (Genesis III, 19) would be quite out of keeping with Zoharic theology. And so would the remark of the pessimist Ecclesiastes: 'And the pre-eminence of man over beast is nought, for all is vanity' (Eccl. III, 19). The whole atmosphere cast by the *Zohar* around these spiritual problems is far warmer and lighter, more cheering and more encouraging. The Mishnah (Aboth III, 1) declares, 'Know whence thou camest: from a putrefying drop; and whither thou art going: to a place of dust, worms, and maggots.' Man's origin is envisaged by the *Zohar* in a far more refined and poetic outlook than this; and as for man's destiny in the hereafter, it is no mere period of judgement before a Heavenly Tribunal, but a series of progressive spiritual experiences in many forms until at the last there is a union of the soul with the Divine source whence it emanated.

Man, says the *Zohar*, was 'created' on the 'sixth day', because he is, in himself, a noble epitome of the cosmos. And he is this by reason of the infinite association of his soul with the *Sefiroth*. The 'upper' and the 'lower' world both find their meeting point in him. He is a *Shekinta Ta-ta-aa*, i.e. a Divine Presence on earth.

The Soul, as a spiritual entity playing the highest of high parts in man's relations with the Unseen, is well brought to the front in all branches of the medieval Cabbalah. The *Zohar* warns us against thinking that man is made up solely of flesh and skin, veins and sinews. Man's skin typifies the firmament, which extends everywhere and covers everything. His flesh typifies the evil side of the universe, i.e. the elements which are purely exterior, of sense. The sinews and veins symbolise the 'Celestial chariot' (the *Merkabah*), being the interior forces of man which are the servitors of God. But all these are merely an outward covering. In the kingdom of man's soul there are processes going on which are the exact counterpart of those going on in the 'upper world'. The soul is threefold. There is (i) *Neshamah*, which is the highest phase of its existence. (ii) *Ruah*, which is the seat of good and evil, the abode of the moral attributes. (iii) *Nefesh*, which is the grosser side of spirit and is *en rapport* with the body and the cause of all the movements and instincts of the physical life. Each of these three constituents of the soul has its source in some one or other of the ten *Sefiroth*.

The soul enjoyed a heavenly pre-existence. This idea is already found in the Talmud and is deduced from certain passages in the Hebrew Bible. Whether the old Rabbis discovered the idea independently, or whether they merely adapted it from the teaching of Plato is a moot point. Complementary to this doctrine of pre-existence is that of the transmigration of the soul—metempsychosis—which is taught in the *Zohar* by way of a solution of the eternally vexing problem of why the wicked prosper. The famous post-Zoharic Cabbalist, Isaac Luria (1534–72), was of opinion that all souls were born with Adam, and that every human being received at birth, through Divine intervention, the soul that fitted it. All souls born with Adam constituted originally one and one only great soul. When Adam sinned through disobedience, this one comprehensive soul born with him and of which every future human being was, at birth, to receive a microscopic fragment, became involved in sin. But all these tainted souls possess the potentiality and hence have the duty of cleansing themselves and working themselves up to a high level of destiny. This tenet was widely held by the Cabbalists and suggested to them their many strange theories about the chequered wanderings of the soul. The soul's dross cannot be cast off in the course of one lifetime. It must pass through many bodies and experience many terrestrial existences, each one higher than the other, before it can reach the pinnacle of perfection—union with God—which is its predestined end.

The Cabbalistic successors of Luria went even further, and said that souls wandered on earth and could sometimes enter the bodily framework of some living person, so as to help him to fulfil certain religious duties which he had neglected.

The soul, says the mystic of all ages and creeds, seeks to enter consciously into the Presence of God. And this idea of the soul's unquenchable yearning to be united with its Divine source is reiterated under many forms in all parts of the *Zohar* and lends to it a charm as well as a lightness of touch which serve as a relief to the excessively sombre and solemn tone of most of the book. It is the poetry of the *Zohar*. Man's intimacy with God, the soul's union with Him, are described in sexual terminology. It is the union of the male with the female. The symbolism is sometimes liable to strike the reader as offensively crude in some of its details; and the *Zohar* has more than once had to suffer for this the cheap sneers of detractors. But this is only the result of shallow knowledge and false perspective. On deeper study and reflection these sexual references will be found to be just as admissible as are the sexual similes and analogies which pervade the writings of the most refined and elegant of poets and romancers. For the *Zohar* speaks throughout of cosmic union—a coming together, a fusion, of all the manifold universes 'above' and 'below'. The worlds above are 'married' to the worlds below. And man, who, mainly by reason of his soul, is a denizen of these multiple worlds, becomes, whilst striving after communion with the Divine, a sharer in these cosmic acts of intercourse. Of course, it will be recollected that the amorous sentiments which find such bold expression in the Old Testament book of the Song of Songs were made to bear a strongly allegoric-mystic interpretation in the old homilies of the Midrashic literature. And there can be little doubt that these pictures of conjugal relations as applied to express man's consummated longing for the Divine must have largely prepared the way for those numerous and often obscure allusions which constitute what has been called the 'sex-mystery' of the *Zohar*.

That much of the mystic speculation to be found in the *Zohar* dates back to the early centuries before and after the destruction of the second Temple is a point upon which there is now unanimous agreement amongst scholars. The early Jewish Apocalyptic and magical literature, the Palestinian and Babylonian Talmuds, the huge and variegated crop of Midrashic literature which continued to spring up for many years after the completion of the Talmud—all these monuments of early Jewish interpretative activity scintillate with mystic allusions which found incorporation in many modified forms in the pages of the *Zohar*. Much of this early speculation was never committed to writing. It was transmitted orally from generation to generation. Herein, by the way, lies the meaning of *Cabbalah:* oral tradition. And the *Zohar* was probably the first important book in which these floating traditions were preserved in writing. Schools and circles wherein Cabbalah was meditated upon had started as early as the sixth century in Galilee, and these, after disappearing for some centuries owing to the fluctuating fortunes of the Jews, were revived in the twelfth and thirteenth centuries under the influence of such great Talmudic luminaries as Moses Nahmanides, Solomon ben Adrath, and others. In the middle of the sixteenth century, Isaac Luria, who had learnt Cabbalah in Egypt, founded a new mystical school at

Safed, in Galilee, then the centre of Jewish learning. He gathered round him a host of disciples, many of them, like Elijah de Vidas and Joseph Hagiz, being themselves distinguished writers of Cabbalistic works. Luria himself wrote nothing. His utterances were taken down in writing by his most prominent disciple, Hayyim Vital Calabreze, whose book *Ets Hayyim* shows how Luria developed many of the leading ideas of the *Zohar* and inaugurated a new mystic system in Judaism, a system wherein Messianic theology and Messianic expectations held a central place. Luria's enlarged and elaborated conceptions of Cabbalah found numerous enthusiastic disciples; and the *Zohar*, as the result of a too extravagant emphasis on certain Messianic comments contained within it, emerged, by an unhappy fate, as the source whence the pseudo-Messiah, Sabbatai Zevi (1626–76), presumed to have drawn the warrant for his dramatically pretentious career.

It goes without saying that the mysticism of the *Zohar*, emphasising as it does the efficacy of prayer, must have influenced considerably the Hebrew Prayer Book, as well as the Divine Service of the Synagogue and certain aspects of Jewish ceremonial observance. Much of the extravagant Zoharic angelology came to find a place in the liturgy, as also much Zoharic doctrine concerning the secrets of the supra-mundane universe and the mysteries, both painful and pleasurable, of the life hereafter. Many mystical formulas, mystical names and symbols intermixed with many arithmetical and astrological references, also became interpolated within the pages of the Prayer Book. Most of this highly pictorial type of prayer material has been eliminated from the modern worship of the Synagogue because of its incongruity with the prevailing conceptions of the Deity; but in spite of this weeding-out, it may still be said that our Jewish liturgy of to-day scintillates with many a Zoharic phrase and idea which are a decided gain to the spirituality of Jewish home or synagogue ritual. One is inclined to differ in this respect from Leopold Zunz when he says: 'Although the more respectable mystics did something for spiritual religion and for devotion as opposed to thoughtless formalism, yet the liturgy lost more than it gained by their influence' (*D. Ritus*, p. 24). The ceremony of blowing the *Shofar* on *Rosh Ha-Shanah* gains rather than loses in impressiveness by the accompanying Zoharic prayers which ask that 'the angels emanating from the *Shofar* may bring the prayers of Israel to the Divine hearing'. Taken literally, the idea jars, of course, on our intelligence. But the Zoharic mysticism, like the mysticism of all other religions and literatures, demands the higher interpretation. And on this basis the blowing of the *Shofar*, far from being a mere stereotyped act of observance of the letter of the Law, rises to become the outward expression of one more of the many mystical beliefs in the unseen spiritual agencies uniting the human with the Divine—an outstanding Zoharic doctrine. Similarly in the case of the prayer, *B'rich Sh'meh Ve'athreh*, recited before the Reading of the Law on Sabbaths and Festivals. The *Zohar* introduces it with these words: 'When the scroll is taken out in the assembly to read therein, the Gates of the heavens of mercy open and the celestial love awakes.' The prayer is a truly noble one, teeming with a vivid sense of the nearness of God, combined with an ever-felt and never-satisfied longing for communion with Him by means of the Torah—a thought which is ubiquitous in the *Zohar*. A modified and modernised adoption of a little more Zoharic sentiment to the Jewish liturgy of to-day would be a welcome improvement! By thus introducing a tinge of 'Ecstasy', of direct intuition of God, into Jewish prayer; by making it less of a merely external religious exercise and more of a means for transcending earthly affairs for a time, there would be restored to prayer something of the position it must have occupied in the days of the Hebrew Psalmist, as well as something of the intensely individual and devotional part which it played in the neo-Hassidic mysticism of the eighteenth century.

Besides influencing the liturgy, the *Zohar*, as is only to be expected from a book which stimulates the imagination and the feelings, has left numerous traces in the medieval religious poetry outside the synagogue. Its allegorism, its symbolism, its erotic terminology, proved excellent material for portraying the ceaseless yearnings of the human heart for union with the Infinite; and the reader is often startled at the ingenuity with which many a simple and innocent Biblical word or phrase is poetically worked up to indicate the physical as well as the spiritual mysteries which surround the Deity and the effort of man to become finally absorbed in Him by means of prayer, Torah study and contemplation.

For some centuries after its first appearance, the *Zohar* was generally regarded by the Jews as an integral part of the literature of Torah, like the Talmud and the Midrash, and, like them, it was considered one of the subjects of religious study, of *talmud torah*. It was, in fact, generally known as the 'Midrash of R. Simeon ben Yohai'. Unlike the Talmud, however, it was what might be called an optional subject in the curriculum of Torah study; a man could be a great Jewish scholar without knowing anything of the *Zohar* or the Cabbalah. Still, there was a merit in studying them also. A breach, however, arose between the Talmudists and the Cabbalists after the failure of the Messianic movement of Sabbatai Zevi in the middle of the seventeenth century. The extravagances of Zevi and his followers were largely inspired by the *Zohar*, and this work in consequence fell into suspicion and disfavour with a large number of Talmudists. This antipathy to the *Zohar* found its culmination in a treatise (in *Mitpahat Sefarim*) written in the middle of the eighteenth century by the great Talmudical scholar, Jacob Emden of Altona, in which it is denounced as being for the most part the work of an impostor. Emden was led to investigate the *Zohar* through his desire to extirpate the Shabbetaean heresy which still lingered in his day. His examination of the *Zohar* shows considerable critical acumen, and his conclusions have been adopted by a large number of orthodox Jews.

The place to be assigned to the *Zohar* in the scheme of Jewish study is also one of the fundamental points at issue between the sect of Hassidim, founded by Israel Baalshem in the eighteenth century, and their opponents in Poland and Lithuania, known as the 'Mithnagedim'. The controversy between the two sects is interesting not only in itself but also for the light it sheds upon many aspects of the Jewish religious and social life of those times. It was a struggle for supremacy between Rabbinic orthodoxy, based upon the authority of the Talmud, and the mystic-emotional-spiritual Judaism founded upon the Zoharic interpretation of the Torah. It was a contest between two principles in Judaism, the formalism of dogmatic ritual and the direct religious sentiment. Whilst Rabbinical orthodoxy, without rejecting the *Zohar*, regarded the ideal Jewish life as one of obedience to law founded upon the study of the Talmud and the Codes, Hassidic Judaism based itself upon the *Zohar*, maintaining that the quintessence of the Jewish religion lay in the cultivation of a sincere love of God, combined with a warm faith and deep belief in the efficacy of prayer. This does not imply that the Hassidim despised Talmudic scholarship or flouted the traditional Rabbinic ordinances. What it does imply is that Hassidism aimed at altering the centre of gravity of the Jewish religious life by introducing into it a new 'spirituality'. This 'spirituality' derived from the *Zohar* consisted in the conviction that there is an unbroken intercourse between the world of the Deity and the world of humanity; that these worlds have a reciprocal influence upon one another; and that prayer should be an ecstatic communion with God, so as to unite the human life with Him who is 'the life of all worlds'. It is not given to all men to attain this exalted state. But the man who attains it is, in the Hassidic sense, the *Tsaddik* who, as a result, possesses a degree of prophetic insight and a power to work miracles.

The study of the *Zohar*, as well as of the Cabbalistic writings which succeeded it, attracted a great many noted Christian scholars of the past. William Postel, who translated the *Sefer Yetsirah* into Latin (Paris, 1552), seems to have been the first Christian to introduce the mysteries of the Cabbalah to the learned circles of Europe. But the first Christian into whose hands the *Zohar* came was Pico della Mirandola, who wrote short theses in Latin about it. He was, too, the first Christian to declare that the *Zohar* contains elements which are capable of a Christian construction. He seems to have believed that the doctrines concerning the Trinity, Original Sin, and the Incarnation could be deduced from its pages. John Reuchlin, another ardent student of

Jewish occultism, wrote *De Arte Cabalistica*, which he dedicated to Leo X, and the object of which was to prove from the post-Zoharic writers on Cabbalism that the Messiah had already appeared. Petrius Galatinus, a contemporary of Reuchlin, published, in 1516, *De Arcanis Catholicae Veritatis*, in which the Zoharic teachings are made to reflect many of the cardinal doctrines of Christianity. The complete list of all the other Christian students would be too long to mention here. Outstanding names are those of Alabaster, Gasparellus, and Athanasius Kircher. But the greatest of all these was Knorr von Rosenroth, whose *Kabbalah Denudata*, first published at Sulzbach in 1677–8 and translated into English by S. L. Macgregor Mathers (London, 1887), contains much valuable material and has proved particularly useful to Christian scholars unable to read the Hebrew and Aramaic originals. A new French translation of the whole of the *Zohar* has recently been made by M. Jean de Pauly and published posthumously by M. Emil Lafuma-Giraud (1906). Grateful reference is also due to the many writings on all aspects of the *Zohar* by the celebrated Scholar, Mr. Arthur Edward Waite.

It is unnecessary to mention here that many of the leading Jewish theologians of the nineteenth century have done much in the way of giving an enlightened and objective presentation of the mysterious and uncanny world in which the *Zohar* lives and moves and has its being. Adolph Franck's *La Kabbale*, first published in Paris in 1843, contains long and representative extracts from the *Zohar* in a beautifully phrased French translation. In German there are numerous monographs and partial translations by Zunz, Jost, Jellinek, Joel, Graetz, and Steinschneider. In Hebrew, Rapaport, Harkavy, and others have made important contributions. During the present century there has been a distinct revival of interest in the literature of the Hassidim from the time of Baalshem, and much has been written by Kahana, Horodetsky, Dubnow, and others, mainly in Hebrew, to show that these devotees of the mystic side of Jewish life and religion were not, as is popularly supposed, half-crazy visionaries living in a universe peopled by the figments of their own degenerate brains, but men of intellect, scholarship, and sound sense who aimed at bringing back to Jewish organised communal life a breath of that mystic sentiment and emotion which are the aromatic life-essence of religion, and which are indispensable to Judaism if it is to continue to play its predestined part of bringing mankind 'under the wings of the Shekinah'.

It has been said that every man is born either a Platonist or an Aristotelian. This means that there is an innate predisposition in every one of us to assimilate certain fixed forms of thought from which we cannot be diverted, no matter what future training, education, or experience we may receive. The Jews during the Middle Ages, both before and after the appearance of the *Zohar*, were (largely through the influence of Maimonides) amongst the staunchest supporters of Aristotle. Whilst the Aristotelian philosophy stands immortalised in the writings of the leading Jewish theologians of medieval times, the philosophy of Plato finds but a mere handful of exponents, eminent though these be. Hence there has arisen the commonly accepted belief that Jews are by nature rationalists rather than mystics. Is this belief correct? Does it square with the facts? I think not. Judaism is unquestionably and supremely a religion of reason. But, paradoxically enough, it only made its appeal to the Jew and held him tightly in its grip because he was—and is—by nature and inclination a mystic. The *Moreh Nebuchim* of Maimonides was the great Jewish philosophical exposition in the Middle Ages, of the 'Supremacy of Reason' in Judaism. But the Jew in the mass knew it not. It was never a people's book. But the *Zohar* was a people's book. It struck a chord in whose music the Jew heard:

> The bubblings of the springs
> That feed the world.

And the impress went down to the roots of his being. However much in accord with reason Judaism may have appeared to the Jew, there were always crises and catastrophes in which he felt that reason failed to solve the tantalising problems involved—problems of pain and suffering, of reward and punishment, of the relation between the human and the

Divine, of the life here and the life hereafter. The Jew, as a pure rationalist, would have quailed in the face of these enigmas; and Judaism might by now have been but a pale memory. But the Jew believed and lived not by logic but by love, not by ratiocination but by intuition. It was by these standards that he was led on

> To see one changeless Life in all the Lives,
> And in the Separate, One Inseparable.

In his great book *Belief in God*, Canon Gore says: 'It is by feeling or intuition that the supreme artist gains his profound vision of experience and of God.' The Jew was this supreme artist. For was he not of the spiritual lineage of the Psalmist, who said: 'My heart and my flesh sing for joy unto the living God. With my whole heart have I sought thee; O let me not err from thy commandments'? Though he could not know God, he nevertheless felt that it was given to him to transcend the crushing weight of earthly affairs, to be raised above the grosser hindrances of sense and to become an organ reflecting the Divine life. Such is the standpoint of the true mystic of all the ages. The Jew had it in overflowing measure. And the Jewish book which first and more than any other crystallised these feelings and gave them their overpowering momentum was the *Zohar*.

J. ABELSON

Leeds
September 1931

TRANSLATORS' PREFACE

The aim of this translation is, on the one hand, to make the *Zohar* accessible to English readers, on the other hand, to afford assistance to those who struggle with its intricacies in the original. For the sake of the latter a good deal has been included which, as far as the former are concerned, might perhaps have been spared, especially if they have never studied the Hebrew Bible. The greater part, however, will probably be intelligible enough, even to those who have no knowledge of Hebrew.

As has been pointed out above, the printed editions of the *Zohar* contain intercalations from other, allied, works, which are paged along with the *Zohar* itself. These are not included in the present translation, which confines itself to what may be called the *Zohar* proper. Certain individual passages have also been omitted for reasons given where they occur. There are also minor omissions (indicated by the sign . . .) of passages containing plays upon Hebrew words and similar matter unsuitable for translation. With these qualifications, the translation may be regarded as complete for the part of the text covered by the first volume, viz. up to the end of *Vayera* (p. 120b).

Certain parts of the *Zohar*—notably the comments on the opening sections of Genesis—are highly enigmatical, and in the absence of an authentic tradition their true meaning is a matter of conjecture. An attempt has been made to give a faithful translation of these also, accounting for practically every word in the original. The result has perhaps been to reproduce only too faithfully the tenebrosity of the original, for which the reader may not be thankful. But he will know, at any rate, that he is getting the authentic *Zohar* and not the translators' own ideas; and he may find assistance in an appendix and a glossary in which the translators indicate their own view of the general trend and purpose of these passages.

In printing the Biblical quotations with which the *Zohar* abounds, a device has been adopted which it is hoped the reader will find useful. The main text-headings, that is to say, the verses from the Pentateuch which the *Zohar* sets out to expound in regular order, are printed in small capitals. The subsidiary text-headings, that is to say, other verses from the Bible which are made the subject of disquisitions illustrative of the main text, are printed in italics. Repetitions of these texts, or incidental quotations, are printed in ordinary type between quotation marks. This distinction will enable the reader to see at a glance where he is and with what subject the *Zohar* is dealing at any point.

A further effort has been made to bring order and system into the text by careful paragraphing and by a judicious use of parentheses. (It should be remembered that in the original text not only these aids, but even punctuation marks, including full stops, are inserted very sparingly, and then not infrequently at the wrong place!) The result, it is hoped, will be to show that the *Zohar* is by no means such a jumble as is usually supposed, that with all its discursiveness it follows a well-defined course, and that there is a reason why most of its reflections are inserted just where they are and not somewhere else.

The Biblical references are in all cases to the Hebrew text (or to the American Jewish translation). The renderings have also been taken where possible from this version or the English Revised Version. In many cases, however, it has been necessary to give the Hebrew quite a different rendering, in order to make it accord with the lesson which the *Zohar* seeks to derive from it—often in lordly disregard of the context or even the rules of grammar.

The translation has been made in the main from the Mantuan text of the *Zohar*, but occasionally a reading has been adopted from the Amsterdam text. The paging of the Mantuan text has also been inserted.

THE ZOHAR

PROLOGUE[1]

Rabbi Hizkiah opened his discourse with the text: *As a lily among thorns, etc.* (S. S. II, 2). 'What', he said, 'does the lily symbolise ? It symbolises the Community of Israel. As the lily among thorns is tinged with red and white, so the Community of Israel is visited now with justice and now with mercy; as the lily possesses thirteen leaves, so the Community of Israel is vouchsafed thirteen categories of mercy which surround it on every side. For this reason, the term *Elohim* (God) mentioned here (in the first verse of Genesis) is separated by thirteen words from the next mention of *Elohim*, symbolising the thirteen categories of mercy which surround the Community of Israel to protect it. The second mention of *Elohim* is separated from the third by five words, representing the five strong leaves that surround the lily, symbolic of the five ways of salvation which are the "five gates". This is alluded to in the verse "I will lift up the cup of salvation" (Ps. CXVI, 13). This is the "cup of benediction" ,which has to be raised by five fingers and no more, after the model of the lily, which rests on five strong leaves in the shape of five fingers. Thus the lily is a symbol of the cup of benediction. Immediately after the third mention of *Elohim* appears the light which, so soon as created, was treasured up and enclosed in that *b'rith* (covenant) which entered the lily and fructified it, and this is what is called " tree bearing fruit wherein is the seed thereof": and this seed is preserved in the very sign of the covenant. And as the ideal covenant was formed through forty-two copulations, so the engraven ineffable name is formed of the forty-two letters of the work of creation.'

IN THE BEGINNING. R. Simeon opened his discourse with the text: *The blossoms appeared on the earth, etc.* (S. S. II, 12). ' "The blossoms", he said, 'refer to the work of creation.

[1] This chapter, a preliminary exposition of Gen. 1, serves to introduce the reader to the circle of R. Simeon and his colleagues, and to give him an idea of the scope and nature of their discussions. It is somewhat more discursive and fanciful than the main body of the *Zohar*.

"Appeared on the earth": when ? On the third day, as it is written, "And the earth brought forth": they thus then appeared on the earth. "The time of pruning is come" alludes to the fourth day in which "the pruning of the overbearing" (Is. xxv, 5) took place. "And the voice of the turtle" alludes to the fifth day, as it is written, "Let the waters swarm, etc., to produce living creatures". "Is heard" points to the sixth day, as it is written, "Let us make man" (namely him who was destined to say first "we will do" and then "we will hear", for the expression [1b] in our text, na'aseh, "Let us make man", finds its echo in the expression "na'aseh (we will do) and hear" (Exod. xxiv, 7)); "In our land" implies the day of the Sabbath, which is a copy of the "land of the living" (the world to come, the world of souls, the world of consolations). The following is an alternative exposition: "The blossoms" are the patriarchs who pre-existed in the thought of the Almighty and later entered the world to come, where they were carefully preserved; from thence they issued secretly to become incarnate in the true prophets. Thus when Joseph entered the Holy Land he planted them there, and thus they "appeared on the earth" and revealed themselves there. When do they become visible ? When the rainbow betokens that "the time of pruning is come", to wit, the time when the sinners are due to be cut off from the world; and they only escape because "the blossoms appear on the earth": if not for their appearance the sinners would not be left in the world and the world itself would not exist. And who is it that upholds the world and causes the patriarchs to appear ? It is the voice of tender children studying the Torah; and for their sakes the world is saved. . . .'

IN THE BEGINNING. R. Eleazar opened his discourse with the text: *Lift up your eyes on high and see: who hath created these ?* (Is. XL, 26). ' "Lift up your eyes on high": to which place ? To that place to which all eyes are turned, to wit, *Petah 'Enaim* ("eye-opener"). By doing so, you will know that it is the mysterious Ancient One, whose essence can be sought, but not found, that created these: to wit, *Mi* (Who ?), the same who is called "from (Heb. *mi*) the extremity of heaven on high", because everything is in His power, and because He is ever to be sought, though mysterious and unrevealable, since further we cannot enquire. That extremity of heaven is called *Mi*, but there is another lower extremity which is called *Mah* (What?). The difference between the two is this. The first is the real subject of enquiry, but after a man by means of enquiry and reflection has reached the utmost limit of knowledge, he stops at *Mah* (What?), as if to say, what knowest thou? what have thy searchings achieved? Everything is as baffling as at the beginning. In allusion to this, it is written "I, *Mah*, testify against thee, etc." (Lam. II, 13). When the Temple was destroyed a voice went forth and said: "I, *Mah*, have testified against thee day by day from the days of old," as it is written, "I called heaven and earth to witness against you." (Deut. XXX, 19.) Further, I, *Mah*, likened myself to thee; I crowned thee with holy crowns, and made thee ruler over the earth, as it is written, "Is this the city that men call the perfection of beauty? etc." (Lam. II, 15), and again, "I called thee Jerusalem that is builded as a city compact together". Further, I, *Mah*, am equal to thee; in the same plight in which thou, Jerusalem, art here, so I am, as it were, above; just as the holy people does not go up to thee any more in sacred array, so, I swear to thee, I will not ascend on high until the day when thy throngs will again stream to thee here below. And this may be thy consolation, inasmuch as to this extent I am thy equal in all things. But now that thou art in thy present state "thy breach is great like the sea" (*Ibid.* 13). And lest thou sayest there is for thee no abiding and no healing, "*Mi* will heal thee" (*Ibid.*). Of a surety the veiled One, the most High, the sum of all existence will heal thee and uphold thee—*Mi*, the extremity of heaven above, *Mah*, as far as the extremity of heaven below. And this is the inheritance of Jacob, he being the "bolt that passes from extremity to extremity" (Exod. XXVI, 28), that is, from the higher, identical with *Mi*, to the lower, identical with *Mah*, as he occupies a position in the middle. Hence "*Mi* (Who) created these".'

Said R. Simeon, 'Eleazar, son of mine, cease thy discourse, that there may be revealed the higher mysteries which remain sealed for the people of this world.' R. Eleazar then fell into silence. R. Simeon wept a while and then said: 'Eleazar, what is meant by the term "these"? Surely not the stars and the other heavenly bodies, since they are always visible, and were created through *Mah*, as we read, "By the word of the Lord were the heavens made" (Ps. XXXIII, 6). Nor can it imply the things inaccessible to our gaze, since the vocable "these" obviously points to things that are revealed. This mystery remained sealed until one day, whilst I was on the sea-shore, Elijah came and said to me, "Master, what means '*Mi* (Who?) created these?'" I said to him, "That refers to the heavens and their hosts, the works of the Holy One, blessed be He, works through the contemplation of which man comes to bless Him, as it is written, 'When I behold thy heavens, the work [2a] of thy fingers, etc. O Lord our God, how glorious is thy name in all the earth!'" (Ps. VIII, 4-10). Then he said to me, "Master, the Holy One, blessed be He, had a deep secret which He at length revealed at the celestial Academy. It is this. When the most Mysterious wished to reveal Himself, He first produced a single point which was transmuted into a thought, and in this He executed innumerable designs, and engraved innumerable gravings. He further graved within the sacred and mystic lamp a mystic and most holy design, which was a wondrous edifice issuing from the midst of thought. This is called *MI*, and was the beginning of the edifice, existent and non-existent, deep-buried, unknowable by name. It was only called *MI* (Who?). It desired to become manifest and to be called by name. It therefore clothed itself in a refulgent and precious garment and created *ELeH* (these), and *ELeH* acquired a name. The letters of the two words intermingled, forming the complete name *ELoHIM* (God). (When the Israelites sinned in making the golden calf, they alluded to this mystery in saying '*Eleh* (these are) thy Gods, O Israel' (Exod. XXXII, 4).) And once *MI* became combined with *ELeH*, the name remained for all time. And upon this secret the world is built." Elijah then flew away and vanished out of my sight. And it is from him that I became possessed of this profound mystery.'

R. Eleazar and all the companions came and prostrated themselves before him, weeping for joy and saying, 'If we had come into the world only to hear this we should have been content.' R. Simeon said further: 'The heavens and their hosts were created through the medium of *Mah* (What ?), as it is written, "When I behold thy heavens, the work of thy fingers, etc. . . . O Lord our God (*Adon*), *Mah*, glorious is thy name in all the earth, whose majesty is rehearsed above the heavens." (Ps. VIII, 4, 2). God is "above the heavens" in respect of His name, for He created a light for His light, and one formed a vestment to the other, and so He ascended into the higher name; hence "In the beginning *Elohim* (God) created", that is, the supernal *Elohim*. Whereas *Mah* was not so, nor was it built up until these letters *Eleh* (from the name *Elohim*) were drawn from above below, and the Mother lent the Daughter her garments and decked her out gracefully with her own adornments. When did she so adorn her ? When all the males (of Israel) appeared before her in accordance with the command "all thy males shall appear before the Lord (*Adon*) God" (Exod. XXXIV, 23). This term Lord (*Adon*) is similarly used in the passage "Behold the Ark of the covenant of the Lord (*Adon*) of all the earth" (Jos. III, 11). Then the letter *Hé* (of *Mah*) departed and her place was taken by *Yod* (making *Mi*), and then she decked herself in male garments, harmonizing with "every male in Israel". Other letters, too, Israel drew from on high to that place. Thus it says: "These (*Eleh*) I remember" (Ps. XLII, 5), i.e., I make mention with my mouth and I pour out my tears, and thus "I make them (the letters) flit" from on high "unto the house of *Elohim*" (*Ibid.*) to be *Elohim* (God) after his form. And with what ? "With the voice of song and praise and amidst a festive throng" (*Ibid.*).' Said R. Eleazar, 'My keeping silence was the means of building the sanctuary above and the sanctuary below. Verily "speech is worth a *sela*, silence two". Speech is worth a *sela*, namely, my exposition and remarks on the subject; but silence is worth two, since through my silence two worlds were built together.'

R. Simeon said: 'We will go on to expound the conclusion of the verse, viz. *He who bringeth forth by number their host*

(Is. XL, 26). There are two grades which have to be distinguished, one of *Mah* and one of *Mi*—one of the higher and the other of the lower sphere. The higher is singled out here in the words, "He who bringeth forth by number their host". "He who" expresses something definite and absolute, a being universally recognized and without equal. (Corresponding to this is the expression "He who bringeth forth bread from the earth": here also "He who" implies the universally acknowledged one, though here visualised as the lower grade; the two, however, are one.) "By number": six hundred thousand are they, and they have in turn produced according to their kinds beyond all number. "All of them", whether the six hundred thousand or the rest of the hosts, "He calls by name". This cannot mean by *their* names, for if it were so, it should have been written "by names". What it means is that as long as this grade did not assume a name, and was still called *Mi*, it was unproductive, and did not bring into actuality the latent forces within it, each according to its kind. But as soon as it created *ELeH* (these), and assumed its rightful name and was called *ELoHIM* (God), then, by force of that name, it produced them in their complete form. This is the meaning of "calls by name", to wit, He proclaimed His own name so as to bring about the emergence of each sort of being in its full form. (Analogous to this we read, "See, I have called by name" (Exod. XXXI, 2), to wit, I have bestowed my name on *Bezalel* (in the shadow of God) so that his work should emerge in perfection. Further, the words "by the abundance of powers" (Is. XL, 26) refer to the supreme grade whereto all the volitions ascend [2b] by a mysterious path. "And mighty of strength": the word "strength" (*KoaH*) symbolizes the supernal World which assumed the name *Elohim* (God), as already said. "No one is missing" of the six hundred thousand which emerged by the power of the Name. And because no one is missing, therefore whenever Israelites died on account of a national sin, the people were afterwards numbered, and it was found that the number of six hundred thousand had not been diminished even by one, so that the likeness to the supernal prototype was still complete; just as no one was missing above, so no one was missing here below.

IN THE BEGINNING. Rab Hamnuna the Venerable said: 'We find here a reversal of the order of the letters of the Alphabet, the first two words *bereshith bara*—"in-the-beginning He-created"—commencing with *beth*, whereas the two words following, *Elohim eth*—"God the"—commence with *aleph*. The reason is as follows. When the Holy One, blessed be He, was about to make the world, all the letters of the Alphabet were still embryonic, and for two thousand years the Holy One, blessed be He, had contemplated them and toyed with them. When He came to create the world, all the letters presented themselves before Him in reversed order. The letter *Tau* advanced in front and pleaded: May it please Thee, O Lord of the world, to place me first in the creation of the world, seeing that I am the concluding letter of *EMeTh* (Truth) which is engraved upon Thy seal, and seeing that Thou art called by this very name of *EMeTh*, it is most appropriate for the King to begin with the final letter of *EMeTh* and to create with me the world. The Holy One, blessed be He, said to her: Thou art worthy and deserving, but it is not proper that I begin with thee the creation of the world, since thou art destined to serve as a mark on the foreheads of the faithful ones (*vide* Ezek. IX, 4) who have kept the Law from *Aleph* to *Tau*, and through the absence of this mark the rest will be killed; and, further, thou formest the conclusion of *MaWeTh* (death). Hence thou art not meet to initiate the creation of the world. The *Shin* then came to the fore and pleaded: O Lord of the world, may it please Thee to begin with me the world, seeing that I am the initial letter of Thy name *ShaDDaI* (Almighty), and it is most fitting to create the world through that Holy Name. Said He in reply: Thou art worthy, thou art good, thou art true, but I may not begin through thee the creation of the world, since thou formest part of the group of letters expressing forgery, *ShekeR* (falsehood), which is not able to exist unless the *Koph* and *Resh* draw thee into their company. (Hence it is that a lie, to obtain credence, must always commence with something true. For the *shin* is a letter of truth, that letter by which the Patriarchs communed with God; but *koph* and *resh* are letters belonging to the evil side, which in order to stand firm attach to themselves the *shin*, thus forming a conspiracy (*QeSheR*).) Having heard all this, the *shin* departed. Enters the *Zadé* and says: O Lord of the world, may it please Thee to create with me the world, inasmuch as I am the sign of the righteous (*Zadikim*) and of Thyself who art called righteous, as it is written, "For the Lord is righteous, he loveth righteousness" (Ps. XI, 7), and hence it is meet to create the world with me. The Lord made answer: O *Zadé*, thou art *Zadé*, and thou signifiest righteousness, but thou must be concealed, thou mayest not come out in the open so much lest thou givest the world cause for offence. For thou consistest of the letter *nun* surmounted by the letter *yod* (representing together the male and the female principles). And this is the mystery of the creation of the first man, who was created with two faces (male and female combined). In the same way the *nun* and the *yod* in the *zadé* are turned back to back and not face to face, whether the *zadé* is upright or turned downwards. The Holy One, blessed be He, said to her further, I will in time divide thee in two, so as to appear face to face, but thou wilt go up in another place. She then departed. The letter *Pé* presented herself and pleaded thus: May it please Thee, O Lord of the world, to create through me the world, seeing that I signify redemption and deliverance (*Purkana, Peduth*), which Thou art to vouchsafe to the world. It is, hence, meet that through me the world be created. The Lord answered: Thou art worthy, but thou representest transgression (*Pesha*), and moreover thou art shapen like the serpent, who had his head curled up within his body, symbolic of the guilty man who bends his head and extends his hand. The letter '*Ayin* was likewise refused as standing for iniquity ('*Awon*), despite her plea that she represents humility ('*Anavah*). Then the *Samekh* appeared and said: O Lord of the world, may it please Thee to create through me the world, inasmuch as I represent upholding (*Semikah*) of the fallen, as it is written, "The Lord upholdeth all that fall" (Ps. CXLV, 14). The Lord answered her: This is just the reason why thou shouldst remain in thy place, for shouldst thou leave it, what will be the fate of the fallen, seeing that they are upheld by thee? She immediately departed. The

Nun entered and pleaded her merits as being the initial letter in " Fearful (*Nora*) in praises" (Ex. xv, 11), as well as in "Comely (*Nawa*) is praise for the righteous" (Ps. XXXIII, 1). The Lord said: O *Nun*, return to thy place, for it is for thy sake (as representing the falling, *Nofelim*) that the *Samekh* returned to her place. Remain, therefore, under her support. The *Nun* immediately returned to her place. The *Mim* came up and said: O Lord of the world, may it please Thee to create by me the world, inasmuch as I commence the word *Melekh* (King) which is Thy title. The Lord replied: It is so assuredly, but I cannot employ thee in the creation of the world for the reason that the world requires a King. Return, therefore, to thy place, thou along with the *Lamed* and the *Kaph*, since the world cannot exist without a *MeLeKh* (King). At that moment, the *Kaph* descended from its throne of glory and quaking and trembling said: O Lord of the universe, may it please Thee to begin through me the creation of the world, seeing that I am Thine own *Kabod* (honour). And when *Kaph* descended from its throne of glory, two hundred thousand worlds began to shake, the throne trembled, and all the worlds quaked and were about to fall in ruins. Said to her the Holy One, blessed be His Name: *Kaph*, *Kaph*, what doest thou here? I will not create the world with thee. Go back to thy place, since thou standest for extermination (*Kelayah*). Return, then, to thy place and remain there. Immediately she departed and returned to her own place. The letter *Yod* then presented herself and said: May it please Thee, O Lord, to vouchsafe me first place in the creation of the world, since I stand first in the Sacred Name. The Lord said to her: It is sufficient for thee that thou art engraven and marked in Myself and that thou art the channel of My will; thou must not be removed from My Name. The *Teth* then came up and said: O Lord of the universe, may it please Thee to place me at the head in the creation of the world, since through me Thou art called Good (*Tob*) and upright. The Lord said to her: I will not create the world through thee, as the goodness which thou representest is hidden and concealed within thyself, as it is written, "O how abundant is thy goodness which thou hast laid up for them that fear thee" (Ps. XXXI, 20). Since then it is treasured within thyself, it has no part in the world which I am going to create, but only in the world to come. And further, it is because thy goodness is hidden within thee that the gates of the Temple sank into the ground, as it is written, "Sunk (*Tabe'u*) in the ground are her gates" (Lam. II, 9). And furthermore, the letter *Ḥeth* is at thy side, and when joined you make sin (*ḤeT*). (It is for that reason that these two letters are not to be found in the names of any of the tribes.) She departed immediately. Then the *Zayin* presented herself and put forth her claim, saying, O Lord of the World, may it please Thee to put me at the head of the creation, since I represent the observance of the Sabbath, as it is written, "Remember (*Zakhor*) the day of the Sabbath to keep it holy" (Ex. XX, 8). The Lord replied: I will not create the world through thee, since thou representest war, being in shape like a sharp-pointed sword, or a lance. The *Zayin* immediately departed from His presence. The *Vau* entered and put forth her claim, saying: O Lord of the world, may it please Thee to use me first in the creation of the world, inasmuch as I am one of the letters of Thy name. Said the Lord to her: Thou, *Vau*, as well as *Hé*, suffice it to you that you are of the letters of My name, part of the mystery of My name, engraven and impressed in My name. I will therefore not give you first place in the creation of the world. Then appeared the letter *Daleth* as well as the letter *Gimel* and put forth similar claims. The Lord gave them a similar reply, saying: It should suffice you to remain side by side together, since "the poor will not cease from the land" (Deut. XV, 11), who will thus need benevolence. For the *Daleth* signifies poverty (*Dalluth*) and the *Gimel* beneficence (*Gemul*). Therefore separate not from each other, and let it suffice you that one maintains the other. The *Beth* then entered and said: O Lord of the world, may it please Thee to put me first in the creation of the world, since I represent the benedictions (*Berakhoth*) offered to Thee on high and below. The Holy One, blessed be He, said to her: Assuredly, with thee I will create the world, and thou shalt form the begnning in the creation of the world. The letter *Aleph* remained in her place without presenting herself. Said the Holy One, blessed be His name: *Aleph, Aleph,* wherefore comest thou not before Me like the rest of the letters? She answered: Because I saw all the other letters leaving Thy presence without any success. What, then, could I achieve there? And further, since [3b] Thou hast already bestowed on the letter *Beth* this great gift, it is not meet for the Supreme King to take away the gift which He has made to His servant and give it to another. The Lord said to her: *Aleph, Aleph,* although I will begin the creation of the world with the *beth,* thou wilt remain the first of the letters. My unity shall not be expressed except through thee, on thee shall be based all calculations and operations of the world, and unity shall not be expressed save by the letter *Aleph.* Then the Holy One, blessed be His name, made higher-world letters of a large pattern and lower-world letters of a small pattern. It is therefore that we have here two words beginning with *beth* (*Bereshith bara*) and then two words beginning with *aleph* (*Elohim eth*). They represent the higher-world letters and the lower-world letters, which two operate, above and below, together and as one.'

BERESHITH (In the beginning). Said R. Yudai: 'What is the meaning of *Bereshith*? It means "with Wisdom", the Wisdom on which the world is based, and through this it introduces us to deep and recondite mysteries. In it, too, is the inscription of six chief supernal directions, out of which there issues the totality of existence. From the same there go forth six sources of rivers which flow into the Great Sea. This is implied in the word *BeReSHiTH*, which can be analysed into *BaRa-SHiTH* (He created six). And who created them? The Mysterious Unknown.' R. Hiya and R. Jose were walking along the road. When they reached the open country, R. Hiya said to R. Jose, 'What you said about *bereshith* signifying *bara-shith* (created six) is certainly correct, since the Torah speaks of six primordial days and not more. The others are hinted at but not disclosed; nevertheless, from what is told us we can perceive the following. The Holy and Mysterious One graved in a hidden recess one point. In that He enclosed the whole of Creation as one who locks up all his treasures in a palace, under one key, which is therefore as valuable as all that is stored up in that palace; for it is the key which shuts and opens. In that palace there are hidden treasures, one greater than the other. The palace is provided with fifty mystic gates. They are inserted in its four sides to the number of forty-nine. The one remaining gate is on none of its sides and it is unknown whether it is on high or below: it is hence called the mysterious gate. All these gates have one lock, and there is one tiny spot for the insertion of the key, which is only marked by the impress of the key. It is this mystery which is implied in the words "In the beginning created God", "In the beginning" (*bereshith*): this is the key which encloses the whole and which shuts and opens. Six gates are controlled by this key which opens and shuts. At first it kept the gates closed and impenetrable; this is indicated by the word *bereshith*, which is composed of a revealing word (*shith*) with a concealing word (*bara*). *Bara* is always a word of mystery, closing and not opening,' Said R. Jose: 'Assuredly it is so, and I have heard the Sacred Lamp say the same, to wit, that *bara* is a term of mystery, a lock without a key, and as long as the world was locked within the term *bara* it was not in a state of being or existence. Over the whole there hovered *Tohu* (chaos), and as long as *Tohu* dominated, the world was not in being or existence. When did that key open the gates and make the world fruitful? It was when Abraham appeared, as it is written, "These are the generations of the heavens and of the earth *behibaream*" (when they were created) (Gen. II, 4). Now, *BeHiBaReAm* is an anagram of *BeABeRaHaM* (through Abraham), implying that what was hitherto sealed up and unproductive in the word *bara* has by a transposition of letters become serviceable, there has emerged a pillar of fruitfulness: for *BaRa* has been transformed into *AiBeR* (organ), which is the sacred foundation on which the world rests. Further, in the same way, as *AiBraHaM* contains *AiBeR*, a transformation of *BaRA*, so it is with the splendour of the name of the Most High and most Concealed One. This is implied in the words *MI BaRA AiLeH*. Add the other sacred name *MaH*. Transpose *BaRA* into *AiBeR*. We have *AiLeH* on one side and

AiBeR on the other side. Add the *Hé* (of *MaH*) to *AiBeR* and the *Yod* (of *MI*) to *AiLeH*. When we take now the *Mim* of both *MI* and *MaH* and join each to each we have complete the sacred name *AeLoHiM* and also the name [4a] *ABRaHaM*. According to another view, the Holy One, blessed be He, took *MI* and joined it to *AiLeH*, so that there was shaped *AeLoHiM*; similarly He took *MaH* and joined it to *AiBeR* and there was shaped *ABRaHaM*. And thus He made the world unfold itself, and made the name complete, as it had not been hitherto. This is meant by the verse "These are the generations (i.e. unfoldings) of the heaven and of the earth *BeHiBaReaM* (when they were created)". That is, the whole creation was in suspense until the name of *ABRaHaM* was created, and as soon as the name of Abraham was completed the Sacred Name was completed along with it, as it says further, "in the day that the Lord God made earth and heaven".'

R. Hiya then prostrated himself on the earth, kissed the dust, and said weeping: 'Dust, Dust, how stiffnecked art thou, how shameless art thou that all the delights of the eye perish within thee! All the beacons of light thou consumest and grindest into nothingness. Fie on thy shamelessness! That Sacred Lamp that illuminated the world, the mighty spiritual force by whose merits the world exists, is consumed by thee. Oh, R. Simeon, thou beacon of light, source of light to the world, how hast thou turned to dust, thou leader of the world whilst alive!' After falling for a moment into a reverie, he continued, 'O dust, dust! pride not thyself, for the pillars of the world will not be delivered into thy power, nor will R. Simeon perish within thee.'

R. Hiya then arose weeping and set out in company with R. Jose. He fasted from that day for forty days, in order that he might see R. Simeon. 'Thou canst not see him' was all the answer to his supplication. He then fasted another forty days, at the end of which he saw in a vision R. Simeon and his son R. Eleazar discussing the very subject which R. Jose had just explained to him, while thousands were looking on and listening. Meanwhile, there appeared a host of huge winged celestial beings upon whose wings R. Simeon and his son R. Eleazar were borne aloft into the heavenly Academy, whilst those beings remained at the threshold, awaiting them. Their splendour was constantly renewed, and they radiated a light exceeding that of the sun. R. Simeon then opened his mouth and said, 'Let R. Hiya enter and behold what the Holy One, blessed be He, has prepared for the rejoicing of the righteous in the world to come. Happy is he who enters here without misgiving, and happy is he who is established as a strong pillar in the world to come.' On entering he (R. Hiya) noticed that R. Eleazar and the other great scholars that were sitting near him stood up. He drew back in some embarrassment, and sat down at the feet of R. Simeon. A voice thereupon went forth, saying, 'Lower thine eyes, raise not thy head and do not look.' He lowered his eyes and discerned a light shining afar. The voice went forth again, saying 'O, ye unseen celestials, ye open-eyed who sweep to and fro throughout the world, behold and see! O, ye terrestrial beings who are sunk deep in slumber, awake! Who among you laboured to turn darkness into light and bitter into sweet before you entered here? Who among you awaited every day the light that shall break forth what time the King shall visit his beloved gazelle, when He will be glorified and called King by all the kings of the world? He who did not thus wait every day in the world below will have no share here.' Meanwhile he beheld a number of his colleagues gather round, even all the mighty pillars of wisdom, and he saw them ascend to the heavenly Academy, while others in turn descended. At the head of them all he saw the chief of the winged angels, who approached him and solemnly declared that he had heard 'from behind the curtain' that the King visits each day and remembers his gazelle which is trodden in the dust, and that at the moment He does so He strikes the three hundred and ninety heavens so they all quake and tremble [4b] before Him: for her fate He sheds tears hot as burning fire, which fall into the great sea. From these tears arises and is sustained the presiding genius of the sea, who sanctifies the name of the Holy King, and who has pledged himself to swallow up all the waters of the creation and to gather them all within himself on that day when all the nations shall assemble against the holy people, so that they shall be able to pass on dry land. Anon he heard a voice proclaiming, 'Make room, make room, for King Messiah is coming to the Academy of R. Simeon.' For all the righteous there have been heads of Academies on earth, and have become disciples of the heavenly Academy, and the Messiah visits all these Academies and puts his seal on all the expositions that issue from the mouths of the teachers. The Messiah then entered wearing heavenly diadems, with which he had been crowned by the heads of the Academy. All the colleagues stood up, along with R. Simeon, from whom a light shot up to the empyrean. The Messiah said to him, 'Happy art thou, for thy teaching mounts on high in the form of three hundred and seventy illuminations, and each illumination subdivides itself into six hundred and thirteen arguments, which go up and bathe themselves in streams of pure balsam. And the Holy One, blessed be He, Himself places His seal on the teaching of thy Academy and of the Academy of Hezekiah, King of Judah, and of the Academy of Ahijah of Shiloh. I come not to set my seal in thy Academy, since it is the chief of the winged angels who comes here; for I know that he does not visit any but thy Academy.' After that R. Simeon told him what the chief of the winged angels had so solemnly declared. Thereupon the Messiah fell a-quaking, and he cried aloud, and the heavens quivered, and the great sea quaked and the Leviathan trembled, and the world was shaken to its foundations. His eye then fell upon R. Hiya, who was sitting at the feet of R. Simeon. 'Who has brought here this man,' he asked, 'who still wears the raiment of the other world?' R. Simeon answered, 'This is the great R. Hiya, the shining lamp of the Torah.' 'Let him then,' said the Messiah, 'be gathered in, together with his sons, and let them become members of the Academy.' R. Simeon said, 'Let a time of grace be granted to him.' A time of grace was then granted to him, and he went forth from thence trembling, with tears running from his eyes, saying as he wept, 'Happy is the portion of the righteous in that world and happy is the portion of the son of Yohai who has merited such glory. It is concerning such as he that it is written, "That

I may cause those who love me to inherit a lasting possession; and their treasures will I fill" (Prov. VIII, 21.)'

IN THE BEGINNING. R. Simeon opened his discourse with the text: *And I put my words in thy mouth* (Is. LI, 16). He said: 'How greatly is it incumbent on a man to study the Torah day and night! For the Holy One, blessed be He, is attentive to the voice of those who occupy themselves with the Torah, and through each fresh discovery made by them in the Torah a new heaven is created. Our teachers have told us that at the moment when a man expounds something new in the Torah, his utterance ascends before the Holy One, blessed be He, and He takes it up and kisses it and crowns it with seventy crowns of graven and inscribed letters. When a new idea is formulated in the field of the esoteric wisdom, it ascends and rests on the head of the "*Zaddik*, the life of the universe", and then it flies off and traverses seventy thousand worlds until it ascends to the "Ancient of Days". And inasmuch as all the words of the "Ancient of Days" are words of wisdom comprising sublime and hidden mysteries, that hidden word of wisdom that was discovered here when it ascends is joined to the words of the "Ancient of Days", and becomes an integral part of them, and enters into the eighteen mystical worlds, concerning which we read "No eye hath seen beside thee, O God" (*Ibid*. LXIV, 3). From thence they issue and fly to and fro, until finally arriving, perfected and completed, before the "Ancient of Days". At that moment the "Ancient of Days" savours that word of wisdom, and finds satisfaction therein above all else. He takes that word and crowns it with three hundred and seventy thousand crowns, and it flies up and down until it is made into a sky. And so each word of wisdom is made into a sky which presents itself fully formed before the "Ancient of Days", who calls them "new heavens", that is, heavens created out of the mystic ideas of the sublime wisdom. As for the other new expositions of the Torah, they present themselves before [5a] the Holy One, blessed be He, and ascend and become "earths of the living", then they descend and become absorbed into one earth, whereby a new earth emerges through that new discovery in the Torah. This is implied in the verse, "For as the new heavens and the new earth, which I am making, rise up before me, etc." (*Ibid.* LXVI, 22). It is not written "I *have* made", but "I *am* making", signifying continual creation out of the new ideas discovered in the Torah. Further, it is written, "And I have placed my words in thy mouth, and with the shadow of my hand have I covered thee, to plant a heaven and to lay the foundations of an earth" (*Ibid.* LI, 16). It does not say "*the* heaven", but "*a* heaven".' Said R. Eleazar: 'What signifies "with the shadow of my hand have I covered thee"?' He replied: 'When the Torah was delivered to Moses, there appeared myriads of heavenly angels ready to consume him with their fiery breath, but the Holy One, blessed be He, sheltered him. Similarly now when the new word ascends and is crowned and presents itself before the Holy One, blessed be He, He covers and protects that word, and also shelters the author of that word, so that the angels should not become aware of him and so be filled with jealousy, until that word is transformed into a new heaven and a new earth. That is the meaning of the passage "and with the shadow of my hand have I covered thee, to plant a heaven and to lay the foundations of an earth". From this we learn that each word of which the purpose is not obvious contains some lesson of special value, as it is written: "And with the shadow of my hand have I covered thee." Why is it covered and hidden from our view? For an ulterior purpose, to wit, "to plant a heaven and to lay the foundation of an earth", as already explained. The verse continues: "And to say to Zion thou art '*Ami*, my people" (*Ibid.*). This means, to say to those gates of study and those words of Zion (distinction) "thou art '*Ami*". The word '*Ami* (my people) may be read '*Imi* (with me), meaning "to be a collaborator with Me"; for just as I made heaven and earth by a word, as it says: "By the word of the Lord the heavens were made" (Ps. XXXIII, 6), so dost thou. Happy are those who devote themselves to the study of the Torah! You should not think, however, that all this applies even to one who is no true scholar. Not so. When one who is a stranger to the mysteries of the Torah makes pseudo-discoveries based on an incomplete understanding, that "word" rises, and is met by the perverse One, the Demon of the false tongue, who emerges from the cavern of the great abyss and makes a leap of five hundred parasangs to receive that word. He takes it and returns with it to his cavern, and shapes it into a spurious heaven which is called *Tohu* (chaos). That Demon then traverses in one swoop the whole of that heaven, a space of six thousand parasangs. As soon as that heaven is formed, the Harlot emerges, and lodges herself in it, and joins forces with it, and issuing from thence she slays thousands and tens of thousands. For as long as she is lodged in that heaven she has authority and power to swoop through the world in the twinkling of an eye. This is implied in the words, "Woe unto them that draw iniquity with cords of vanity" (Is. v, 18). The word for "iniquity", *'Avon*, being of the masculine gender, designates the Demon. In the next part of the verse, "and sin, as it were, with a cart rope", the word for "sin", *ḥattaah*, being of the feminine gender, signifies the female, the Harlot who rushes to execute slaughter on the sons of men. Concerning her we also read, "For she hath caused to fall many deadly wounded" (Prov. VII, 26), namely, that *ḥattaah* (sin) who slays the sons of men. And the ultimate cause is the unripe scholar who is not qualified to teach and yet does so. May God save us from him!' Said R. Simeon to the colleagues: 'I beseech you not to let fall from your mouth any word of the Torah of which you are not certain and which you have not learnt correctly from a "great tree", so that you may not be the cause of that Harlot slaying multitudes of the sons of men.' They answered in unison, 'God forbid, God forbid!' R. Simeon proceeded: 'See now, it was by means of the Torah that the Holy One created the world. That has already been derived from the verse, "Then I was near him as an artisan, and I was daily all his delight" (Prov. VIII, 30). He looked at the Torah once, twice, thrice, and a fourth time. He uttered the words composing her and then operated through her. That is a lesson for men, how to study the Torah properly. This lesson is indicated by the verse, "Then did he see, and declare it; he established it, yea, and searched it out." (Job. XXVIII, 27). Seeing, declaring, establishing and searching out correspond to these four operations which the

Holy One, blessed be He, went through before entering on the work of creation. Hence the account of the creation commences with the four words *Bereshith Bara Aelohim Aith* ("In-the-beginning created God the"), before mentioning "the heavens", thus signifying the four times which the Holy One, blessed be He, looked into the Torah before He performed His work.'

R. Eleazar was journeying to visit his father-in-law, R. Jose, son of R. Simeon son of Lakunya [5*b*]. He was accompanied by R. Abba, and another man was leading their baggage-ass behind them. Said R. Abba, 'Let us open a discourse on the Torah, the time and place being propitious.' R. Eleazar then began thus: 'It is written: *Ye shall keep my Sabbaths* (Lev. XIX, 30). Consider this: the Holy One, blessed be He, created the world in six days and each day revealed a part of His work, and functioned through the energy imparted to it. But none of the work was actually disclosed nor the energy functioning until the fourth day. The first three days were undisclosed and imperceptible, but when the fourth day came the product and energy of all of them was brought out into the open. Fire, water, and air, as three primordial elements, were still in suspense, their activity not having become visible until the earth disclosed them and so made knowable the workmanship of each one of them. You may object that in the account of the third day it is written, "Let the earth put forth grass", as well as "And the earth put forth". The answer is that, though ascribed to the third day, this actually took place on the fourth day, and it was included in the account of the third day merely to indicate the unbroken continuity of the creation. From the fourth day onwards He disclosed His work and produced an artificer for the function of each one (for the fourth day is the symbol of the fourth leg of the celestial Throne). Furthermore, the activities of all the days, whether of the first or the second triad, were made dependent on the day of the Sabbath, as it is written, "And on the seventh day God finished." This is the Sabbath, and this is the fourth foot of the celestial Throne. What, then, you may ask, is implied in "My *Sabbaths* ye shall observe", which seems to point to two Sabbaths? The answer is that the plural form indicates the eve of Sabbath and the Sabbath itself, which merge into each other without a break.'

At this point the driver who was following them interposed with the question: 'What is meant by "And ye shall reverence my sanctuary" (*Ibid.*)?' R. Abba replied: 'This designates the sanctity of the Sabbath.' 'What then,' he said, 'is the sanctity of the Sabbath?' 'It is the sanctity which was conferred upon it from above.' 'If that is so' (argued the stranger) 'thou makest the Sabbath to possess no sanctity of its own but only such as rests on it from above.' 'It is indeed so' (said R. Abba), 'as it is written, "And call the Sabbath a delight, and the holy of the Lord honourable" (Is. LVIII, 13), where the "Sabbath" and the "holy of the Lord" are mentioned each separately.' 'What, then, is the "holy of the Lord"?' 'It is the holiness which descends from above to rest on it.' 'But' (argued the stranger) 'if the holiness emanating from on high is called "honourable", evidently the Sabbath itself is not so called, and yet it is written, "And thou shalt honour it" (*Ibid.*).' Said R. Eleazar to R. Abba, 'Cease arguing with that man, for he seems to know some mystery of which we are ignorant.' They then said to him: 'Say what thou hast to say.' He commenced thus: 'It is written: *'eth Shabthothai* ("My sabbaths") (Lev. XIX, 30). The particle *eth* indicates that in the precept of the Sabbath is to be included the limit of the Sabbath walk, which is two thousand cubits in all directions. "My Sabbaths" is a reference to the higher Sabbath and the lower Sabbath, which are two joined together as one. There was still one Sabbath left unmentioned. Feeling humiliated, she pleaded before the Creator, saying, "O Lord of the universe, since the time when Thou didst create me, I have been called merely 'day of Sabbath', but surely a day must have for companion a night." Said the Lord to her, "O my daughter, thou art Sabbath, and Sabbath I will call thee. But I will confer on thee an even more glorious crown." He then made proclamation, "And ye shall fear my sanctuary" (*Ibid.*). This is a reference to the Sabbath of the eve of Sabbath, which inspires fear, and upon which fear rests. And it is the Holy One, blessed be He, Himself who identified Himself with her, saying "I am the Lord" (*Ibid.*). I have further heard' (continued the stranger) 'the following exposition from my father. He stressed the particle *eth* as signifying the limit of the Sabbath walk. "My Sabbaths," he said, denotes the circle and the square within,[1] and corresponding to these two the sanctification recital consists of two parts, one the verses Genesis II, 1-3, commencing *Vaikhulu* (and were completed) and the other the sanctification proper (*Kiddush*). *Vaikhulu* contains thirty-five words, and the *Kiddush* contains thirty-five words, making together seventy, corresponding to the seventy names of the Holy One, blessed be He, by which the congregation of Israel is crowned. On account of this circle and square, the Sabbaths here referred to come under the injunction of the word "keep" used in the second version of the Ten Commandments (Deut. V, 12) as it is written here, "ye shall *keep* my Sabbaths". For the other, the highest Sabbath does not come under the injunction of *Shamor* (keep), but is under that of *Zakhor* (remember), which is used in the first version of the Ten Commandments (Exod. XX, 8), since the Supreme King is hinted at in the word *Zakhor* (remember). For this reason He is called "the King with whom Peace dwells", and His peace is within the injunction of *zakhor* (remember). And this is why there is no contention in the supernal realm, because of the twofold peace here below, one for Jacob and one for Joseph, as it is written, "Peace, Peace, to him that is far off and to him that is near" (Is. LVII, 19): "to him that is far off" refers to Jacob [6a], "and to him that is near" refers to Joseph. "To him that is far" is parallel to "From afar the Lord appeared unto me" (Jer. XXXI, 3), as well as to "And his sister stood afar off" (Exod. II, 4); "and to him that is near" is parallel to "new gods who came up since a near time" (Deut. XXXII, 17). "From afar" signifies the supernal point which is situated in His palace, and in regard to which it is said "ye shall keep", thus bringing it under the injunction of *shamor* (*keep*). "And my sanctuary ye shall fear" refers to the point which is situated in the centre and which is most to

---

[1] The circle, square, and point were used by the Cabbalists to symbolise the three highest *Sefiroth*.

be feared, as the penalty of transgression is death, as it is written, "Everyone that profaneth it shall surely be put to death" (Ex. XXXI, 14); i.e. those who penetrate into the space of the circle-square, treading on the spot where the central point is situated and damaging it—these shall surely be put to death. Of this it is written, "Ye shall fear." That point is called *Ani* (I) (Lev. XIX, 30), and upon it rests the unknown, the Most High, the unrevealed One which is *YHWH* (the Lord), both being one.' R. Eleazar and R. Abba came up to the stranger and kissed him. They said: 'With all this profound knowledge thou hast displayed, is it meet that thou shouldst journey behind us ? Who art thou ?' they asked him. 'Do not ask,' he said, 'but let us proceed on our way and together let us discourse on the Torah. Let each one say some word of wisdom to illumine our way.' They asked him, 'Who charged thee to make this journey as an ass-driver ?' He said to them, 'The letter *Yod* waged war with the letters *Kaph* and *Samekh*, to make them join me. The *Kaph* refused to leave its place, since it could not exist for a moment elsewhere. The *Samekh* refused to move from its place lest it should cease to support those that fall. The *Yod* then came to me all alone and kissed and embraced me. He wept with me and said, "My son, what shall I do for thee? I will go and load myself with a plenitude of good things and of precious, sublime and mystic symbols, and then I will come to thee and help thee and put thee in possession of two celestial letters superior to those that have departed, to wit the word *Yesh* (plentifulness), consisting of a celestial *Yod* and a celestial *Shin*, so that thou wilt become possessed of stores of riches of all kinds. Go then, my son, and load thy ass." This is why I am travelling in this manner.' R. Eleazar and R. Abba rejoiced; they also wept and said to him, 'Go, ride in front and we will follow thee on the ass.' He said to them, 'Have I not told you that it is the command of the King that I should continue thus until he who will ride on an ass shall appear ?' They said to him, 'Thou hast not told us thy name, nor thy habitation.' He answered, 'My habitation is a good one and an exalted one for me—a mighty and imposing tower suspended in the air. In that tower there reside the Holy One, blessed be He, and a certain poor man: and that is my place of habitation. But I have left it and am become an ass-driver.' R. Abba and R. Eleazar gazed at him, and he discoursed to them words as sweet as manna and honey. They said to him, 'If thou wouldst tell us the name of thy father we would kiss the dust of thy feet.' He said to them, 'Why so? It is not my habit to pride myself on a knowledge of the Torah, but my father inhabited the great sea, he was a huge fish who embraced the great sea from one end to the other; he was mighty and noble and ancient of days so that he would swallow up all the other fishes in the sea and then release them again alive and filled with all the good things of the world. Like a mighty swimmer he could traverse the whole sea in one second. He shot me out like an arrow in the hand of a bowman and hid me in the place I told you of, and he himself returned to his place and is hid in that sea.' R. Eleazar pondered a little and said, 'Thou art the son of the sacred lamp, thou art the son of the venerable Rab Hamnuna, thou art the son of the light of the Torah, and yet thou drivest behind us!' They both wept together and they kissed him and went forward on their way. They further said to him, 'May our master be pleased to let us know his name.' He thereupon began to discourse on the verse: *And Benaiah the son of Jehoiada, etc.* (II Sam. XXIII, 20). 'This verse', he said, 'has been well explained—in addition to its literal meaning—to signify high mysteries of the Torah. "Benaiah the son of Jehoiada" (i.e. son of God, son of knowing-God) contains an allusion to wisdom, and is a symbolic appellation which influences its bearer. "The son of a living man" indicates the "*Zaddik*, the life of the universe". "Mighty of deeds" signifies the Master of all actions and of all celestial hosts, since all proceed from him; He is the "Lord of hosts", the insignia of all His hosts, yet distinguished and exalted above all. He is "mighty of deeds, from Kabzeel", as if to say: "that great and most mighty tree, from what place comes it, from what grade does it issue? From Kabzeel" (lit. gathering of God), from the highest and hidden grade [6*b*] where "no eye hath ever seen, etc." (Is. LXIV, 3), a grade which contains the whole and which is the focus of the supernal light, and from which everything issues. That light is the sacred and hidden temple (*Hekal*) wherein is concentrated that divine essence from which all the worlds draw sustenance, and all divine hosts are nourished and so subsist. "He smote the strong lion of Moab" is a reference to the two Temples that existed for His sake and drew their strength from Him, namely, the first Temple and the second Temple. But as soon as He departed, the flow of blessing from above ceased; "He", as it were, "smote" them, destroyed them, made an end of them, and the sacred Throne was overturned, as it is written, "as I was among the captives" (Ezek. I, I), implying that that divine essence called "I" was in captivity. "On the river Khebar" (*Ibid.*) (*Khebar*=long ago) means the stream that was once flowing, but the waters and sources of which were cut off so that it flows no more as formerly. The same is implied in the verse "and the river faileth and drieth up" (Job. XIV, 11): "faileth", referring to the first Temple, and "drieth up" to the second Temple. And so "He smote the two strong lions of Moab" (Moab = *Meab*, of the father), namely the Temples of the Father in heaven, by whom they were now destroyed, so that all lights which illuminated Israel were now darkened. Further, "He went down and smote the lion": formerly when that stream flowed down to here below, Israel was free from care, offering peace-offerings and sin-offerings to atone for his soul; and from on high descended the image of a lion visible to all, crouching on his prey, consuming the offerings like a mighty giant. All the dogs kept themselves out of sight, fearing to venture abroad. But when sin prevailed He descended to the regions here below and slew that lion, not desiring any more to provide his portion as formerly. He, as it were, slew him: "He smote the lion", most assuredly, "into the pit", that is to say, in the sight of the "evil monster". The same evil monster, seeing this, sent a dog to consume the offerings. The name of the lion is Ariel, as his face is that of a lion; and the name of the dog is Baladon (not-man), for it is a dog and has the face of a dog. "In a day of snow", that is, in the day when on account of Israel's sins sentence was pronounced by the Court on high. (The same is implied in the verse "She is not afraid of the snow for her household" (Prov. XXXI, 21), that is to say, of the judgement on high; why so? "for all her household are clothed with scarlet", and hence can endure the strongest fire.) Such is the mystical meaning of this verse. The next verse reads: "And he smote an Egyptian, a man of good appearance, etc." The mystical meaning of this verse is that every time Israel sins, God leaves them and withholds from them all the blessings and all the lights which illumined them. "He smote an Egyptian": this signifies the light of Israel's great luminary, to wit, Moses, who is called an Egyptian, as it is written, "And they said, an Egyptian delivered us, etc." (Exod. II, 19), for there he was born, there he was brought up and there he was vouchsafed the higher light. "A man of good appearance" (*mar'eh*) also signifies Moses, of whom it is written "*ou-mar'eh* (by clear appearance) and not in dark speeches" (Num. XII, 8); so too "man" (*ish*), as he is called "man of God" (Deut. XXXIII, 1), the husband, as it were, of the Divine glory, leading it whereso he would upon the earth, a privilege no other man had ever enjoyed. "And the Egyptian had a spear in his hand," to wit, the divine rod that was delivered into his hand, as we read: "With the rod of God in my hand" (Exod. XVII, 9), which is the same rod that was created in the twilight of the eve of Sabbath, and on which there was engraven the Divine Name in sacred letters. With the same rod Moses sinned by smiting the rock, as we read: "And he smote the rock with his rod twice" (Num. XX, 11). The Holy One, blessed be He, said to him "I have not given the rod for that purpose; by thy life, from henceforward it will not be in thy hand any more." Immediately "He went down to him with a rod", i.e. He judged him rigidly, "and plucked the spear out of the Egyptian's hand," for from that moment he lost it and never more regained it. "And slew him with his spear," i.e. through the sin of smiting the rock with that rod he died without entering the Holy Land, and thereby that illumination was withheld from Israel. "He was more honourable than the thirty" (II Sam. XXIII, 23) alludes to the thirty celestial years from which he was taken to be sent down below. "But he attained not to the first three", that is, they (the patriarchs) came to him and gave him whatever he craved, but he did not come to them; and although he did not enter into their number, yet "David put him into his service", that is, David never detached him from his heart, [7a] nor will there ever be any separation between the two. David turned his heart towards him, but he did not turn his towards David, in the same manner as the moon addresses her praises and hymns towards the sun, drawing him to herself to set up, as it were, his abode with her. This is implied in the words "And David put him into his service".'

R. Eleazar and R. Abba prostrated themselves before the stranger. Of a sudden they saw him not. They arose and looked on every side, but they saw him not. They sat down and wept and were unable to exchange a word. After a while R. Abba said: 'It is assuredly true as we have been taught, that whenever the righteous on their journey busy themselves with expositions of the Torah, they are favoured by visits from the other world; for it is clear that it was the venerable Rab Hamnuna who appeared to us from the other world to reveal to us all these things, and now before we could recognize him, he has vanished.' They arose and tried to drive the asses, but could not make them go, and again tried, but could not. They became frightened and left the animals behind. That spot is called until this day 'Asses' place.

R. Eleazar commenced to discourse thus: *O how great is the abundance of thy goodness which thou hast laid up for them that fear thee, etc.* (Ps. XXXI, 20). 'How great is the heavenly bounty which the Holy One, blessed be He, hath reserved for those who excel in righteousness, who shun sin and devote themselves to the study of the Torah, when they ascend to the world to come. It is not written simply "thy goodness", but "*abundance of* thy goodness", the same expression as in the verse "They utter the fame of the abundance of thy goodness" (Ps. CXLV, 7), to wit, the delight which the righteous enjoy in the world to come in the presence of the Everlasting who is "abundant in goodness towards the house of Israel" (Is. LXIII, 7). We may also find enshrined in this passage a mystery of wisdom, in which all other mysteries are enclosed. We translate: "O *Mah*, great is thy goodness, etc." *Mah*

("How" or "What") has already been explained. *Rab* ("abundant" or "great") alludes to the strong and mighty tree: there is another and a smaller tree, but this one is tall, reaching into the highest heaven. "Thy goodness" alludes to the light that was created on the first day. "Which thou hast laid up for those who fear thee", since He has treasured it up for the righteous in the world to come: "which thou hast wrought" alludes to the higher *Gan-Eden* (Garden-of-Eden, Paradise), as it is written, "The place, O Lord, which thou hast wrought for thy dwelling" (Exod. xv, 17), to wit, "Thou hast wrought for them that trust in thee". "In the sight of the sons of men" alludes to the lower *Gan-Eden* where all the righteous abide, as spirits clad in a resplendent vesture resembling their corporeal figure in this world; this is meant by "in the sight of man", i.e. presenting the likeness of the people of this world. They stay there for a time, then rise in the air and ascend to the celestial Academy, which is the *Gan-Eden* above; then they rise again and bathe in the dewy rivers of pure balsam, and then descend and remain below, and sometimes they appear to men to perform for them miracles in the manner of angels, as we have just seen the light of the "Sacred Lamp", without, however, being vouchsafed an insight into the mysteries of Wisdom, so far as we could have wished.' R. Abba said: 'It is written, "And Manoah said unto his wife, We shall surely die, because we have seen God" (Judg. xiii, 22). Although Manoah was ignorant of the object of the apparition, he nevertheless argued, "Since it is written 'for man shall not see me and live' (Exod. xxxiii, 20), and as we certainly saw Him, we shall therefore die." And we were privileged to see that light which accompanied us, and we are still alive, because the Holy One, blessed be He, sent it to us in order to reveal to us the mysteries of Wisdom. Happy is our portion!'

They continued their journey and reached a certain hill at sunset. The branches of the trees on the hill began to shake and rustle and broke forth into hymns. Whilst walking, they heard a resounding voice proclaim: 'Holy sons of God, who are interspersed among the living of yonder world, ye who are the lamps of the Academy, reassemble into your places to regale yourselves, under the guidance of your Master, in the study of the Torah.' In fear and trembling they stopped and sat down. Meanwhile, a voice went forth again and proclaimed: 'O, ye mighty rocks, exalted hammers, behold the Lord, lo, Him whose appearance is as a broidered pattern of many colours, mounted on His throne: enter then into your place of assembly.' At that moment they heard a loud and mighty sound issuing from between the branches of the trees, and they uttered the verse: 'The voice of the Lord breaketh the cedars' (Ps. XXIX, 5). R. Eleazar and R. Abba fell upon their faces and a great fear came over them. They then arose in haste and went on their way, and heard nothing more. They left the hill, and when they reached the house of R. Simeon the son of Lakunya they saw there R. Simeon the son of Yohai, and they rejoiced [7b] exceedingly. R. Simeon said to them, 'Assuredly ye traversed a path of heavenly miracles and wonders, for as I was sleeping just now I had a vision of you and of Benaiah the son of Jehoiada, who was sending you two crowns by the hand of a certain elder to crown you withal. Assuredly the Holy One, blessed be He, was on that path. Further, I saw your faces as if transfigured.' R. Jose remarked: 'Well have ye said that "the sage is superior to the prophet".' R. Eleazar then approached and put his head between the knees of his father and told him all that had happened to them. R. Simeon trembled and wept. ' "O Lord, I have the report of thee, and I am afraid" ' (Habak. III, 2), he said. 'This verse did Habakkuk exclaim at the time when he reflected on his own death and his resurrection through Elisha. Why was he named HaBaKkuK? Because it is written, "At this season when the time cometh round, thou shalt be embracing (HoBeKeth) a son" (II Kings IV, 16), and he—Habakkuk—was the son of the Shunammite. He received indeed two embracings, one from his mother and one from Elisha, as it is written, "and he put his mouth upon his mouth" (*Ibid.* 34). In the Book of King Solomon I have found the following: He (Elisha) traced on him the mystic appellation, consisting of seventy-two names. For the alphabetical letters that his father had at first engraved on him had flown off when the child died; but when Elisha embraced him

he engraved on him anew all those letters of the seventy-two names. Now the number of those letters amounts to two hundred and sixteen, and they were all engraved by the breath of Elisha on the child so as to put again into him the breath of life through the power of the letters of the seventy-two names. And Elisha named him Habakkuk, a name of double significance, alluding in its sound to the twofold embracing, as already explained, and in its numerical value (H. B. K. V. K. = 8. 2. 100. 6. 100) to two hundred and sixteen, the number of the letters of the Sacred Name. By the words his spirit was restored to him and by the letters his bodily parts were reconstituted. Therefore the child was named Habakkuk, and it was he who said: "O Lord, I have heard the report of thee, and I am afraid" (Habak. III, 2), that is to say, I have heard what happened to me, that I tasted of the other world, and am afraid. He then commenced to supplicate for himself, saying, "O Lord, Thy work" which Thou hast accomplished for me, "in the midst of the years", I pray, "let its life be". For he who is bound up with the cycles of past years has life bound up with him. "In the midst of the years make it known", to wit, that stage in which there is no life.'
R. Simeon then wept and said: 'I also from what I have heard am seized with fear of the Holy One, blessed be He.' He then raised his hands above his head and said, 'What a privilege it was for you to see face to face the venerable Rab Hamnuna, the light of the Torah—a privilege I have not been granted.' He then fell on his face and saw him uprooting mountains, and kindling the lights in the temple of the Messiah. R. Hamnuna, addressing him, said, 'Master, in this other world thou wilt be the neighbour of the teachers of the Law in the presence of the Holy One, blessed be He.' From that time onward R. Simeon named R. Eleazar his son and R. Abba Peniel (face of God), in allusion to the verse, "For I have seen God face to face" (Gen. XXXII, 31).

IN THE BEGINNING. R. Hiya opened his discourse thus: *The beginning of wisdom is the fear of the Lord; A good understanding have all they that do hereafter. His praise endureth for ever* (Ps. CXI, 10). He said: 'Instead of "the beginning of wisdom" it would be more appropriate to say "the *end* of wisdom is the fear of the Lord", since the fear of the Lord is the final object of wisdom. The Psalmist, however, speaks of the highest order of wisdom, which can only be reached through the gate of the fear of God. This is implied in the verse "Open to me the gates of righteousness. . . . This is the gate of the Lord . . ." (Ps. CXVIII, 19-20). Assuredly, without entering through that gate one will never gain access to the most high King. Imagine a king greatly exalted who screens himself from the common view behind gate upon gate, and at the end, one special gate, locked and barred. Saith the king: He who wishes to enter into my presence must first of all pass through that gate. So here the first gate to super-Wisdom is the fear of God; and this is what is meant by *reshith* (beginning). The letter *Beth* (=2) indicates two things joined together, namely two points, one shrouded in mystery and one capable of being revealed; and as they are inseparable they therefore are both joined in the single term *reshith* (beginning), i.e. they are one and not two, and he who takes away the one takes away the other as well. For He and His name are one, as it is written "That they may know that thou and thy name of Lord art alone" (Ps. LXXXIII, 19). Why is this first gate called "the fear of the Lord"? Because it is the tree of good and evil. If a man deserves well it is good, and if he deserves ill it is evil. [8a] Hence in that place abides fear, which is the gateway to all that is good. "Good" and "understanding" are two gates which are as one.' R. Jose said: 'The term "A good understanding" alludes to the tree of life which is the knowledge of good without evil. "To all that do hereafter": these are "the sure mercies of David" (Is. LV, 3), viz. they who support the study of the Torah. For they who support the study of the Torah are, we may say, *doing* something, whereas those who are merely occupied in its study are for the time being not *doing*. Through this activity "his praise endureth for ever", and the Throne abides on its base securely.'

R. Simeon was sitting and studying the Torah during the night when the bride was to be joined to her husband.[1] For

---

[1] i.e. the eve of Pentecost.

we have been taught that all the members of the bridal palace, during the night preceding her espousals, are in duty bound to keep her company and to rejoice with her in her final preparations for the great day: to study all branches of the Torah, proceeding from the Law to the Prophets, from the Prophets to the Holy Writings, and then to the deeper interpretations of Scripture and to the mysteries of Wisdom, as all these represent her preparations and her adornments. The bride, indeed, with her bridesmaids, comes up and remains with them, adorning herself at their hands and rejoicing with them all that night. And on the following day she does not enter under the canopy except in their company, they being called the canopy attendants. And when she steps under the canopy the Holy One, blessed be He, enquires after them and blesses them and crowns them with the bridal crown: happy is their portion!

Hence R. Simeon and all the companions were chanting the Scripture with exultation, each one of them making new discoveries in the Torah. Said R. Simeon to them, 'O my sons, happy is your portion, for on the morrow the bride will not enter the bridal canopy except in your company; for all those who help to prepare her adornments to-night will be recorded in the book of remembrance, and the Holy One, blessed be He, will bless them with seventy blessings and crown them with crowns of the celestial world.' R. Simeon opened his discourse thus: *The heavens declare the glory of God, etc.* (Ps. XIX, 2). He said: 'The inner meaning of this verse is as follows. When the bride awakes on the morn of her wedding day, she begins to prepare her ornaments and decorations with the aid of the companions who have rejoiced with her all that night, as she with them. On that day there assemble in her honour hosts upon hosts, awaiting each one of those who have helped in her adornment on the previous night. As soon as the bride beholds her spouse, "the heavens declare the glory of God". "The heavens" are the bridegroom, who enters under the bridal canopy. "Declare" (*meSaPeRim*) signifies that they radiate a brilliance like that of a sapphire, sparkling and scintillating from one end of the world to the other. "The glory of *El*" (God) signifies the glory of the bride which is called *El* (God), as it is written "and *El* (God) hath indignation every day" (Ps. VII, 12); all the days of the year it is called *El* (God), but now when she enters under the bridal canopy it is called Glory. It is also at the same time still called *El* (God), signifying glory on glory, splendour on splendour, and dominion on dominion. Thus, at that time when heaven enters into the canopy and irradiates her, all those companions who joined in her adornment have their names recorded there above, as it is written, "and the firmament showeth his handiwork" (*Ibid.* XIX, 2), the words "his handiwork" being an allusion to those who have entered into a covenant with the bride. The confederates of the covenant are called " the works of his hands", as we read " the work of our hands establish thou it" (Ps. XC, 17) This is an allusion to the covenant that is engraven on man's body.'

Rab Hamnuna discoursed thus: *Suffer not thy mouth to bring thy flesh into guilt* (Eccl. v, 5). 'This is a warning to man not to utter with his mouth words that might suggest evil thoughts and so cause to sin the sacred body on which is stamped the holy covenant. For he who does this is dragged into Gehinnom. The angel presiding over Gehinnom is called Duma, and there are tens of thousands of angels of destruction under him. He stands at its door, but those who have carefully guarded the sign of the holy covenant he has no power to touch. David, after his affair with Uriah, was in great fear. Duma entered into the presence of the Holy One, blessed be He, and said: [8*b*] "O Lord of the universe, it is written in the Torah: 'And the man that committeth adultery with another man's wife, etc.' (Lev. XX, 10), and it is also written 'And with thy neighbour's wife, etc.' (*Ibid.* XVIII, 20). Now, David has misused the sign of the holy covenant; what shall be done to him ?" Said the Holy One, blessed be His name: "David is pure, and the holy covenant remains untouched inasmuch as at the creation of the world it was revealed before Me that Bath-Sheba was assigned to him."

' "If before Thee it was revealed, yet it was not revealed to him."

' "And further, what was done was done lawfully, since

every one who goes out to war first gives a bill of divorcement to his wife."

' "Even so, he ought to have waited three months, which he did not."

' "That rule only applies where there is a risk that she may be pregnant. In this case, however, it is known to Me that Uriah never came in unto her, in witness whereof My name is sealed in his, as he is sometimes called *URiYaH* and sometimes *URiYaHU*, to show that he never had intercourse with her."

' "O Lord of the universe, I must repeat my plea. If to Thee it was manifest that Uriah never came in unto her, was it manifest unto David? He ought then to have waited three months. Further, if David was aware that he never came near her, why then did he send an order to him to go home and visit his wife, as it is written, 'Go down to thy house and wash thy feet' (II Sam. XI, 8)?"

' "He certainly was not aware of it, and indeed he waited even more than three months, namely, four months, as we have been taught: The twenty-fifth day of Nisan David called the people to arms, and the people assembled under Joab on the seventh of Sivan, when they went and smote the Ammonites. They remained there the months of Sivan, Tamuz, Ab, and Elul, and on the twenty-fourth of Elul happened the incident of Bath-Sheba. And on the day of Kippur (Atonement) the Holy One, blessed be He, forgave him that sin. According to another account, on the seventh day of Adar David called the people to arms, and they assembled on the fifteenth of Iyar, and on the fifteenth of Elul happened the incident of Bath-Sheba, and the day of Kippur he was vouchsafed the message: 'The Lord also hath put away thy sin: thou shalt not die' (*Ibid.* XII, 13), to wit, thou shalt not die at the hand of Duma."

' "O Lord of the universe, I have still one argument, that he himself pronounced his doom, saying: 'As the Lord liveth, the man that hath done this deserveth to die' (*Ibid.* 5). He thereby condemned himself, and my charge against him stands."

' "Thou hast no power over him since he made confession

to Me and said 'I have sinned against the Lord', although he was not guilty. As for his sin in the matter of Uriah, I prescribed a penalty for him which he suffered immediately."

'Duma returned then crestfallen to his place. It is in regard to this that David said: "Unless the Lord had been my help, but a little would have been wanting that my soul had dwelt in *duma*" (silence) (Ps. XCIV, 17). That is, if the Lord had not been my advocate, "it wanted but little, etc." Only by the hairbreadth which is between me and the "Sinister Power" did my soul escape from the clutches of Duma. A man should therefore be on his guard not to let slip an incautious word like David, since he will not be able to plead with Duma "that it was an error" (Eccl. v, 5), like David, who was vindicated by the Holy One, blessed be His Name; "wherefore should God be angry at thy voice, and destroy the work of thy hands?" (*Ibid.*), i.e. the flesh of the holy covenant which the man has defiled and which, as a punishment, is stretched in Gehinnom at the hand of Duma.'

[R. Simeon resumed:] 'The words "And the firmament showeth his handiwork" (Ps. XIX, 2) are an allusion to the companions who kept the bride company and are the custodians of her covenant. Every one of them He telleth and inscribeth. The "firmament" here mentioned is that one wherein are the sun, the moon, the stars, and constellations, and which constitutes the Recording Book. He telleth and inscribeth every one of them as denizens of the heavenly Palace, whose desires shall always be accomplished. "Day unto day uttereth speech" (*Ibid.* 3); each sacred day of the heavenly days utters the praises of the companions and repeats each word of exposition which was exchanged between them: day unto day expresses that word and extols it. "And night unto night revealeth knowledge" (*Ibid.*): that is, all the forces ruling in the night extol to one another the deep knowledge of the companions, and become their devoted friends. "There is no speech, there are no words, neither is their voice heard" (*Ibid.* 4): this refers to worldly conversation, which is not heard by the holy King, nor does He desire to hear it. But as for those words of wisdom, "their line is gone out through all the earth" (*Ibid.* 5), they trace [9a] the measure and the plan of all celestial and all terrestrial habitations: it is indeed through those words that the heavens were made, and it is through the praises sung in those words that the earth was made. Nor think that they rest only in one spot: we are told "and their words to the end of the earth" (*Ibid.*). Who, then, inhabits the heavens made by them? "In them hath he set a tent for the sun" (*Ibid.*): the sacred sun has made his habitation in them and is crowned in them. Thus we read "And he is as a bridegroom coming out of his chamber" (*Ibid.* 6), gaily coursing through those heavens. When he emerges from them and hastens to another tower in another place, "his going forth is from the end of the heavens" (*Ibid.* 7), he issues from the supernal world, which is as the "extremity of heaven" above. "His circuit" (*Ibid.*) is the extremity of heaven" below, viz. the circuit of the year, which goes completely round and extends from the heaven to our firmament. "And there is nothing hid from his heat" (*Ibid.*), i.e. from the heat of this circuit, and from the circuit of the sun, which embraces every side; from this "nothing is hid", i.e. no one of all the upper grades is hid from him, since all come round to him, and not one is hidden "from his heat" when he returns to them in full strength. All this praise and laudation is on account of the Torah (Law), as we read, "The Law of the Lord is perfect, etc." (*Ibid.* 8–10). We find in this passage six times the mention of the Lord (*tetragrammaton*) as well as six verses from "The heavens declare" up to "The Law of the Lord is perfect". Likewise the first word of the Torah, *bereshith* (in the beginning) consists of six letters, and the rest of the first verse, "created God the heaven and-the earth", also consists of six words. The six verses of our text correspond to the six letters, and the six mentions of the Name correspond to the six words.'

Whilst they were sitting there entered his son, R. Eleazar, and R. Abba. He said to them: 'Of a certainty the face of the Shekinah has arrived, and it is for this reason that I named you Peniel, because you have seen the Shekinah face to face. And now that you have learnt the secret of the verse concerning Benaiah the son of Jehoiada, an exposition indeed emanating from the Ancient and Holy One, as well as of the verse following, I am going to expound to you another even more mysterious verse in another passage.' He then opened his discourse thus: 'It is written, *And he slew an Egyptian, a man of great stature, five cubits high* (1 Chr. XI, 23). There is here the same hidden meaning as in the verses just mentioned. By "the Egyptian" is meant that well-known figure who was "very great in the land of Egypt in the eyes of the servants, etc." (Exod. XI, 3). He was great and honoured, as Rab Hamnuna explained. In the heavenly Academy, however, the words *ish middah* (man of dimension) were explained as "one whose dimensions extended from one end of the world to the other", which were the dimensions of the first man, Adam. Those "five cubits", then, must have been such as to extend from one end of the world to the other. To return, however: "And in the Egyptian's hand was a spear like a weaver's beam" (1 Chr. XI, 23). This alludes to the divine rod which was in Moses' hand, and on which there was engraved the divine ineffable Name radiating in various combinations of letters. These same letters were in possession of Bezalel, who was called "weaver", and his school, as it is written: "Them hath he filled with wisdom of heart . . . of the craftsman and the skilled workman, and the weaver, etc." (Exod. XXXV, 35). So that rod had engraved on it the ineffable Name on every side, in forty-two various combinations, which were illumined in different colours. The rest of the verse is as he already explained. Happy is his portion! Come, dear friends, come and let us renew the preparations of the bride in this night. For everyone who keeps vigil with her in this night will be guarded above and below and will complete the year in peace. It is of them that it is written: "The angel of the Lord encampeth round about them that fear him and delivereth them: O consider and see that the Lord is good." (Ps. XXXIV, 8–9).'

R. Simeon opened his discourse thus: 'It is written, *In the beginning God created.* This verse must be well laid to heart, for he who affirms that there is another god will be destroyed from the world. It is written: *Thus shall ye say unto them: The gods that have not made the heavens and the earth, these shall perish from the earth and from under the heavens*. (Jer. x, 11). Why has this verse [9b] been written in Aramaic, with the exception of the last word? It cannot be because the holy angels do not pay attention to Aramaic and do not understand it, for then all the more was it appropriate for this verse to be written in Hebrew, so that the angels should acknowledge its doctrine. The true reason certainly is that the angels, since they do not understand Aramaic, shall not come to be jealous of man and do him evil. For in this verse the holy angels are comprised, as they are called *Elohim* (gods, powers), and yet they have not made heaven or earth. Instead of *wearka* (and the earth) there should have been written the proper Aramaic word *wear'a*. *Arka*, however, is one of the seven nether earths, the place inhabited by the descendants of Cain. When Cain was banished from the face of the earth, he descended into that land and there propagated his kind. That earth consists of two sections, one enveloped in light, the other in darkness, and there are two chiefs, one ruling over the light, the other over the darkness. These two chiefs were at perpetual war with each other, until the time of Cain's arrival, when they joined together and made peace; and therefore they are now one body with two heads. These two chiefs were named '*Afrira* and *Kastimon*. They, moreover, bear the likeness of holy angels, having six wings. One of them had the face of an ox and the other that of an eagle. But when they became united they assumed the image of a man. In time of darkness they change into the form of a two-headed serpent, and crawl like a serpent, and swoop into the abyss, and bathe in the great sea. When they reach the abode of 'Uzza and 'Azael they stir them up and rouse them. These then leap into the "dark mountains", thinking that their day of judgement has come before the Holy One, blessed be His Name. The two chiefs then swim about in the great sea, and when night comes they fly off to Na'amah, the mother of the demons (*shedim*), by whom the first saints were seduced; but when they think to approach her she leaps away six thousand parasangs, and assumes all shapes and forms in the midst of the sons of men, so that the sons of men may be led astray after her. These two chiefs then fly about through the world, and return to their abode, where they arouse sensual desires in the descendants of Cain to bear children. The heaven above that earth is not like ours, nor are the seasons of seed and harvest the same as ours, but they only return after cycles of many years. "These *Elohim*", then, "who have not made heaven and earth [may] perish from" the upper earth of the universe, so that they should have no dominion there, should not traverse it and should not cause men to pollute themselves "through anything that chanceth by night"; and for that "they will perish from the earth and from underneath the heaven" which were made in the name of *Eleh*, as has been explained above. It is for that reason that this verse has been written in Aramaic, so that the angels should not think that they are alluded to and so bring accusations against us. This, too, is the secret of the last word, to wit, *Eleh*, which being a sacred name, could not be altered into Aramaic.'

R. Eleazar said to his father: 'Regarding what is written in the same passage, *Who will not fear thee, O King of the Gentiles? For it befitteth thee* (Jer. x, 7), is this such a high eulogy?' His father said to him: 'Eleazar, my son, this passage has been variously explained, but for its full meaning we must go to its continuation, which reads: *For among all the wise men of the Gentiles, and in all their royalty, there is none like unto thee.* (*Ibid.*) The purpose of this verse is to express the view of the sinners, who fancy that God does not know their thoughts, and to answer them according to their folly. Once,' he continued, 'a Gentile philosopher came to visit me and argued with me thus: You say that your God rules in all the heights of heaven, and that all the heavenly hosts and legions cannot approach Him and do not know His place. If so, then this verse, saying "For among all the wise men of the Gentiles, and in all their royalty there is none like unto thee", does not extol Him very highly, for what special glory is there for Him not to find among perishable men His like? [10a] And further, you infer from the passage which says "And there hath not arisen a prophet since in Israel like unto Moses" (Deut. xxxiv, 10), that only in Israel hath there not arisen, but among the other nations of the world there did arise one like him; and on this analogy I am justified in inferring that only among the wise of the Gentiles there is none like Him, but among the wise of Israel there is. If that is so, such a God, the like unto whom is to be found among the wise men of Israel, cannot be all-powerful. Look closely into the verse and you will find that it bears out my inference. I replied to him: Indeed, what you say is actually true. Who raises the dead to life? Only the Holy One alone, blessed be He; yet Elijah and Elisha came and raised the dead to life. Who causes rain to fall? Only the Holy One alone, blessed be He; yet Elijah came and kept back the rain and then made it descend again, through his prayer. Who made heaven and earth? The Holy One alone, blessed be He; yet Abraham came and they were firmly established for his sake. Who regulates the course of the sun? None but the Holy One, blessed be He; yet Joshua came and ordered it to stand still in its place and it stood still, as it is written, "And the sun stood and the moon stayed" (Jos. x, 13). The Holy One, blessed be He, issues decrees, but similarly Moses issued decrees, and they were fulfilled. Further, the Holy One, blessed be He, pronounces judgements and the righteous of Israel annul them, as it is written, "The righteous ruleth the fear of God" (II Sam. XXIII, 3). And further, He commanded them to follow literally in His ways, and to be like Him in every way. That philosopher then went to K'far Shekalim and became a proselyte, and was given the name of Jose Katina (humble), and he studied the Torah diligently until he became one of the most learned and pious men of that place.'

'Now,' continued R. Simeon, 'we must look more closely into this verse. We remark at once that another passage says: "All the nations are as nothing before him" (Is. XL, 17). What special glorification is then here expressed? Is He only the King of the Gentiles and not the King of Israel? the explanation is this. We find in every place in the Scriptures that the Holy One, blessed be He, has desired to be glorified only by Israel and has attached His name to Israel only; so it is written: "The God of Israel", "the God of the Hebrews" (Exod. v, 1, 3), and further: "Thus saith the Lord, the King of Israel" (Is. XLIV, 6). The nations of the world therefore said: We have another Patron in heaven, since your King has dominion only over you alone and not over us. Hence the verse comes and says: "Who would not fear thee, O King of the Gentiles ? Forasmuch as among all the wise men of the nations", alluding thereby to the great chiefs in heaven appointed over the Gentiles. The expression "and in all their royalty there is none like unto thee" alludes to the celestial government, inasmuch as there are four rulers on high who, by the will of God, rule over all the other nations; and for all that, not one of these has the power to do the smallest thing except as He commands them, as it is written: "And he doth according to his will in the host of heaven, and among the inhabitants of the earth" (Dan. IV, 32). "The wise ones of the Gentiles" are, then, the heavenly superintendents from whom they draw their wisdom; and the phrase "and in all their royalty" implies the heavenly over-lords of the nations, as has just been explained. This is the plain meaning of the passage. But in ancient books I have found it expounded as follows. Although these heavenly hosts and legions (who are "the wise of the nations and their royalty") have the control of the affairs of this world and have each their mission allotted to them, who of them can accomplish the least thing "like unto thee" ? For Thou excellest in Thy work on high and below above all of them. "There is not like unto thee, O Lord", that is, What Holy Unknown is there who acts and is like Thee above and below, and is on an equality with Thee in all respects ? The work of the Holy King is heaven and earth, but "they are vanity, and their costly idols cannot profit" (Is. XLIV, 9). Of the Holy One, blessed be He, it is written, "In the beginning God created etc.", but of the lower royalty it is written "And the earth was chaos and confusion".'

Said R. Simeon to the companions: 'Come all you that participate in this bridal festivity, let each one of you prepare a decoration for the bride.' To R. Eleazar his son he said: 'Eleazar, offer a present to the heavenly bride so that on the morrow thou mayest be deemed worthy to behold her when she enters under the bridal canopy amidst the songs and hymns of the heavenly retinue.' R. Eleazar then opened his discourse thus: *Who is this that cometh up ('Olah) out of the wilderness?* (S. S. III, 6). The words *Mi* (Who?) and *zoth* (this) denote the separate holinesses of the two worlds joined in firm bond and union; and this union is said to be *'olah* (a burnt-offering), and so holy of holies. For *Mi* is holy of holies, and *zoth* through its union with this becomes a burnt-offering (*'olah*), which is holy of holies. "Out of the wilderness": because she had to come forth from there in order to become the heavenly bride and to enter under the nuptial canopy. Further, the term *midbar* (wilderness) signifies speech, as we read, "and thy speech (*oumidbarekh*) is comely" (*Ibid.* IV, 3): by that *midbar* which is the utterance [10b] of the lips she goes up. Further, we have been taught as follows: It is written "these mighty gods; these are the gods that smote the Egyptians with all manner of plagues in the wilderness" (*bamidbar*) (1 Sam. IV, 8). What does this verse mean? Was it only in the wilderness that the Lord showed them all His great deeds, and not in inhabited country? Not so, only the term *bamidbar* means "by means of the word", analogous to the expression "and thy speech (*oumidbarekh*) is comely" (S. S. IV, 3), or to the expression "and from the word (*oumimidbar*) did the mountains arise" (Ps. LXX, 7). Similarly here, "she rises up out of the word", that is, by means of uttered words she mounts up and nestles between the wings of the Mother, and then by the same means she descends and rests on the heads of the holy people. Her ascent is effected thus. At the beginning of the day, when a man rises in the morning, it is his duty to bless his Master as soon as he opens his eyes. The pious men of old used to have by them a cup of water, and when they awoke in the night they washed their hands and rose and occupied themselves in the study of the Torah, having first pronounced the appropriate blessing. When the cock crows it is precisely midnight, and at that moment the Holy One, blessed be He, is to be found in company with the righteous in the Garden of Eden (*Gan-Eden*). It is therefore proper then to pronounce the benediction and study the Torah; but one may not pronounce the benediction with unclean hands. So, too, at any time that one rises up from his sleep. For whilst a man is asleep his soul departs from him and an impure spirit comes forth and settles on his hands and defiles them: hence one may not pronounce a blessing without first washing them. Why then, one may ask, is it forbidden, after one has been in a privy, to pronounce a blessing or to read even one word of the Torah, even in the daytime, without washing the hands, although one has not been asleep, so that one's soul did not depart, and one's hands have not been defiled by an evil spirit? Why is it forbidden even if one's hands are quite clean? The answer is: woe to those who pay no heed to the majesty of their Master, and do not realise on what this world is founded. There is in every privy a spirit which feasts on filth and excrement, and settles forthwith on the fingers of a man's hands.'

R. Simeon further discoursed as follows: 'He who rejoices on the festivals but does not give to the Holy One, blessed be He, His due share, is selfish, the Satan tries to injure him and accuses him before heaven, compasses his downfall, and causes him endless trouble. To give the portion of the Holy One, blessed be He, means to make glad the poor, according to one's ability. For on these days the Holy One, blessed be He, goes to look at those broken vessels of His: He comes to them, and, seeing that they have nothing with which to rejoice on the festival, He weeps over them and reascends on high with intent to destroy the world. The members of the heavenly Academy then present themselves before Him and plead: "O Lord of the universe, Thou art called gracious and merciful, let Thy compassion be moved upon Thy children." The Lord makes answer: "Verily I have made the world only on the foundation of mercy, as it is written: 'I have said, the world is built on mercy' (Ps. LXXXIX, 3), and the world is established on it." Then the heavenly angels proceed: "O Master of the universe, behold so-and-so, who eats and drinks and is in a position to give charity but neglects to do so." Then the Accuser comes and, having claimed and obtained permission, sets out in pursuit of that man. Whom have we in the world greater than Abraham, whose benevolence extended to all creatures? Once, we are told, he prepared a feast, as it is written: "And the child grew, and was weaned. And Abraham made a great feast on the day that Isaac was weaned" (Gen XXI, 8). To that feast Abraham invited all the great men of the age. Now we have been taught that whenever a banquet is given, the Accuser comes to spy out whether the owner has first dispensed charity and invited poor people to his house. If he finds that it is so, he departs without entering the house. But if not, he goes in and surveys the merry-making, and having taken note that no charity had been sent to the poor nor had any been invited to the feast, he ascends above and brings accusations against the owner. Thus, when Abraham invited to his feast the great men of the age, the Accuser came and appeared at the door in the guise of a poor man, but no one took notice of him. Abraham was attending on the kings and magnates; Sarah was giving suck to all their babes; for people did not believe that she had born a child, and said that it was only a foundling from the street, and so all the guests brought their infants with them, and Sarah suckled them in the presence of all, as it is written, "Who would have said [11a] unto Abraham that Sarah should give children suck ?" (*Ibid.* 7) (note the plural "children"). The Accusing Angel was still standing at the door when Sarah said: "God hath made laughter for me" (*Ibid.* 6). The Accusing Angel then presented himself before the Holy One, blessed be He, and said to Him: "O Master of the world, Thou hast said 'Abraham is my friend'; behold, he has made a feast and has not given anything to Thee nor to the poor, nor hath he offered up to Thee so much as one pigeon ; and further, Sarah said that Thou hast made mock of her." The Lord made answer: "Who in this world can be compared to Abraham ?" Nevertheless the Accusing Angel did not stir from thence until he had spoilt all the festivity; and the Lord after that commanded Abraham to offer up Isaac as an offering, and it was decreed that Sarah should die from anguish on account of her son's danger—all this because Abraham did not give anything to the poor.'

R. Simeon further discoursed thus: 'It is written, *Then Hezekiah turned his face to the wall, and prayed unto the Lord.* (Is. XXXVIII, 2.) Observe how powerful is the might of the

Torah, and how it surpasses any other force. For whoso occupies himself in the study of the Torah has no fear of the powers above or below, nor of any evil haps of the world. For such a man cleaves to the tree of life, and derives knowledge from it day by day, since it is the Torah that teaches man to walk in the true path, and gives him counsel how to repent and return to his Master so that He may annul the evil decreed against him; nay, even if it has been further decreed that it shall not be annulled, yet it is annulled and no longer threatens that man in this world. Hence it is incumbent upon a man to occupy himself in the study of the Torah day and night without cessation, in accordance with the text, "and thou shalt meditate therein day and night" (Jos. I, 8); and if he abandons such study, it is as though he abandoned the tree of life. Here, then, is a wise counsel for man. When a man goes to bed of a night, he should acknowledge wholeheartedly the kingship of heaven, and should entrust his soul to the keeping of heaven: he will then immediately be guarded against all diseases and evil spirits, and they will have no power over him. In the morning, when he rises from his bed, he should bless his Master, proceed to His house, bow down before His sanctuary with awe, and then offer up his prayer. For this, he must take counsel of the holy patriarchs, as it is written: "But as for me, in the abundance of thy lovingkindness will I come into thy house: I will bow down towards thy holy temple in the fear of thee" (Ps. v, 8). This verse has been interpreted to imply that a man should not enter the Synagogue without first taking counsel of Abraham, Isaac, and Jacob, for the reason that it is they who instituted prayer to the Holy One, blessed be He. Thus, in the verse just mentioned, the words "but as for me, in the abundance of thy lovingkindness will I come into thy house" are an allusion to Abraham; "I will bow down towards thy temple", to Isaac; "in the fear of thee", to Jacob. It is fitting, then, to invoke their names first and then enter the synagogue to offer up one's prayer. Of such a one it is written: "And he said unto me, Thou art my servant, Israel, in whom I will be glorified" (Is. XLIV, 3).

R. Phineas was a frequent visitor at the house of R. Rehumai, who lived on the shore of the lake of Gennesareth. He was a man of note, well advanced in years, and had lost his sight. Said he one day to R. Phineas: 'Verily I have heard that our colleague Yohai possesses a precious jewel.[1] I did look at that jewel, and it flashed like the radiance of the sun when he emerges from his sheath, and flooded the world with a light which radiated from heaven to earth and spread to the whole world, until the Ancient of Days was duly enthroned. That light is wholly contained in thy household, and from that light there emanates a tiny and tenuous ray which is shed abroad and illumines the whole world. Happy is thy portion! Go forth, my son, go forth and try to find that gem which illumines the world, for the hour is propitious.' R. Phineas took his leave and embarked in a boat in the company of two other men. He noticed two birds which were flying to and fro over the sea, and cried to them: 'Birds, birds, ye that fly about over the sea, have ye seen anywhere the resting-place of the son of Yohai?' He paused a while and then said: 'Birds, birds, go your way and bring me answer.' They flew away and disappeared in the distance, but before R. Phineas left the boat they returned, and one of them was holding in its mouth a written note stating that the son of Yohai had left the cave together with his son Eleazar. R. Phineas then went to visit him, and found him sadly changed, with his body full of sores. He wept [11b] and said: 'Woe unto me that I see thee thus!' He replied: 'Happy is my portion that thou seest me thus, for otherwise I would not be what I am.' R. Simeon then opened his discourse on the precepts of the Torah. He said: 'The precepts of the Torah which the Holy One has given to Israel are all laid down in the first chapter of Genesis in summary.

In the Beginning God created.[2] This contains the first precept of all, to wit, the fear of the Lord, as it is written: "The fear of the Lord is the beginning of wisdom" (Ps. CXI, 10), as well as: "The fear of the Lord is the beginning of

---

[1] His son, R. Simeon. [2] The remainder of this chapter is more in the style of the *Ra'yah Mehemnah* than of the *Zohar*.

knowledge" (Prov. I, 7). It is the beginning and the gateway of faith, and on this precept the whole world is established. There are three types of fear: two have no proper root, while the third is the real fear. There is the man who fears the Holy One, blessed be He, in order that his children may live and not die, or lest he be punished in his body or his possessions; and so he is in constant fear. Evidently this is not the genuine fear of God. Another man fears the Holy One, blessed be He, because he is afraid of punishment in the other world and the tortures of Gehinnom. This is a second type which is not genuine fear. The genuine type is that which makes a man fear his Master because He is the mighty ruler, the rock and foundation of all worlds, before whom all existing things are as nought, as it has been said: "and all the inhabitants of the earth are as nought" (Dan. IV, 32), and place his goal in that spot which is called *yir'ah* (fear).' R. Simeon here wept and said: 'Woe to me if I tell and woe to me if I do not tell! If I tell, then the wicked will know how to worship their Master; and if I do not tell, then the companions will be left in ignorance of this discovery. Corresponding to the "holy fear" there is an "evil fear" below which scourges and accuses, and which is a lash for punishing the wicked. Now he whose fear is of punishment and accusation is not endowed with that fear of God which leads to life. The fear which rests upon him is that evil fear of the lash, but not the fear of the Lord. For this reason the spot which is called "the fear of the Lord" is also called "the beginning of knowledge". Hence this precept is laid down here, as it is the principle and root of all the other precepts of the Torah. He who cherishes fear observes the whole Torah, and he who does not cherish fear does not observe the other precepts of the Torah, since it is the gate of all. Therefore it is written: *Bereshith*, through a beginning, that is, fear, God created heaven and earth. For he who transgresses this transgresses all the precepts of the Torah; and his punishment is to be scourged by the evil lash. This is implied in the words: "And the earth was chaos and confusion (*tohu wabohu*), and darkness was upon the face of the abyss." This is an allusion to the four kinds of punishment which are meted out to the wicked: *tohu* (chaos) alludes to strangulation, as it is written: "a line of (*tohu*) chaos" (Is. XXXIV, 11), meaning a measuring cord. *Bohu* (confusion) alludes to stoning ("stones of confusion", *ibid.*) by the stones which are sunk in the great abyss for the punishment of the wicked; "Darkness" is burning, as it is written: "And it came to pass, when ye heard the voice out of the midst of the darkness, while the mountain did burn with fire" (Deut. V, 20), also: "and the mountain burned with fire into the heart of heaven and darkness, etc." (*Ibid.* IV, 11): this is the fire that rests on the heads of the wicked to consume them. The "wind" alludes to beheading by the sword, which whirls round the wicked like a tempest, as it is said: "and the flaming sword which is turned every way" (Gen. III, 24). These punishments are meted out to those who transgress the precepts of the Torah, and the words which allude to them follow immediately after the word "beginning", which symbolises the fear of God, which is the summary of all the precepts. Then follow all the other precepts of the Torah.

'The *second precept* is the one which is indissolubly bound up with the precept of fear, namely, love; that a man should love his Master with a perfect love, that which is called "great love". This is implied in the command: "walk before me, and be thou wholehearted" (Gen. XVII, 1), to wit, in love. This is implied also in the verse: *And God said, Let there be light*, which alludes to the perfect love, called great love. Herein, then, is the precept for man to love his Master truly.' Said R. Eleazar, 'Father, I have heard a definition of perfect love.' His father said to him 'Expound it, my son, whilst R. Phineas is present, for he truly practises it.' R. Eleazar then explained thus: ' "Great love" is the love which is complete through the union of two phases, without which it is not [12a] genuine love; and this is signified by the dictum that the love of the Holy One, blessed be He, has two aspects. There is, for instance, the man who loves Him because he has riches, length of life, children, power over his enemies, success in all his undertakings—all these form the motive of his love. Should the Holy One, blessed be He, turn the wheel of fortune against him and bring suffering upon him, he will change and his love will be no more. This kind of love has no root. Perfect love is the kind which remains steadfast in both phases, whether of affliction or prosperity. The right way of loving one's Master is expressed in the traditional teaching which says: "even if he deprive thee of thy life". This is, then, perfect love, embracing two phases. It was for this reason that the light of creation which first emerged was afterwards withdrawn. When it was withdrawn suffering emerged, in order that there might be this perfect love.' R. Simeon embraced his son and kissed him; R. Phineas also came and kissed him and blessed him, saying: 'Of a surety, the Holy One, blessed be He, sent me hither, and this is the meaning of the "tiny light" which I was told was somewhere in my household and would illumine the whole world.' Said R. Eleazar: 'Assuredly, fear must not be forgotten in any of the precepts, least of all in this precept of love, which requires the association of fear. How is this to be achieved? In this way. Love, as has been said, may in one phase be inspired by favours, such as riches, length of life, children, plenty, and affluence. In such cases a man should be ever haunted by the fear lest sin may cause a reversal. Of such a one it is written: "Happy is the man that feareth alway" (Prov. XXVIII, 14), since he combines fear and love. The "adverse influence" (*sitra ahra*) which brings suffering and chastisement is therefore necessary in the world, since it rouses in man fear: for through chastisement a man becomes filled with the true fear of God, and does not harden his heart; for if he does, then "he that hardeneth his heart shall fall into evil" (*Ibid.*), to wit, into the hands of that "adverse influence" which is called "evil". Thus we have a love which is complete in both phases, and from this results a true and perfect love.

'The *third precept* is to acknowledge that there is a God, all-powerful and ruler of the universe, and to make due proclamation of his unity every day, as extending in the six supernal directions, and to unify them all through the six words contained in the *Shema Israel*, and in reciting these to devote oneself wholly to God. The word *Ehad* therefore must be dwelt on to the length of six words. This is implied in the passage, *Let the waters under the heaven be gathered together unto one place*: that is, let the grades beneath the heaven be unified in it so as to form one whole, perfect in all the six directions. With God's unity one must further associate fear, for which reason one must dwell on the *daleth*, the last letter of *Ehad*, the *daleth* being for that reason written larger than the other letters. And this is implied in the words "and let the dry land be seen", that is, let the *daleth*, which is a "dry land", be associated with that unity. After forming this union on high it is necessary to repeat the process for the lower world through all its multiplicity in the six lower directions. This is expressed in the verse we recite after the *Shema*, viz. "Blessed-be the-name-of the-glory-of His-Kingdom for-ever and-ever", which contains another six words expressive of the unity. In this way, what was dry land becomes fertile soil to produce fruits and flowers and trees. This is implied in the passage: "And God called the dry land earth", that is, by the manifestation of God's unity here below the earth was duly perfected. It is for this reason that in the account of the third day the expression "that it was good" appears twice, once for the manifestation of the unity above and once for the manifestation of the unity below. As soon as that unity was made manifest at both ends, the text says "Let the earth put forth grass", that is, the earth was then fitted to produce fruits and flowers according to its capacity.

'The *fourth precept* is to acknowledge that the Lord is God, as we read: "Know this day, and lay it to thy heart that the Lord, he is God" (Deut. IV, 39); namely, to combine the name *Elohim* (God) with the name *Jehovah* (Lord) in the consciousness that they form an indivisible unity. And this is the inner meaning of the text: *Let there be lights in the firmament of heaven*. The omission of the *vau* from the word *emoroth* (lights) points to complete unity, to the black light and the white light being only two manifestations of one indivisible light. [12b] The same is symbolised by the "white cloud by day" and the "cloud of fire by night" (Exod. XIII, 21); the two phases of day and night are complementary to each other, both forming one whole, in order—as we read—"to give light upon earth". Herein consisted the sin of the primeval serpent who united below but divided above, and so caused the mischief we still lament. The right way, on the contrary, is to recognise diversity below but unity above, so that the black light becomes wholly merged above and afterwards unified in respect of its diverse elements, and so is kept away from the evil power. It is therefore necessary for man to acknowledge that "God" and "the Lord" are one and the same without any cleavage whatever: "The Lord he is God" (1 Kings XVIII, 39); and when mankind will universally acknowledge this absolute unity, the evil power (*sitra ahra*) itself will be removed from the world, and exercise no more influence on earth. This is hinted in the word *meoroth*, which is made up of *or* (light), surrounded by *môth* (death), just as the brain, symbolic of light, is enveloped in a membrane symbolic of the baneful power (*sitra ahra*) which is death. Should the light (*or*) be removed, the letters on either side would coalesce and form death (*môth*). . . .

'The *fifth precept*. It is written: *And God said, Let the waters swarm with the movement of living creatures*. This verse contains three precepts—to labour in the study of the Torah, to beget children, and to circumcise a male child on the eighth day by removing the foreskin. It behoves a man to labour in the study of the Torah, to strive to make progress in it daily, so as thereby to fortify his soul and his spirit: for when a man occupies himself in the study of the Torah, he becomes endowed with an additional and holy soul, as it is written: "the movement of living creatures", that is, a soul (*nefesh*) derived from the holy centre called "living" (*hayah*). Not so is it with the man who does not occupy himself with the study of the Torah: such a man has no holy soul, and the heavenly holiness does not rest upon him. But when a man earnestly studies the Torah, then the motion of his lips wins for him that "living soul" and he becomes as one of the holy angels, as it is written: "Bless the Lord, ye angels of his" (Ps. CIII, 20), to wit, those who occupy themselves in the study of the Torah, and who are therefore called His angels on earth. The same are alluded to in the words: "and let birds fly on the earth". So much for his reward in this world. As regards the other world, we have been taught that the

Holy One, blessed be He, will provide them with wings as of eagles, enabling them to fly across the whole universe, as it is written: "But they that wait for the Lord shall renew their strength, then shall mount up with wings as eagles" (Is. XLIV, 31). This, then, is the interpretation of that which is written: "Let the waters swarm with the movement of living creatures": the Torah, which is symbolised by water, possesses the virtue of implanting in her devotees a mobile soul derived from the place called "living" (ḥayah), as has already been said. David alluded to this when he said: "Create in me a clean heart, O God", so that I may be devoted to the Torah, and thus "renew a steadfast spirit within me" (Ps. LI, 12).

'The *sixth precept* is to be fruitful and multiply. For he who performs this precept causes the stream (of existence) to be perennially flowing so that its waters never fail, and the sea is full on every side, and new souls are created and emerge from the "tree" (of life) and the celestial hosts are increased in company with those souls. This is implied in the words: *Let the waters swarm with the movement of living souls.* This is an allusion to the holy and imperishable covenant, to the perennially rushing stream, the waters of which continually swell and produce new swarms of souls for that "living" (ḥayah). Along with the souls as they arise there appear many winged beings who fly about all over the world, and whenever a soul descends into this world the winged being that issued together with it from that tree accompanies it. Two accompany each soul, one on its right hand, and one on its left. If the man is worthy they constitute themselves his guardians, as it is written: "For he will give his angels charge over thee" (Ps. XCI, 11), but if not, they act as his accusers.' Said R. Phineas: 'Three [13a] is the number of angels who keep guard over a man who is worthy, as it is written: "If there be for him an angel, an intercessor, one among a thousand, to vouch for man's uprightness" (Job. XXXIII, 23). "If there be for him an angel" signifies one; "an intercessor" signifies another one; "one among a thousand to vouch for man's uprightness" is a third one.' R. Simeon said : 'Five angels, since it is written further: "And He is gracious unto him, and saith". "And he is gracious unto him" implies one, "and saith" implies another one.' R. Phineas replied: 'It is not so, as the expression "And he is gracious unto him" refers only to the Holy One, blessed be He, no one else having the power to dispense grace.' Said R. Simeon: 'You are right. Now' (he continued) 'he who refrains from propagating his kind derogates, if one might say so, from the general form in which all individual forms are comprehended, and causes that river to cease its flow and impairs the holy covenant on all sides. Of such a one it is written, "And they shall go forth and look upon the carcasses of the men that have rebelled against me" (Is. LXVI, 24)—"against me" assuredly. This is the punishment for the body, and as for his soul, she will not enter at all "within the curtain", and will be banished from the next world.

'The *seventh precept* is to circumcise the male child on the eighth day after birth and thereby to remove the defilement of the foreskin. The "living" (ḥayah) of which we have spoken forms the eighth grade in the scale, and hence the soul which has flown away from it must appear before it on the eighth day. And in this way it is made clear that this is really a "living soul", emanating from that holy "living" and not from the "unholy region". And this is alluded to in the words: *Let the waters swarm*, which in the Book of Enoch are explained thus: Let the water of the holy seed be stamped with the stamp of the "soul of the living", which is the form of the letter *yod* impressed on the holy flesh in preference to all other marks. The words, "and let winged beings fly on the earth" are a reference to Elijah, who traverses the universe in four swoops in order to be present at the initiation of the child into the holy covenant. It is proper to prepare for him a seat and to proclaim, "This is the throne of Elijah"; otherwise he will not be present. The words "And the Lord created the two great fishes" refer to the two operations, circumcision and uncovering, which represent the male and female principles; "and every living soul that moves" refers to the stamping of the sign of the holy covenant, which is a holy living soul, as has been explained. "Wherewith the waters swarmed": to wit, the supernal waters which were drawn towards that distinguishing mark. And it is for that reason that the Israelites were stamped with that sign of holiness and purity; for just as the supernal holy beings are marked in such a way as to distinguish between the "holy region" and the impure "unholy region", so the Israelites are marked in order to distinguish between the holy people and the idolatrous nations who are derived from the impure "unholy region", as has been already explained. And in the same way as the Israelites themselves are marked, so are the clean animals and birds permitted to them for food marked off from the other animals and birds eaten by the Gentiles. Happy the portion of Israel!

'The *eighth precept* is to love the proselyte who comes to be circumcised and to be brought under the wings of the "Divine Presence" (*Shekinah*), which takes under its wings those who separate themselves from the impure "unholy region" and come near unto her, as it is written: *Let the earth bring forth a living soul according to its kind*. Think not that the same "living soul" which is found in Israel is assigned to all mankind. The expression "after its kind" denotes that there are many compartments and enclosures one within the other in that region which is called "living", beneath its wings. The right wing has two compartments, which branch out from it for two other nations who approach Israel in monotheistic belief,[1] and therefore have entrance into these compartments. Underneath the left wing there are two other compartments which are divided between two other nations, namely Ammon and Moab. All these are included in the term "soul of the living". There are besides under each wing other concealed enclosures and divisions from whence there emanate souls which are assigned to all the proselytes who enter the fold—these are indeed termed "living soul", but "according to its kind": they all enter under the wings of the Shekinah, and no farther. The soul of Israel, on the other hand, emanates from the very body of that tree and from thence flies off into the very bowels of that earth. This is hinted in the words: "For ye shall be a delightsome land" (Mal. III,

---

[1] Al. "are most closely related to Israel."

12). It is for that reason that Israel is called a "darling son", for whom the bowels, as it were, of the Shekinah yearn, and that the children of Israel are called "those who are born from the womb", and not merely from the outer wings. Furthermore, [13b] the proselytes have no portion in the celestial tree, much less in the body of it; their portion is only in the wings and no more. The righteous proselytes, therefore, rest underneath the wings of the Shekinah and are united to it there, but penetrate no further, as has already been explained. Therefore we read: *Let the earth bring forth a living soul according to its kind*, namely, *cattle, and creeping thing, and beast of the earth after its kind*, that is to say, all derive their soul from that source called "living", but each according to its kind, from the grade appropriate to itself.

'The *ninth precept* is to show kindness to the poor and to provide them with their needs, as it is written: *Let us make man in our image, after our likeness;* that is, "let us make man", as a compound being, including the male and female, "in our image", to wit, the rich; "after our likeness", to wit, the poor. For the rich are from the male side and the poor from the female. For as the male and the female act in co-operation, showing compassion to each other and mutually exchanging benefits and kindnesses, so must man here below act rich and poor in co-operation, bestowing gifts upon each other and showing kindness to each other. We have seen the following mystical observation in the Book of King Solomon. He who of his own impulse shows pity to the poor will retain for ever unchanged the original form of the first man, and by that impress of the likeness of Adam he will exercise dominion over all creatures of the world. This is implied in the words: "And the fear of you and the dread of you shall be upon every beast of the earth, etc." (Gen. IX, 2), that is, all and every one will be in fear and in dread of that image which characterises man. For this is a noble precept, by means of which man can rise in the image of Adam above all other creatures. This we know from Nebuchadnezzar who, in spite of the dream that he had seen, as long as he showed mercy to the poor suffered no evil effects; but as soon as he selfishly neglected the poor, what do we read about him? "While the word was in the King's mouth, etc." (Dan. IV, 28), his image changed and he was driven from men. . . .

'The *tenth precept* is to put on *tephillin* (phylacteries), and thereby to attain in oneself the perfection of the divine image, according to that which is written: *And the Lord created man in His own image*.' R. Simeon discoursed in this connection on the text "Thy head upon thee is like Carmel" (S. S. VII, 6). 'This verse,' he said, 'has already been explained in a way, but its true meaning is as follows: "Thy head upon thee is like Carmel" alludes to the phylactery worn on the head above, containing four sections of the Torah which represent each one of the four letters of the Divine Name (*Tetragrammaton*) of the most high King. Our teachers have told us that the verse: "that the name of the Lord is called upon thee, and they shall be afraid of thee" (Deut. XXVIII, 10) alludes to the phylactery worn on the head which represents the Divine Name in order of its letters. Thus, the first section, "Sanctify unto me all the first-born, etc." (Exod. XIII, 2) represents the *Yod*, which is the first of all the supernal sanctities; "whatsoever openeth the womb" (*Ibid.*) is an allusion to the slender stroke underneath the *yod* which opens the womb to bring forth fitting fruit. The second section, "And it shall be when the Lord shall bring thee, etc." (*Ibid.* 5) represents the *Hé*, significant of the palace the womb of which was opened by the *Yod*. It is through fifty mysterious gates and forecourts and enclosures that the *Yod* makes an opening and enters that palace, causing the sound to issue from the great *Shofar*. For the *Shofar* was closed on all sides and the *Yod* came and opened it to cause the emission of its sound; and as soon as he opened it he emitted a blast as a signal for the freeing of the slaves. It was at the blowing of that *Shofar* that the Israelites went forth from Egypt. And the same will be repeated at the end of days. Indeed, every deliverance is preceded by the blowing of that *Shofar*. Hence the deliverance from Egypt is included in this section, since it resulted from that *Shofar* when under the pressure of the *Yod* it opened its womb and produced its sound as a signal for the deliverance of the slaves. So much as regards the *Hé*, the second letter of the Divine

Name. The third section contains the mystery of the unity in the proclamation: "Hear, O Israel, etc." (Deut. VI, 4), and is represented by the *Vau*, which is the summary of all, expressive of absolute unity, combining and absorbing all. The fourth section "And it shall come to pass if ye shall hearken, etc." (*Ibid.* XI, 13-21) presents the two influences [14a] to which the Congregation of Israel—the manifestation of God's power below—is subjected. This, then, is represented by the second *Hé*, which takes up the previous letters and contains them. The phylacteries are thus literally the counterpart of the letters of the Divine Name. Hence "Thy head upon thee is like Carmel" is an allusion to the phylactery worn on the head; and the "hair (*dallath*, lit. poverty) of the head" signifies the phylactery worn on the hand, which is poor in comparison to that worn on the head above, but which nevertheless has its own perfection like that which it symbolises above. "The King is held captive in the tresses thereof", that is, the heavenly King is duly enshrined in these compartments of the Tephillin through the Divine Name therein contained in manner due. Thus he who equips himself with them is a man made in the image of God, for just as the letters of Holy Name are united to express the divine essence, so in a degree they are united by him (through the phylacteries). "Male and female he created them" is a reference to the phylactery of the head and the phylactery of the hand, which together make one whole.

'The *eleventh precept* is to give the tithe of the produce of the land. This includes two precepts, one the tithing of the land and the other the giving of the first fruits of the trees; for it is written: *Behold I have given you every herb yielding seed, which is upon the face of all the earth.* The expression "I have given" is applied to tithe in the passage: "And unto the children of Levi, behold, I have given all the tithe in Israel" (Num. XVIII, 21), and it is written besides: "And all the tithe of the land, whether of the seed of the land, or of the fruit of the tree, is the Lord's" (Lev. XXVII, 30).

'The *twelfth precept* is to bring as an offering the fruits of the tree, which is alluded to in the words: *and every tree in which is the fruit of a tree yielding seed,* that is, although whatever is consecrated to God may not be eaten by man, yet God permitted them (the Levites) to enjoy all His tithe and the first fruit of the tree. *I have given to you;* that is, to you and not to the generations in the future.

'The *thirteenth precept* is to redeem the first-born son so as to attach him firmly to life. For every man is attended by two angels, one of life and one of death, and by redeeming his first-born son the father ransoms him from the angel of death, who therefore has no power over him. This is hinted in the words: *And God saw everything that he had made*, to wit, creation as a whole, *and, behold it was good;* this alludes to the angel of death. Through the act of redemption, then, the life-angel is strengthened, whilst the death-angel is weakened. By means of this redemption the child obtains life, as has already been stated; the evil power leaves him and has no more hold on him.

'The *fourteenth precept* is to observe the Sabbath day, which was the day of rest from all the works of Creation. This precept comprises two parts, one to rest on the Sabbath, and one to invest it with holiness. We have to observe that day as a day of rest, as has already been said, for the reason that it was a day of rest from the beginning, the whole work of Creation having been completed before this day was sanctified. After the day was sanctified there was left a residue of spirits for which no bodies had been created. Why, it may be asked, could not God have waited to sanctify the day until He had created bodies for those spirits? The reason is that from the tree of the knowledge of good and evil there went forth the "evil power" to seize control of the world, and so a number of diverse spirits set out to acquire for themselves bodies by force. As soon as the Holy One, blessed be He, saw this, He raised out of the tree of life a wind that blew and lashed against the other tree so that the "beneficent power" arose and the day was sanctified. For the creation of bodies and the stirring of spirits on that night comes about under the influence of the "beneficent power" and not of the "evil power". Had the "evil power" forestalled on that night the "beneficent power", the world could not exist, on account of the evil spirits, for an instant. But the Holy One, blessed be He, provided the cure in advance; He hastened the sanctification of the day before the evil power prevailed, and so the world was established, and instead of the evil power becoming master of the world as it thought to be, on that night it was the "beneficent power" which obtained the victory, and therefore sacred bodies and spirits are being built up on that night under the influence of the "beneficent power". It is for that reason that the marital intercourse of the wise and learned men who know this [14b] is weekly, from Sabbath to Sabbath. It is, moreover, the night on which the "evil power", being supplanted by the "beneficent power", roams about the world, accompanied by his many hosts and legions, and pries into all places where people perform their conjugal intercourse immodestly and by the light of a candle, with the result that the children born of such intercourse are epileptics, being possessed by spirits of that "evil power", which are the nude spirits of the wicked, called demons (*shedim*) ; these are pursued and killed by the demon Lilith. As soon as the day is sanctified the evil power becomes weakened and withdraws into hiding all the night and day of the Sabbath, with the exception of Assimon and his band, who roam about to spy out indecent intercourses and then go and hide themselves in the cave of the great abyss. As soon as Sabbath ends, innumerable hosts and companies of them commence to fly and roam to and fro through the world, and it is to ward them off that the recitation of the Hymn against Calamities (Ps. xci) has been instituted, so as to destroy their power over the holy people. When, after issuing precipitately to obtain dominion over the holy people, they see them engaged in prayer and hymns, reciting the "Separation" (*Habdalah*) in the course of the prayer and afterwards over the cup, they flee and wander about until they reach the wilderness. May the Merciful One deliver us from them and from the evil power ! Our teachers, of blessed memory, said: There are three persons who bring evil upon themselves. One is the man who utters a curse against himself; a second, he who throws on the floor pieces of bread of the size of an olive; the third, he who lights his candle at the close of the Sabbath before the congregation has reached the recital of the "Sanctification" at the close of the service, for thereby he causes the fire of Gehinnom to be kindled by that light before its time. There is a place in Gehinnom assigned for those who profane the Sabbath, and those who undergo there their punishment curse the man who has lighted a candle before the time and pronounce against him the verse: "Behold the Lord will hurl thee up and down with a man's throw, yea, he will wind thee round and round" (Is. XXII, 17). For it is not lawful to kindle a light at the close of the Sabbath before Israel has pronounced the "Separation Blessing" in the prayer and the "Separation Blessing" over the cup, as until that time it is still Sabbath, and the sanctity of the Sabbath still rests on us. At the moment, however, when we recite the "Separation Blessing" over the cup, all the armies and camps which have charge over the weekdays return each to its place and to its appointed service. For with the entrance of the Sabbath and at the moment when it is sanctified, holiness awakens and spreads its dominion over the world, and worldliness is divested of its rule, and until the close of the Sabbath they do not return to their place; and even when the Sabbath closes they do not return to their places until the Israelites pronounce the words, "Blessed art Thou, O Lord, who separatest the holy from the profane." Then holiness withdraws and the armies appointed over the weekdays rouse themselves and return each to its place and office. But yet they do not assume control until they become illumined through the light of the candle, for which reason they are called "fiery lights", because they spring from the fiery element, which gives them the power to rule over the terrestrial world. All this is only when a man lights a candle before the congregation has finished the recital of the "Sanctification" at the close of prayer. But when he waits until the close of that recital, the wicked in Gehinnom acknowledge the justice of the Holy One, blessed be He, and confirm for that man the blessings which the congregation recite in the words "So God give thee of the dew of heaven, etc." (Gen. XXVII, 28), as well as: "Blessed shalt thou be in the field, etc." (Deut. XXVIII, 3).

' "Happy is he that considereth the poor, the Lord will deliver him in the day of evil" (Ps. XLI, 2). We should have expected "in the evil day"; but the expression "the day of evil" alludes to the day when the "evil power" obtains permission to seize man's soul. Hence, "Happy is he that considereth the poor", to wit, the man sick of soul, so as to heal him of his sins before the presence of the Holy One, blessed be He. According to an alternative interpretation, "the day of evil" alludes to the last day of judgement of the world from which such a one will be delivered, as it says: "in the day of evil the Lord will deliver him", to wit, the day when the world is placed in the power of that evil one to chastise it.'[1]

---

[1] The text breaks off here abruptly.

BERESHITH[1]

Gen. I, I–VI, 8

At the outset the decision of the King made a tracing in the supernal effulgence, a lamp of scintillation,[2] and there issued within the impenetrable recesses of the mysterious limitless a shapeless nucleus[3] enclosed in a ring, neither white nor black nor red nor green nor of any colour at all. When he took measurements, he fashioned colours to show within, and within the lamp there issued a certain effluence from which colours were imprinted below. The most mysterious Power enshrouded in the limitless clave, as it were, without cleaving its void, remaining wholly unknowable until from the force of the strokes there shone forth a supernal and mysterious point. Beyond that point there is no knowable, and therefore it is called *Reshith* (beginning), the creative utterance which is the starting-point of all.

It is written: *And the intelligent shall shine like the brightness of the firmament, and they that turn many to righteousness like the stars for ever and ever* (Dan. XII, 3). There was indeed a "brightness" (*Zohar*). The Most Mysterious struck its void, and caused this point to shine. This "beginning" then extended, and made for itself a palace for its honour and glory. There it sowed a sacred seed which was to generate for the benefit of the universe, and to which may be applied the Scriptural words "the holy seed is the stock thereof" (Is. VI, 13). Again there was *Zohar*, in that it sowed a seed for its glory, just as the silkworm encloses itself, as it were, in a palace of its own production which is both useful and beautiful. Thus by means of this "beginning" the Mysterious Unknown made this palace. This palace is called *Elohim*, and this doctrine is contained in the words, "By means of a beginning (it) created *Elohim*." The *Zohar* is that from which were created all the creative utterances through the extension of the point of this mysterious brightness. Nor need we be surprised at the use of the word "created" in this connection, seeing that

---

[1] *v*. Appendix I.   [2] al. 'darkness'; al. 'measurement'.   [3] al. 'vapour'.

we read further on, "And God created man in his image" (Gen. I, 27). A further esoteric interpretation of the word *bereshith* is as follows. The name of the starting-point of all is *Ehyeh* (I shall be). The holy name when inscribed at its side is *Elohim*, but when inscribed by circumscription[1] is *Asher*, the hidden and recondite temple, the source of that which is mystically called *Reshith*. The word *Asher* (i.e. the letters, *Aleph, Shin, Resh* from the word *bereshith*) is anagrammatically *Rosh* (head), the beginning which issues from *Reshith*. So when [15b] the point and the temple were firmly established together, then *bereshith* combined the supernal Beginning with Wisdom. Afterwards the character of that temple was changed, and it was called "house" (*bayith*). The combination of this with the supernal point which is called *rosh* gives *bereshith*, which is the name used so long as the house was uninhabited. When, however, it was sown with seed to make it habitable, it was called *Elohim*, hidden and mysterious. The *Zohar* was hidden and withdrawn so long as the building was within and yet to bring forth, and the house was extended only so far as to find room for the holy seed. Before it had conceived and had extended sufficiently to be habitable, it was not called *Elohim*, but all was still included in the term *Bereshith*. After it had acquired the name of *Elohim*, it brought forth offspring from the seed that had been implanted in it.

What is this seed ? It consists of the graven letters, the secret source of the Torah, which issued from the first point. That point sowed in the palace certain three vowel-points, *holem, shureq*, and *hireq*, which combined with one another and formed one entity, to wit, the Voice which issued through their union. When this Voice issued, there issued with it its mate which comprises all the letters; hence it is written *Eth hashammaim* (the heavens), to wit, the Voice and its mate. This Voice, indicated by the word "heaven", is the second *Ehyeh* of the sacred name, the *Zohar* which includes all letters and colours, in this manner. Up to this point the words "The Lord our God the Lord" (*Yhvh Elohenu Yhvh*) represent three grades corresponding to this deep mystery of

---

[1] i.e. between the two *Ehyeh's*. *v.* Ex. III, 14.

bereshith bara Elohim. *Bereshith* represents the primordial mystery. *Bara* represents the mysterious source from which the whole expanded. *Elohim* represents the force which sustains all below. The words *eth hashammaim* indicate that the two latter are on no account to be separated, and are male and female together. The word *eth* consists of the letters *aleph* and *tau*, which include between them all the letters, as being the first and last of the alphabet. Afterwards *hé* was added, so that all the letters should be attached to *hé*, and this gave the name *attah* (Thou); hence we read "and Thou (*ve-attah*) keepest all of them alive" (Neh. IX, 6). *Eth* again alludes to *Adonai* (Lord), who is so called. *Hashammaim* is *Yhvh* in its higher signification. The next word, *ve-eth*, indicates the firm union of male and female; it also alludes to the appellation *ve-Yhvh* (and the Lord), both explanations coming to the same thing. *Ha-aretz* (the earth) designates an *Elohim* corresponding to the higher form, to bring forth fruit and produce. This name is here found in three applications, and thence the same name branches out to various sides.

Up to this point only extend the allusions to the Most Mysterious who carves out and builds and vivifies in mysterious ways, through the esoteric explanation of one verse. From this point onwards *bara shith*, "he created six", from the end of heaven to the end thereof, six sides which extend from the supernal mystic essence, through the expansion of creative force from a primal point. Here has been inscribed the mystery of the name of forty-two letters.

And the intelligent shall shine (Dan. XII, 3). This "shining" corresponds to the movement given by the accents and notes to the letters and vowel-points which pay obeisance to them and march after them like troops behind their kings. The letters being the body and the vowel-points the animating spirit, together they keep step with the notes and come to a halt with them. When the chanting of the notes marches forward, the letters with their vowel-points march behind them, and when it stops they also stop. So here: "the intelligent" correspond to the letters and the vowel-points; "the brightness" to the notes; "the firmament" to the flow of the chant through the succession of notes; while "they that turn to righteousness" correspond to the pausal notes, which stop the march of the words and bring out clearly the sense. These "cause to shine" letters and vowels, so that they all flow together in their own mystical manner through secret paths. From this impetus the whole was extended. Again, the words "and the intelligent shall shine as the brightness of the firmament" may be referred to the pillars and sockets of the "celestial palanquin" (*apiryon*).[1] The "wise and intelligent" as the supernal pillars and sockets, since they ponder with understanding all things needful for the upholding of the palace. This use of the term "intelligent" (*maskilim*) has its parallel in the passage: "Blessed is he that considereth (*maskil*) the poor" (Ps. XLI, 2). "They will shine", for if they do not shine and give light, they cannot well consider and ponder the needs of the palace. "As the brightness of the firmament", [16a] namely, of that firmament which rests upon those "intelligent" we have mentioned, and of which it is written, "And over the head of the *Hayyah* there was the likeness of a firmament, like the colour of the terrible ice" (Ezek. I, 22). "The brightness" is that which illumines the Torah, and which illumines also the heads of the *Hayyah*, those heads being the "intelligent", who shine continually and ever contemplate the "firmament" and the light which issues therefrom, to wit, the light of the Torah which radiates perpetually without cease.

Now the earth had been void and without form. The word *hoithah* (was), being a pluperfect, implies that the earth *had been* previously. There was snow in the midst of water, from the action of which was produced a slime. Then a mighty fire beat upon it and produced in it a refuse. So it was transformed and became *Tohu* (chaos), the abode of slime, the nest of refuse, and also *Bohu* (formlessness), the finer part which was sifted from the *Tohu* and rested on it. The word "darkness" in the text alludes to this mighty fire. This darkness covered the *Tohu*, namely the refuse, and was buoyed up by it. The "spirit of God" is a holy spirit that proceeded from *Elohim Hayyim* (living God),

[1] v. p. 110.

and this "was hovering over the face of the waters". When this wind blew, a certain film detached itself from the refuse, like the film which remains on the top of boiling broth when the froth has been skimmed off two or three times. When *Tohu* had thus been sifted and purified, there issued from it "a great and strong wind rending the mountains and breaking in pieces the rocks", like that which Elijah saw (1 Kings XIX, 11, 12). Similarly *Bohu* was sifted and purified, and there issued from it earthquake, as with Elijah. Then what we call "darkness" was sifted, and there was contained in it fire, just as to Elijah there appeared "after the earthquake fire". When what we call "spirit" was sifted, there was contained in it a still, small voice. *Tohu* is a place which has no colour and no form, and the esoteric principle of "form" does not apply to it. It seems for a moment to have a form, but when looked at again it has no form. Everything has a "vestment" except this. *Bohu*, on the other hand, has shape and form, namely, stones immersed in the chasm of *Tohu*, but sometimes emerging from the chasm in which they are sunk, and drawing therefrom sustenance for the world. Through the form of their vestment they draw sustenance from above to below, and ascend from below above, and therefore they are hollow and strong. These are suspended in the expanse; that is to say, sometimes they are suspended in the expanse when they rise out of the chasm, and sometimes they are hidden, to wit, on the "day of cloud", when they draw waters from the abyss to supply therewith *Tohu*, for then there is joy that *Tohu* was spread in the universe. "Darkness" is a black fire, strong in colour. There is a red fire, strong in visibility; a yellow fire, strong in shape; and a white fire, the colour which includes all. "Darkness" is the strongest of all fires, and this it was which took hold of *Tohu*. "Darkness" is fire, but fire is not darkness, save when it takes hold of *Tohu*. The symbol for this is, "his eyes were dim so that he could not see, and he called Esau, etc." (Gen. XXVII, 1). Here, too, "the countenance of the evil one was darkened" because it countenanced the evil one. Hence this fire is called "darkness" because it rested upon *Tohu* and took hold of it; this is the inner meaning of the words "and darkness on the face of the abyss". "Spirit" is the voice which rests on *Bohu*, and grasps it and guides it as required. This is symbolised in the words "The voice of the Lord is on the waters" (Ps. XXIX, 3); and so, too, "the spirit of the Lord was hovering over the face of the waters". By "face of the waters" is meant stones sunk in the abyss, so called because waters issue from them. Thus each was provided as befitted. *Tohu* is under the ægis of the name *Shaddai* ; *Bohu*, under that of *Zebaoth* ; Darkness, under that of *Elohim* ; Spirit, under that of *Yhvh*. We now understand what happened to Elijah: "there was a strong wind breaking the mountains, but the Lord was not in the wind", because this name was not in it, since *Shaddai* presides over it through the mystic nature of *Tohu*. "After the wind there was a quaking, but the Lord was not in the quaking", since over it presides the name of *Zebaoth*, through the mystic nature of *Bohu* (which is called "quaking" (*ra'ash*), because it quakes continually. "After the quaking there was a fire, but the Lord was not in the fire", because over it presides the name *Elohim* from the side of darkness. "And after the fire there was a small still voice"; and here at last was found the name *Yhvh*. There are in this verse four clauses corresponding to the four so-called "sections of the body" and "limbs" which, being four, are resolvable into twelve. Here, too, is the graven name of twelve letters which was transmitted to Elijah in the cave. [16*b*]

AND GOD SAID, LET THERE BE LIGHT; AND THERE WAS LIGHT. From this point we can begin to discover hidden things relating to the creation of the world in detail. For up to this point the Creation has been described in general, and lower down the general description is repeated, so that we have a combination of general-particular-general.[1] Up to this point the whole was suspended in the void in direct dependence on the limitless. When, however, energy had been extended through the supernal palace alluded to in the name *Elohim*, the term "saying" is used in connection with it, in

---

[1] i.e. according to the Rabbinical system of hermeneutics, the 'general' (heaven-and-earth) is of the same nature as the 'particular' (days), being like them the product of a 'saying'.

the words "And God said". For to that which is beyond no detailed "saying" is ascribed; for although the word *bereshith* is a creative utterance (*maamar*), the actual words "and said" are not used in connection with it. This expression "and said" (*vayomer*) opens the door to inquiry and understanding. We define this "saying" as an energy that was culled, as it were, in silence from the mystic limitless through the mystic power of thought. Hence "and God said" means that now the above-mentioned palace generated from the holy seed with which it was pregnant. While it brought forth in silence, that which it bore was heard without. That which bore, bore in silence without making a sound, but when that issued from it which did issue, it became a voice which was heard without, to wit, "Let there be light." Whatever issued came forth under this category. The word *Yehi* (let there be) indicates that the union of the Father and Mother symbolised by the letters *Yod Hé* became now a starting-point (symbolised by the second *Yod*) for further extension.

LIGHT, AND THERE WAS LIGHT. These words imply that there had already been light. This word, *awr* (light), contains in itself a hidden significance. The expansive force proceeding from the hidden recesses of the secret supernal ether opened a path and produced from itself a mysterious point (or, rather, the *En Sof* (Limitless) clave its own ether and disclosed this point), *Yod*. When this expanded, that which was left of the mysterious *AWIR* (ether) was found to be *AWR* (light). When the first point had developed from it, it showed itself upon it, touching and yet not touching it. When it expanded, it emerged into being, and thus was light (*awr*) left from ether (*awir*); and this is what we mean by saying that it "had been" previously; and so it remained. It went up and was stored away, and there was left of it one dot, which continually approaches by invisible paths the other point, touching and yet not touching, illuminating it in the manner of the first point from which it issued. Therefore the whole is linked together, and it illumines both one and the other. When it ascends, all ascend and are attached to it, and it reaches the place of *En Sof*, where it is stored away, and all becomes one.

This dot of the word *Awr* is Light. It extended, and there shone forth in it seven letters of the alphabet, which did not solidify and remained fluid. Afterwards Darkness issued, and there issued in it seven other letters of the alphabet, and they too were not solidified and remained fluid. There then issued the Firmament, which prevented discord between the two sides. In it there issued eight other letters, making twenty-two in all. Seven letters jumped from one side and seven from the other, and all were graven in this Firmament, where they remained for a time fluid. When the firmament solidified, the letters were also solidified, and took material shape. Thus there was graven there the Torah to shine abroad. "Let there be light": to wit, *El Gadol* (great God), that which emerged from the primal ether. "And there was": this signifies Darkness, which is called *Elohim*. "Light": signifying that the Left was included in the Right, and so from that which we call *El* was produced *Elohim*. Right was included in Left and Left in Right.

AND GOD SAW THE LIGHT THAT IT WAS GOOD. This is the Central Column: *Ki Tob* (that it was good) threw light above and below and on all other sides, in virtue of *Yhvh*, the name which embraces all sides. AND GOD DIVIDED: He put away strife, so that the whole was in perfect order. AND GOD CALLED. The word "called" here means "called to" or "invited". God summoned to issue forth from this complete Light which was in the centre a certain radiance which is the foundation of the world, and on which worlds are established. From that complete Light, the Central Pillar, extended the foundation, the Life of worlds, which is day from the side of the Right. AND THE DARKNESS HE CALLED NIGHT. He summoned to issue from the side of Darkness a kind of female moon which rules over the night and is called night, and is associated with *Adonai*, the Lord of all the earth. The Right entered into the complete Pillar of the centre united with the Left, and the primal point thereupon ascended on high and there seized [17*a*] the energy of three dots, the *holem*, the *shureq*, and the *hireq*, the seed of holiness (for no seed has been sown save from this source).

The whole was then united in the Central Pillar, and it produced the foundation of the world, which therefore is called *Kol* (all), because it embraces the whole in the radiation of desire. Meanwhile the Left flamed forth with its full power, producing at all points a kind of reflection, and from this fiery flame came forth the female moonlike essence. This flaming was dark because it was from Darkness. These two sides produced these two grades, one male and one female. Unity was retained in the Central Pillar from that surplus of light which was in it. For since that Central Pillar was complete in itself and made peace on all sides, additional light was lent to it from above and from all sides through the universal joy in it. From that additional joy came forth the foundation of worlds, which was also called *Musaf* (additional). From this issue all the lower powers and spirits and holy souls, alluded to in the expressions, "Lord of hosts" (*Yhvh Zebaoth*) and "God the God of spirits" (Num. XVI, 22). "Night" is "the Lord of all the earth" from the side of the left, from Darkness. It was because the desire of Darkness was to merge itself in the Right, and it was not strong enough, that night spread from it. When night began to spread, and before it was complete, Darkness went and merged itself in the right, and the night was left defective. Just as it is the desire of Darkness to merge itself in Light, so it is the desire of night to merge itself in day. Darkness abated its light, and therefore it produces a grade which was defective and not radiant. Darkness does not radiate save when it is merged in Light. So night which issued from it is not light save when it is merged in day. The deficiency of night is only compensated by the *Musaf*. What is added in one place is subtracted from the other. The *Musaf* contained a symbolism of the supernal point and of the Central Pillar, and therefore two letters were added in respect of it which were lacking in respect of the night, viz. the *vau yod* of *vayikra* (and he called). Herein is an allusion to the name of seventy-two letters, the tracing of the supernal crown.

AND GOD SAID, LET THERE BE A FIRMAMENT IN THE MIDST OF THE WATERS. Here in the particular (day) there is an allusion to the separation of the upper from the lower waters through that which is called " the Left". Here, too, discord was created through that which is called "the Left". For up to this point the text has alluded to the right, but now it alludes to the left; and therefore there was an increase of discord between this and the right. It is the nature of the right to harmonize the whole, and therefore the whole is written with the right, since it is the source of harmony. When the Left awoke there awoke discord, and through that discord the wrathful fire was reinforced and there emerged from it the Gehinnom, which thus originated from the left and continues there.

Moses in his wisdom pondered over this and drew a lesson from the work of creation. In the work of creation there was an antagonism of the left against the right, and the division between them allowed the Gehinnom to emerge and to fasten itself to the left. Then the Central Column, which is the third day, intervened and allayed the discord between the two sides, so that the Gehinnom descended below, and the Left became absorbed in the Right and there was peace over all. Similarly the quarrel of Korah with Aaron was an antagonism of the left against the right. Moses, reflecting on what had happened during the Creation, said: 'It seems proper to me to compose the difference between the right and the left.' He therefore endeavoured to effect an accord between the two. The left, however, was not willing, and Korah proved obdurate. Moses thereupon said: 'Assuredly the Gehinnom is embittering this quarrel. The left ought to strive upwards and absorb itself in the right. Korah has no wish to attach himself to the higher influences and to merge himself in the right. Let him, then, descend below in the impetus of his wrath.' The reason why Korah refused to allow the quarrel to be composed by the intervention of Moses was that he had not entered upon it for a truly religious motive, and that he had scant regard for the glory of God, and refused to acknowledge His creative power. When Moses perceived that he had thus placed himself outside the pale, he "was very wroth" (Num. XVII, 15). He was "wroth" because he was not able to compose the quarrel;

he was "very wroth" because they denied the creative power of God. Korah denied [17b] this power wholly, both in the higher and the lower sphere, as implied in the phrase: "when they strove against the Lord" (Num. XXVI, 9). Hence Korah clave to that which was meet for him. A dispute that was composed on the pattern of the supernal dispute, that became more and not less worthy as it proceeded, and that perpetuated itself rightfully, was that between Shammai and Hillel. The Holy One, blessed be He, approved of their dispute, for the reason that its motive was lofty and that it therefore resembled that which took place at the Creation. Hence, like the latter, the dispute between Shammai and Hillel has survived to this day. Korah, on the other hand, denied the Creation, fought against heaven itself and sought to confute the words of the Torah. He certainly was of the following of the Gehinnom, and therefore remained attached to it. All this is brought out in the Book of Adam. It says there that when Darkness asserted itself, it did so with fury, and created the Gehinnom, which attached itself to it in that quarrel we have mentioned. But as soon as the wrath and the fury abated there arose a quarrel of another kind, to wit, a quarrel of love. Thus the dispute fell into two distinct parts. It is the way of the righteous to enter on a dispute stiffly and end it amicably. Korah continued the dispute as he began it, in wrath and passion; and therefore clung to Gehinnom. Shammai conducted his dispute in that spirit of calm which should follow on the first burst of passion; it therefore became a quarrel of love and obtained the approval of Heaven. This is indicated by our text. It says first: "Let there be a firmament in the midst of the waters, and let it divide, etc." This refers to the beginning of quarrel, the outburst of passion and violence. There was a desire for reconciliation, but meanwhile the Gehinnom arose before the wrath and passion cooled down. Then "God made the firmament, etc."; that is, there emerged a quarrel of love and affection which made for the permanence of the world. And in this category is the dispute between Shammai and Hillel, the result of which was that the Oral Law approached in a loving mood the Written Law, so that they mutually supported each other.

As regards separation, it always proceeds from the left. Here it is written, "and let it separate", as well as, "and he separated"; and in connection with Korah it is written, "Is it a small thing unto you that the God of Israel hath separated you from the congregation of Israel, etc."; and it is also written, "At that time the Lord separated the tribe of Levi" (Deut. x, 8). In all these texts we find separation associated with the second (day or tribe), which is the place of the left. It may be objected that Levi was the third and not the second tribe; separation, then, should have been associated, not with Levi, but with Simeon, he being the second. The answer is that in the eyes of Jacob (who, on the first night of his nuptials, was unaware that Leah was substituted for Rachel) Levi was the second (from Leah). Hence the separation of the tribe of Levi was perfectly correct. There is a "separation" on every outgoing of the Sabbath, between the powers that have sway on week-days and on the Sabbath respectively. As soon as the Sabbath ends, there ascends from the Gehinnom, from the grade called Sheol, a party of evil spirits who strive to mingle among the seed of Israel and to obtain power over them. But when the children of Israel perform the ceremonies of the myrtle and the cup of blessing, and recite the separation prayer (*Habdalah*), that evil spirit departs to his place in Sheol, the region where Korah and his accomplices abide, as it is written: "And they and all that appertained to them went down alive into the Sheol" (pit) (Num. XVI, 33). These, too, did not descend to the Sheol before the Israelites had performed a separation (*Habdalah*), as it is said: "Separate yourselves from among this congregation" (*Ibid.* 21). "Separation" is thus associated with the second, which is symbolic of the left, at its first impetus, when it first enters on a quarrel in wrath and violence, giving birth to Gehinnom before the fury subsides. It was on the second that, before the discord was allayed, the Gehinnom was created. Then also were created all the angels who revolted against their Master, and whom the fire of the Gehinnom consumed and destroyed; likewise all those others who vanish away and do not endure and are consumed by fire.

LET THERE BE A FIRMAMENT: i.e. let there be a gradual extension. Thereupon *El* (God), the "right cluster",[1] *El Gadol* (Great God), spread forth from the midst of the waters to complete this name *El* and to combine with this extension, and so *El* was extended into *Elohim* (=*El*+*H, Y, M*). These *H, Y, M*, extended and became reversed so as to form lower waters, *Y, M, H*. This extension which took place on the second day is the upper waters. The *hé, yod, mim*, form *hayam* (the sea), which is the upper waters. The reversal of these letters, *yamah* (seaward), is the lower waters. When they were firmly established, all became one whole, and this name was extended to a number of places. The upper waters are male and the lower waters female. At first they were commingled, but afterwards they were differentiated into upper and lowers waters. This is the meaning of "*Elohim* upper waters", and this is the meaning of "*Adonai* lower waters"; and this is the meaning of upper *Hé* and lower *Hé*. It is further written: AND GOD MADE THE FIRMAMENT. That is to say, this extension took this name. *Elohim* is the upper waters, and the lower waters [18a] are *Adonai*; nevertheless, since the upper waters were completed by the lower, this name spread to the whole.

Even after the separation between the waters, the discord did not cease till the third day, when peace was restored and everything was settled in its place. It is on account of this strife, necessary as it was for the existence of the world, that the phrase "that it was good" is not applied to the work of the second day, because it was not completed. So long as the upper and lower waters were commingled, there was no production in the world: this could only be when they were separated and made distinct. They then produced, and in this way, although on the second day there was separation and discord, the third day brought complete harmony. This is the name which is graven with the lettering of *Yhvh*, to reconcile the upper with the lower waters, the upper with the lower *Hé;* the insertion of the *Vau* between them harmonises the two sides. Symbolic of this is the crossing by the Israelites of the Jordan (Josh. III, 16): "the waters (of the

[1] al. 'shoulder' : in either case a designation of the grade *Ḥesed* (kindness).

Jordan)" corresponds to the upper waters; "rose up in one heap" corresponds to the lower waters, which descended into the sea, whilst the Israelites passed between the two.

Five "firmaments" are mentioned in this section, and the Life of the World passes among them and leads them, and they are all interwoven. But for this discord, however, which was composed by the mediator, they would not have been intertwined or harmonised. They correspond to the five hundred years to which the Tree of Life clings in order to become a source of growth and fruitfulness to the world. All the waters of creation which issue from the original source branch out from its foot. King David similarly takes the whole and subsequently distributes it, as we read: "And he distributed among all the people, even among the whole multitude, etc." (II Sam. VI, 19); likewise we read: "That thou givest them they gather" (Ps. CIV, 28); also: "She rises also while it is yet night, and giveth meat to the household" (Prov. XXXI, 15).

At the time when discord was stirred by the violence of the left, the Avenging Spirit was reinforced. There issued from it (two) demons which immediately became solidified without any moisture, one male and one female. From them were propagated legions of demons, and to this is due the inveteracy of the unclean spirit in all those demons. It is they who are symbolised by the foreskin (*orlah*); the one is called *Ef'eh* (adder) and the other is called *Nahash* (serpent), the two, however, being but one. The *Ef'eh* bears offspring from the *Nahash* after a period of seven years' gestation. Herein is the mystery of the seven names borne by the Gehinnom as well as by the "evil tempter" (*yetser-hara'*); and from this source impurity has been propagated in many grades through the universe. All this proceeds from the mystic power of the left, which dispenses good and evil, thereby rendering the world habitable. Here we have the engraven Name of eighteen letters, which presides over the gentle and beneficent rains for the well-being of the world.

AND GOD SAID, LET THE WATERS FLOW: The word flow (*yikavvu*) implies that they were to go in a line (*kav*) so as to take a straight path. For from the first mystic point the Whole issues in secret, until it reaches and is gathered in to the supernal Palace, and from there it issues in a straight line to the other grades, until it comes to that place which collects the whole in a union of male and female; this is the "Life of worlds". THE WATERS: to wit, those that issue from on high, from under the upper *Hé*. FROM UNDER THE HEAVEN: this is the lesser *Vau* (hence the word *yikavvu* is spelt with two *vau's*, one for "the heaven" and one for "under the heaven"). In consequence: LET THE DRY LAND APPEAR. This is the lower *Hé*. This is disclosed and all the rest is undisclosed; from this last we conclude by inference to that which is undisclosed. TO ONE PLACE: so called because it is here that the whole of the upper World is linked into one.

It is written: *The Lord (Yhvh) is one and his name is One* (Zech. XIV, 9). Two unifications are here indicated, one of the upper World in its grades, and one of the lower World in its grades. The unification of the upper World is consummated at this point. The Life of Worlds was there firmly based, and through its unity the upper World was bound together, and therefore it is called "one place". All grades and all members were gathered there and became in it one without any separation; nor is there any grade in which they are embraced in one unification save this. In it, too, they all mysteriously conceal themselves in one desire. In this grade the disclosed World is linked with the undisclosed. The disclosed World is similarly unified below, and the disclosed World is, in fact, a lower world. Hence such expressions as: "I saw the Lord" (Is. VI, 1), "And they saw the God of Israel" (Ex. XXIV, 10), "And the glory of the Lord appeared" (Num. XIV, 10: XVII, 7), "So was the appearance of the brightness round about; this was the appearance of the likeness of the glory of the Lord" (Ezek. I, 28). This, too, is the inner meaning of the words here, "and let the dry land appear". The same is referred to in the words, "My bow I have set in the cloud" (Gen. IX, 13): to wit, from the day on which the world was created. On the day [18b] of cloud, when the bow, "the appearance of the likeness of the glory of the

Lord" appeared, the Left arose in might. Then "Rachel went forth and had pain in childbirth". With her appeared Michael on one side, Raphael on another, and Gabriel on a third, these being the colours which appeared in the "likeness". Hence "the appearance of the brightness round about", to wit, the radiance which is hidden in the pupil of the eye, becomes "the appearance of the likeness of the glory of the Lord", to wit, corresponding colours, so that the lower unity is formed in correspondence with the upper unity. This is signified by the formula, "The Lord our God the Lord" (Deut. VI, 4). The mysterious and undisclosed colours which are linked "in one place" form one higher unity; the colours of the bow below in which are united white, red, and yellow, corresponding to those other mysterious colours, form another unity, signified by the formula "and his name is One". Further, the form "Blessed be the name of the glory of his kingdom for ever and ever" signifies the lower unity, while the upper unity is signified by the form "Hear, O Israel, the Lord our God the Lord is one." These forms correspond, each having six words.[1] . . .

LET THE EARTH PUT FORTH GRASS, HERB, ETC. At this behest the "earth" put forth a host through those waters which were gathered together in one place and flowed mysteriously through it, so that there issued in it hidden celestial beings and sacred existences which are upheld and sustained and constantly renewed by the faithful among mankind through the worship they offer to their Master. This mystery is indicated by the verse: "Who causest the grass to spring up for the *B'hema*" (cattle), etc. (Ps. CIV, 14). This refers to Behemoth that crouches on a thousand mountains and for whom these mountains produce each day what is here called "grass", by which is meant those angelic beings whose existence is ephemeral, and who were created on the second day as destined food for that Behemoth, which is "fire consuming fire". The Psalmist continues, "and herb for the service of man", indicating by "herb" the angelic orders named *Ofanim* (wheels), *Hayyoth* (animal-shaped), and

---
[1] i.e. in the original Hebrew.

Cherubim, all of whom are upheld, sustained, and confirmed whenever mortal beings come to worship their Master with sacrifices and prayers, in which consists the "service of man", and as they are reinforced by virtue of that service of man, there springs up food and sustenance for the world, as it is written: "to bring forth bread out of the earth" (*Ibid.*). The same is implied here by the words HERB YIELDING SEED. For "grass" does not yield seed, but is only destined for food for the sacred fire, whereas "herb" helps to maintain the world. All this has for its purpose "to bring forth bread from the earth", i.e. to provide, by virtue of the service offered to their Master by human beings, food and sustenance out of the earth for this world, so that the heavenly blessings should descend on mankind. FRUIT TREE BEARING FRUIT. One degree above another, these combining male and female. Just as " fruit tree" produced the host of "trees bearing fruit", so the latter in turn produced "Cherubim and Pillars". "Pillars" are those that go up in the smoke of the sacrifices and derive their strength therefrom, and hence are called "pillars of smoke", and all of them exist permanently for the "service of man", whereas the "grass" has no permanence, being destined to be consumed as food, as it is written: "Behold now Behemoth, which I made with thee; he eateth grass as an ox" (Job XL, 15). The words "fruit tree bearing fruit" indicate the form of male and female in combination. Their faces are "like the face of a man" (Ezek. I, 10), but they are not like the Cherubim, having large faces covered with beards, whereas the Cherubim have little faces like those of tender children.

All forms are comprised in these, because they are "large faces". On them are traced forms like the tracings of the Divine Name on the four cardinal points, East, West, North, and South. Michael is imprinted on the South, and all faces are turned towards him, viz. "the face of a man . . . the face of a lion . . . the face of an ox . . . the face of an eagle" (*Ibid.*). "Man" implies the union of male and female, without which the name "man" (*Adam*) is not applied. By him are formed the figures of the chariot of God, as it is written: "(On) the chariot of God are myriads of thousands of *Shin'an* (angels)"

(Ps. LXVIII, 15): the word *SHiN'AN* expresses by means of its initials all the figures, the *Shin* standing for *Shor* (ox), the *Nun* for *Nesher* (eagle), and the *Aleph* for *Aryeh* (lion), and the final *Nun* representing by its shape man, [19a] who walks erect, and who mystically combines male and female. All those thousands and myriads of angels issue from those symbolised by the name *Shin'an*, and from these types they diverge in their several groups, each to its appropriate side. These four are all interlaced and intertwined in one another, to wit, ox, eagle, lion, man. Their activity is directed by four graven names, which they ascend to contemplate. "Ox" ascends to seek guidance and gaze in the face of "Man". There ascends with him a certain name crowned and engraved in two mystic forms, which represent the name *El* (God). Then it turns back and the throne engraves and traces it and it is imprinted thereon to be under the guidance of this mystic name. "Eagle" ascends to seek guidance and gaze in the face of "Man". There ascends with it another name, which is crowned and engraved in two mystic forms, to shine forth and to mount and be crowned on high; this represents the attribute "Great". Then it turns back and the throne engraves it and it is imprinted thereon to be under the guidance of this mystic name. "Lion" ascends to seek guidance and to gaze in the face of "Man". Another name ascends with it and is crowned and engraved in two mystic forms to be endowed with strength and power, representing the attribute of "Mighty". It turns back and the throne engraves it and it is imprinted thereon to be under the guidance of this mystic name. "Man" contemplates all of them, and all ascend and contemplate him. Thus they all become engraved in this form in the one mystic name known as "Tremendous" (*Nora*). Thus it is written concerning them, "And the likeness of their faces is as the face of man" (Ezek. I, 10). They are all embraced in that likeness, and that likeness embraces them all. In virtue of all this the Holy One, blessed be He, is called the Great, Mighty, and Tremendous God, since these names are engraved above on the supernal chariot which is comprised in the four letters of the Tetragrammaton, which is the name that comprises all. These likenesses are engraved on the throne, and the throne is decorated with them, one to the right, one to the left, one in front, and one behind, corresponding to the four quarters of the world. The throne when it ascends is stamped with these four likenesses. These four supernal names bear along the throne, and the throne is comprised in them, and collects a harvest of longing desires. When it has collected these desires, it descends with its burden like a tree laden with branches on all sides and full of fruit. As soon as it descends, these four likenesses come forth in their several shapes emitting bright flashes which scatter seed over the world. Hence it is written, "herb yielding seed", because these scatter seed over the world. But of the issuing forth of the likeness of man which comprises all the other likenesses it is written, "fruit tree yielding fruit after its kind, the seed of which is in it on the earth". It produces no seed save for propagation. The term "in it" should be noticed. It teaches us that man may not emit his seed idly. This is hinted in the word "verdure", which does not "yield seed", and hence has no permanency like the others, not having any likeness which can be shaped or engraved in any manner at all. Such things show themselves but to vanish: they have not acquired form and likeness, and have no permanency; they exist only for a moment and then are consumed in that fire which devours fire, and are continually renewed and devoured.

Man here below possesses an ideal form and likeness, but he is not so permanent as those supernal beings. These are formed in their proper shape without any outer covering to modify it. Hence they are changeless; whereas man below assumes form through the medium of an outer covering. Hence he endures for a while, and every night the spirit is divested of that garment and ascends and is consumed by that consuming fire, and then reverts to its former state and takes the same outer shape again. Hence they have not the same permanency as those supernal forms, and in allusion to this it is written, "new every morning" (Lam. III, 23), i.e. human beings who are renewed every day. [19b] The reason is that "great is thy faithfulness" (*Ibid.*)—great and not little. "Great is thy faithfulness": assuredly great, since it can support all the creatures of the world and comprise them all in itself, upper and lower alike. It is of infinite expanse, it absorbs all and becomes no fuller. This is alluded to in the verse, "All the rivers run into the sea, yet is the sea not full, etc." (Eccl. I, 7). They run into the sea, and the sea receives and swallows them and is not filled, and then it restores them to their former state. Hence "great is thy faithfulness". In the account of this (third) day it is written twice "that it was good", the reason being that this day became intermediary between two opposing sides, and removed discord. It said to this side "good", and to the other side "good", and reconciled the two. Hence we find twice written in the account of it, "and he said". Connected with this day is the secret of the name of four letters engraved and inscribed, which can be made into twelve (by permutations), corresponding to the four images on the four sides inscribed on the holy throne.

AND GOD SAID, LET THERE BE LIGHTS, ETC. The word for "lights" (*meoroth*) is written defectively, as if *me'eroth* (curses), for the reason that the children's disease, croup, was through them created. For after the primordial light was withdrawn there was created a "membrane for the marrow", a *k'lifah*, and this *k'lifah* expanded and produced another. As soon as this second one came forth she went up and down till she reached the "little faces".[1] She desired to cleave to them and to be shaped as one of them, and was loth to depart from them. But the Holy One, blessed be He, removed her from them and made her go below. When He created Adam and gave him a partner, as soon as she saw Eve clinging to his side and was reminded by his form of the supernal beauty, she flew up from thence and tried as before to attach herself to the "little faces". The supernal guardians of the gates, however, did not permit her. The Holy One, blessed be He, chid her and cast her into the depths of the sea, where she abode until the time that Adam and his wife sinned. Then the Holy One, blessed be He, brought her out from the depth of the sea and gave her power over all those children, the "little faces" of the sons of men, who are liable to punishment for the sins of their fathers. She then wandered

---

[1] v. p. 79.

up and down the world. She approached the gates of the terrestrial paradise, where she saw the Cherubim, the guardians of the gates of Paradise, and sat down near the flashing sword, to which she was akin in origin. When she saw the flashing sword revolving, she fled and wandered about the world and, finding children liable to punishment, she maltreated and killed them. All this is on account of the action of the moon in diminishing her (original) light. When Cain was born this *k'lifah* tried for a time without success to attach herself to him, but at length she had intercourse with him and bore spirits and demons. Adam for a hundred and thirty years had intercourse with female spirits until Naamah was born. She by her beauty led astray the "sons of God", Uzza and Azael, and she bore them children, and so from her went forth evil spirits and demons into the world. She wanders about at night time, vexing the sons of men and causing them to defile themselves. Wherever these spirits find people sleeping alone in a house, they hover over them, lay hold of them and cleave to them, inspire desire in them and beget from them. They further inflict diseases on them without their being aware—all this through the diminution of the moon. When the moon was restored, the letters of *meoroth* (lights) were reversed to form *imrath* (word), as it is written, "the word (*imrath*) of the Lord is tried, he is a shield to those that trust in him" (Ps. XVIII, 31), i.e. He is a shield against all those evil spirits and demons that wander about the world at the waning of the moon, unto those that hold fast to their faith in the Holy One, blessed be He. King Solomon, when he "penetrated into the depths of the nut garden" (as it is written, "I descended into the nut garden", S. S. VI, 11), took a nut-shell (*klifah*) and drew an analogy from its layers to these spirits which inspire sensual desires in human beings, as it is written, "and the delights of the sons of men (are from) male and female demons" (Eccl. II, 8). This verse also indicates that the pleasures in which men indulge in the time of sleep give birth to multitudes of demons. The Holy One, blessed be He, found it necessary to create all these things in the world to ensure its permanence, so that there should be, as it were, a brain with many membranes encircling it. The whole world is constructed on this principle, upper and lower, from the first mystic point up to the furthest removed of all the stages. They are all [20a] coverings one to another, brain within brain and spirit within spirit, so that one is a shell to another. The primal point is the innermost light of a translucency, tenuity, and purity passing comprehension. The extension of that point becomes a "palace" (*Hekal*), which forms a vestment for that point with a radiance which is still unknowable on account of its translucency. The "palace" which is the vestment for that unknowable point is also a radiance which cannot be comprehended, yet withal less subtle and translucent than the primal mystic point. This "palace" extends into the primal Light, which is a vestment for it. From this point there is extension after extension, each one forming a vestment to the other, being in the relation of membrane and brain to one another. Although at first a vestment, each stage becomes a brain to the next stage. The same process takes place below, so that on this model man in this world combines brain and shell, spirit and body, all for the better ordering of the world. When the moon was in connection with the sun, she was luminous, but as soon as she separated from the sun and was assigned the charge of her own hosts, she reduced her status and her light, and shells upon shells were created for covering the brain, and all for the benefit of the brain. Hence *meoroth* is written defectively. All this was for the benefit of the world, and hence it is written, "to give light upon the earth".

AND GOD MADE THE TWO GREAT LIGHTS. The word "made" signifies the due expansion and establishment of the whole. The words "the two great lights" show that at first they were associated as equals, symbolising the full name *Jehovah Elohim* (although the latter part is not revealed, but is known inferentially). The word "great" shows that at their creation they were dignified with the same name, so that through them the name of the Whole was called *Mazpaz Mazpaz*,[1] the two highest names of the thirteen categories of mercy.[2] These were invested with greater dignity, and they

[1] If the Hebrew alphabet is inverted, $M = Y$, $Z = H$, $P = V$. [2] v. Ex.xxxiv, 6.

are placed at the head because they derive from on high and ascend for the benefit of the world and for the preservation of worlds. Similarly the two lights ascended together with the same dignity. The moon, however, was not at ease with the sun, and in fact each felt mortified by the other. The moon said "Where dost thou pasture?" (S. S. 1, 7). The sun said "Where dost thou make thy flock to rest at noon? (*Ibid.*) How can a little candle shine at midday?" God thereupon said to her, "Go and diminish thyself." She felt humiliated and said "Why should I be as one that veileth herself?" (*Ibid.*). God then said "Go thy way forth in the footsteps of the flock." Thereupon she diminished herself so as to be head of the lower ranks. From that time she has had no light of her own, but derives her light from the sun. At first they were on an equality, but afterwards she diminished herself among all those grades of hers, although she is still head of them; for a woman enjoys no honour save in conjunction with her husband. The "great light" corresponds to *Yhvh*, and the "lesser light" to *Elohim*, which is the last of the degrees and the close of the Thought. At first it was inscribed above among the letters of the sacred Name, in the fourth letter thereof, but afterwards it took a lower rank with the name *Elohim;* nevertheless, it still ascends in all directions above in the letter *Hé* in the union of the letters of the sacred Name. Afterwards degrees extended on this side and on that. The degrees that extended upwards were called "the dominion of the day", and the degrees that extended downwards were called "the dominion of the night". "The stars" are the remainder of the forces and the hosts which, countless in number, are all suspended in that "firmament of the heaven" which is the "life of the universe", as it is written, "and God placed them in the firmament of the heaven to give light upon the earth. . . ." This is the lower earth, which derives light from them as they from above. On this (the fourth) day the kingdom of David was established, the fourth leg and support of the (divine) throne, and the letters (of the divine Name) were firmly fixed in their places. Yet withal until the sixth day, when the likeness of man was fully formed, the throne was not firmly fixed in its place; but then at last both the upper and the lower thrones were established, and all the worlds were settled in their places, and all the letters were fixed [20b] in their spheres by the extension of the primordial vapour. The fourth day was "rejected of the builders", because on it this luminary degraded itself and abated its radiance, and the outer shells were reinforced. All those radiating lights are suspended in that firmament of the heaven, that by them the throne of David may be established.

Those lights are formative agents in the lower world to perfect the shape of all those who are included in the term "man". This is the name given to every interior shape; and thus every shape which is comprised in this extension is called "man", which properly indicates man's spirit emanating from the realm of holiness, to which his body is a vestment, as we read, "Thou clothest me in skin and flesh" (Job x, 11). Hence we often meet the expression "flesh of man", implying that the real man is within and the flesh which is his body is only a vestment. The lower beings which have been compounded with this spirit assume shapes which are clothed in another vestment, such as the forms of clean animals, ox, sheep, goat, deer, etc. They would fain partake of the vestment of man, corresponding to their inner nature, but their forms are covered by the name applied to their bodies; so we find "flesh of ox", "ox" being the inner element of that body, while the "flesh" is the vestment; and so with all. Similarly with the "other side": the spirit which is found in the idolatrous nations issues from the realm of uncleanliness and is not, properly speaking, "man"; therefore it is not covered by this name and has no portion (in the future world). Its body, which is the vestment of that unclean thing, is unclean flesh, and the spirit is unclean within the flesh that clothes it. Therefore as long as that spirit is within that body it is called "unclean". When the spirit emerges from that covering it is not called "unclean", and the vestment does not bear the name of man. The lower beings compounded with this spirit assume shapes which clothe themselves in another vestment, such as the forms of unclean animals, of which the Law says "this shall be unclean to you", such as the pig and unclean birds, and beasts of that side. The spirit is covered by the name of the body in which it is clothed, and the body is called "flesh of pig"—pig within the flesh which clothes it. Consequently these two groups are sharply separated, one side being embraced under the category "man" and the other under the category "unclean", and the individuals flock each to its kind and return to their kind. Thus the supernal lights radiate in that "firmament of the heaven" to fashion in the lower world the requisite shapes, as it is written, "and God set them in the firmament of the heaven . . . and to rule by day and by night".

It is fit and proper that two lights should rule, the greater light by day and the lesser light by night. The lesson we derive is that the male rules by day to regulate his household and to bring food and sustenance into it. When night arrives, the female takes command, and she rules the house, as it is written, "she rises while it is still night and giveth food to her house" (Prov. XXXI, 15)—she and not he. Thus the dominion of the day belongs to the male and the dominion of the night to the female. Further it is written, AND THE STARS. As soon as the wife has given her orders and retired with her husband, the direction of the house is left to the maidens, who remain in the house to look after all its requirements. Then when day comes the man again duly takes command.

"And God made the two lights." There are two kinds of luminaries. Those which ascend above are called "luminaries of light", and those which descend below are called "luminaries of fire". These latter belong to the lower sphere and rule over the weekdays. It is for this reason that at the expiry of Sabbath a blessing is said over the lamp, because rule is then restored to these luminaries. Man's fingers symbolise the mystic grades of the upper world, which are divided into front and back. The latter are outside, and are symbolised by the finger-nails, and therefore it is [21*a*] permissible to look at the finger-nails at the expiry of Sabbath by the light of the candle. But it is not permissible to look at the fingers from the inside by the light of the candle. This is hinted in the verse, "Thou shalt see me from the back, thou shalt not see my face" (Ex. XXXIII, 23). Therefore a man should not look at his fingers from the inside when he recites the blessing "Creator of the light of the fire". On the Sabbath day God rules alone by means of those inner grades upon His throne of glory, and all of them are comprised in Him and He assumes dominion. Therefore on this day He accorded rest to all worlds. As part of the legacy of this day the holy and unique people has inherited the "luminaries of light" from the side of the Right, which is the primal light that was on the first day. For on the Sabbath day those luminaries of light shine alone and have dominion, and from them everything is illumined below. When Sabbath expires the luminaries of light are withdrawn and the luminaries of fire assume sway each in its place. They rule from the expiry of one Sabbath till the commencement of the next. For this reason it is proper to use the light of the lamp at the expiry of Sabbath.

It is said of the *Hayyoth* that "they run to and fro" (Ezek. I, 14), and so no eye can follow them. The *Hayyoth* which disclose themselves are those in the midst of which there is an *Ofan* (wheel), which is *Metatron*, who is more exalted than all the other hosts. The *Hayyoth* which are never disclosed are those which are under the two undisclosed letters *Yod*, *Hé*, which rule over *Vau*, *Hé*, these being the pedestal of the former. The most mysterious and incomprehensible essence rules over all and is mounted upon all. The *Hayyoth* which disclose themselves are below those which remain undisclosed and derive light from them and follow them. The celestial *Hayyoth* are all comprised in the "firmament of the heaven", and are referred to in the words "let there be lights in the firmament of the heaven", "and they shall be for lights in the firmament of the heaven". They are all suspended in that firmament. But there is also a firmament above the heavens of which it is written, "and a likeness upon the heads of the *Hayyah*, a firmament like the ice, etc." (Ezek. I, 22). This is the first *Hé* beyond which it is impossible for the human mind to penetrate, because what is further is enveloped in the thought of God, which is elevated above the comprehension of man. If that which is within the Thought cannot be comprehended, how much less the

Thought itself! What is within the Thought no one can conceive, much less can one know the *En Sof*, of which no trace can be found and to which thought cannot reach by any means. But from the midst of the impenetrable mystery, from the first descent of the *En Sof* there glimmers a faint undiscernible light like the point of a needle, the hidden recess of thought, which even yet is not knowable until there extends from it a light in a place where there is some imprint of letters, and from which they all issue. First of all is *Aleph*, the beginning and end of all grades, that on which all the grades are imprinted and which yet is always called "one", to show that although the Godhead contains many forms, it is still only one. This is the letter on which depend both the lower and the upper entities. The top point of the *Aleph* symbolises the hidden supernal thought, in which is contained potentially the extension of the supernal firmament. When *Aleph* issues from that firmament in a form symbolising the commencement of Thought, there issue in its middle bar six grades, corresponding to the hidden supernal *Hayyoth* which are suspended from the Thought. One is the light which shone and was withdrawn. This is the "heat of the day" which Abraham felt when he was sitting at "the door of his tent", the door which opens the way from below to above, and on which shone "the heat of the day". A second light is that which fades away at eventide, to restore which was the object of Isaac's prayer, as it is written, "Isaac went forth into the field to meditate at eventide" (Gen. XXIV, 63). A third light is that which combines these other two, [21*b*] and shines for healing, and it is hinted at in the verse which says of Jacob that "the sun rose upon him, etc." (Gen. XXXII, 32). Of a surety it was after he had attained the degree of "eventide". From this point he was "halting on his thigh", i.e. he attained imperfectly to the conception of the "strength (*Nezah*) of Israel". It is written "on his thigh" and not "on his thighs"; this is the fourth degree, by which no prophet was inspired till Samuel came, of whom it is written, "and also the strength (*Nezah*) of Israel, etc." (I Sam. XV, 29). Thus he restored to its pristine strength that which was weak from the time that Jacob was injured by the guardian angel of Esau. "He touched the hollow of his thigh." When he came to Jacob, he derived strength from that "eventide" which is associated with the attribute of stern justice. Jacob, however, being embraced in that grade, was proof against him. "He saw that he could not prevail against him and he touched the hollow of his thigh." He found a weak spot in the thigh, because that is outside of the trunk, which is the symbolical name of Jacob, whose body was therefore under the protection of two degrees symbolised by the name "man". So when the angel found a point of attack outside the trunk, straightway "the hollow of Jacob's thigh sank", and no man received prophetic inspiration from that source till Samuel came. Joshua derived prophetic inspiration from the majesty of Moses, as it is written, "thou shalt confer of thy majesty upon him" (Num. XXVII, 20); this, then, is the fifth grade. Neẓaḥ is the left thigh, the grade of Jacob, and therefore David came and united it with the right, as it is written, "bliss in thy right hand is Neẓaḥ". The reason why Jacob's thigh was weak was because the side of impurity touched it and deprived it of its strength; and it remained weak till the time of Samuel. Hence Samuel spoke of the Neẓaḥ of Israel; and hence, too, he spoke always with severity. Later, however, God brought him under the ægis of Hod, after he had anointed kings. On this account he is ranked with Moses and Aaron, since he combined two lower grades, as they combined two upper grades, though all the grades are linked with one another.[1] [22a]

All those supernal lights exist in their image below—some of them in their image below upon the earth; but in themselves they are all suspended in the "firmament of the heaven". Here is the secret of two names combined which are completed by a third and become one again.

AND GOD SAID, LET US MAKE MAN.[2] It is written, "The

[1] Here in the text follows a passage (up to *behai' alma*, p. 22a) dealing with the prophetic grades of Moses and Jacob as typified respectively by the 'Jubilee' and the 'Shemitah'. It has been omitted from the translation as being both highly technical and in the nature of a digression.

[2] The commentator, Derekh Emeth, remarks that from here to 29a (*bereshith teninan*) is obviously, from its style, not an intrinsic part of the

secret of the Lord is to them that fear him" (Ps. xxv, 14). That most reverend Elder opened an exposition of this verse by saying 'Simeon Simeon, who is it that said: "Let us make man?" Who is this *Elohim?*' With these words the most reverend Elder vanished before anyone saw him. R. Simeon, hearing that he had called him plain "Simeon", and not "Rabbi Simeon", said to his colleagues: 'Of a surety this is the Holy One, blessed be He, of whom it is written: "And the Ancient of days was seated" (Dan. VII, 9). Truly now is the time to expound this mystery, because certainly there is here a mystery which hitherto it was not permitted to divulge, but now we perceive that permission is given.' He then proceeded: 'We must picture a king who wanted several buildings to be erected, and who had an architect in his service who did nothing save with his consent. The king is the supernal Wisdom above, the Central Column being the king below: *Elohim* is the architect above, being as such the supernal Mother, and *Elohim* is also the architect below, being as such the Divine Presence (*Shekinah*) of the lower world. Now a woman may not do anything without the consent of her husband. When he desired anything built in the way of emanation (*aziluth*), the Father said to the Mother by means of the Word (*amirah*), "let it be so and so", and straightway it was so, as it is written, "And he said, *Elohim*, let there be light, and there was light": i.e. one said to *Elohim*, let there be light: the master of the building gave the order, and the architect carried it out immediately; and so with all that was constructed in the way of emanation. When he came to the "world of separation", which is the sphere of individual beings, the architect said to the master of the building: "Let us make man in our image, according to our likeness." Said the master of the building: "Truly, it is well that he should be made, but he will one day sin before thee, because he is foolish: so it is written, 'A wise son rejoiceth his father, and a foolish son is a heaviness to his mother' (Prov. x, 1)." She replied: "Since his guilt is referred to the mother and not the father, I desire to create him in my likeness." Hence it is

Zohar. It seems, however, to fill a gap in the Zoharic exposition, and therefore most of it has been translated.

written, "And *Elohim* created man in his image", the Father not being willing to share in his creation. Thus in reference to his sin it is written, [22b] "and through your transgression your *Mother* is dismissed" (Is. L, 1). Said the king to the mother, "Did I not tell thee that he was destined to sin?" At that time he drove him out and drove out his mother with him; and so it is written, "A wise son rejoiceth his father and a foolish son is the heaviness of his mother." The wise son is Man formed by emanation, and the foolish son is man formed by creation (*beriah*).'

The colleagues here interrupted and said, 'Rabbi, Rabbi, is there such a division between Father and Mother that from the side of the Father Man has been formed in the way of emanation, and from the side of the Mother in the way of creation?' He replied, 'My friends, it is not so, since the Man of emanation was both male and female, from the side of both Father and Mother, and that is why it says, "And God said, Let there be light, and there was light": "let there be light" from the side of the Father, "and there was light" from the side of the Mother; and this is the man "of two faces". This "man" has no "image and likeness". Only the supernal Mother had a name combining light and darkness—light, which was the supernal vestment and which God created on the first day and then stored away for the righteous, and darkness, which was created on the first day for the wicked. On account of the darkness, which was destined to sin against the light, the Father was not willing to share in man's creation, and therefore the Mother said: "let us make man in our image after our likeness". "In our image" corresponds to light, "after our likeness", to darkness, which is a vestment to light in the same way that the body is a vestment to the soul, as it is written, "Thou didst clothe me with skin and flesh." ' He then paused, and all the colleagues rejoiced and said: "Happy is our lot that we have been privileged to hear things which were never disclosed till now.'

R. Simeon then proceeded, taking as his text: *See now that I, I am he, and Elohim is not with me, etc.* (Deut. XXXII, 39)". He said: 'Friends, here are some profound mysteries which I desire to reveal to you now that permission has been given to utter them. Who is it that says, "See now that I, I am he"? This is the Cause which is above all those on high, that which is called the Cause of causes. It is above those other causes, since none of those causes does anything till it obtains permission from that which is above it, as we pointed out above in respect to the expression, "Let us make man". "Us" certainly refers to two, of which one said to the other above it, "let us make", nor did it do anything save with the permission and direction of the one above it, while the one above did nothing without consulting its colleague. But that which is called "the Cause above all causes", which has no superior or even equal, as it is written, "To whom shall ye liken me, that I should be equal?" (Is. XL, 25), said, "See now that I, I am he, and *Elohim* is not with me", from whom he should take counsel, like that of which it is written, "and God said, Let us make man".' The colleagues here interrupted him and said, 'Rabbi, allow us to make a remark. Did you not state above that the Cause of causes said to the Sefirah *Kether*, "Let us make man"?' He answered, 'You do not listen to what you are saying. There is something that is called "Cause of causes", but that is not the "Cause above all causes" which I mentioned, which has no colleague of which it should take counsel, for it is unique, prior to all, and has no partner. Therefore it says: "See now that I, I am he, and *Elohim* is not with me", of which it should take counsel, since it has no colleague and no partner, nor even number, for there is a "one" which connotes combination, such as male and female, of whom it is written, "for I have called him one" (Is. LI, 2); but this is one without number and without combination, and therefore it is said: "and *Elohim* is not with me".' They all rose and prostrated themselves before him, saying, 'happy the man whose Master agrees with him in the exposition of hidden mysteries which have not been revealed to the holy angels.'

He proceeded: 'Friends, we must expound the rest of the verse, since it contains many hidden mysteries. The next words are: *I kill and make alive, etc.* That is to say, through the *Sefiroth* on the right side I make alive, and through the *Sefiroth* on the left side I kill; but if the Central Column does not concur, sentence cannot be passed, since they form a court of three. Sometimes, [23a] even when they all three agree to condemn, there comes the right hand which is outstretched to receive those that repent; this is the *Tetragrammaton*, and it is also the Shekinah, which is called "right hand", from the side of *Ḥesed* (kindness). When a man repents, this hand saves him from punishment. But when the Cause which is above all causes condemns, then "there is none that delivers from my hand".' Withal the colleagues explained the word *Elohim* in this verse as referring to other gods, and the words "I kill and make alive" as meaning "I kill with my Shekinah him who is guilty, and preserve by it him who is innocent." What, however, has been said above concerning the Supreme Cause is a secret which has been transmitted only to wise men and prophets. See now how many hidden causes there are enveloped in the *Sefiroth* and, as it were, mounted on the *Sefiroth*, hidden from the comprehension of human beings: of them it is said, "for one higher than another watcheth" (Eccl. v, 7). There are lights upon lights, one more clear than another, each one dark by comparison with the one above it from which it receives its light. As for the Supreme Cause, all lights are dark in its presence.

Another explanation of the verse " Let us make man in our image after our likeness" was given by the colleagues, who put these words into the mouth of the ministering angels. Said R. Simeon to them, 'Since they know what has been and what will be, they must have known that he was destined to sin. Why, then, did they make this proposal ? Nay more, Uzza and Azael actually opposed it. For when the Shekinah said to God "Let us make man", they said, "What is man that thou shouldst know him ? Why desirest thou to create man, who, as thou knowest, will sin before thee through his wife, who is the darkness to his light, light being male and darkness female ?" The Shekinah answered them: "You yourselves shall commit the very crime of which you accuse him"; and so it is written, "and the sons of God saw the daughters of man that they were comely", and they went astray after them and were degraded by the Shekinah from their holy estate.' Said the colleagues: 'Rabbi, after all, Uzza and Azael were not wrong, because man was really destined to sin through woman.' He replied, 'What the Shekinah said was this: "You have spoken worse of man than all the rest of the heavenly host. If you were more virtuous than man, you would have a right to accuse him. But whereas he will sin with one woman, you will sin with many women, as it is written, 'and the sons of God saw the daughters of man'—not a daughter, but daughters; and further, if man sinned, he was ready to repent and to return to his Master and repair his wrong."' Said the colleagues, 'If so, why was he after all created?' He replied: 'If God had not created man in this way, with good and evil inclination, which correspond to light and darkness, created man would have been capable neither of virtue, nor of sin; but now that he has been created with both, it is written, "see, I have set before thee this day life and death"' (Deut. xxx, 19). They said to him: 'Still, why all this? Would it not have been better that he should not have been created and so not have sinned, thereby causing so much mischief above, and that he should have had neither punishment nor reward?' He replied: 'It was just and right that he should be created in this way, because for his sake the Torah was created in which are inscribed punishments for the wicked and rewards for the righteous, and these are only for the sake of created man.' They said: 'Of a truth we have heard now what we never knew before. Certainly God created nothing which was not required.' What is more, the created Torah [23b] is a vestment to the Shekinah, and if man had not been created, the Shekinah would have been without a vestment like a beggar. Hence when a man sins it is as though he strips the Shekinah of her vestments, and that is why he is punished; and when he carries out the precepts of the Law, it is as though he clothes the Shekinah in her vestments. Hence we say that the fringes (*tsitith*) worn by the Israelites are to the Shekinah in captivity like the poor man's garments, of which it is said, "for that is his only covering, it is his garment for his skin, wherein shall he sleep?" (Ex. xxii, 26).

Prayer which is not whole-hearted is pursued by numbers of destructive angels, according to the Scriptural expression:

"all her pursuers have overtaken her, etc." (Lam. I, 3). Therefore it is well to preface one's prayer with the verse, "but he is merciful and forgiveth iniquity, etc." (Ps. LXXVIII, 38). The word "iniquity" signifies Samael, who is the serpent; "he will not destroy" signifies the destroyer; "he turneth his anger away" refers to the demon *Af* (anger); "and doth not stir up all his wrath" refers to the demon *Hemah* (wrath). To these powers are attached many destructive angels, which are under seven chiefs with seventy under-chiefs, dispersed in every firmament, and under them are myriads of others. When an Israelite wearing fringes and phylacteries prays with devotion, then the words of the Scripture are fulfilled: "All the peoples of the earth shall see that the name of the Lord is called upon thee and they shall fear thee" (Deut. XXVIII, 10). We have agreed that "the name of the Lord" refers to the phylactery of the head; and when the destructive angels see the name of Jehovah on the head of him who is praying, they at once take to flight, as it is written, "a thousand shall fall at thy side" (Ps. XCI, 7).

Jacob foresaw the oppression of the last captivity in the end of days, and therefore "he prayed in that place and tarried there because the sun had set" (Gen. XXVIII, 11), i.e. the night of captivity had come. David, referring to the captivity, said "hungry and weary and thirsty in the wilderness". He saw the Shekinah parched and withered and dried, and was in deep sorrow on its behalf. When he saw Israel returning in joy, he composed ten kinds of chants, and at the end of all he exclaimed: "A prayer for the poor man when he fainteth" (Ps. CII, 1). This is the prayer which comes before God before all the others. Which is the "prayer of the poor man"? This is the evening prayer, which is single, without a husband; and because she is without a husband she is poor and dry. Like her is the just man, poor and parched; this is the seed of Jacob, which is in subjection to all nations and resembles the evening prayer, which typifies the night of captivity. The Sabbath prayer is a kindness to this poor man. Therefore a man when reciting the *Amidah* prayer during the weekdays should stand like a poor man at the king's gate on account of the Shekinah, and he should clothe it with the vestment of the fringes, and he should stand in his phylacteries like a beggar at the gate when he begins with the word *Adonai* (Lord). When he opens his mouth to utter the evening prayer an eagle comes down on the weekdays to take up on its wings the evening prayer. This is the angel called Nuriel when coming from the side of *Ḥesed* (Kindness), and Uriel when coming from the side of *Geburah* (Force), because it is a burning fire. For the morning prayer also a lion comes down to receive it in his winged arms: this is Michael. For the afternoon prayer an ox comes down to take it with his arms and horns: this is Gabriel. On Sabbath God himself comes down with the three patriarchs to welcome his only daughter. At that moment the celestial beings who are called by the name of the Lord exclaim "Lift up your heads, O ye gates, and be exalted, ye everlasting doors", and straightway the doors of seven palaces fly open. The first palace is the palace of love; the second, of fear; the third, of mercy; the fourth, of prophecy through the clear mirror [24a]; the fifth, of prophecy through the hazy mirror; the sixth, of righteousness; the seventh, of justice.[1]   [24b]

THESE ARE THE GENERATIONS OF THE HEAVENS AND THE EARTH. We have laid down that the expression "these are" denotes that those mentioned before are henceforth of no account. In this case what is referred to is the products of *tohu* (emptiness) hinted at in the second verse of the first chapter, "and the earth was *tohu* and *bohu*". These it is of which we have learnt that "God created worlds and destroyed them". On account of this the earth was "dazed" (*tohah*) and "bewildered" (*bohah*), as if to say, "How could God create worlds to destroy them? It were better not to create them." Similarly it is said of the heavens, "the heavens have vanished like smoke" (Is. LI, 6). But in fact we have here an indication of what is meant by the expression "destroyed them", showing that God does not really destroy the works of His hands. The explanation is this. God created the world

---

[1] From here to *razin t'mirin* on 24b is a dissertation on the relation of prayer to the various *Sefiroth*, involving much manipulation of Hebrew letters and vowel-points, and therefore unsuitable for translation.

by means of the Torah, that is to say, in so far as it is called *Reshith*. By this *Reshith* He created the heavens and the earth, and He supports them by it, because the word *bereshith* contains the word *brith* (covenant); this covenant is referred to in the verse: "Were it not for my covenant with the day and night, I had not appointed the ordinances of heaven and earth" (Jer. XXXIII, 25). This heaven is that of which it is said "the heavens are the heavens of the Lord" (Ps. cxv, 16), and this earth is the "land of the living" comprising seven lands of which David said: "I will walk before the Lord in the lands of the living" (*Ibid.* cxvi, 9). Afterwards He created a heaven and an earth [25a] resting on *Tohu* (emptiness), and having no foundation, i.e. "covenant", to support them. For this reason God sought to give to the nations of the world the Law containing the covenant of the circumcision, but they were not willing to accept it, and consequently the earth remained parched and desolate. Hence we read: "Let the waters be gathered to one place, and let the dry land appear." By "the waters" we understand in this connection the Torah; by "one place" we understand Israel, whose souls are attached to that place of which it is written, "blessed is the glory of the Lord from his place". The glory of the Lord is the lower Shekinah; "his place" is the upper Shekinah; and since their souls are from that quarter, the name of the Lord rests upon them, and it is said of them, "for the portion of the Lord is his people". In this way "the waters were gathered to one place". The Torah is the salvation of the world, and the Gentiles who did not accept it were left dry and parched. It is in this way that God created worlds and destroyed them, viz. those who do not keep the precepts of the Law; not that He destroys His own works, as some fancy. For why indeed should He destroy His sons, of whom it is written: *behibar'am* (when they were created) in this passage, which may be analysed into *behé beraam*, "He created them by means of *Hé*" (symbolising the attribute of mercy)? This refers to those of the Gentiles who embrace Judaism. Moses, before leaving Egypt, sought to enrol proselytes, thinking that they were of those who had been thus created through the letter *Hé*, but they were not sincere, and therefore they caused him to be degraded, as it is written, "Go, get thee down, for the people (i.e. thy proselytes) have dealt corruptly" (Ex. XXXII, 7). There are five sections among the "mixed multitude", *Nefilim, Gibborim, Anakim, Refaim*, and *Amalekites*. The *Amalekites* are those who are left from the time of the Flood, from those of whom it is written, "and he blotted out all living substance"; those who have been left from this class in this fourth captivity make themselves leaders by main force, and are scourges to Israel; of them it is written, "for the earth was full of violence because of them". These are the *Amalekites*. Of the *Nefilim* (lit. fallen ones) it is said: "and the sons of God saw the daughters of man that they were fair" (*Ibid.*). These form a second category of the *Nefilim*, already mentioned above, in this way When God thought of making man, He said: "Let us make man in our image, etc." i.e. He intended to make him head over the celestial beings, who were to be his deputies, like Joseph over the governors of Egypt (Gen. XLI, 41). The angels thereupon began to malign him and say, "What is man that Thou shouldst remember him, seeing that he will assuredly sin before Thee." Said God to them, "If ye were on earth like him, ye would sin worse." And so it was, for "when the sons of God saw the daughters of man", they fell in love with them, and God cast them down from heaven. These were [25*b*] Uzza and Azael; from them the "mixed multitude" derive their souls, and therefore they also are called *nefilim*, because they fall into fornication with fair women. For this, God casts them out from the future world, in which they have no portion, and gives them their reward in this world, as it is written, "He repays his enemies to their faces" (Deut. VII, 10). The *Gibborim* (mighty ones) are those of whom it is written: "they are the mighty ones . . . men of name" (Gen. VI, 4). They come from the side of those who said "Come, let us build a city and make to us a name" (Gen. XI, 4). These men erect synagogues and colleges, and place in them scrolls of the law with rich ornaments, but they do it not for the sake of God, but only to make themselves a name, and in consequence the powers of evil prevail over Israel (who should be humble like the dust of the earth), according to the verse: "and the waters prevailed very much upon the earth" (Gen. VII, 19). The *Refaim* (lit. weak ones), the fourth section of the "mixed multitude", are those who, if they see Israel in trouble, abandon them, even though they are in a position to help them, and they also neglect the Torah and those who study it in order to ingratiate themselves with the non-Jews. Of them it is said, "They are *Refaim* (shades), they shall not arise" (Is. XXVI, 14); when redemption shall come to Israel, "all their memory shall perish" (*Ibid.*). The last section, the *Anakim* (lit. giants), are those who treat with contumely those of whom it is written, "they shall be as necklaces (*anakim*) to thy neck". Of them it is said, "the *Refaim* are likewise counted as *Anakim*", i.e. they are on a par with one another. All these tend to bring the world back to the state of "*tohu* and *bohu*", and they caused the destruction of the Temple. But as "*tohu* and *bohu*" gave place to light, so when God reveals Himself they will be wiped off the earth. But withal redemption will not be complete until Amalek will be exterminated, for against Amalek the oath was taken that "the Lord will have war against Amalek from generation to generation" (Ex. XVII, 16).

The following is another explanation of the words: "These are the generations of heaven and earth." The expression "these are" here corresponds to the same expression in the text: "these are thy gods, O Israel" (Ex. XXXII, 4). When these shall be exterminated, it will be as if God had made heaven and earth on that day; hence it is written, "on the day that God makes heaven and earth". At that time God will reveal Himself with the Shekinah and the world will be renewed, as it is written, "for as the new earth and the new heaven, etc." (Is. LXVI, 22). At that time "the Lord shall cause to spring from the ground every pleasant tree, etc.", but before these are exterminated the rain of the Torah will not descend, and Israel, who are compared to herbs and trees, cannot shoot up, as is hinted in the words: "no shrub of the field was yet in the earth, and no herb of the field, etc." (Gen. II, 5), because "there was no man", i.e. Israel were not in the Temple, "to till the ground" with sacrifices. According to another explanation, the words "no shrub of the field was yet in the earth" refer to the first Messiah, and the words "no herb of the field had yet sprung up" refer to the second Messiah. Why had they not shot forth? Because Moses was not there to serve the Shekinah—Moses, of whom it is written, "and there was no man to till the ground". This is also hinted at in the verse "the sceptre shall not depart from Judah nor the ruler's staff from between his feet", "the sceptre" referring to the Messiah of the house of Judah, and "the staff" to the Messiah of the house of Joseph. "Until Shiloh cometh": this is Moses, the numerical value of the two names Shiloh and Moses being the same. It is also possible to refer the "herbs of the field" to the righteous or to the students of the Torah. . . . [26a]

AND THE LORD GOD FORMED MAN. "Man" here refers to Israel, whom God shaped at that time both for this world and for the future world. Further, the word *vayizer* (and he formed) implies that God brought them under the ægis of His own name by shaping the two eyes like the letter *Yod* and the nose between like the letter *Vau*. . . . Forthwith at that time He planted Israel in the holy Garden of Eden, as it is said: "and the Lord God planted" (Gen. II, 8). The two names here refer to the Father and the Mother; the "Garden" is the Shekinah on earth, and "Eden" is the supernal Mother; "the man" is the Central Column; the Shekinah was to be his plantation, his spouse who was never to depart from him and was to be his perpetual delight. Thus God at that time planted Israel as a holy shoot, as it is written, "the branch of my planting, the work of my hands, in which I glory".

AND THE LORD GOD CAUSED TO GROW. The two names may be referred to the Father and the Mother; "every pleasant tree" refers to the *Zaddik;* "good to eat" refers to the Central Column, through which He provided food for all, and from which alone the *Zaddik* is nourished, as the Shekinah from him. These have no need of the lower world, but, on the contrary, all below are nourished from him. For in this period of captivity the Shekinah and "the Life of the universe" are only nourished by the eighteen blessings of

Israel's prayer, but at the time he will be food for all. A N D
THE TREE OF LIFE. This means that at that time the Tree
of Life will be planted in the Garden, so that "he shall take
also of the Tree of Life and eat and live for ever" (Gen. III, 22).
The Shekinah will no longer be in the power of the "evil
influence", i.e. the mixed multitude who are "the tree of the
knowledge of good and evil", and shall no longer receive into
itself anyone unclean, to fulfil what is written, "the Lord
alone shall lead him and there shall be no strange god with
him" (Deut. XXXII, 12). For this reason proselytes will no
longer be admitted in the days of the Messiah. The Shekinah
will be like a vine on which there cannot be grafted any shoot
from another species, and Israel shall be "every tree pleasant
to see", and their former beauty shall be restored to them,
of which we are told: "He cast from heaven to earth the
beauty of Israel" (Lam. II, 1). "The tree of the knowledge
of good and evil" shall be thrust from them and shall not
cleave to them or mingle with them, for of Israel it is said:
"and of the tree of the knowledge of good and evil ye shall
not eat". This tree is the "mixed multitude", and God
pointed out to them that through mixing with them they
suffered two losses, of the first and of the second Temple,
as it is said: "and on the day that thou eatest of it thou shalt
surely die". They caused the *Zaddik* to be left parched and
desolate by the loss of the first Temple, which is the Shekinah
in heaven, and by the loss of the second Temple, which is
the Shekinah on earth. Hence it is written, "and the river
shall be drained dry"; i.e. the river *vau* shall dry in the
lower *hé*, so as to deprive it of the flow of *yod* issuing from
En-Sof. But as soon as Israel shall go forth from captivity,
that is, the holy people alone, then that river which was dried
up shall become "the river that goes forth from Eden to water
the garden". This river is the Central Column; "goes forth
from Eden" is the supernal Mother; "to water the garden"
is the Shekinah on earth. In reference to that time it is said
of Moses and Israel, "Then thou shalt delight in the Lord",
and the words shall be fulfilled, "then Moses shall sing"
(Ex. XV, 1). [26*b*] . . . Further, the river "shall part from
thence and become four heads" (Gen. II, 10). The first of

these is *Ḥesed* (Kindness), which is the right arm. From this shall drink the camp of Michael, and with it the tribe of Judah and his two accompanying tribes. The second is *Geburah* (Force), and from it shall drink the camp of Gabriel, and with it the tribe of Dan and his two accompanying tribes. The third is *Neẓaḥ* (Victory), the right leg, and from it shall drink the camp of Nuriel, and with it the tribe of Reuben and his two accompanying tribes. The fourth is *Hod* (Majesty), the "left leg" (referred to in what was said of Jacob, that "he halted on his left thigh"), and from it shall drink the camp of Raphael, whose mission is to heal the ills of the captivity, and with it the tribe of Ephraim and his two accompanying tribes.[1] [27a]

AND THE LORD GOD TOOK THE MAN AND PUT HIM IN THE GARDEN OF EDEN, ETC. From whence did he take him? He took him from the four elements which are hinted at in the verse "and from there it parted and became four heads". God detached him from these and placed him in the Garden of Eden. So does God do now to any man created from the four elements when he repents of his sins and occupies himself with the Torah; God takes him from his original elements, as it is said, "and from there he parts", i.e. he separates himself from the desires which they inspire, and God places him in his garden, which is the Shekinah, "to dress it", by means of positive precepts, "and to keep it", by means of negative precepts. If he keeps the law, he makes himself master of the four elements, and becomes a river from which they are watered, and they obey him and he is their ruler. But if he transgresses the law, they are watered from the bitterness of the tree of evil, which is the evil inclination, and all his limbs are full of bitterness; but when the members of the body are kept holy from the side of good, it may be said of them that "they came to Marah and were not able to drink waters from Marah, for they were bitter" (Ex. xv, 23). Similarly, the study of the Talmud is bitter

---

[1] Here follows a digression (up to *abathreh*, p. 27a) on a saying of R. Akiba about the esoteric study, too technical for translation into English.

compared with that of the esoteric wisdom, of which it is said, "And God showed him a tree" (*Ibid.*); this is a tree of life, and through it "the waters were sweetened". Similarly of Moses it is written, "And the staff of God was in his hand." This rod is *Metatron*, from one side of whom comes life and from the other death. When the rod remains a rod, it is a help from the side of good, and when it is turned into a serpent it is hostile, so that "Moses fled from it", and God delivered it into his hand. This rod typifies the Oral Law which prescribes what is permitted and what is forbidden. When Moses struck the rock God took it back from him, and "he went down to him with a rod" (II Sam. XXXIII, 21), to smite him with it, the "rod" being the evil inclination, which is a serpent, the cause of the captivity. A further lesson can be derived from the words "and from there it parted": happy is the man who devotes himself to the Torah, for when God takes him from this body, from the four elements, he is detached from them and ascends to become the head [27b] of the four *Hayyoth*, as it is written, "and they shall bear thee on their hands" (Ps. XCI, 12).

AND THE LORD GOD COMMANDED THE MAN, SAYING. It is agreed that the term "command" in the Scripture always has reference to the prohibition of idolatry. This sin has its root in the liver, which is the seat of anger, and it has been laid down that "to fall into a passion is like worshipping idols". The expression "the man" designates bloodshed, on the analogy of the verse: "by man shall his blood be shed" (Gen. IX, 6). This sin has its root in the gall, the sword of the angel of death, after the verse: "her latter end is bitter like gall, piercing like a two-edged sword" (Prov. V, 4). The expression "saying" refers to incest, which has its root in the spleen, as it is written, "Such is the way of the adulterous woman, she eats and wipes her mouth" (*Ibid.* XXX, 20). Although the spleen has no mouth or suckers, yet it absorbs the black turbid blood of the liver; so the adulterous woman wipes her mouth and leaves no trace. The murderer is incited by the bile and sucks from the blood of the heart. All who see bile recoil from it, but unchastity is covered in darkness, in the black blood of the spleen. Whoever sins by murder, idolatry, and incest bans his soul through the liver, the gall, and the spleen, and is punished in Gehinnom in these three members, through three chief demons, *Mashith* (destroyer), *Af* (anger), and *Hemah* (wrath). . . . Before Israel went into captivity, and while the Shekinah was still with them, God commanded Israel: "thou shalt not uncover thy mother's nakedness" (Lev. XVIII, 7), and this captivity is the uncovering of the nakedness of the Shekinah, as it is written, "On account of your sins your mother has been put away" (Is. L, 1), i.e. for the sin of unchastity Israel has been sent into captivity and the Shekinah also, and this is the uncovering of the Shekinah. This unchastity is Lilith, the mother of the "mixed multitude". It is they who separate the two *Hé*'s of the sacred name, and prevent the *Vau* from entering between them; so it is written, "the nakedness of a woman and her daughter thou shalt not uncover", referring to the upper and lower Shekinah. When the "mixed multitude" are between the one *Hé* and the other, the Holy One, blessed be He, cannot link them together, and consequently "the river becomes dry and parched"—dry in the upper *Hé* and parched in the lower *Hé*, in order that the "mixed multitude" may not be nourished by the *Vau*, which is the Tree of Life. Therefore the *Vau* does not link together the two *Hé*'s when the mixed multitude is between them, and the letter *Yod* is not able to draw near to the second *Hé;* thus the precept "thou shalt not uncover the nakedness of thy daughter-in-law" is transgressed. Further, they separate the *Yod* from the upper *Hé*, and so break the command "thou shalt not uncover the nakedness of thy father's wife", the *Yod* being the father, the first *Hé* the mother, *Vau* the son and the second *Hé* the daughter. Therefore it is ordained with regard to the upper *Hé*, "thou shalt not uncover the nakedness of thy father's wife"; "the nakedness of thy sister the daughter of thy father" refers to the lower *Hé;* "her son's daughter and her daughter's daughter" refers to the *Hé* and *Hé* which are the children of *Hé;* "the nakedness of the father's brother" refers to the *Yod*, which is the product of the letter *Yod*, a brother to *Vau*. In a word, when the "mixed multitude" are mingled with Israel, the letters of the name *YHVH* cannot be joined and linked together; but as soon as they are removed from the world, then it is said of the letters of God's name that "On that day the Lord shall be one and his name one" (Zech. XIV, 9). This is why Adam, who is Israel, is closely linked with the Torah, of which it is said, "It is a tree of life to those who take hold on it"; this tree is the Matron, the Sefirah *Malkhuth* (Kingship), through their connection with which Israel are called "sons of kings". On this account God said, "It is not good that the man should be alone; I will make him an help meet for him" (Gen. II, 18). This help is the Mishnah (the oral Law), the handmaid of the Shekinah. If Israel deserve well, it is a help to them in the captivity from the side of the permitted, the clean, and the proper; if they do not deserve well, it is a hindrance to them from the side of the unclean, the unfit, and the forbidden, the clean, the permitted, and the fit signifying the good inclination, and the unfit, the unclean, and the forbidden signifying the evil inclination. Thus the Mishnah resembles the woman, who has both pure and impure blood of menstruation. But the Mishnah is not the spouse of his real union, for real union is denied to him until the "mixed multitude" shall be removed from the earth. On account of this Moses was buried outside of the Holy Land.... [28a]

AND THE LORD GOD FORMED FROM THE GROUND ALL THE BEASTS OF THE FIELD AND ALL THE FOWL OF THE HEAVEN. Said R. Simeon, 'Alas for the stupidity and the blindness of men who do not perceive the mysteries of the Torah, and do not know that by "the beasts of the field and the fowl of the heaven" are designated the unlearned. Even those of them who are "a living soul" are of no service in the Captivity to the Shekinah or to Moses who is with her, for all the time that she is in exile he does not quit her.' Said R. Eleazar, 'Are we justified in applying what is said of Adam to Moses and Israel?' R. Simeon answered: 'My son, is it you who speak thus? Have you forgotten the text, "He announceth the end from the beginning" (Is. XLVI, 10)?' He replied: 'You are certainly right; and that is why we are told that Moses did not die, and that he was called Adam; and in reference to him in the last captivity it is written, "and for Adam he found no help", but all was "against him". So, too, of the Central Column it is written, "and for the man he found no help", viz. to bring the Shekinah out of captivity; therefore it is written, "And he turned this way and that and saw that there was no man" (Ex. II, 12), Moses being after the pattern of the Central Column. At that time "the Lord God caused a deep sleep to fall upon the man" (Gen. II, 21). "Lord God" designates the Father and the Mother; the "deep sleep" is the "captivity", as it is said, "and a deep sleep fell upon Abraham" (*Ibid*. XV, 12). "And he took one of his sides." Whose sides? What is referred to is the maidens of the Matron. The Father and the Mother took one of these, a white side, fair as the moon, "and closed up the place with flesh"; this is the flesh of which it is written, "seeing that he also is flesh" (Gen. VI, 3), which refers to Moses.

AND THE LORD GOD BUILT THE SIDE. Here is an allusion to the law of the deceased husband's brother, in regard to whom the Sages said, "If he refuses to build once, he shall not build any more", as it is written, "thus shall be done to the man who shall not build his brother's house" (Deut. XXV, 9). But of God it is written, "And the Lord God built", i.e. the Father and the Mother built the son, as it is written, "God buildeth Jerusalem", i.e. *Vau*, which is the son, is built by *Yod Hé*, which are the Father and Mother. Hence it says, "And the Lord God built the side which he had taken from the man", viz. the Central Column, "and brought it to the man", i.e. he brought to the side which he had taken from *Hé* its maiden, and of her it is said, "And I shall be to her, saith the Lord, a wall of fire round about" (Zech. II, 9). It is because the future Temple will be built on this rock by the hands of the Holy One, blessed be He, that it will endure for all generations. Of this Temple it is written, "greater shall be the glory of this latter house than of the former", for the former was built by the hands of man, but this one shall be built by the hands of the Holy

One, blessed be He. . . . The words "and the Lord God built the side" can also be applied to Moses, in so far as he is from the side of *Ḥesed* (Kindness). "And he closed the place of it with flesh": flesh being red, symbolises *Geburah* (Force), and so in Moses both were combined. THIS TIME BONE OF MY BONE AND FLESH OF MY FLESH. This is said of the Shekinah, the betrothed maiden, by the Central Column, as though to say, "I know that this is bone of my bone and flesh of my flesh; so this of a surety shall be called woman, from the supernal realm, which is Mother, for she was taken from the realm of the Father, which is *Yod*." And as with the Central Column, so with Moses below. At that time every Israelite will find his twin-soul, as it is written, "I shall give to you a new heart, and a new spirit I shall place within you" (Ezek. XXXVI, 26), and again, "And your sons and your daughters shall prophesy" (Joel III, 1); these are [28*b*] the new souls with which the Israelites are to be endowed, according to the dictum, "the son of David will not come until all the souls to be enclosed in bodies have been exhausted", and then the new ones shall come. At that time the mixed multitude shall pass away from the world, and it will be possible to say of Moses and of Israel, each in reference to his twin-soul, "and the man and his wife were both naked and were not ashamed", because unchastity shall pass away from the world, namely those who caused the captivity, the mixed multitude. Of them it is further said, AND THE SERPENT WAS MORE SUBTLE THAN ANY BEAST OF THE FIELD WHICH THE LORD GOD HAD MADE; i.e. they are more subtle for evil than all the Gentiles, and they are the offspring of the original serpent that beguiled Eve. The mixed multitude are the impurity which the serpent injected into Eve. From this impurity came forth Cain, who killed Abel. . . . From Cain was descended Jethro, the father-in-law of Moses, as it is written, "And the sons of the Kenite the father-in-law of Moses" (Jud. I, 16), and according to tradition he was called Kenite because he originated from Cain. Moses, in order to screen the reproach of his father-in-law, sought to convert the "mixed multitude" (the descendants of Cain), although God warned him, saying, "They are of an evil stock; beware of them." Through them Moses was banished from his proper place and was not privileged to enter the land of Israel, for through them he sinned in striking the rock when he was told to speak to it (Num. xx, 8); it was they who brought him to this. And withal God takes account of a good motive, and since Moses' motive in converting them was good, as has been said, therefore God said to him, "I shall make thee a nation greater and mightier than he" (*Ibid*. XIV, 12). In regard to them it is written, "Whoso hath sinned against me, him will I blot out of my book" (Ex. XXXII, 33), for they are of the seed of Amalek, of whom it is said, "thou shalt blot out the memory of Amalek" (Deut. xxv, 19): it was they who caused the two tablets of the Law to be broken, whereupon, AND THE EYES OF BOTH OF THEM WERE OPENED AND THEY KNEW THAT THEY WERE NAKED, i.e. Israel became aware that they were sunk in the mire of Egypt, being without Torah, so that it could be said of them "and thou wast naked and bare" .... Next it says, AND THEY SEWED FIG LEAVES, that is to say, they sought to cover themselves with various husks from the "mixed multitude"; but their real covering is the fringes of the *Tzitzith* and the straps of the phylacteries, of which it is said, AND THE LORD GOD MADE FOR THE MAN AND HIS WIFE COATS OF SKIN AND COVERED THEM; this refers more properly to the phylacteries, while the fringes are designed in the words AND THEY MADE FOR THEMSELVES GIRDLES.

AND THEY HEARD THE VOICE OF THE LORD GOD, ETC. This alludes to the time when Israel came to Mount Sinai as it is written, "Hath a people heard the voice of God speaking from the midst of the fire, etc." The mixed multitude then perished, those who said to Moses, "Let not God speak with us lest we die" (Ex. xx, 16). These are the prototypes of the unlearned (*Am haaretz*), of whom it is said, "cursed is he that lieth with any manner of beast" (Deut. XXVII, 21), because they are from the side of the serpent, of which it is said, "cursed art thou from among all the beasts" (Gen. III, 14). Various impurities are mingled in the composition of

Israel, like animals among men. One kind is from the side of the serpent; another from the side of the Gentiles, who are compared to the beasts of the field; another from the side of *mazikin* (goblins), for the souls [29a] of the wicked are literally the *mazikin* (goblins) of the world; and there is an impurity from the side of the demons and evil spirits; and there is none so cursed among them as Amalek, who is the evil serpent, the "strange god". He is the cause of all unchastity and murder, and his twin-soul is the poison of idolatry, the two together being called Samael (lit. poison-god). There is more than one Samael, and they are not all equal, but this side of the serpent is accursed above all of them.

AND THE LORD GOD CALLED TO THE MAN AND SAID, WHERE ART THOU? The word *aiekah* (where art thou) has the same letters as the word *aikah* (how), which commences the book of Lamentations, and thus foreshadows the destruction of the Temple and the lamentation over it. But in the days to come God will sweep away all evil growths from the world, as it is written, "He hath swallowed up death for ever" (Is. XXV, 8), and everything shall be restored to its rightful place, as it is written, "On that day the Lord shall be one and his name one" (Zech. XIV, 9).

IN THE BEGINNING.[1] We have been taught that wherever the name Solomon occurs in the Song of Songs, it refers to "the King to whom peace belongs", while the term "king", simply, refers to the Female. The lower is contained in the upper, and the mnemonic is that the lower is heir to the upper, so that both are as one, together constituting *beth* (=*bayith*, house), as it is written, "With wisdom a house (*bayith*) is builded" (Prov. XXIV, 3). Now it is written: *The king Solomon made him a palanquin of the trees of Lebanon* (S. S. III, 9). The "palanquin" is the maintenance of the lower world through the agency of the upper world. Before God created the world, His name was enclosed within Him, and therefore He and His name enclosed within Him were not one. Nor could this unity be effected until He created the world. Having, therefore,

[1] v. Appendix, p. 383.

decided to do so, He traced and built, but the aim was not attained until He enfolded Himself in a covering of a supernal radiance of thought and created therefrom a world. He produced from the light of that supernal radiance mighty cedars of the upper world, and placed His chariot on twenty-two graven letters which were carved into ten utterances and infixed there. Hence it is written, "from the trees of Lebanon", and it is also written, "the cedars of Lebanon which he hath planted" (Ps. CIV, 16). It says in our text, "King Solomon made for himself." The words "for himself" indicate that He made it for His own behoof, for His own advantage, to display His glory, to show that He is one and His name one, as it is written, "and they shall know that it is thou alone whose name is the Lord" (Ps. LVIII, 19). Through the blows of His light various realms were made intelligible. He glanced at this side above, He glanced to the right, He turned to the left and descended below, and so to all four cardinal points. Thus His kingdom spread above and below and in all four directions, since a certain supernal stream flowed downwards and formed a great sea, as it says, "all the rivers flow into the sea and the sea is not full" (Eccl. I, 7), for it gathers the Whole and draws it into its midst, as it is written, "I am the rose of Sharon" (S. S. II, 1), Sharon being the basin of the great sea which draws to itself all the waters of the World and absorbs them. Thus the one discharges and the other collects, and one shines through the other in a specified manner. Of this relationship it is written, "By wisdom is the house built"; hence the *beth* (=2) of *bereshith*, implying that the upper house is built in wisdom and the lower one also. The upper house, which is the greater, makes the world habitable, and is called *Elohim;* the lower one is called simply "king". It is written, "The king shall rejoice in *Elohim*" (Ps. LXIII, 12): to wit, when the supernal *Geburah* (Force) bestirs itself to embrace him and draw him to himself, so that all should be one. Again, the words may be taken to refer to the gladness of the stream which issues in one hidden and secret path and enters as two which are one, thus rendering the world complete and whole. Or again, "The king shall rejoice in *Elohim*", i.e. the lower world rejoices in the upper recondite world which sent forth life to all, which was called the life of the king. This is the foundation [29b] of the house. This house built the house of the world, and built a world. This is what is meant by "in the beginning God created": "in the beginning", to wit, in Wisdom.

When it collected the whole into itself, it became the great sea, a sea of which the waters were congealed, those waters which had flowed in from the upper source, as we indicate by the verse, "From the womb of Whom (*Mi*) came forth the ice" (Job. XXXVIII, 29), its waters congealing in it in order to draw in others. This ice was a frozen sea the waters of which did not flow until the force of the South reached it and drew it to itself. Then the waters which were congealed in the side of the North were relaxed and commenced to flow; for it was on the side of the North that the waters were frozen, and on the side of the South that they thawed and began to flow, in order to water all the "beasts of the field", as it is written, "they give water to all the beasts of the field" (Ps. CIV, 11). These are called *haré bather* (mountains of separation), and all are watered when the side of the South begins to approach and to make the water flow. Through the streaming of this supernal energy all were in gladness. When it so pleased the thought of the Most Mysterious, a river flowed forth therefrom, and when one joined the other by a path which cannot be traced either above or below, herein was the beginning of all, and *Beth* (= second), which is plain "king", was completed from this beginning, and one was like the other. With this energy God created the heavens, a hidden point the waters of which flow forth without, and produced therefrom a voice which is called the voice of the *Shofar*. Hence it says, "God created the heavens", to wit, the voice of the *Shofar*. The heavens control the life of the supernal King upon the earth (as indicated by the catchword, "the son of Jesse is alive upon the earth", since life depends upon the son of Jesse). It is through *Vau* that life flows to it, and it controls all and the earth is fed therefrom; hence it is written, "and (*v-*) the earth", the *vau* being added to control the sustenance of the earth. The word *eth* refers to something in the upper world, to wit, the power of the totality of the twenty-two letters, which *Elohim* produced and gave to the heavens (as it says, "with the crown with which his mother crowned him on the day of his espousals"); hence, "the (*eth*) heavens", to associate and combine one with the other, so as to be established together by the "life of the king", that the heavens should be fed therefrom. The words "and (*ve-eth*) the earth" indicate the union of male and female, which were traced with individual letters, and the "life of the king" which flowed from the heavens, the heavens pouring them forth to maintain the earth and all its denizens.

In this way the so-called supernal *Elohim* made a heaven and earth for permanency, and produced them together by the supernal energy, the starting-point of all. The supernal essence then descended to a lower grade, and this latter made a heaven and earth below. The whole process is symbolised by the letter *beth*. There are two Worlds and they created worlds, one an upper world and one a lower world, one corresponding to the other; one created heaven and earth and the other created heaven and earth. In this way the letter *beth* signifies two further worlds; one produced two worlds and the other produced two worlds; and all through the energy of the supernal *reshith*. When the upper descended into the lower, it was filled from the channel of a certain grade which rested on it, corresponding to that hidden, secret and recondite path above, the difference being that one is a narrow path and the other a way. The one below is a way, like "the way of the righteous which is as a shining light" (Prov. IV, 18), whereas the one above is a narrow path, like "the track which the vulture knoweth not" (Job XXVIII, 7). The mnemonic for the whole is the verse, "who maketh a way in the sea and a path in the mighty waters" (Is. XLIII, 16); and similarly it is written, "Thy way is in the sea and thy path is in great waters".

When the upper world was filled and became pregnant, it brought forth two children together, a male and a female, these being heaven and earth after the supernal pattern. The earth is fed from the waters of the heaven which are poured into it. These upper waters, however, are male, whereas the lower are female, and the lower are fed from the male and the lower waters call to the upper, like a female that receives the male, and pour out water to meet the water of the male to produce seed. Thus the female is fed from the male, as it is written, "and the earth", with the addition of *vau*, as we have explained.

Letters were imprinted [30a] on the fabric of the Whole, on the upper and on the lower fabric. Afterwards the letters were distinguished and inscribed in the Scripture—*beth* in *bereshith bara*, and *aleph* in *Elohim eth*. *Beth* is female, *aleph* male. As *beth* created, so *aleph* produced letters. "The heavens" are the totality of twenty-two letters. The letter *hé* produced the heavens to give them life and to water them and the earth. The letter *vau* produced the earth to give it food and to provide for it its requirements. The word *ve-eth* (and) signifies that *vau* took *eth*, which embraces the twenty two letters, and the earth absorbed them, as it is written, "all the rivers go to the sea", and was thus fed. Thus the heavens and the earth are united and the earth is fed. When the flaming fire goes forth and the Left is awakened, smoke also goes up, as it says, "Now mount Sinai was altogether on smoke, because the Lord descended upon it in fire" (Ex. XIX, 18); because when fire descends, smoke and fire are intermingled, and so the whole is on the side of the left. This is the inner meaning of the verse, "Yea, my *hand* hath laid the foundations of the earth, and my *right hand* hath spread out the heavens" (Is. XLVIII, 13), i.e. by the power of the Right above; for the heavens are male and the male comes from the side of the right, and the female from the side of the left.

It says: *Lift up your eyes on high and see, Who hath created these* (Is. XL, 26). This is the limit of inquiry. For Wisdom was completed from *ayin* (nothing), which is no subject of inquiry, since it is too deeply hidden and recondite to be comprehended. From the point at which its light begins to extend it is the subject of inquiry, although it is still more recondite than anything beneath, and it is called the interrogative pronoun, "Who?" Hence, "Who (*Mi*) created these", and also, "From the womb of Whom (*Mi*) came forth the ice"; as much as to say, that about which we can inquire but find no answer.

We have analysed the word *bereshith* into the letter *beth* and the word *reshith*. Is *reshith* a creative utterance, or are we to say that *bereshith* is the creative utterance? The truth is that so long as its energy had not emerged and spread and everything was still latent in it, it was *bereshith*, and that was a creative utterance. But when being emerged and spread from it, it was called *reshith*, and that became a creative utterance. Similarly, the interrogative *Mi* created *eleh* (these); but subsequently when it extended and completed itself, it became *Yam* (sea), and created a lower world after the pattern of the upper, the two being represented by the letter *beth* (=2). It is written: *While the king sat at his table, my spikenard sent forth its fragrance* (S. S. 1, 12). This describes how the King delights himself in the company of the lower king, in their affectionate companionship in the celestial Eden, in that hidden and concealed path which is filled from him and issues in certain specified streams. "My spikenard gave its fragrance": this is the lower king, who created a lower world after the pattern of the upper. So there goes up a goodly fragrance to direct and to perform, and it acquires power and shines with supernal light.

The world was created in two fashions, with the right and with the left, in six supernal days. Six days were created to illumine, as it says, "for into six days the Lord made the heavens and the earth", and they trod out paths and made sixty openings into the great abyss, to conduct the waters of the streams into the abyss. Hence the Rabbinic dictum that "the openings (under the altar) were from the six days of creation", and they brought peace to the world.

AND THE EARTH WAS VOID AND WITHOUT FORM. This describes the original state—as it were, the dregs of ink clinging to the point of the pen—in which there was no subsistence, until the world was graven with forty-two letters, all of which are the ornamentation of the Holy Name. When they are joined, letters ascend [30b] and descend, and form crowns for themselves in all four quarters of the world, so that the world is established through them and they through it. A mould was formed for them like the seal of a ring; when they went in and issued, and the world was created, and when they were joined together in the seal, the world was established. They struck against the great serpent, and penetrated under the chasms of the dust fifteen hundred cubits. Afterwards the great deep arose in darkness, and darkness covered all, until light emerged and cleft the darkness and came forth and shone, as it is written, "He uncovereth deep things out of darkness, and bringeth out to light the shadow of death" (Job XII, 22). The waters were weighed in a balance. Fifteen hundred times three fingers flowed into the balance, half for preservation and half to go below. At first one side of the balance rose and the other fell. When, however, the lower side was raised by the hand, the balance was even and did not incline to left or right; hence it is written, "Who hath measured the waters in the hollow of his hand?" (Is. XL, 12). At first all the powers of the earth were latent and not productive, and the waters were frozen in it and did not flow. They only spread abroad when a light from above was shed upon the earth, for when this struck it with its rays its powers were released. So it says, "And God said, Let there be light, and there was light." This is the supernal primordial light which was already existing; from this came forth all powers and forces, and through this the earth was firmly established and subsequently brought forth its products. When this light shone on what was below, its radiance spread from one end of the world to the other; but when it observed the sinners of the world, it hid itself away, and issued only by secret paths which cannot be discovered.

AND GOD SAW THE LIGHT THAT IT WAS GOOD. We have learnt that every dream which contains the term *tob* (good) presages peace above and below, provided the letters are seen in their proper order. . . .[1] These three letters were afterwards combined to signify "the Righteous one (*Zaddik*) of the world", as it is written, "Say of the righteous one that he is good", because the supernal radiance is contained therein.

---

[1] Here follow some lines on the inner significance of the letters of the word *tob*, viz. *teth*, representing the ninth grade (from the end, i.e. Wisdom) *vau*, the heavens, and *beth*, the two worlds.

IN THE BEGINNING GOD CREATED. The word *reshith* (beginning) refers to the supernal Wisdom; the letter *beth* (i.e. *bayith*, house) designates the world, which is watered from that stream which enters it, and which is alluded to in the verse, "A stream went forth from Eden to water the garden." This stream gathers all the waters from a supernal hidden source, and flows perenially to water the Garden. (This hidden source is the First Temple.) In *reshith* all the letters were enclosed by a secret path hidden within it. From this source went forth two entities, as it is written, "the heavens and the earth". The earth was at first included in the heavens, and they emerged together, clinging to one another. When the first illumination came, the heavens took the earth and put it in its place. Thereupon the earth, being separated [31a] from the side of the heavens, was amazed and dumbfounded, desiring to cleave to the heavens as before, because she saw the heavens bathed in light while she was enveloped in darkness. At length, however, the celestial light descended upon her, and from her place she looked at the heavens face to face; and so the earth was firmly established. Light came forth on the right side and darkness on the left, and God afterwards separated them in order again to unite them, as it is written, "And God divided the light from the darkness." This does not mean that there was an absolute separation, but that day came from the side of light, which is the right, and night from the side of darkness, which is the left, and that, having emerged together, they were separated in such a way as to be no longer side by side but face to face, in which guise they clung to one another and formed one, the light being called day and the darkness night, as it says, "And God called the light day and the darkness he called night." This is the darkness that is attached to night, which has no light of its own, although it comes from the side of the primordial fire which is also called "darkness". It remains dark until it is illumined from the side of day. Day illumines night, and night will not be light of itself until the time of which it is written, "the night shineth as the day, the darkness is even as the light" (Ps. CXXXIX, 12).

¹ R. Eleazar came forward first and expounded the verse: *The voice of the Lord is upon the waters: the God of glory thundereth, even the Lord upon many waters* (Ps. XXIX, 3). He said, ' "The voice of the Lord" is the supernal voice presiding over the waters, which flow from grade to grade until they are all collected in one place and form one gathering. It is this voice which sends them forth each in its course, like a gardener who conducts water through various channels to the requisite spots. "The God of glory thundereth": this is the side that issues from *Geburah* (Force), as it is written, "Who can understand the thunder of his mighty deeds (*geburotov*)?" (Job. XXVI, 14). "The Lord upon many waters": this is the supernal Wisdom, which is called *Yod*, and which is "upon the many waters", the secret source that issues therefrom.'

R. Simeon explained the difference, and said: 'It is written, "Close by the border shall the rings be, for places for the staves" (Ex. XXV, 27). The "border" is a secret place accessible only by one narrow path known to a few. It is, therefore, filled with gates and lit with lamps. This is the future world, which, being hidden and stored away, is called *misgereth* (border, lit. closed). The "rings" are the supernal chain of water, air, and fire, which are linked with one another and emerge from one another like so many rings of a chain. They all turn to the "border", with which is connected that supernal stream which waters them, and with which they are thus connected. Further, these supernal rings are "places for the staves", to wit, the lower chariots, of which some are from the side of fire, some of water, and some of air, so that they should be a chariot to the ark. Hence anyone who approaches should proceed only as far as the staves, but should not penetrate further, save those who are qualified to minister within, and to whom permission has been given to enter for that purpose.'

R. Jose propounded the question: 'What are the "six days of *bereshith*" of which the Rabbis speak so often ?' R. Simeon answered: 'These are, in truth, "the cedars of Lebanon which he has planted". As the cedars spring from Lebanon, so these six days spring from *bereshith*. These are the six

¹ There seems to be here a lacuna in the text.

supernal days which are specified in the verse: "Thine, O Lord, are the Greatness (*Gedulah*), the Might (*Geburah*), the Beauty (*Tifereth*), the Victory (*Nezah*), and the Majesty (*Hod*)" (I Chron. XXIX, 11). The words "For all" refer to the *Zaddik* (righteous one), who is *Yesod* (foundation of the world).... [31b] The word *bereshith* we interpret to mean "the second, i.e. *Hokmah* (Wisdom) is the starting-point", because the supernal *Kether* (Crown), which is really first, is too recondite and therefore is not counted; hence the second is the starting-point. Again, the word *be-reshith* indicates that there are two *reshith*'s, because as the upper Wisdom is a *reshith* (starting-point), so the lower Wisdom is a *reshith*. Further, we reckon *bereshith* as a *maamar* (creative utterance), and six days issued from it and are comprised in it, and bear the names of those others. The next words, *Created Elohim*, are analogous to the verse "and a river went forth from Eden to water the garden", i.e. to water it and keep it and attend to all its needs. Thus this *Elohim* is *Elohim Hayyim* (the living God), and we render "*Bereshith* created *Elohim*" by means of that stream, as the agent for producing the world and vivifying it. Further, the two words *eth hashamaim* (the heavens) signify the fitting union of male and female. After this a lower world was created through the agency of the heavens, and through it *Elohim* gave being to all. More precisely, the heavens produced *eth*, which is the Whole. When the Whole was settled in its place, this last link in the chain became in turn a starting-point (*reshith*), through which *Elohim* released the stream, and the waters began to flow to the lower world, so that we can now render "by means of *reshith* God created", viz. the lower world; by its means He produced radiances and gave being to all.' R. Judah said: 'In allusion to this it is written, "should the axe boast itself against him that heweth therewith?" (Is. x, 15). Surely it is the craftsman who is entitled to boast. So here, seeing that by means of this *reshith* the supernal *Elohim* created the heavens, it is God to whom the glory belongs....'

AND GOD SAID, LET THERE BE LIGHT, AND THERE WAS LIGHT. This is the original light which God created.

This is the light of the eye. It is the light which God showed to Adam, and through which he was able to see from one end of the world to the other. It was the light which God showed to David, who on seeing it burst forth into praise, saying, "Oh, how abundant is thy goodness which thou hast laid up for them that fear thee" (Ps. XXXI, 20). It is the light through which God showed to Moses the Land of Israel from Gilead to Dan. When God foresaw that three sinful generations would arise, namely the generation of Enosh, the generation of the Flood, and the generation of the Tower of Babel, He put it away so that they should not enjoy it, and gave it to Moses for the first three months after he was born when his mother hid him. When he was brought before Pharaoh God withdrew it from him, and only restored it to him when he stood upon the mountain of Sinai to receive the Torah. From that time he had the use of it for the rest of his life, so that the Israelites could not approach him till he put a veil over his face (Ex. XXXIV, 30).

LET THERE BE LIGHT, AND THERE WAS LIGHT. Anything to which the term *vayehi* (and there was) is applied is found in this world and the next world. R. Isaac said: 'The radiance which God produced at the time of the Creation illumined the world from one end to the other, but was withdrawn, in order that the sinners of the world might not enjoy it, and it is treasured up for the righteous, i.e. for the *Zaddik*, [32a] as it is written, "light is sown for the *Zaddik*" (Ps. XCVII, 11); then worlds will be firmly established and all will form a single whole, but until the time when the future world shall emerge this light is hidden and stored up. This light issued from the darkness which was carved out by the strokes of the Most Recondite; and similarly from that light which was stored away there was carved out through some hidden process the lower-world darkness in which light resides. This lower darkness is what is called "night" in the verse, "and the darkness he called night" (Gen. 1, 5). Hence the Rabbinical exposition of the text: "He uncovereth deep things out of darkness" (Job. XII, 22)', on which R. Jose said: 'This cannot be the original darkness, since all the supernal crowns contained therein are still undisclosed, and we call them "deep things". The term "uncovereth" can be applied to those supernal mysteries only in so far as they are contained in that darkness which is in the category of night. For all those deep and hidden things which issue from (God's) thought and are taken up by the Voice are not disclosed till the Word reveals them. This Word is Speech, and this Speech is called Sabbath, because this Speech seeks to dominate and not to let any other do so. It is this Speech which comes from the side of darkness that discloses hidden things from that darkness.' Said R. Isaac: 'If so, what is the meaning of the text, "And God divided the light from the darkness"?' He replied: 'Light produced day and darkness produced night. Afterwards He joined them together and they were one, as it is written, "And there was evening and there was morning one day", i.e. night and day were called one. As for the words, "And God divided the light from the darkness", this means that He prevented dissension between them.' Said R. Isaac: 'Up to this point the male principle was represented by light and the female by darkness; subsequently they were joined together and made one. The difference by means of which light is distinguished from darkness is one of degree only; both are one in kind, as there is no light without darkness and no darkness without light; but though one, they are different in colour.' R. Simeon said: 'The world is created and established on the basis of a covenant, as it is written, "If not for my covenant with the day and night, I had not appointed the ordinances of heaven and earth" (Jer. XXXIII, 25). This covenant is the *Zaddik* (righteous one), the foundation of the world, and therefore the world is established on the covenant of day and night together, as stated in our text, the "ordinances of heaven" being those which flow and issue forth from the celestial Eden.' R. Simeon discoursed here on the text: *From the (place of) the voice of those who mediate between the water drawers, there they shall rehearse the kindnesses of the Lord, etc.* (Judges V, 11). 'This voice', he said, 'is the voice of Jacob, which rests between those who draw waters from on high, and takes hold of both sides and unites them in itself. "There they shall rehearse the kindnesses of the

Lord": i.e. there is the place for faith to cleave fast; there the kindnesses of the Lord draw sustenance. The verse proceeds: "The kindnesses of him who is generous to Israel." This is the "Righteous One of the world", who is everlasting and holy, and who draws in to Himself the stream of the Whole and disperses the supernal waters into the great sea. "In Israel": because Israel inherited this covenant, and God gave it to them for an everlasting inheritance. When Israel deserted it through performing the ceremony of circumcision without drawing back the flesh, there was applied to them the verse, "then the people of the Lord went down to the gates" (*Ibid.*): these are the gates of righteousness in which they sat without entering further. Of that time [32*b*] it is written, "and the children of Israel forsook the Lord" (Judges II, 12), until Deborah came and restored the proper performance of the ceremony. Hence Deborah speaks of herself as a "mother in Israel", to indicate that she brought down the supernal waters from above to establish both worlds through Israel, thus showing that the world rests only on this covenant. We see from all this how three issue from one and one is established on three; one enters between two, two give suck to one, and one feeds many sides, and so all are one. Hence it is written, "and there was evening and there was morning one day", i.e. a day that embraces both evening and morning, thus indicating the covenant of day and night and rendering the whole a unity.'

AND GOD SAID, LET THERE BE A FIRMAMENT IN THE MIDST OF THE WATERS, AND LET IT DIVIDE WATERS FROM WATERS. R. Judah said: 'There are seven firmaments above, all in the realm of supernal holiness, and the Holy Name is completed through them. The firmament mentioned here is in the midst of the waters; it rests upon other *Hayyoth*, separating the upper from the lower waters. The lower waters call to the upper and drink them in through the medium of this firmament, because all the upper waters are collected in it, and it then transmits them to these *Hayyoth*, and so they draw from there. It is written: "A garden shut up is my sister, my bride, a spring shut up, a fountain sealed" (S. S.

iv, 12). This firmament is called a "garden shut up", because the whole is enclosed and embraced in it. It is called a "spring shut up", because the supernal stream as it courses enters it but cannot issue, the waters being congealed. For the north wind blows on them, and so they become congealed and cannot issue, being made into ice; nor would they ever issue were it not for a wind from the South which breaks up the ice. The appearance of this highest firmament is like that of the ice which collects all the waters. Similarly it collects waters and separates the upper from the lower waters. When we said above that it was in the middle, this refers to that firmament which was produced from this one, but this one is above and rests on the heads of the *Hayyoth*.' Said R. Isaac: 'There is a membrane in the inside of the human body which separates the upper from the lower part of the trunk, and which imbibes from the upper part and distributes to the lower part; so is this firmament between the waters. . . .' R. Abba illustrated from the text: 'Who lays the beams of his upper chambers in the waters, etc." (Ps. CIV, 3), the "waters" mentioned here being the supernal waters through which the "house" was built up, as it is written, "through wisdom a house is builded and through understanding it is established" (Prov. XXIV, 3). In the following clause, "Who makes the clouds his chariot", R. Yesa divided the word *abim* (clouds) into *ab* (cloud), and *yam* (sea), interpreting it to mean "the cloud", viz. darkness from the Left, "resting on this sea". "Who walketh upon the wings of the wind": this is the spirit of the supernal sanctuary. . . . R. Jose said: 'It is written, "and he meteth out waters by measure" (*middah*), implying that God literally measured them out, so that they were for the well-being of the world when they came from the side of *Geburah* (Force).' R. Abba said: 'When the scholars of old came to this place, they used to say: "The lips of the wise move but they say nothing lest they bring down punishment on themselves".' R. Eleazar said: 'The first of the letters was flitting over the face of the ethereal expanse, and was crowned above and below, and went up [33*a*] and down, and the waters were graven into their shapes and were settled in their places, and enfolded in one another;

and so all the letters were combined with one another and crowned with one another until a firm building was erected on them. When they were all built and crowned, the upper waters and the lower waters, which were still mingled together, produced the habitation of the world. And the waters continued going up and down until this firmament came into being and separated them. The division took place on the second (day), on which was created Gehinnom, which is a blazing fire, and which is destined to rest upon the heads of sinners.' Said R. Judah: 'From this we learn that every division (of opinion) in which both sides act for the glory of heaven endures, since here we have a division which was for the sake of heaven. Through the firmament the heavens were established, as it is written, "and God called the firmament heaven", since this divides the more from the less holy, like the curtain in the Tabernacle.'

LET THE WATERS UNDER THE HEAVEN BE GATHERED: i.e. those "under the heaven" only. TO ONE PLACE: i.e. to the place which is called "one", namely, the lower sea, which completes the formation of One, and without which God would not be called One. R. Yesa said: " 'One place" is the place of which it is written, "my covenant of peace shall not be removed" (Is. LIV, 10), for this takes the Whole and casts it into the sea, whereby the earth is established, as it is written, AND LET THE DRY LAND APPEAR, which is the earth, as it is written, AND GOD CALLED THE DRY LAND EARTH. The earth is called "dry" because it is "bread of the poor one" (*Yesod*), and it remains dry until this place fills it, and then the waters commence to flow from their sources.'

AND THE GATHERING TOGETHER OF THE WATERS CALLED HE SEAS. This is the upper reservoir of the waters where they are all collected and from which they all flow and issue forth. R. Hiya said: 'The gathering place of the waters is the *Zaddik* (righteous one), because it is written in connection with it, AND GOD SAW THAT IT WAS GOOD, and it is written elsewhere, "say ye of the righteous that he is good" (Is. III, 10).' R. Jose said: 'This *Zaddik* is also referred to in the words, "he called seas", because he takes all the streams and sources and rivers and he is the source of all; hence he is called "waters". Hence it says: AND GOD SAW THAT IT WAS GOOD. And since the *Zaddik* is designated with the words "that it is good", there is a gap between the first and the third days, and on the day between it is not written, "that it was good", since on the third day the earth brought forth produce from the impulse of that *Zaddik*, as it is written, AND GOD SAID, LET THE EARTH PUT FORTH GRASS, HERB YIELDING SEED, AND FRUIT TREE BEARING FRUIT AFTER ITS KIND. By "fruit tree" is meant the tree of the knowledge of good and evil, which put forth blossoms and fruit. "Bearing fruit" is the *Zaddik*, the basis of the world. "After its kind" means that all human beings who have in them the spirit of holiness which is the blossom of that tree are stamped as being of its kind. This stamp is the covenant of holiness, the covenant of peace, and the faithful enter into that kind and do not part from it. The *Zaddik* generates, and that tree conceives and brings forth fruit after his kind, i.e. after the kind of the producer, so as to be like him. Blessed he that resembles these his mother and his father. The holy seal is therefore set upon him on the eighth day that he may resemble his "mother" (who is the eighth grade), and the flesh is turned back to show the holy seal in order that he may resemble the "father". So by "fruit tree" we understand the mother, by "producing" the father, by "fruit" the holy covenant, and by "to its kind", the resemblance to the father. WHOSE SEED IS IN IT UPON THE EARTH. Instead of *zar'o* (whose seed), we may read *zera'vau* (the seed of *Vau*), which has literally been cast upon the earth. Blessed is the lot of Israel, who are holy and resemble the holy angels, wherefore it is written, "and thy people are all righteous" (Is. LX, 21), truly righteous, for from such they issue and such they resemble. Happy they in this world and in the world to come.' [33*b*] R. Hiya said: 'It is written, "God maketh the earth by his strength" (Jer. X, 12). He who "maketh the earth" is the Holy One, blessed be He, above; "by his strength" means by the *Zaddik;* "he establishes the universe", this is the earth beneath; "by his wisdom", refers to *Zedek* (justice). Also it is written, "makes the earth", and not "made", because God constantly regulates the earth and its activities through the agency of His "strength", as just explained. . . .' R. Isaac said: 'It is written, "By the word of the Lord the heavens were made and by the breath of his mouth all their hosts." The "heavens" mentioned here are the lower heavens, which were made by the word of the upper heavens, through the spirit which sent forth a voice until it reached that stream which issues and flows perennially. By "all their hosts" is meant the lower world, which exists through that "breath", which is male. A similar lesson is derived from the verse, "Who watereth the mountains from his upper chambers, the earth is full of the fruit of thy works" (Ps. CIV, 13). The "upper chambers" we have already explained, and the term can be further illustrated by the verse, "Who lays the beams of his upper chambers in the waters." The expression "the fruit of thy works" alludes to that stream which ever flows and issues forth; hence it is written, "Yielding fruit whose seed is in it," as explained.'

LET THERE BE LIGHTS IN THE FIRMAMENT OF THE HEAVEN TO GIVE LIGHT UPON THE EARTH. The word *meoroth* (lights) is written defectively. R. Hizkiah says that this indicates that this firmament is the home of the rigour of justice. R. Jose says that the defective spelling indicates the lowest, namely the moon, which is the cause of croup in children. It is also the cause of other misfortunes, because it is the smallest of all the luminaries, and sometimes it is obscured and receives no light at all. IN THE FIRMAMENT OF HEAVEN. This is the firmament which includes all the others, since it receives all lights and it illumines the one which has no light of its own. R. Isaac said: 'Even that firmament which has no light of its own is called by us "the kingdom of heaven" and "the land of Israel" and "the land of the living". It is the heaven which illumines this firmament. Hence the word *meoroth* is written defectively, to show that without *Vau* there would be death to the world. Everything is included in it, and through it Lilith also finds a place in the world. (We derive this from the recurrence of the word "there" in the sentences: "the small and the great are *there*" (Job. III, 19). "The Lord shall be with us *there* in majesty" (Is. XXXIII, 21), and "Lilith reposeth *there*" (Is. XXXIV, 14).') R. Eleazar said: 'The word *meoroth* (lights), being written defectively, indicates a shining body which has no light of its own, but only reflects the light of other more luminous bodies. It is written: "Behold, the ark of the covenant, the Lord of all the earth" (Josh. III, 11). The ark here is the "unclear mirror"; the covenant is the "clear mirror". The ark is the receptacle for the Written Torah, whereas the covenant is the sun that illumines it. The covenant is the "lord of all the earth"; and on its account the ark is also called [34a] *Adon* (lord), which is the same as *Adonai* (the Lord). Observe that stars and planets exist through a covenant which is the firmament of the heaven, in which they are inscribed and engraved.' R. Yesa the Elder used to explain thus: 'The words "let there be lights" refer to the moon, which is suspended in the firmament of the heaven. The words "and let them be for lights" indicate the sun. "They shall be for seasons", because seasons, holydays, new-moons and Sabbaths are determined by them. There are seven planets corresponding to seven firmaments, and by all the world is regulated. The supernal world is above them. There are two worlds, an upper world and a lower world, the lower being on the pattern of the upper. There is a higher king and a lower king. It is written: "The Lord reigneth, the Lord hath reigned, the Lord will reign for evermore", i.e. "the Lord reigneth" above, "the Lord hath reigned" in the middle, "the Lord will reign" below.' R. Aha said: ' "The Lord" refers to the supernal Wisdom; "reigneth", to the supernal world which is the world to come. "The Lord hath reigned" refers to the "beauty of Israel"; "the Lord will reign" signifies the ark of the covenant. At another time David reversed the order and said, "The Lord is king for ever and ever" (Ps. X, 16), i.e. "the Lord is king", below, "for ever", in the middle, "and ever", above, for there is the reunion and the perfection of all. God "is king" above, and "will reign" below.'

R. Abba said: 'All those lights are collected in the firmament of the heaven to give light on the earth. What is this firmament that gives light upon the earth? It is, of course, that stream which flows and issues forth from Eden, as it is written, "And a river went forth from Eden to water the garden." For when the moon is dominant and is illumined by that stream which flows and issues forth, all the lower heavens and their hosts receive increased light, and the stars which have charge of the earth all function and cause plants and trees to grow, and enrich the earth, and even the waters and the fishes of the sea are more productive. Many emissaries of divine justice also traverse the world, because all are in good spirits and full of energy when there is gladness in the king's palace, and even the beings which hover on the outskirts are glad and fly about the world; and therefore it is necessary to take special care of young children.'

AND GOD SET THEM IN THE FIRMAMENT OF THE HEAVEN. R. Aha said: 'When all of them were there they rejoiced in one another. Then the moon diminished its light in presence of the sun; all the light which it receives from the sun is to shine upon the earth, as it is written, "to give light upon the earth".' R. Isaac said: 'It is written, "The light of the moon shall be as the light of the sun, and the light of the sun as the light of the seven days" (Is. xxx, 26). These seven days are the seven days of the Creation.' R. Judah said: 'They are the seven days of the consecration of the Tabernacle, when the world was restored to its original completeness, and the moon was not impaired by the evil serpent. This will again be at the time when "God shall swallow up death for ever" (Is. xxv, 8), and then "the Lord will be one and his name one".'

LET THE WATERS SWARM WITH SWARMS OF LIVING CREATURES. R. Eleazar said: 'These are the lower waters, which brought forth species corresponding to those above, so that there was a lower order and a higher order.' R. Hiya said: 'It was the upper waters which brought forth a "living soul", to wit, the soul of the first man, as it is written, "and the man became a living soul" (Gen. II, 7).' AND FOWL TO FLY ABOVE THE EARTH. These are the emissaries from the upper world which appear to men in visible shape. For there are others of whose existence man knows only by conjecture. These latter are referred to in the next verse in the words, "every winged fowl after its kind". The words "after its kind" are used in connection with the latter and not with the former, because the latter never take the forms of another species, whereas the former do. Nevertheless, they do differ one from another. AND GOD CREATED THE GREAT SEA MONSTERS. These are the Leviathan and its female. AND EVERY LIVING CREATURE THAT CREEPETH. This is the soul of the creature which creeps to the four quarters of the globe, to wit, Lilith. WHEREWITH THE WATERS SWARMED, AFTER ITS KIND. It is the waters which nourish them. For when the wind blows from the South, the waters are released and flow to all sides, and ships pass to and fro, as it is written, "there go the ships, there is Leviathan whom thou hast formed to sport therein" (Ps. CIV, 26). EVERY WINGED FOWL AFTER ITS KIND: this refers, as already said, to the angels, as in the verse, "for a bird of the air shall carry the voice, and that which hath wings shall tell the matter" (Eccl. X, 20),' R. Jose said: 'They all have six wings, and never change their shape; hence it is written of them, "to their kind". i.e. that they are always angels. It is these who sweep through the world with six beats of their wings, who observe the actions of men and record them above; hence the Scripture says, "even in thy thought curse not the king, etc." (*Ibid.*).' R. Hizkiah said: 'Just as it is written here, "living creature that creepeth", so elsewhere (Ps. CIV, 20) it is written, "wherein creep all the beasts (*haytho*) of the field." Just as here we interpret the word *hayah* of Lilith, so there we interpret the word *haytho* of the *Hayyoth*. For they all have sway when she has sway; they commence to chant at each of the three watches of the night and go on without cessation, and of them it is written, "Ye that are the Lord's remembrancers, take ye no rest" (Is. LXII, 6).'

R. Simeon arose and spoke thus: 'My meditation disclosed

to me that when God came to create man, all creatures trembled above and below. The sixth day was proceeding on its course when at length the divine decision was formed. Then the source of all lights shone forth and opened the gate of the East, for thence light issues. The South displayed in full power the light which it had inherited from the commencement, and joined hands with the East. The East took hold of the North, and the North awoke and spread forth and called aloud to the West to come and join him. Then the West went up into the North and united with it, and afterwards the South took hold of the West, and the South and the North, which are the fences of the Garden, surrounded it. Then the East approached the West, and the West was rejoiced and said to the others, "Let us make man in our image, after our likeness", embracing like us the four quarters and the higher and the lower. Then the East united with the West and produced him. Hence our Sages have said that man emerged from the site of the Temple. Further, the words "let us make man" may be taken to signify that God imparted to the lower beings who came from the side of the upper world the secret of forming the divine name "Adam", which embraces the upper and the lower in virtue of its three letters, *aleph*, *daleth*, and *mim* final. When these three letters descended below, together in their complete form, the name Adam was found to comprise male and female. The female was attached to the side of the male until God cast him into a deep slumber, during which he lay on the site of the Temple. God then sawed her off from him and adorned her like a bride and brought her to him, as it is written, "And he took one of his sides and closed up the place with flesh." (Gen. II, 21). I have found it stated in an old book that the word "one" here means "one woman", to wit, the original Lilith, who was with him and who conceived from him. Up to that time, however, she was not a help to him, as it is written, "but for Adam there was not found an help meet for him." Observe that Adam came last of all, it being fitting that he should find the world complete on his appearance.'

AND NO PLANT OF THE FIELD WAS YET IN THE EARTH ETC. R. Simeon said further: 'These are [35a] the great trees which were planted out later, but as yet were tiny. We have stated that Adam and Eve were created side by side. Why were they not created face to face? Because "the Lord God had not yet caused it to rain upon the earth" (Gen. II, 5), and the union of heaven and earth was not yet firmly established. When the lower union was perfected and Adam and Eve were turned face to face, then the upper union was consummated. We know this from the case of the Tabernacle, of which we have learnt that another tabernacle was erected with it, and that the upper one was not raised till the lower one was raised; and similarly here. Further, since all was not yet in order above, Adam and Eve were not created face to face. The order of verses in the Scripture proves this: for first we read, "For the Lord God had not caused it to rain upon the earth", and then "there was not a man to till the ground", the meaning being that man was still defective, and only when Eve was perfected was he also perfected. This is further indicated by the fact that in the word *vayisgor* (and he closed) the letter *samekh*, which means "support", occurs for the first time in this section, as if to say that they now supported one another, as male and female. Similarly the lower and the upper world mutually support one another. For until the lower world was completed, that other world of which we have spoken was not completed. When this lower world was turned face to face to the upper, it became a support to the upper, for previously the work had been defective, because "the Lord God had not caused rain to fall upon the earth". Next, A MIST WENT UP FROM THE GROUND, to repair the deficiency below, by "watering the whole face of the ground". The rising of the mist signifies the yearning of the female for the male. According to another explanation, we supply the word "not" from the previous clause after "mist", the meaning being that God did not send rain because a mist had not gone up, etc., it being necessary for the impulse from below to set in motion the power above. So vapour first ascends from the earth to form the cloud. Similarly, the smoke of the sacrifice rises and creates harmony above, so that all unite, and in this way there is completion in the supernal realm. The impulse commences from below, and from this all is perfected. If the Community of Israel did not give the first impulse, the One above would not move to meet her, for by the yearning from below completion is effected above.'

THE TREE OF LIFE ALSO IN THE MIDST OF THE GARDEN, AND THE TREE OF THE KNOWLEDGE OF GOOD AND EVIL. The Tree of Life, according to a tradition, extends over five hundred years' journey, and all the waters of Creation issue from its foot. This tree was in the middle of the Garden, and it collected all the waters of Creation, which afterwards flowed from it in different directions. For the perennially flowing stream rests upon this Garden and enters it, and the waters issuing from it divide into numbers of streams below which water the "beasts of the field", just as the waters originally issued from the supernal world and watered the celestial "mountains of pure balsam". THE TREE OF GOOD AND EVIL. This tree was not in the middle. It is called by this name because it draws sustenance from two opposite sides, which it distinguishes as clearly as one distinguishes sweet and bitter, and therefore it is called "good and evil". All those other plants rest upon it. Other supernal plants are also attached to it, which are called "cedars of Lebanon"; these are the six supernal days, the six days of the Creation which we have mentioned, which were indeed saplings which God first planted and then transferred to another place, [35b] where they were firmly established. R. Abba here remarked: 'How do we know that Adam and Eve were also planted out? From the verse, "the branch of my planting, the work of my hands, wherein I glory" (Is. LX, 21). They are called "the work of God's hands" because no other creatures were concerned in their formation. We have been taught that the plants at first were like the antennæ of grasshoppers, and their light was feeble, until they were planted and firmly established, when their light was augmented and they were called "cedars of Lebanon". Adam and Eve also when they were first planted were not swathed in light nor did they emit a sweet odour; of a surety they were uprooted and replanted and duly established.'

AND THE LORD GOD COMMANDED. According to our teachers, the word "commanded" here contains a prohibition of idolatry; "the Lord", of blasphemy; "God", of the perversion of justice; "the man", of murder; "saying", of adultery and incest; "from all the trees of the garden", of robbery; "thou mayest freely eat", of eating flesh from a living animal; and so we agree. OF ALL THE TREES OF THE GARDEN THOU SHALT SURELY EAT. This means that he was permitted to eat them all together, for, as we see, Abraham ate, Isaac and Jacob ate, and all the prophets ate and remained alive. This tree, however, was a tree of death, in so far that he who ate it by itself was bound to die, since he took poison. Hence it says, IN THE DAY THAT THOU EATEST THEREOF THOU SHALT SURELY DIE, because thereby he would be separating the shoots. R. Judah asked R. Simeon: 'What is the meaning of the dictum of the teachers, that Adam drew his foreskin?' He said: 'It means that he removed the holy covenant from its place; he abandoned the holy covenant and clung to the *orlah* and allowed himself to be seduced by the serpent.' The words OF THE FRUIT OF THE TREE (Gen. III, 3) signify the woman, of whom it is written, "Her feet go down to death, her steps take hold of the nether world" (Prov. v, 5). On this tree there was fruit, but not on a certain other. R. Jose said: 'That tree which we mentioned was nurtured and fostered from above, and rejoiced thereat, as it says: "A river went forth from Eden to water the garden." The "garden" designates woman; this river entered it and watered it, and up to this point there was complete unity, for it is from this point onward that there is separation, as it is written, "and from there it parted".'

AND THE SERPENT. R. Isaac said: 'This is the evil tempter.' R. Judah said that it means literally a serpent. They consulted R. Simeon, and he said to them: 'Both are correct. It was Samael, and he appeared on a serpent, for the ideal form of the serpent is the Satan. We have learnt that at that moment Samael came down from heaven riding on this serpent, and all creatures saw his form and fled before him. They then entered into conversation with the woman, and the two brought death into the world. Of a surety Samael brought curses on the world through Wisdom and destroyed the first tree that God had created in the world. This responsibility rested on Samael until another holy tree came, namely Jacob, who wrested the blessings from him, in order that Samael might not be blessed above and Esau below. For Jacob was the reproduction of Adam, and he had the same beauty as Adam. Therefore as Samael withheld blessings from the first tree, so Jacob, who was such another tree as Adam, withheld blessings, both upper and lower, from Samael; and in doing so Jacob but took back his own. It is written: AND THE SERPENT WAS SUBTLE. This serpent is the evil tempter and the angel of death. It is because the serpent is the angel of death that it brought death to the world.' AND HE SAID TO THE WOMAN, YEA (*af*). R. Jose said: 'He commenced with *af*, and he brought *af* (wrath) upon the world. He said [36a] to the woman: "With this tree God created the world; eat therefore of it, and ye shall be like God, knowing good and evil, for through this knowledge he is called God."' Said R. Judah: 'This was not the way he spoke, for had he said that God created the world through this tree, he would have spoken correctly, for the tree was really "like the axe in the hand of him that hews with it". What he said, however, was that God ate of the tree and so built the world. "Therefore," he went on, "eat you of it and you shall create worlds. It is because God knows this that He has commanded you not to eat of it, for every artisan hates his fellow of the same craft."' R. Isaac said: 'The speech of the serpent was one tissue of falsehoods. His first remark, "Surely God hath said that ye shall not eat of all the trees of the garden" was a lie, because God had said, "of all the trees of the garden thou shalt surely eat", and all was permitted to him.' R. Jose said: 'With reference to the dictum quoted above, that God prohibited to Adam idolatry, injustice, murder, incest, and so forth, why should all this have been necessary, seeing that Adam was still alone in the world? The answer is that all these prohibitions had reference to the tree alone, and were applicable to it. For whoever takes of it causes separation and associates himself with the lower hordes which are attached to it. He renders himself guilty of idolatry, murder, and adultery. Of idolatry, because he acknowledges the superior chieftains; of bloodshed, because that is inspired by this tree, which is of the side of *Geburah* (Force), under the charge of Samael; and of adultery, because the tree is of the female principle and is called "woman", and it is forbidden to make an appointment with a woman without her husband, for fear of suspicion of adultery. Hence all the prohibitions had reference to this tree, and when he ate of it he transgressed them all.' R. Judah said: 'The way in which the serpent seduced Eve was as follows. He said to her: "See, I have touched the tree and yet am not dead; you also put your hand on it and you will not die" (for it was he who added on his own account the words "neither shall ye touch it").' AND THE WOMAN SAW THAT IT WAS GOOD. R. Isaac said that "saw" here means "perceived", to wit, through the pleasant odour that the tree emitted, which inspired in her a desire to eat of it. R. Jose said that she really "saw". Said R. Judah to him, 'How can this be, seeing that it says later that "their eyes were opened"?' He answered: 'This "seeing" means really that she made a mental picture of the tree, seeing it and yet not seeing. THAT IT WAS GOOD. She saw that it was good, but this was not enough for her, so SHE TOOK OF ITS FRUIT, but not of the tree itself; she thus attached herself to the place of death, and brought death upon the world, and separated life from death. This sin, too, is the cause of the menstruation which keeps a woman apart from her husband.' (The Voice should never be separated from the Utterance, and he who separates them becomes dumb, and, being bereft of speech, returns to dust. R. Simeon said: 'It is written: "I was dumb with silence, I held my peace, having no good things to say, and my sorrow was stirred" (Ps. XXXIX, 3). This is the exclamation of the Community of Israel in exile; for then Voice is separated from Utterance, and no word is heard, and therefore Israel is "dumb with silence, etc." And Israel further say: "To thee praise is silent" (Ps. LXV, 2), i.e. the psalm of David is silent in exile and without voice.) According to a tradition, Eve pressed grapes and gave to Adam, and in this way brought death into the world. For death is attached to this tree. Its sway is by night, [36b] and during that time all creatures taste of death save those faithful ones who first entrust their souls to God, so that they are in due course restored to their place; hence it is written, "And thy faithfulness is at night" (Ps. XCII, 3).'

AND THE EYES OF BOTH OF THEM WERE OPENED. R. Hiya says, their eyes were opened to the evil of the world, which they had not known hitherto. Then they knew that they were naked, since they had lost the celestial lustre which had formerly enveloped them, and of which they were now divested. AND THEY SEWED FIG LEAVES. They strove to cover themselves with the (delusive) images from the tree of which they had eaten, the so-called "leaves of the tree". AND THEY MADE THEMSELVES GIRDLES. R. Jose said: 'When they obtained knowledge of this world and attached themselves to it, they observed that it was governed by those "leaves of the tree". They therefore sought in them a stronghold in this world, and so made themselves acquainted with all kinds of magical arts, in order to gird themselves with weapons of those leaves of the tree, for the purpose of self-protection.' R. Judah said: 'In this way three came up for judgement and were found guilty, and the terrestrial world was cursed and dislodged from its estate on account of the defilement of the serpent, until Israel stood before Mount Sinai.' Afterwards God clothed Adam and Eve in garments soothing to the skin, as it is written, HE MADE THEM COATS OF SKIN ('or). At first they had had coats of light ('or), which procured them the service of the highest of the high, for the celestial angels used to come to enjoy that light; so it is written, "For thou hast made him but little lower than the angels, and crownest him with glory and honour" (Ps. VIII, 6). Now after their sins they had only coats of skin ('or), good for the body but not for the soul.

When they begat children, the first-born was the son of the

(serpent's) slime. For two beings had intercourse with Eve, and she conceived from both and bore two children. Each followed one of the male parents, and their spirits parted, one to this side and one to the other, and similarly their characters. On the side of Cain are all the haunts of the evil species, from which come evil spirits and demons and necromancers. From the side of Abel comes a more merciful class, yet not wholly beneficial—good wine mixed with bad. The right kind was not produced until Seth came, who is the first ancestor of all the generations of the righteous, and from whom the world was propagated.

From Cain come the shameless and wicked sinners of the world. R. Eleazar said: 'When Cain sinned, he was in great terror because he saw before him figures like armed warriors coming to kill him. When he repented, he said: BEHOLD THOU HAST DRIVEN ME OUT THIS DAY FROM THE FACE OF THE GROUND, AND FROM THY FACE SHALL I BE HID. By these words he meant: "I shall be kept away from my proper building." R. Abba said: 'The word "face" here has the same meaning as in the verse, "and he hid not his *face* from him" (Ps. XXII, 25), i.e. providential care. Consequently he said, WHOSOEVER FINDETH ME SHALL SLAY ME. Therefore THE LORD APPOINTED A SIGN FOR CAIN. This sign was one of the twenty-two letters of the Torah, and God set it upon him to protect him.'

R. Judah said: 'Cain rose up against Abel and killed him because he inherited his nature from the side of Samael, who brought death into the world. He was jealous of Abel on account of his female, as indicated by the words, "and it came to pass when they were in the field", the word "field" signifying woman.' On R. Hiya objecting that, according to the text, Cain was wroth because his offering was not accepted, R. Judah answered that this was a further reason. R. Judah further expounded the words, "If thou doest well, shall there not be an uplifting?" 'The word "uplifting",' he said, 'means the dignity which is due to a first-born, provided his actions warrant it. In the next clause, "If thou doest not well, sin coucheth at the door", this door [37a] is the door on high from which issue the chastisements for evil deeds in this world. The "sin" which couches at that door is the angel of death, who is ready to punish thee. The word "door" (*petah*, lit. opening) further contains an allusion to the New Year, the day of judgement, on which Adam was born.' "Unto thee is his desire", i.e. he will not be content until thou art destroyed. "And thou shalt rule over him": the word "thou" contains a mystic allusion to the Almighty, who is also called "Thou". There is a dictum that God is supreme only when the wicked are destroyed, but our text indicates that when the angel of death destroys them, God "rules over him" to prevent him from ruining the world. R. Judah, however, explained the words "thou shalt rule over him" to mean "through repentance".

R. Jose said: 'When the descendants of Cain spread through the world, they used to cut up the soil, and they had traits in common both with the upper and the lower beings.' R. Isaac said: 'When Uzza and Azael fell from the abode of their sanctity above, they saw the daughters of mankind and sinned with them and begat children. These were the *Nefilim* (giants), of whom it is said, THE NEFILIM WERE IN THE EARTH (Gen. VI, 4).' R. Hiya said: 'The descendants of Cain were "the sons of God" (*Ibid*. 2). For Cain was born from Samael and his aspect was not like that of other human beings, and all who came from his stock were called "sons of God".' R. Judah said that the *Nefilim* were also called so. THE SAME WERE THE MIGHTY MEN. There were sixty on the earth, corresponding to the number above, as it is written, "Threescore mighty men are about it" (S.S. III, 7). WHICH WERE OF OLD, THE MEN OF NAME. R. Jose saw in the word "name" an indication that they were from the upper world, while R. Hiya saw in the word *meʿolam* ("of old" or "from the world") an indication that they were from the terrestrial world, and that from there God moved them.

R. Yesa asked the meaning of the words THIS IS THE BOOK OF THE GENERATIONS OF ADAM (Gen. V, 1). Said R. Abba to him: 'There is here a very recondite allusion. According to the Rabbinical dictum, "three books are opened on New Year, one of the wholly righteous, [37b] etc." One is the supernal book from which issued the Whole, and from which issues also writing. The middle book unites the higher and the lower; it embraces all sides and is called the Written Torah of the first man. The third book is called that of the generations of man, and this is the book of the completely righteous.' IN THE DAY THAT GOD CREATED MAN IN THE LIKENESS OF GOD: for thereby indeed the whole was completed above and below, and both were established after one pattern. MALE AND FEMALE HE CREATED THEM: the one included in the other. R. Abba said: 'God did indeed send down a book to Adam, from which he became acquainted with the supernal wisdom. It came later into the hands of the "sons of God", the wise of their generation, and whoever was privileged to peruse it could learn from it supernal wisdom. This book was brought down to Adam by the "master of mysteries", preceded by three messengers. When Adam was expelled from the Garden of Eden, he tried to keep hold of this book, but it flew out of his hands. He thereupon supplicated God with tears for its return, and it was given back to him, in order that wisdom might not be forgotten of men, and that they might strive to obtain knowledge of their Master. Tradition further tells us that Enoch also had a book, which came from the same place as the book of the generations of Adam. . . .[1] This is the source of the book known as "the book of Enoch". When God took him, He showed him all supernal mysteries, and the Tree of Life in the midst of the Garden and its leaves and branches, all of which can be found in his book. Happy are those of exalted piety to whom the supernal wisdom has been revealed, and from whom it will not be forgotten for ever, as it says, "The secret of the Lord is with them that fear him, and his secret to make them know it."'

AND THE LORD SAID, MY SPIRIT SHALL NOT STRIVE WITH MAN FOR EVER, FOR THAT HE ALSO IS FLESH. R. Aha said: 'At that time the stream which perennially flows used to draw forth the celestial spirit from the tree of life and pour it into the tree which harbours death, and so

---

[1] Here follows a highly allusive passage identifying Enoch with "the lad" (v. Prov. XXII, 6), i.e. *Metatron*.

the spirit was continued in the body of men for great length of days, until they turned out bad and inclined to sin. Then the celestial spirit departed from that tree at the moment of the soul's entry into the sons of men.' R. Eleazar said that the word *beshagam* (for that he) signifies Moses, who caused the moon to shine, and this enabled men to abide in the world for great length of days. AND HIS DAYS SHALL BE A HUNDRED AND TWENTY YEARS. This is an allusion to Moses, through whose agency the Law was given and who thus bestowed life on men from the tree of life. And in truth had Israel not sinned, they would have been proof against death, since the tree of life had been brought down to them. All this was through Moses, who is called *beshagam*, and hence we have learnt: "Moses did not die, but he was gathered in [38a] from the world, and caused the moon to shine", being in this respect like the sun, which also after setting does not expire, but gives light to the moon. According to another explanation we translate, "for that it, to wit, the spirit, is also flesh", i.e. it is long converted into flesh, in the sense of following the body and seeking the pleasures of this world.

R. Isaac said: 'The generations which followed in the steps of Seth were all pious and righteous. Subsequently, as mankind spread and multiplied, they learnt the arts of war, which they practised until Noah came and taught them the arts of peace and agriculture; for at first they used not to sow or reap, but afterwards they found this necessary, as it is written, "While the earth remaineth, seedtime and harvest, etc. (Gen. VIII, 22).'

R. Eleazar said: 'God will one day re-establish the world and strengthen the spirit of the sons of men so that they may prolong their days for ever, as it is written, "For as the days of a tree shall be the days of my people, etc." (Is. LXV, 22), and also, "He hath swallowed up death for ever, and the Lord God will wipe away tears from all faces, and the reproach of his people shall he take away from off all the earth, for the Lord hath spoken it" (*Ibid.* xxv, 8).'[1] [39b]

---

[1] Here closes the second exposition of the section *Bereshith*. A third commences on the fifth line of p. 39b, goes on to the eighth line of p. 40a,

IN THE BEGINNING.[1] R. Judah said: 'There were two houses, the first house and the second house, one higher and one lower. There are two *hé*'s, one higher and one lower; all, however, form only one. The higher *beth* opens the gates to every side, and when combined with *reshith* forms the "beginning" in the list of the component parts of the building.' R. Isaac said in the name of R. Eleazar: 'This *bereshith* is the comprehensive form in which all forms are embraced. This is the inner meaning of the words, "this was the appearance of the likeness of the glory of the Lord" (Ezek. I, 28); to wit, the appearance in which the six others are discernible. Hence we analyse the word *bereshith* into *bara shith* (created six). When the six colours enter into this appearance, it makes itself ready to reflect them, and through them to keep the world going. Yet the credit for this must be ascribed not to this grade alone, but to all the six.' R. Jose quoted here the verse, *The flowers appear on the earth, the time of singing is come, and the voice of the turtle is heard in our land* (S. S. II, 12). ' "The flowers",' he said, 'allude to the six grades. The words "they appear on the earth" mean that they are forms which are reflected by the grade so called. It is then that "the time of singing is come", to wit, of praise and laudation.' R. Abba said: 'The uppermost world is shrouded in mystery, and all its attributes likewise, because it forms a day separate from all other days. When it created and produced, it produced those other six. On account of its incomprehensibility, the Scripture opens with the word *bereshith*, "it created six", without saying *what* created. But when it came to the lower creation, it gave a name to the creator, who was now discoverable, and said: "*Elohim* created the heavens and the earth." Thus the first, which is the higher, remains shrouded in mystery, while the lower is disclosed, so that the work of

---

and is then interrupted and resumed towards the end of p. 45*b*. Pp. 38*a*–39*b* and 40*a*–45*b* contain a dissertation, or rather three allied dissertations, on the abodes of the righteous in Paradise, and of the angels (*Hekaloth* and *Medorin*), and on the halls of prayer (also called *Hekaloth*). These really constitute a separate work called *Hekaloth*, and therefore have not been included in this translation.

[1] Gen. I, I.

the Holy One, blessed be He, should be ever both hidden and disclosed. Similarly, the holy name is also, in the esoteric doctrine, both hidden and disclosed.'

THE (*eth*) HEAVENS: the particle *eth* indicates that the lower heavens were also created for the lower world. Similarly, the word *ve-eth* in AND THE EARTH points to the lower earth and all its products after the supernal pattern.

NOW THE EARTH WAS FORMLESS AND VOID, as we have explained. "The earth" here is the upper earth, which has no light of its own. It "was" at first in its proper state, but now "void and without form", having diminished itself and its light. *Tohu* (formlessness), *bohu* (void), "darkness", and "spirit" were the four elements of the world which were comprised in it. Hence, "the earth was formless and void and darkness and spirit". [45*b*]

AND GOD SAID, LET THERE BE LIGHT. R. Isaac said: 'We learn from these words that God uprooted those shoots of which we have spoken[1] and replanted them; hence the expression "and there was light", implying that light had already existed.' R. Judah confirmed this idea from the verse "light is sown for the *Zaddik*" (Ps. XCVII, 11), this being the one mentioned in the verse "Who aroused Righteousness (*zedek*) from the East, etc." (Is. XLI, 2).

AND GOD SAW THE LIGHT AND DIVIDED. Said R. Isaac: 'This implies, as we have explained, that he foresaw the works of the wicked and stored the light away.' R. Abba said: 'He saw its radiance flashing from one end of the world to the other, and concluded that it was better [46*a*] to store it away in order that sinners might not have the benefit of it.' R. Simeon said: 'The expression "God saw the light that it was good" means really "God decided that the light should be only good", that is, that it should never be an instrument of wrath (cf. "that it *was good* in the eyes of the Lord to *bless* Israel", Num. XXIV, 1); and this is proved by the end of the

[1] *v.* p. 131.

verse, "And God divided the light from the darkness." For although He afterwards united light and darkness, yet this light continued to emanate from the supernal radiance, and through that radiance to bring gladness to all. This also is the Right Hand through which the most deeply graven letters[1] are crowned, as has been explained. The treasuring up of this primal light is referred to in the verse, "How great is thy goodness which thou hast laid up for them that fear thee, which thou hast wrought for them that trust in thee" (Ps. XXXI, 20).'

AND THERE WAS EVENING AND THERE WAS MORNING, ONE DAY: evening from the side of darkness and morning from the side of light; and because they are joined together, the Scripture speaks of "one day". R. Judah said: 'The reason why it is written "and there was evening and there was morning" for each day is to show that there is no day without night and no night without day, and the two cannot be separated.' R. Jose said: 'The day in which the primal light emerged extended into all the other days; hence the word "day" is repeated with all of them.' R. Eleazar said: 'We learn this from the fact that the term "morning" is used in connection with all of them, and "morning" proceeds only from the side of the primal light.' R. Simeon said: 'The first day accompanies all the others, and all are embraced in it, to show that there is no break between them and they all merge into one another.' Another explanation of the words "let there be light" is: "let there be an extending of this light downwards, to form the angels, who were created on the first day, and who have permanent existence on the right side." Further, the word *eth* in the fourth verse may be taken to indicate that the "unclear mirror" was created along with the "clear mirror". R. Eleazar says that it points to the creation of all the angels, who proceed from the side of light and who all continue to shine as brightly as at first.

LET THERE BE A FIRMAMENT IN THE MIDST OF THE WATERS. R. Judah said: 'By this the "upper waters" were

[1] The letters *Yod, Hé, Vau,* of the sacred name.

separated from the "lower waters", the firmament being an extending of the waters, as has been explained. Similarly, "let it divide", to wit, the "upper waters" from the "lower waters".'

AND GOD MADE THE FIRMAMENT: the word "made" indicates that God exercised upon it particular care, and invested it with great power. R. Isaac said: 'On the second day was created Gehinnom for sinners; on the second day, too, was created conflict. On the second day the work begun was not finished, and therefore the words "and it was good" are not used in connection with it. Not till the third day was the work of the second finished; hence in the account of that day we find twice the expression "that it was good", once in reference to its own proper work, and once in reference to that of the second day. On the third day the deficiency of the second day was made good: discord was removed on it, and mercy was extended to the sinners in Gehinnom, the flames of which were moderated. Hence the second day is embraced in and completed by the third.' While studying one day with R. Simeon, R. Hiya said to him: 'You say that light was on the first day and darkness on the second, and the waters separated and discord arose on it—why was not the whole work finished on the first day, when the Right still comprised the Left?' He answered: 'That is the very reason why there was discord, and hence it was necessary for the third day to intervene and to restore their amity.'

LET THE EARTH PUT FORTH GRASS: this indicates the union of the upper with the lower waters so as to bear fruit. The upper waters generate, and the lower call to them as the female to the male, because the upper waters are male and the lower female. R. Simeon said: 'All this takes place both above and below.' Said R. Jose, 'If so, seeing that we have posited *Elohim hayyim* (living God) above, are we to posit plain *Elohim* below? Not so, but the truth is that generation is only below [46b] (according to our explanation of the words "these are the generations of the heavens and the earth when they were created (*behibaream*)", or, as we explain, "which were created with *hé*"), while the one above is the father of all; the other is a creation, and therefore it is the earth which brought forth products (*toledoth*), being made pregnant like a female by a male.' R. Eleazar said: 'All forces were latent in the earth from the first, but it did not bring forth its products till the sixth day, as it is written, "let the earth bring forth living soul". True, it is written that on the third day "the earth brought forth grass", but this only means that it brought its forces into a state of preparedness, and all its products remained latent in it till the due time. First it was "void and without form", then it was duly prepared and furnished with seeds and with grass, plants, and trees, and finally it put them forth. Similarly the luminaries did not emit their light till the due time.'

LET THERE BE LIGHTS IN THE FIRMAMENT OF THE HEAVEN. The omission of the *vau* from the word *meoroth* (so that it can be read *meeroth* (curses)) indicates the inclusion of the evil serpent which befouled the moon and separated it from the sun, thus causing the earth to be cursed (Gen. III, 17). The word *yehi*, being in the singular, shows that the word 'lights' refers to the moon, while 'the firmament of the heaven' refers to the sun. Thus the whole expression indicates that both were meant to be coupled together so as to illumine worlds both above and below, as shown by the expression 'above' ('*al*) the earth. All calculation (of time) is by the moon. R. Simeon said: 'Measurements and the determination of seasons and intercalary days are all made by the moon, and not by the higher spheres.' Said R. Eleazar to him: ' Is that so ? Do not our colleagues make all kinds of calculations and measurements (by the higher spheres) ?' He answered, 'No. Calculation is made by the moon, and this is a basis for proceeding further.' R. Eleazar further objected that it is written 'and *they* shall be for *signs*'. R. Simeon answered that the word for signs (*othoth*) is written defectively (showing that only one is meant), while the expression '*they* shall be' alludes to the many phases of the moon, which make it as it were a storehouse full of various objects, though it is always the one moon which is the basis of reckoning. Consider this. There is a certain point which is the beginning of number, and which cannot be further analysed. There is one point above, unrevealed and unknowable, which is the starting-point for numbering all entities hidden and recondite. Corresponding to it there is a point below which is knowable and which is the starting-point for all calculation and numbering; here, consequently, is the place for all measurements and determinations of seasons and intercalary days and festivals and holy-days and Sabbaths. Israel who cleave to God reckon by the moon, and so they ascend above, as it is written, 'and ye who clave unto the Lord your God, etc.' (Deut. IV, 4).

LET THE WATERS TEEM WITH SWARM OF LIVING CREATURES. R. Eleazar said: 'We have already explained that these (lower) waters teemed and produced, like those above; and so it is agreed.' AND BIRDS TO FLY ABOVE THE EARTH. The form *yeofef* (to fly) is peculiar. R. Simeon said: 'There is here a mystic allusion. "Birds" refers to the angel Michael, of whom it is written, "And one of the Seraphim flew to me" (Is. VI, 6). "To fly" refers to Gabriel, of whom it is written, "The man Gabriel whom I had seen at first in a vision being caused to fly quickly." (Dan. IX, 21).' UPON THE EARTH: R. Abba says, 'This is Raphael (lit. healer of God), who is charged to heal the earth, and through whom the earth is healed so as to furnish an abode for man, whom also he heals of his maladies.' ON THE FACE OF THE FIRMAMENT OF THE HEAVEN: this is Uriel. (All these names can be found in the text.) Hence the text proceeds: AND GOD CREATED THE GREAT SEA-MONSTERS. Said R. Eleazar: 'These are the seventy great chieftains appointed for the seventy nations, and for this they were created, to be in control of the earth.' AND EVERY LIVING CREATURE THAT MOVETH: these designate Israel, whose [47a] souls actually are derived from the 'living' (*hayah*) of which we have spoken, and who are called 'one nation on the earth'. WHICH THE WATERS BROUGHT FORTH ABUNDANTLY AFTER THEIR KINDS. This designates those who study the Torah. AND EVERY WINGED FOWL AFTER ITS KIND:

these are the righteous among them, in virtue of whom they are 'living soul'. According to another explanation, these are the angels sent as God's messengers into the world, of whom we have already spoken. R. Abba said that 'living soul' designates Israel because they are children to the Almighty, and their souls, which are holy, come from Him. From whence, then, come the souls of other peoples? R. Eleazar said: 'They obtain souls from those sides of the left which convey impurity, and therefore they are all impure and defile those who have contact with them.'

AND THE LORD SAID, LET THE EARTH BRING FORTH LIVING SOUL, ETC. This includes all the other animals (except man), each after its kind. R. Eleazar said: 'The repetition of the words "after its kind" confirms what we have said before, that "living soul" refers to Israel, who have holy living souls from above, and " cattle and creeping thing and beast of the earth" to the other peoples who are not "living soul", but who are as we have said.'

LET US MAKE MAN IN OUR IMAGE, AFTER OUR LIKENESS, i.e. partaking of six directions, compounded of all, after the supernal pattern, with limbs arranged so as to suggest the esoteric Wisdom, altogether an exceptional creature. 'Let us make man': the word *adam* (man) implies male and female, created wholly through the supernal and holy Wisdom. 'In our image, after our likeness': the two being combined, so that man should be unique in the world and ruler over all.

AND GOD SAW ALL (*eth kol*) THAT HE HAD MADE, AND BEHOLD, IT WAS VERY GOOD. Here the word 'very' makes good the omission of the words 'that it was good' in the account of the second day. On the second day death was created, and, according to our colleagues, the expression 'very good' refers to death, 'And God saw, etc.' Assuredly He had seen all before, but the Scripture here indicates by the accusative particle *eth* that God now saw also all the generations which were to be, and everything which was to happen in the world in each generation before it came into existence. 'Which he had made': these words indicate all the works of the creative period (recounted in the section *Bereshith*), in which was created the foundation and basis of all that was to be and come to pass in the world subsequently. God foresaw all, and placed all potentially in the work of the creation. The word *ha-shishi* (the sixth) here contains the definite article, which was not used in numbering the other days. This is to indicate that when the world was finished the male and female were united so as to form a single whole—*hé* with 'sixth', which is the foundation. 'Were finished': this indicates that they were completed in every detail; they were completed from every side, and fully equipped with everything.

R. Eleazar discoursed on the text: *How great is thy goodness which thou hast laid up for them that fear thee, thou hast wrought for them that put their trust in thee, before the sons of men* (Ps. XXXI, 20). He said: 'God created man in the world and gave him the faculty to perfect himself in His service and to direct his ways so as to merit the enjoyment of that celestial light which God has hidden and reserved for the righteous, as it is written, "Eye has not seen, O Lord, besides thee what thou wilt do for him that waits for thee" (Is. LXIV, 3). It is through the Torah that man can make himself worthy of that light. For whoever studies the Torah every day is earning a share in the future world, and is even accounted a builder of worlds, because through the Torah the world has been built and completed; so the Scripture says, "The Lord founded the earth with Wisdom (i.e. the Torah), he established the heavens with Understanding" (Prov. III, 19), and again, "And I (the Torah) was a craftsman with him, and I was his delight every day" (*Ibid.* VIII, 30). Thus whoever studies the Torah completes the world and preserves it. Further, God made the world through a breath, and through a breath it is preserved—the breath of those who assiduously study the Torah, and still more the breath of school-children, when reciting their lesson. By "great goodness" in this verse is meant the stored-up blessing, and by "those that fear Thee", those that fear sin. "Thou hast wrought for them that trust in Thee": the implied object of "wrought" is the work of creation.' R. Abba says, it is the Garden of Eden, which God has cunningly wrought upon the earth after the supernal pattern for the righteous to seize and hold [47b]; hence it is written "before the sons of men", since this one is in the presence of men, while the other is in the presence of the holy angels. R. Simeon said: 'The Garden of Eden above is said to be "before the sons of men" because in it are gathered the righteous who perform the will of their Master'.

AND WERE FINISHED: implying that all the work which was to be done, both above and below, was finished. THE HEAVEN AND THE EARTH: above and below. R. Simeon said: 'These words designate the general fabric of the Written Law, and the general fabric of the Oral Law. The words AND ALL THEIR HOSTS designate the details of the Torah, the seventy alternative explanations of the Torah; while the words AND THEY WERE COMPLETED imply that the two Torahs are complementary to one another. Or again, "heaven and earth" may be interpreted as the general and the particular, and "all their hosts" as the inner meanings of the Torah, its rules concerning clean and unclean, etc. AND GOD FINISHED BY MEANS OF THE SEVENTH DAY: this is the Oral Law, which is the "seventh day", and through which the world was completed and the whole is preserved. HIS WORK WHICH HE HAD MADE, but not *the whole* of His work, because it was the Written Torah which produced the Whole through the power of the Writing which issued from Wisdom. The words "on the seventh day" are used here three times, viz. "and God finished on the seventh day", "and he rested on the seventh day", and "and God blessed the seventh day". The "seventh day" in the first of these quotations is the Oral Torah, because with this seventh day the world was completed, as we have said. "And he rested on the seventh day" refers to the "Foundation of the world". In the book of R. Yeba the Elder it says that this is the Jubilee, and hence it is written here "from the whole of his work" because the Whole issues from it. We, however, interpret it of the Foundation, because this is the chief source of rest and contentment. And "God blessed the seventh day" refers to the

High Priest, who blesses all, and who always takes the first share, as we have learnt: "The High Priest takes the first share, and blessings open with him, and he is called seventh." R. Yesa the Elder says: These two mentions of the "seventh day" refer one to the Foundation of the world and one to the Column of the centre. AND HE SANCTIFIED IT: the word *otho* (it) means also "his sign" (cf. II Sam. XV, 25), and so refers to the place in which the sign of the covenant is fixed. This is the abode of all the celestial sanctifications, and from it they descend upon the community of Israel to bestow upon it all kinds of luxuries and dainties. This may be illustrated from the verse "From Asher his bread is fat, and he shall give the dainties of a king" (Gen. XLIX, 20). "Asher" we interpret as the perfect covenant. "His bread is fat" means that what was bread of affliction has been converted into bread of luxury. The "king" is the community of Israel, to whom it gives all the luxuries in the world. FOR ON IT HE RESTED: in it all find rest and contentment, upper and lower, and in it is the Sabbath for rest. WHICH GOD CREATED TO MAKE: As "remembering" finds its fulfilment in "keeping", so here "creating" is implemented by "making", to establish firmly the work of the world; "to make" indicates the world's artificer, through whom the whole is carried on.'
R. Simeon further explained the verse as follows. He said: 'It is written, *Who keepeth the covenant and the kindness* (Deut. V, 10). "Who keepeth" indicates the community of Israel; "the covenant" indicates the Foundation of the world; "kindness" indicates Abraham. The community of Israel is that which keeps the covenant and the kindness, and it is called "keeper of Israel", and guards the gate of the Whole, and on it depend all the works of the world. This it is which "God created to make", i.e. to perfect and finish off the whole, and to bring forth spirits and souls and even spirits and demons. Do not think that these also are not for the good of the world, for they serve for the punishment of the wicked, whom they find out and admonish; for he who proceeds towards the left becomes entangled in the left side, and is set upon by them. Hence they are of use.

'We read that God said with regard to Solomon, "I will

chasten him with the rod of men and with the plagues of the children of men" (II Sam. VII, 14). These "plagues of the children of men" are the demons. They were created just at the moment when the Sabbath was sanctified.¹ and they were left spirit without body. These are the creatures which were not [48a] finished; they are from the left, dross of gold, and because they were not finished and remained defective, the holy name is not mentioned in connection with them, and they do not cleave to it, and are in great terror of it. The holy name does not rest upon anything defective. Hence a man who departs from life defective through not having left a son behind him cannot attach himself to the holy name, and is not admitted within the curtain, because he is defective, and a tree which has been uprooted must be planted over again; for the holy name is perfect on every side, and no defect can attach to it. Those creatures we have mentioned are rejected both above and below, and therefore they have no sure place either above or below. It is these which are meant by the words "which God created to make", i.e. they were not made into finished beings either above or below. You may ask, seeing that they are spirits, why were not these beings finished off above? The answer is that they were not finished below on the earth, and therefore they were not finished above. They all have their origin in the side of the left; they are invisible to men and hover round them to do them mischief. They have three features in common with the angels and three in common with human beings, as has been laid down elsewhere. After they had been created, they were left behind the millstones of the chasm of the great abyss during the night and the day of Sabbath. When the sanctity of the day expired, they came out into the world in their unfinished state and commenced flying about in all directions. They became a great danger to the world, because with them the whole of the left side roused itself and the fire of Gehinnom began to flash, and all the denizens of the left side commenced to roam about the world. They sought to clothe themselves in bodies, but were not able. Hence we require protection against them, and therefore the recital of

---

¹ v. p. 59.

the "hymn of accidents" (Ps. XCI) has been prescribed for every occasion when danger is threatened from them. For when the Sabbath is sanctified on Friday evening, a tabernacle of peace descends from heaven and is spread over the world. This tabernacle of peace is the Sabbath, and when it comes down, all evil spirits and demons and all the creatures which defile hide themselves within the orifice of the millstones of the chasm of the great abyss. For when sanctity spreads over the world, the spirit of uncleanliness remains inactive, since the two shun one another. Hence the world is under special protection (on the Sabbath eve), and we do not require to say the prayer "who keepeth his people Israel for ever, amen". This prayer has been prescribed for week-days, when protection is needed. But on Sabbath a tabernacle of peace is spread over the world, which is thus sheltered on all sides. Even the sinners in Gehinnom are protected, and all beings are at peace, both in the upper and lower spheres, and therefore we conclude our prayer this day with the words "who spreads a tabernacle of peace over us and over all his people Israel and over Jerusalem". (The reason why Jerusalem is mentioned is because it is the abode of the tabernacle.) Thus it behoves us to invite that tabernacle to spread itself over us and to rest upon us and to shield us as a mother shields her children, so that we should feel secure on every side. See now, when Israel by reciting this blessing invite this tabernacle of peace to their homes as a holy guest, a divine sanctity comes down and spreads its wings over Israel like a mother encompassing her children. Then all evil spirits disappear from the world, and Israel are at rest under the sheltering sanctity of their Master. Further, this tabernacle of peace imparts new souls to her children. For souls have their abode in her and issue from her, and so when she comes down and spreads her wings over her children, it sheds a new soul on each one of them.' R. Simeon said further: 'It is on this account that, as we have learnt, Sabbath is a mirror of the future world. For this same reason, too, the Sabbatical year and the Jubilee mirror one another. This additional soul descends from the mystic force implied in the word *zachor* (remember) upon the tabernacle of peace, being taken [48*b*] from the future world, and the tabernacle gives it to the holy people, who are gladdened by it and enabled to forget all worldly matters and all their troubles and sorrows, thus realising the words of the prophet, "on the day that the Lord shall give thee rest from thy sorrow, and from thy trouble, and from the hard service, etc." (Is. XIV, 3). Therefore on Friday night a man should have a full-course meal, to show that this tabernacle of peace has been formed by a union of all principles, provided only that he leaves himself enough for one meal the next day, or, according to others (and this is more correct), for two meals. All the more so, of course, if he has more than enough left for the next day. For children two dishes are enough;[1] and so the colleagues agreed. The function of lighting the Sabbath light has been entrusted to the women of the holy people: as the colleagues put it, "woman put out the light of the world and brought darkness, etc."; and so we agree. There is, however, a more esoteric reason. This tabernacle of peace is the Matron of the world, and the souls which are the celestial lamp abide in her. Hence it behoves the matron to kindle the light, because thereby she is attaching herself to her rightful place and performing her rightful function. A woman should kindle the Sabbath light with zest and gladness, because it is a great honour for her, and, further, she qualifies herself thereby to become the mother of holy offspring who will grow to be shining lights of learning and piety and will spread peace in the world, and she also procures long life for her husband. Hence she should be very careful to observe this ceremony. Observe that the words "remember" and "keep" in the commandment of the Sabbath (Ex. XX, 8, and Deut. V, 12). Both apply equally to the day and to the night; nevertheless "remember" has a more special application to the man and "keep" to the woman, whose chief observance is at night.'

AND THE LORD GOD BUILT (*vayiven*) THE SIDE WHICH HE HAD TAKEN FROM THE MAN, ETC. Said R. Simeon: 'It is written, *God understandeth the way thereof and he knoweth the place thereof* (Job XXVIII, 23). This verse may be

---

[1] al. Two dishes should be the minimum.

taken in many ways. One is that the word "understood" (*hevin*) has the same sense as *vayiven* in the second chapter of Genesis. Hence the "side" here is the Oral Law, which forms a "way", as it is written, "who maketh a way in the sea" (Is. XLIII, 16). Similarly, "place" here can be interpreted as the Written Law, which is a source of knowledge. The double name "Lord God" is used to show that it was completed in all details, Hence it is called both *Hokmah* (wisdom) and *Binah* (understanding). "The side" (*ẓela'*) is the unclear mirror, as it is written, "they rejoiced at my *halting* (*be-ẓal'i*) and gathered together" (Ps. XXXV, 15). "Which he took from the man": because the Oral Law issued from the Written Torah. INTO A WOMAN: to be linked with the flame of the left side, because the Torah was given from the side of *Geburah*. Further, *ishah* (woman) may be analysed into *esh hé* (fire of *hé*), signifying the union of the two. AND HE BROUGHT HER TO THE MAN: as much as to say that the Oral Torah must not be studied by itself, but in conjunction with the Written Torah, which then nourishes and supports it and provides all its needs. (We have similarly explained the words "and the earth".) We learn from this passage that when a man gives his daughter in marriage, up to the time of the wedding the father and mother are responsible for her upkeep, but once she is married the husband has to support her and provide all her necessaries. For it first says here that the Lord God built up the side, i.e. that the Father and Mother provided for her, but afterwards "he brought her to the man", that they might be closely united to one another, and the man might thenceforth provide all her requirements. According to another explanation this verse has a deep esoteric meaning, viz. that the primal point is unknowable save to God, who "understands its way", i.e. the future world, while "He", i.e. the great inscrutable called *hu* (he) "knows its place".'

AND THE LORD GOD FORMED THE MAN. At this point he was completely formed so as to partake both of the Right and of the Left. We laid down before that he was wholly under the ægis of the good inclination: now God formed him with both good and evil inclination—with the good inclination for himself, and the evil inclination to turn towards the female. Esoterically speaking, we learn from here that the North is always attracted to the female and attaches itself to her, and therefore she is called *isha* (i.e. *esh hé*, fire of *hé*). Observe this. The good inclination and the evil inclination are in harmony only because they share the female, who is attached to both, in this way: first the evil inclination sues for her and they unite with one another, and when they are united the good inclination, which is joy, rouses itself and draws her to itself, and so she is shared by both and reconciles them. Hence it is written, "and the Lord God formed man", the double name being made responsible both for the good and the evil inclination. THE MAN: as we have explained, male and female, together and not separated, so as to turn face to face. Hence it is written DUST FROM THE GROUND. The use of the word "ground" (*adamah*) here must be explained. When the wife is joined with the husband she is called by the name of the husband; thus the correlatives *ish* (man) and *ishah*, *zaddik* (righteous one), and *zedek*, '*ofer* (buck) and '*efar*, *zebi* (hart), and *zibia*. So, too, with the words *asher* (which) and *asherah*. It says, 'Thou shalt not plant thee an *Asherah* (grove) of any kind of tree beside the altar of the Lord thy God which (*asher*) thou shalt make thee.' Are we to suppose that anywhere else it is permitted? The truth is that the *Hé* is called *Asherah*, after the name of its spouse, *Asher*, and the meaning of the verse is therefore: 'thou shalt not plant another *asherah* by the side of the altar which is established upon this.' Observe that throughout the Scriptures the worshippers of the sun are called servants of Baal and the worshippers of the moon servants of Asherah; hence the combination 'to Baal and Asherah.' If this is so (that Asherah is the name of the *Hé*), why is it not used as a sacred name? The reason is that this name brings to mind the words of Leah, 'happy am I, for the daughters will call me happy (*ishruni*)', but this one is not 'called happy' by other nations, and another is set up in its place; nay more, it is written, 'all that honoured her despise her' (Lam. 1, 8). But the real altar is one that is made of earth, as it is written, 'An altar of earth thou shalt make for me.' Hence 'dust from the earth'. AND HE BREATHED INTO HIS NOSTRILS THE BREATH OF LIFE. The breath of life was enclosed in the earth, which was made pregnant with it like a female impregnated by the male. So the dust and the breath were joined, and the dust became full of spirits and souls. AND THE MAN BECAME A LIVING SOUL. At this point he attained his proper form, and became a man to support and nourish the living soul.

AND THE LORD GOD BUILT. Here also the full name of the Deity is used, indicating that the father and mother provided for her until she came to her husband. THE SIDE: 'black but comely'; she was the 'unclear mirror', but the father and mother tricked her out so as to make her acceptable to her husband. AND BROUGHT HER TO THE MAN. From this we learn that it is incumbent on the father and mother of the bride to transfer her to the charge of the bridegroom; so we read 'my daughter I have given to this man' (Deut. XXII, 16). From that point the husband is to come to her, since the house is hers; so it is written 'and he came to her' (Gen. XXIX, 23), 'and he came in to Rachel' (*Ibid.*). Of the father and mother it is written that they 'brought', but of the husband that he 'came', to show that he must obtain her permission. We make a similar reflection on the verse, 'And he prayed in the place and tarried there' (Gen. XXVIII, 11), viz. that Jacob sought permission first. From this we learn that a man who desires his wife's society must first entreat and coax her; and if he cannot persuade her, he must not stay with her, for their companionship must be loving and unconstrained. It says further of Jacob that 'he tarried there because the sun had set', which shows that sexual intercourse is forbidden during the day. Further it says that 'he took of the stones of the place and put it under his head'. From this we learn that even a king who has a bed of gold with precious coverings, if his wife prepares for him a bed of stones, must leave his own bed and sleep on the one which she prepares, as it is written, 'and he lay down in that place'. Observe that it says here AND THE MAN SAID, THIS TIME, ETC., to show that he spoke to her lovingly so as to draw her to him and to win her affections. See how tender and coaxing is his language—'bone of my bone and flesh of my flesh'—to prove to her that they were one and inseparable. Then he began to sing her praises: THIS SHALL BE CALLED WOMAN, this is the peerless and incomparable one; this is the pride of the house, who surpasses all other women as a human being surpasses an ape. This one is perfect in all points, and alone merits the title of woman. Every word is inspired by love, like the verse 'Many daughters have done valiantly, but thou excellest them all' (Prov. XXXI, 29). THEREFORE A MAN SHALL LEAVE HIS FATHER AND HIS MOTHER AND CLEAVE TO HIS WIFE, AND THEY SHALL BE ONE FLESH: all this, too, was to win her affection and to draw her closer.

AND THE SERPENT WAS SUBTLE. After the man had addressed all these words to the woman, the evil inclination awoke, prompting him to seek to unite with her in carnal desire, and to entice her to things in which the evil inclination takes delight, until at last THE WOMAN SAW THAT THE TREE WAS GOOD FOR FOOD, AND THAT IT WAS A DELIGHT FOR THE EYES AND SHE TOOK OF THE FRUIT THEREOF AND ATE—giving ready admission to the evil inclination—AND GAVE ALSO UNTO HER HUSBAND WITH HER: it was she now who sought to awaken desire in him, so as to win his love and affection. This account shows the proceedings of human beings after the model of those above. Said R. Eleazar, 'If so, what are we to make of the evil inclination seizing the female above?' He said: 'It has already been observed that one set (Left and Right) is above and one set below, viz. the good inclination and the evil inclination; the good inclination on the right and the evil inclination on the left. The Left above seizes the female to join with her in the body, as it is written, "his left hand under my head, etc." (S. S. II, 6). In this way the passage can be interpreted as applying both above and below. The rest of the points are not at all recondite, and a child almost could elucidate them; and the colleagues have noted them.'

R. Simeon was once going to Tiberias accompanied by

R. Jose and R. Judah and R. Hiya. On the way they saw R. Phineas coming towards them. When they met, they dismounted and sat down under a large tree. Said R. Phineas, 'Now that I am sitting here, I should like to hear some of those wonderful ideas to which you daily give utterance.' R. Simeon thereupon opened a discourse with the text, *And he went on his journeys from the South even unto Bethel, unto the place where his tent was at first, between Bethel and Ai* (Gen. XIII, 3). He said: 'The word "journeys" is used here where we might have expected "journey", to indicate that the Shekinah was journeying with him. It is incumbent on a man to be ever "male and female", in order that his faith may be firm, and that the Shekinah may never depart from him. What, then, you will say, of a man who goes on a journey and, being absent from his wife, is no longer "male and female"? His remedy is to pray to God before he starts his journey, while he is still "male and female", in order to draw to himself the presence of his Master. When he has offered his prayer and thanksgiving and the Shekinah rests on him, then he can depart, for through his union with the Shekinah he has become "male and female" in the country as he was "male and female" in the town, as it is written: "Righteousness (*zedek*, the female of *zaddik*) shall go before him and shall place his footsteps on the way" (Ps. LXXXV, 14). Observe this. All [50a] the time that a man is on his travels he should be very careful of his actions, in order that the celestial partner may not desert him and leave him defective, through lacking the union with the female. If this was necessary when his wife was with him, how much more so is it necessary when a heavenly partner is attached to him? All the more so since this heavenly partner guards him on the way all the time until he returns home. When he does reach home again, it is his duty to give his wife some pleasure, because it is she who procured for him this heavenly partner. It is his duty to do this for two reasons. One is that this pleasure is a religious pleasure, and one which gives joy to the Shekinah also, and what is more, by its means he spreads peace in the world, as it is written, "thou shalt know that thy tent is in peace, and thou shalt visit thy fold and not sin" (Job. v, 24). (Is it a sin, it may be asked, if he does not visit his wife? The answer is that it is so because he thereby derogates from the honour of the celestial partner who was joined with him on account of his wife.) The other is, that if his wife becomes pregnant, the celestial partner imparts to the child a holy soul, for this covenant is called the covenant of the Holy One, blessed be He. Therefore he should be as diligent to procure this gladness as to procure the gladness of the Sabbath, which is the partner of the Sages. Hence "thou shalt know that thy tent is in peace", since the Shekinah comes with thee and abides in thy house, and therefore "thou shalt visit thy house and not sin", by performing with gladness the religious duty of conjugal intercourse in the presence of the Shekinah. In this way the students of the Torah who separate from their wives during the six days of the week in order to devote themselves to study are accompanied by a heavenly partner in order that they may continue to be "male and female". When Sabbath comes, it is incumbent on them to gladden their wives for the sake of the honour of the heavenly partner, and to seek to perform the will of their Master, as has been said. Similarly again, if a man's wife is observing the days of her separation, during all those days that he waits for her the heavenly partner is associated with him, so that he is still "male and female". When his wife is purified, it is his duty to gladden her through the glad performance of a religious precept. All the reasons we have mentioned above apply to this case also. The esoteric doctrine is that men of true faith should concentrate their whole thought and purpose on this one (the Shekinah). You may object that, according to what has been said, a man enjoys greater dignity when he is on a journey than when he is at home, on account of the heavenly partner who is then associated with him. This is not so. For when a man is at home, the foundation of his house is the wife, for it is on account of her that the Shekinah departs not from the house. So our teachers have understood the verse, "and he brought her to the tent of his mother Sarah" (Gen. XXIV, 67), to indicate that with Rebecca the Shekinah came to Isaac's house. Esoterically speaking, the supernal Mother is found in company with the male only at the time when the house is prepared, and the male and female are joined. Then the supernal Mother pours forth blessings for them. Similarly the lower Mother is not found in company with the male save when the house is prepared and the male visits the female and they join together; then the lower Mother pours forth blessings for them. Hence the man in his house is to be encompassed by two females, like the Male above. There is an allusion to this in the verse "Unto (*'ad*) the desire of the everlasting hills" (Gen. XLIX, 26). This *'ad* is the object of the desire of the "everlasting hills", viz. the supreme female, who is to prepare for him and beatify and bless him, and the secondary female, who is to be conjoined with him and to be supported by him. Similarly below, when the man is married the desire of the "everlasting hills" is towards him, and he is beatified by two females, one of the upper and one of the lower world—the upper one to pour blessings upon him, and the lower one to be supported by him and to be conjoined with him. So much for the man in his house. When, however, he goes forth on a journey, while the celestial Mother still accompanies him, the lower wife is left behind: so when he comes back he has to take measures to encompass himself with two females, as we have said.' Said R. Phineas: 'Even the angels above would not dare to open [50*b*] their mouths before thee.'

R. Simeon proceeded: 'In the same way the Torah is situated between two houses, one recondite and on high, and the other more accessible. The one on high is the "Great Voice" referred to in the verse, "a great voice which did not cease" (Deut. V, 19). This Voice is in the recesses and is not heard or revealed, and when it issues from the throat it utters the aspirate without sound and it flows on without ceasing, though it is so tenuous as to be inaudible. From this issues the Torah, which is the voice of Jacob. The audible voice issues from the inaudible. In due course speech is attached to it, and through the force of that speech it emerges into the open. The voice of Jacob, which is the Torah, is thus attached to two females, to this inner voice which is inaudible, and to this outer voice which is heard.

Strictly speaking, there are two which are inaudible and two which are heard. The two which are not heard are, first, the supernal Wisdom which is located in the Thought and is not disclosed or heard; and secondly the same Wisdom when it issues and discloses itself a little in a whisper which cannot be heard, being then called the "Great Voice", which is very tenuous and issues in a whisper. The two which are heard are those which issue from this source—the voice of Jacob and the articulation which accompanies it. This "Great Voice" which cannot be heard is a "house" to the supernal Wisdom (the female is always called "house"), and the articulation we have mentioned is a "house" to the Voice of Jacob, which is the Torah, and therefore the Torah commences with the letter *beth*, which is, as it were, a "house" to it.' R. Simeon here drew a parallel between the creation of heaven and earth and of woman. ' "In the beginning God created",' he said, 'corresponds to "And the Lord God built the side"; "the heavens" corresponds to "and he brought her to the man"; "and the earth" corresponds to "bone from my bone", since this one assuredly is "the land of the living".'

R. Simeon further gave an exposition of the verse: *The Lord said unto my lord, Sit at my right hand until I make thine enemies thy footstool* (Ps. cx, 1). "The Lord saith unto my lord": 'to wit, the upper grade said to the lower, "sit at my right hand", in order that the West should be linked with the South and the Left with the Right so as to break the power of the Gentiles. Or again, "The Lord" is (the celestial) Jacob, and "to my lord" is "the ark of the covenant, the lord of all the earth" (Josh. III, 11). According to another explanation, "the Lord" refers to the Jubilee and "my lord" to the Sabbatical Year (cf. Ex. XXI, 5, "I love my lord"). The words "sit at my right hand" are appropriate, because the Right is located in the Jubilee, and the Sabbatical Year craves to be linked with the Right. When it first came into being, the Sabbatical Year was not linked securely (to the supreme power) through either the Right or the Left. So when it sought to secure itself, the supreme power stretched forth its right arm to meet it and created this world. It is because it is from the side of the Left that it has no sure basis till the time of the seventh millennium, when at length it will be linked through the Right. Then the Sabbatical Year, between the Right and the Left, will be securely based, there will be a new heaven and a new earth, and it will not depart from there for ever. According to this explanation, we must take the words "sit at my right hand" to refer only to a specified period, viz. "till I make thine enemies thy footstool", but not in perpetuity; for when that event has come to pass, it will not depart from there for ever, as it is written, "for thou shalt spread abroad on the right hand and on the left" (Is. LIV, 3), all being united. Similarly we can interpret the text "the heavens and the earth" to mean that the higher Shekinah and the lower Shekinah will be joined in the union of male and female; this has already been explained, as the colleagues have noted.'

They now rose to depart, but R. Simeon said: 'I have still one thing more to tell you. It says in one place "For the Lord thy God is a consuming fire" (Deut. IV, 24), and in another place "Ye that clave to the Lord your God are all of you alive this day" (Deut. IV, 4). The apparent contradiction between these texts has already been discussed among the colleagues, but here is another explanation. It has already been established among the colleagues that there is a fire which consumes fire and destroys it, because there is one sort of fire stronger than another. Pursuing this idea, we may say that he who desires to penetrate to the mystery of the holy unity should contemplate the flame which rises from a burning coal or candle. The flame cannot rise save [51*a*] from some concrete body. Further, in the flame itself there are two lights: one white and luminous, and the other black, or blue. The white light is the higher of the two and rises steadily. The black or blue light is underneath the other, which rests on it as on a pedestal. The two are inseparably connected, the white resting and being enthroned upon the black. (Herein is the inner significance of the fringe of blue.) This blue or black base is in turn attached to something beneath it which keeps it in flame and impels it to cling to the white light above. This blue or black light sometimes turns red, but the white light above never changes its colour. The lower light, which is sometimes black, sometimes blue, and sometimes red, is a connecting link between the white light to which it is attached above and to the concrete body to which it is attached below, and which keeps it alight. This light always consumes anything which is under it or which is brought in contact with it, for such is its nature, to be a source of destruction and death. But the white light which is above it never consumes or destroys and never changes. Therefore Moses said, "For the Lord thy God is a consuming fire", literally consuming all that is beneath him; that is why he said "thy God" and not "our God", because Moses was in that white light above which does not consume or destroy. Now observe. The impulse through which this blue light is set aflame and attaches itself to the white light comes only from Israel, who cleave to it from below. Further, although it is the nature of this blue or black light to consume everything that is in contact with it beneath, yet Israel are able to cleave to it from below and still exist; so it is written, "and ye that cleave to the Lord your God are all of you alive this day". *Your* God and not *our* God: to wit, that blue or black flame which consumes and destroys all that cleaves to it from below; yet you cleave and are still alive. Above the white light and surrounding it is still another light scarcely perceptible, symbolical of the supreme essence. Thus the ascending flame symbolises the highest mysteries of wisdom.'

R. Phineas approached and kissed him, saying, 'Blessed be God who led my steps here.' They then accompanied R. Phineas on his way for three miles. When they came back, R. Simeon said: 'What I told you before furnishes a symbol of the sacred unification. The second *hé* of the holy name is the blue or black light which is attached to *Yod, Hé, Vau*, which are the white shining light. Sometimes this blue light is not *hé* but *daleth;* that is to say, when Israel do not cleave to it from below so as to make it burn and cling to the white light, it is *daleth*, but when they give it the impulse to cling to the white light, it is *hé*. For where male and female are not found together, *hé* is eliminated and only *daleth* is left (hence in Deut. XXII, 15, the word *na'ar* is used for "maiden" instead of *na'arah*, because she is not united with the male). But when the chain is complete, the *hé* cleaves to the white light and

Israel cleave to it and feed its light without being destroyed. This is the secret of the sacrifice. The ascending smoke kindles the blue light, which then attaches itself [51b] to the white light, so that the whole candle is completely alight. Since it is the nature of this blue light to destroy and consume everything which is in contact with it underneath, when the sacrifice is pleasing and the candle is completely alight, then, as in the case of Elijah, "the fire of the Lord descends and consumes the burnt-offering" (1 Kings XVIII, 38), this being a manifestation that the chain is complete, the blue light both cleaving to the white light and consuming the fat and flesh of the burnt-offering beneath it, for it does not consume what is beneath it save when it ascends and attaches itself to the white light. Then there is peace in all worlds, and the whole forms a unity. When the blue light has consumed all that is beneath it, the priests, the Levites, and the laity assemble at its foot with chanting, with meditation, and with prayer, the lamp burns above them, the lights are welded into one, worlds are illumined, and both those above and those below are blessed. Hence it is that "ye, even while cleaving to the Lord your God, are all alive this day". The word *athem* (you) here is preceded by the letter *vau* (and), to show that whereas the fat and the flesh which cleave to the flame are destroyed by it, you cleave to it and are still alive.'

All colours seen in a dream are of good presage, except blue; this is ever consuming and destroying, being the tree in which death is located. It spreads over the lower world, and because all things are situated beneath it, therefore they are perishable. It is true that it also pervades the heaven, and there are many objects there which are imperishable. These, however, are constituted of this blue light, whereas the lower ones are of coarser material, and constitute a lower world on which the upper one rests. Hence the blue light consumes and destroys them.'[1] [52a]

AND THEY HEARD THE VOICE OF THE LORD GOD WALKING IN THE GARDEN. (Note the form *mithalech*

---

[1] From this point to 52a *ad fin.* is a Cabbalistic interpolation on the origin of the Serpent.

(walking) instead of the usual *mehalech*.) Until he sinned, man was gifted with the wisdom of celestial illumination, and he did not for an instant quit the Tree of Life. But when he was seduced by his desire to know what was below, he weakly followed it until he became separated from the Tree of Life, and knew evil and forsook good: hence the Scripture says 'for thou art not a God that hath pleasure in wickedness, [52b] evil shall not sojourn with thee' (Ps. v. 5). He who is drawn after evil may not abide with the Tree of Life. Before they sinned, the human pair used to hear a voice from above, and were endowed with the higher wisdom; they stood erect with heavenly radiance, and knew no fear. When they sinned, they were not able to stand up even before an earthly voice. A similar thing happened later with the Israelites. When Israel stood before Mount Sinai, the impurity of the serpent was removed from them, so that carnal passion was suppressed among them, and in consequence they were able to attach themselves to the Tree of Life, and their thoughts were turned to higher things and not to lower. Hence they were vouchsafed heavenly illuminations and knowledge which filled them with joy and gladness. Further, God girt them with cinctures of the letters of the Holy Name, which prevented the serpent from gaining power over them or defiling them as before. When they sinned by worshipping the calf, they were degraded from their high estate and lost their illumination, they were deprived of the protective girdle of the Holy Name and became exposed to the attacks of the evil serpent as before, and so brought death into the world. After their sin, it is related that 'Aaron and the children of Israel saw Moses, and behold, the skin of his face shone, and they were afraid to come nigh him' (Ex. xxxiv, 30). Before that, however, we are told that 'Israel saw the great hand' (*Ibid.* xiv, 31) on the Red Sea, and that at Mount Sinai they all saw celestial lights and were illumined with the vision of clear prophecy, as it is written, 'And all the people saw the voices' (*Ibid.* xx, 18), and by the Red Sea they saw God and did not fear, as it is written, 'This is my God and I will praise him' (*Ibid.* xv, 2). But after they sinned, they were not able to look even on the face of the deputy (Moses). How was this? Because 'the children of Israel were deprived of their ornament from Mount Sinai', to wit, of the armour with which they were girt on Mount Sinai in order that the evil serpent should not have power over them. After this had been stripped from them we read that 'Moses took the tent and pitched it without the camp, afar off from the camp' (*Ibid.* XXXIII, 7). R. Eleazar explained the connection thus: 'When Moses perceived that Israel had been deprived of their heavenly armour, he said, "Of a surety the evil serpent will now come to dwell among them, and if the sanctuary remains here among them it will be defiled", and he therefore took the tent and pitched it outside, far from the camp.' 'And he called it the tent of meeting.' It had been such before, but had been called the 'tent', simply. The epithet 'of meeting' was now given to it, according to R. Eleazar, in compliment, according to R. Abba, in disparagement. R. Eleazar defended his view on the ground that *moed* (meeting, appointed time) is the word used of the day when the moon is in full career, when its holiness is increased and it is free from defect; so here, Moses gave the tent this name to show that it had been removed from the contagion of the people. R. Abba argued that the simple name 'tent' has the same implication as in the verse 'a tent that shall not be removed, the stakes of which shall never be plucked up' (Is. XXXIII, 20), i.e. that it designates something which confers eternity on the world and saves it from death, whereas the epithet 'meeting' is used in the same sense as in the phrase 'a house of meeting for all flesh' (i.e. the grave, Job XXX, 23), and indicates that now the life which it conferred was only for a limited period. At first it was unimpaired, but now it was impaired; at first the sun and the moon were in continuous union, but now their union was only from season to season (*moed*); hence the name 'tent of season' (*moed*).

R. Simeon was one night studying the Torah in company with R. Judah, R. Isaac, and R. Jose. Said R. Judah to him: 'We read that "the Israelites took off their ornament from Mount Horeb", and we go on to assert that they thereby brought death upon themselves, and once more placed themselves in the power of the evil serpent from whose clutches they had previously escaped. This may be true of the Israelites; but what of Joshua, who had not sinned ? Are we to say that he was deprived of the armour which he received with them, or not ? [53a] If not, why did he die like other people ? If you say he was deprived, what was the reason, seeing that he had not sinned, as he was with Moses when the people sinned ? And if you say that he did not receive the same crown on Mount Sinai as the rest of the people, again, what was the reason ?' R. Simeon in reply quoted the text: *For the Lord is righteous, he loveth righteousness, he is upright, men shall behold his face* (Ps. XI, 7). He said: 'This verse has been variously explained by our colleagues, but it may be taken in this way. "For the Lord is righteous": to wit, He is righteous and His name is Righteous (*Zaddik*) and therefore He loves righteous deeds. He is also upright, as it is written, "righteous and upright is he" (Deut. XXXII, 4); and therefore all the inhabitants of the world behold His face, that they may amend their ways and walk in the straight path. For when God judges the world, He passes sentence only according to the conduct of the majority. Now when Adam sinned by eating of the forbidden tree, he caused that tree to become a source of death to all the world. He also caused imperfection by separating the Wife from her Husband. This imperfection was exhibited in the moon, until the time when Israel stood before Mount Sinai, when the moon was freed from its defect, and was in a position to shine continually. When Israel sinned by making the calf, the moon reverted to its former imperfection, and the evil serpent was able to seize her and draw her to him. When Moses saw that Israel had sinned and that they had been deprived of their holy armour, he knew full well that the serpent had seized the moon to draw her to him, and that she had become defective, and he therefore took her outside. Thus she has reverted to the defective state into which she was brought by the sin of Adam, and therefore no man can live permanently save Moses, who controls her, and whose death was due to a different cause. Hence she had not power to bestead permanently even Joshua, although he retained his holy armour; and it was therefore that Moses called her "tent of appointed time" (*moed*), to wit, the tent in which is an appointed time for all living. To speak more esoterically: there is a Right above and there is a Right below; there is a Left above and there is a Left below. There is a Right above in the realm of supernal holiness, and there is a Right below located in the "other side". There is a Left above in the realm of supernal holiness to procure indulgence for the moon, so as to link her to the holy place and enable her to shine. There is a Left below which estranges the upper realm from her and prevents her from reflecting the sun's light and drawing near to him. This is the side of the evil serpent, who, when this Left of the lower realm bestirs itself, draws the moon to himself and separates her from the upper world, so that her light is darkened. She then causes death to descend like a stream on all that is below; she cleaves to the serpent and departs from the Tree of Life, and so brings death on all the world. At such time the sanctuary is defiled till an appointed time when the moon is repaired and shines again. Hence the name "tent of appointed time" (*moed*), and hence it is that Joshua died only through the instigation of the serpent, which came up to the tent and rendered it imperfect as at first. This is the inner meaning of the verse, "And Joshua the son of Nun, a lad (*naar*), departed not from out the tent" (Ex. XXXIII, 11). Although he was a "lad" (i.e. attendant) beneath qualified to receive the (celestial) light, he did not depart from out the tent: he shared in its imperfection; although he still had the holy armour, yet when the moon became imperfect, he also was not delivered from the same power which caused that imperfection. Similarly when Adam sinned, God took from him the armour of the bright and holy letters with which he had been encompassed, and then he and his wife were afraid, perceiving that they had been stripped; so it says AND THEY KNEW THAT THEY WERE NAKED. At first they had been invested with those glorious crowns which gave them protection and exemption from death. When they sinned, they were stripped of them, and then they knew that death was calling them, that they had been deprived of their exemption, and that they had brought death on themselves and on all the world.' [53*b*]

AND THEY SEWED FIG LEAVES TOGETHER. This means, as explained elsewhere, that they learnt all kinds of enchantments and magic, and clung to worldly knowledge, as has been said. At that moment the stature of man was diminished by a hundred cubits. Thus a separation took place (of man from God), man was brought to judgement, and the earth was cursed, all as we have explained.

AND HE DROVE OUT THE MAN. R. Eleazar said: 'We naturally suppose that "he" is the subject and "man" the object. The truth is, however, that "man" is the subject and the object is the accusative particle *eth*, so that we render "and the man drove out *eth*". Hence it is written, "And God sent him forth from the Garden of Eden", for the reason that he had divorced *eth*, as we have explained. AND HE PLACED: the subject is still "man"; it was he who fixed the Cherubim in this place, who closed the path to Paradise, who subjected the world to chastisement, and drew upon it curses from that day onward. THE FLAME OF A SWORD WHICH TURNED EVERY WAY: this refers to those beings who are ever in readiness to chastise the world, and who take all manner of shapes, being sometimes male, sometimes female, sometimes flaming fire and sometimes irresistible winds. All this is TO KEEP THE WAY OF THE TREE OF LIFE, so that man should not do any more mischief there. The "flaming sword" denotes those punitive spirits who heap fire on the heads of the wicked and sinners (in hell). They take various forms according to the offences of those who are punished. The word "flaming" (*lahat*) here has its analogy in the verse, "the day that cometh shall burn them up" (*ve-lihat*, Mal. III, 19). The "sword" is that mentioned in the verse, "The sword of the Lord is filled with blood, etc." (Is. XXXIV, 6).' R. Judah said: 'All those punitive spirits that we have mentioned, that assume so many various forms, are charged to maltreat and harry in this world the sinners who deliberately transgress the precepts of their Master. For when a man sins, he draws towards himself numbers of evil spirits and emissaries of punishment, before whom he quails in fear. Solomon was conversant with the mysteries of Wisdom, and God set upon his head the crown of royalty, and the whole world feared him. When, however, he sinned, he drew towards himself numbers of evil and punitive spirits, of whom he was much frightened, so that they were able to maltreat him and to take away his (precious) possessions. In truth, a man by his actions is always drawing to himself some emissary from the other world, good or evil according to the path which he treads. So Adam drew to himself an emissary of defilement who defiled him and all mankind after him. This was the evil serpent who is himself unclean and defiled the world. Our Sages have taught that when he draws the soul out of a man, there is left an unclean body which renders the whole house unclean, and all those that touch it, as it is written, "He that touches a dead body, etc." (Num. XIX, 11). The reason is that when he takes the soul and renders the body unclean, permission is given to all the unclean spirits, which are akin to the evil serpent, to rest upon it, and so the whole place where the evil serpent is present becomes defiled. Further, when men sleep on their beds at night-time and night spreads her wings over the world, they are having a foretaste of death, and in consequence the unclean spirit is let loose in the world, carrying pollution. In particular it rests upon a man's hands and defiles them, so that when he wakes up and his soul is restored to him, everything which he touches with his hands is rendered unclean. Hence a man should be careful when dressing not to take his garments from a person who has not washed his hands, because in this way he draws upon himself the unclean spirit and becomes defiled. This spirit is authorised to settle in every place where there is the merest trace of the side from which it issues. Hence a man should not let water be poured over his hands by one who has not yet washed his own hands, because in this way he draws on himself the unclean spirit, from contact with the one who pours water over him. [54a] Therefore a man should be on his guard on every side against the side of this evil serpent, which otherwise will gain the better of him. God has promised one day to remove it from this world, as it is written, "I will cause the unclean spirit to pass out of the land" (Zech. XIII, 2), and also "He will swallow up death for ever" (Is. XXV, 8).'

AND THE MAN KNEW EVE HIS WIFE. R. Abba discoursed in connection with this verse on the text: *Who knoweth the spirit of man which goeth upwards, and the spirit of the beast which goeth downward to the earth?* (Eccl. III, 21). He said: "This verse can bear many constructions, and so it is with all the words of the Torah: they can all bear several meanings, and all good, and the whole Torah can be expounded in seventy ways, corresponding to seventy sides and seventy wings. We will, however, expound thus. When a man walks in the path of truth, he goes towards the right and attracts to himself a holy spirit from above, which in turn ascends with holy intent to attach itself to the upper world and to cleave to the supernal holiness. When, however, a man walks in the path of evil, he draws to himself an unclean spirit belonging to the left side, which renders him impure; so it is written, "ye shall not make yourselves unclean with them that ye should be defiled thereby" (Lev. XI, 43), i.e. he that first defiles himself is led further into defilement. Further, when a man walks in the right path and attracts to himself a spirit of holiness from above and cleaves to it, he also draws a spirit of holiness on to the son whom he bears into the world, so that he is like to be endowed with the sanctity of his Master (as it is written, "if ye sanctify yourselves, ye shall be holy" (Lev. XI, 44)). Contrariwise, when the man goes to the side of the left and draws to himself the impure spirit and clings to it, he also draws a spirit of uncleanliness on the son that issues from him, so that he is like to be defiled by the impurity of the left side. This is what is meant by the words, "Who knows the spirit of the sons of men, namely that one which ascends on high, etc." When a man cleaves to the right, the spirit mounts aloft, but when he cleaves to the left, the side of the left, which is the spirit of uncleanliness, descends from above and fixes its abode in a man's body, and the son whom he begets in that state of impurity is his son *from* that unclean spirit. Now Adam clave to that unclean spirit, and his wife clung to it at first and received defilement from it. Hence when Adam begat a son, that son was the son of the impure spirit. Thus there were two sons—one from the unclean spirit, and one after Adam had repented. Thus one was from the pure side and one from the impure.' R. Eleazar said: 'When the serpent injected his impurity into Eve, she absorbed it, and so when Adam had intercourse with her she bore two sons—one from the impure side and one from the side of Adam; and Abel bore a resemblance to the higher form and Cain to the lower. Hence it was that their ways in life were different. It was natural, too, that Cain, coming from the side of the angel of death, should kill his brother. He also adhered to his own side, and from him originate all the evil habitations and demons and goblins and evil spirits in the world.' R. Jose said: 'Cain was the nest (*Qina*) of the evil habitations which came into the world from the impure side. Afterwards both Cain and Abel brought sacrifices, each from his appropriate side; hence it is written, AND IT CAME TO PASS AT THE END OF DAYS THAT CAIN BROUGHT OF THE FRUIT OF THE GROUND, ETC.' R. Simeon said: 'This "end of days" is the same as "the end of all flesh" (Gen. VI, 13), who is also the angel of death. Cain brought his offering from this "end of days"; this is indicated by the expression in the text "from the end" (*mi-ketz*). [54*b*] CAIN BROUGHT OF THE FRUIT OF THE GROUND: this is parallel to "of the fruit of the tree" in God's words to Adam.' R. Eleazar said: 'We can apply to Cain the verse, "Woe to the wicked, it shall be ill with him, for the reward of his hands shall be done to him" (Is. III, 11). "The reward of his hands" refers to the angel of death, who is drawn towards them and clings to them so as to slay or defile them. Thus Cain offered from the side appropriate to him. AND ABEL ALSO BROUGHT OF THE FIRSTLINGS: to amplify the higher side which comes from the side of holiness. Hence THE LORD HAD RESPECT UNTO ABEL AND TO HIS OFFERING, BUT TO CAIN AND TO HIS OFFERING HE HAD NOT RESPECT, i.e. God did not accept it, and therefore CAIN WAS VERY WROTH AND HIS COUNTENANCE (presence) FELL, because his presence was not received, being from the side of the left. On the other hand, God received Abel, and therefore it is written, AND IT CAME TO PASS WHEN THEY WERE IN THE FIELD, ETC. "Field" is here a designation for woman; Cain was jealous of the twin sister that was born with Abel (according to the interpretation placed by us on the words "and she bore in addition", IV, 2).' IF THOU DOEST WELL, SHALL THERE NOT BE UPLIFTING? This has already been explained, viz. the word *se'eth* (uplifting) means, according to R. Abba, 'thou shalt mount above and shalt not descend below'. R. Jose said: 'We accept this explanation, which is a good one, but I have also heard another, viz. "this attachment of the impure spirit shall depart (lit. be lifted) from thee and leave thee". If not, then SIN COUCHETH AT THE DOOR. By "door" is meant the heavenly tribunal which is the door through which all enter, as it is written, "open to me the doors of righteousness" (Ps. CXVIII, 19). By "sin coucheth" is meant that the side which clung to thee and was drawn towards thee is lying in watch for thee to exact punishment from thee.' Said R. Isaac: 'When Cain wanted to kill Abel, he did not know how to make him give up the ghost, and he bit him like a snake, as our colleagues have explained. God then cursed him, and he wandered about the world without being able to find any resting-place until, clapping his hands on his head, he repented before his Master. Then the earth found a place for him in one of its lower levels.' R. Jose said: 'The earth allowed him to stay on its surface, as it is written, "And the Lord set upon Cain a sign".' R. Isaac said: 'That is not so. The earth found a place for him in a certain lower level, as it is written, "Behold, thou hast driven me out this day from the *face* of the ground", implying that he was banished from the surface but not from underground. The level on which he found a resting-place was *Arka*, of the denizens of which it is written, "these shall perish from the earth and from beneath the heavens" (Jer. X, 11). There was fixed his habitation, and this is what is meant by the words, AND HE DWELT IN THE LAND OF NOD ON THE EAST OF EDEN.' Said R. Isaac further: 'From the time that Cain killed Abel Adam separated from his wife. Two female spirits then used to come and have intercourse with him, and he bore from them spirits and demons that flit about the world. This need cause no surprise, because now also when a man dreams in his sleep, female spirits often come and disport with him, and so conceive from him and subsequently give birth. The creatures thus produced are called "plagues of mankind"; they appear always under the form of human beings, but they have no hair on their heads. It is they who are referred to in the verse, "and I shall chastise him with the rod of men and with the plagues of the sons of men" (II Sam. VII, 14). In the same way male spirits visit womenfolk and make them pregnant, so that they bring forth spirits which are also called "plagues of the sons of men".

After a hundred and thirty years, Adam again felt drawn [55a] with desire towards his wife, and he begat from her a son whom he called Seth. This name symbolises an end, being composed of the two last letters of the alphabet in regular order.' R. Judah said: 'This name symbolised the reincarnation of the spirit which had been lost, being of the same letters as the word *shath* (set) in the sentence "God hath replaced (*shath*) for me another seed instead of Abel"'. R. Judah further said: 'The words AND HE BEGAT IN HIS OWN LIKENESS AFTER HIS IMAGE indicate that his other sons were not fully after his likeness, but that this one reproduced his qualities both of body and soul. This accords with what R. Simeon said in the name of R. Yeba, the Elder, that his other sons were engendered in defilement through the attachment of the serpent and of its rider, Samael, and therefore they were not a complete reproduction of Adam. We said before, it is true, that Abel was not from the same side as Cain; nevertheless, both were alike in this, that they were not endowed with the full human figure.' R. Jose said: 'This view is borne out by the language of the text, which in regard to the birth of Cain says, "And Adam knew his wife and she conceived and *she* bore Cain", and so of Abel, "and *she* again bore his brother Abel", but of Seth it says, "and *he* bore in his likeness after his image".' R. Simeon said: 'For a hundred and thirty years Adam separated from his wife, and during that time he begat many spirits and demons, through the force of the impurity which he had absorbed. When that impurity was exhausted, he turned once more to his wife and begat from her a son, of whom it is written, "he begat in his own likeness after his image". For when a man goes to the side of the left and walks in impurity, he draws to himself all kinds of impure spirits, and an unclean spirit clings to him and refuses to leave him, since these spirits cling only to those that cling to them first. Happy the righteous who walk in the straight path, they being the truly righteous; their children are also blessed, and of them it is written, "for the upright shall dwell in the earth" (Prov. II, 21).'

AND THE SISTER OF TUBAL CAIN WAS NAAMAH. R. Hiya said: 'Why does the Scripture particularly mention Naamah? The reason is that she was the great seducer not only of men, but also of spirits and demons.' R. Isaac said: 'The "sons of God" mentioned in the Scripture (Gen. VI, 4), who were Uzza and Azael, were seduced by her.' R. Simeon said: 'She was the mother of the demons, being of the side of Cain, and it is she who in company with Lilith brings epilepsy on children.' Said R. Abba to him: 'Did you not say before that her function is to seduce men?' He replied: 'That is so; she disports herself with men, and sometimes bears spirits from them. And she still exists to seduce men.' Said R. Abba to him: 'But do these demons not die like human beings? How then comes she to exist to the present day?' He replied: 'It is so. Lilith and Naamah and Iggereth, the daughter of Mahlath, who originated from their side, will all continue to exist until the Holy One, blessed be He, sweeps away the unclean spirit, as it is written, "I will cause the unclean spirit to pass out of the land" (Zech. XIII, 2).' Said R. Simeon: 'Alas for the blindness of the sons of men, all unaware as they are how full the earth is of strange and invisible beings and hidden dangers, which could they but see, they would marvel how they themselves can exist on the earth. This Naamah was the mother of the demons, and from her originate all those evil spirits which mix with men and arouse in them concupiscence, which leads them to defilement. It is because such a hap comes from the side of the unclean spirit that it entails the need of purification by ablution, as our colleagues have explained.'

THIS IS THE BOOK OF THE GENERATIONS OF ADAM, i.e. those who inherited his likeness. Said R. Isaac: 'God showed Adam the visages of all future generations, of all the wise men and all the kings that were destined to rule over Israel. When he saw David, who was destined to die as soon as he was born, he said, "I will lend him seventy years from my life", and so it came to pass. It was to this that David referred when he said: "For Thou, O Lord, hast made me glad [55b] through thy work, I will triumph in the works of thy hands" (Ps. XCII, 5), the expression "work" and "works of thy hands" in this passage referring to Adam, who was made by God and not by flesh and blood. Hence Adam's days fell short by seventy years of the thousand which he ought by right to have lived. God also showed him the wise men of each generation. When he came to R. Akiba and saw his great learning, he rejoiced, but when he saw his martyrdom he was sorely grieved. Nevertheless, he exclaimed: "How precious in mine eyes are thy companions, O God, how mighty are the chiefs of them" (Ps. CXXXIX, 17). "This is the book": literally so, as we have explained, viz. that when Adam was in the Garden of Eden, God sent down to him a book by the hand of Raziel, the angel in charge of the holy mysteries. In this book were supernal inscriptions containing the sacred wisdom, and seventy-two branches of wisdom expounded so as to show the formation of six hundred and seventy inscriptions of higher mysteries. In the middle of the book was a secret writing explaining the thousand and five hundred keys which were not revealed even to the holy angels, and all of which were locked up in this book until it came into the hands of Adam. When Adam obtained it, all the holy angels gathered round him to hear him read it, and when he began they exclaimed: "Be thou exalted, O Lord, above the heavens, let thy glory be above all the earth" (Ps. LVII, 12). Thereupon the holy angel Hadarniel was secretly sent to say to him: "Adam, Adam, reveal not the glory of the Master, for to thee alone and not to the angels is the privilege given to know the glory of thy Master." Therefore he kept it by him secretly until he left the Garden of Eden. While he was there he studied it diligently, and utilised constantly the gift of his Master until he discovered sublime mysteries which were not known even to the celestial ministers. When, however, he transgressed the command of his Master, the book flew away from him. Adam then beat his breast and wept, and entered the river Gihon up to his neck, so that his body became all wrinkled and his face haggard. God thereupon made a sign to Raphael to return to him the book, which he then studied for the rest of his life. Adam left it to his son Seth, who transmitted it in turn to his posterity, and so on until it came to Abraham, who learnt from it how to discern the glory of his Master, as has been said. Similarly Enoch possessed a book through which he learnt to discern the divine glory.'

MALE AND FEMALE HE CREATED THEM. R. Simeon said: 'Profound mysteries are revealed in these two verses.[1] The words "male and female he created them" make known the high dignity of man, the mystic doctrine of his creation. Assuredly in the way in which heaven and earth were created man was also created; for of heaven and earth it is written, "these are the generations of the heaven and the earth", and of man it is written, "these are the generations of man"; of heaven and earth it is written, "when they were created", and of man it is written, "on the day when they were created": "Male and female he created them." From this we learn that every figure which does not comprise male and female elements is not a true and proper figure, and so we have laid down in the esoteric teaching of our Mishnah. Observe this. God does not place His abode in any place where male and female are not found together, nor are blessings found save in such a place, as it is written, AND HE BLESSED THEM AND CALLED THEIR NAME MAN ON THE DAY THAT THEY WERE CREATED: note that it says *them* and *their* name, and not *him* and *his* name. The male is not even called man till he is united with the female.' R. Judah said: 'Since the destruction of the Temple, blessings have not reached the world, but they go astray every day, as it is written, "The righteous loses", to wit, the blessings which used to rest upon him, as it is written, "blessings on the head of the righteous". AND CALLED HIS NAME SETH. It is to Seth that all the

---

[1] i.e. this one and Gen. 1, 27.

generations which have survived in the world and all the truly righteous of the world trace their descent.' R. Jose said: 'The two last letters of the alphabet were left in their order after the others had been reversed [56a] through Adam's transgression, and therefore when he repented he grasped at these two and called the son who was born in his likeness Seth, a name formed of the last two letters of the alphabet in proper order. Nevertheless, the other letters of the alphabet remained in the inverse order, and not till Israel stood before Mount Sinai did they recover their proper order as on the day when the heaven and earth were created, and the earth was once more securely established.' R. Abba said: 'On the day that Adam transgressed the command of his Master, heaven and earth were like to have been uprooted from their place, being based as they are only on the covenant, as it is written, "But for my covenant day and night, I had not set the statutes of heaven and earth" (Jer. XXXIII, 25), and Adam broke the covenant, as it is written, "And they like Adam transgressed the covenant" (Hos. VI, 7). And had not God foreseen that Israel would one day stand before Mount Sinai to confirm this covenant, the world would not have been preserved.' R. Hizkiah said: 'Whoever confesses his sin thereby procures forgiveness from God. See now, when God created the world, He made this covenant and established the world upon it, as it is written *bereshith*, which we interpret as *bara shith*, "he created the foundation", to wit, the covenant on which the world rests, and which is also called *shith*, because it is a trough from which blessings flow forth to the world. Adam broke this covenant and removed it from its place. This covenant is symbolised by the small letter *Yod*, the root and foundation of the world. When Adam begat a son, he confessed his guilt and called the child Seth; he did not venture to insert a *Yod* and call him "Shith", because he had broken the covenant so symbolised. In recompense, God propagated mankind from Seth, and made him the forefather of all the righteous who have lived since. Note also this. When Israel stood before Mount Sinai, there entered between these two letters (*shin* and *tau*) a symbol of the covenant, to wit, the letter *beth*, and God gave to Israel the word formed of all three letters, which is SaBba'TH, as it is said: "And the children of Israel shall keep the Sabbath, to make the Sabbath throughout their generations a perpetual covenant." In this way these two letters finally obtained their original potency, which had remained in suspense until the world was brought into its complete state and the holy covenant entered between them.' R. Jose said: 'These two letters were indeed fully reinstated through the letter *beth*, but all the letters commenced to return to their proper order with the birth of Seth, and so in every generation until Israel stood before Mount Sinai, when they were finally restored.' R. Judah said: 'They had already been restored below, and in every generation the world was held together by the letters though they were not yet properly settled in their places; but when the Torah was given to Israel, then everything was put right.'

R. Eleazar said: 'In the time of Enosh, men were skilled in magic and divination, and in the art of controlling the heavenly forces. Adam had brought with him from the Garden of Eden the knowledge of "the leaves of the tree", but he and his wife and their children did not practise it. When Enosh came, however, he saw the advantage of these arts and how the heavenly courses could be altered by them, and he and his contemporaries studied them and practised magic and divination. From them these arts descended to the generation of the Flood and were practised for evil purposes by all the men of that time. Relying upon these arts, they defied Noah, saying that divine justice could never be executed upon them, since they knew a way to avert it. The practice of these arts commenced with Enosh, and hence it is said of his time, THEN WAS THE NAME OF THE LORD CALLED UPON PROFANELY. R. Isaac said: 'All the righteous men that were among them sought to restrain them, such as Jered, Methuselah, and Enoch, but without success, and the world became full of sinners who rebelled against their Master saying, "What is the Almighty that we should serve him?" (Job XXI, 15). This is not so foolish as it sounds, for they knew all the arts we have mentioned and all the ruling chieftains in charge of the world, and on this knowledge they relied, until at length God disabused them by restoring the earth to its primitive state [56b] and covering it with water. Later, He again restored it and made it productive, since He looked upon it with mercy, as it is written, "The Lord sat at the Flood"—"the Lord" signifying the attribute of mercy. In the days of Enoch even children were acquainted with these mysterious arts.' Said R. Yesa: 'If so, how could they be so blind as not to know that God intended to bring the Flood upon them and destroy them?' R. Isaac replied: 'They did know, but they thought they were safe because they were acquainted with the angel in charge of fire and the angel in charge of water, and had means of preventing them from executing judgement on them. What they did not know was that God rules the world and that punishment proceeds from Him. They only saw that the world was entrusted to those chieftains and that everything was done through them, and therefore they took no heed of God and His works until the time came for the earth to be destroyed and the Holy Spirit proclaimed every day, "Let sinners be consumed out of the earth and let the wicked be no more" (Ps. CIV, 35). God gave them a respite all the time that the righteous men Jered, Methuselah, and Enoch were alive; but when they departed from the world, God let punishment descend upon them and they perished, as it says, "and they were blotted out from the earth" (Gen. VII, 23).'

AND ENOCH WALKED WITH GOD, AND HE WAS NOT, FOR GOD HAD TAKEN HIM. R. Jose illustrated this verse from the passage: *While the king was still with his company at table, my spikenard sent forth its fragrance* (S. S. I, 12). 'This verse', he said, 'can be expounded as referring to the ways of God. When God sees that a man who cleaves to Him and with whom He abides will one day degenerate, He takes him from the world prematurely, culling, as it were, the odour while it is still sweet; hence it is written, "while the King was with his company, my spikenard gave up its scent." The King is God; the company is the good man who cleaves to Him and walks in His ways; the spikenard indicates the good deeds on account of which he is removed from the world before his time. Of such a case did King Solomon say: "There is a vanity which is done upon the earth, that there be righteous men unto whom it happeneth according to the work of the wicked, etc." (Eccl. VIII, 14). How there are "righteous men to whom it happeneth according to the work of the wicked" we have just explained, viz. that because their deeds are good, God removes them from the world before their time and before they become liable to punishment. The rest of the verse, "there be wicked men to whom it happeneth according to the work of the righteous", means that God gives them a respite and is long-suffering with them. Thus the good die early in order that they may not degenerate, and the wicked live on in order that they may have a chance to repent, or in order that a virtuous progeny may issue from them. See now, Enoch was virtuous, but God saw that he would degenerate, and therefore gathered him in in time, as one "gathers lilies" (S. S. VI, 2) because of their good scent. "And he was not, for God had taken him." This means that he did not live to a great age like his contemporaries, because God took him before his time.' R. Eleazar said: 'God removed Enoch from the earth, and took him up to the highest heavens, and there presented to him wonderful treasures, including forty-five mystical key-combinations of graven letters which are used by the highest ranks of angels, as has been explained elsewhere.'

AND THE LORD SAW THAT THE WICKEDNESS OF MAN WAS VERY GREAT IN THE EARTH, AND THAT EVERY IMAGINATION OF THE THOUGHTS OF HIS HEART WAS ONLY EVIL CONTINUALLY. R. Judah quoted in this connection the verse: *For thou art not a God who hath pleasure in wickedness, evil shall not sojourn with thee* (Ps. V, 5). He said: 'One lesson that may be derived from this verse is that if a man cleaves to the evil imagination and follows after it, not only does he defile himself thereby, but he is led further into defilement, as has already been stated. The men of the time of the Flood committed all kinds of sin, but the measure of their guilt was not full until they wasted their blood (i.e. seed) upon the ground. We know this from the fact that the word *ra'* (evil) is used here, [57*a*] and also in the verse, "and Er the son of Judah was evil (*ra'*) in the sight of the Lord" (Gen. XXXVIII, 7).' Said R. Jose: 'Is not evil (*ra'*) the same as "wickedness" (*resha'*)?' He said: 'No. A man is called "wicked" (*rasha'*) if he merely lifts his hand against his neighbour without doing him any harm, as it is written, "And he said to the wicked one (*rasha'*), why wilt thou smite thy neighbour?", the future tense (wilt smite) implying that he had not yet done anything to him. But only he is called "evil" (*ra'*) who corrupts his way and defiles himself and the earth, and so lends force to the unclean spirit which is called *ra'* (whence it is said that "all their thoughts were for evil", *ra'*). Such a one will never enter the heavenly palace nor gaze upon the Shekinah, for by this sin the Shekinah is repelled from the world. We know this from Jacob, who, when the Shekinah departed from him, concluded that there was some stain attaching to his offspring, on account of which the unclean spirit had acquired strength and the light of the moon had been impaired: for this sin defiles the sanctuary. If on this account the Shekinah departed from Jacob, how much more certain is it that it will depart from one who corrupts his way and defiles himself, so giving power to the unclean spirit. Hence when a man defiles himself he is called *ra'*. Further, when a man defiles himself, he is not favoured with visitation (in dreams) from the Holy One, blessed be He, but on the contrary he is subject at all times to the visits of the spirit called *ra'*, as it is written, "he who sleeps sated (i.e. without evil passion) will not be visited by evil" (Prov. XIX, 23) (as much as to say that when he walks in the right path he will not be visited by *Ra'*.) Hence it is said of the men of the Flood that their thoughts were only evil, and the Psalmist said, "evil shall not sojourn with thee". Those who commit this sin are called *ra'* and not *rasha'*. Hence, too, it is written, "Yea, though I walk through the valley of the shadow of death I will not fear evil (*ra'*), for thou art with me".'

AND IT REPENTED THE LORD THAT HE HAD MADE MAN UPON THE EARTH, AND IT GRIEVED HIM AT HIS HEART. R. Jose illustrated from the verse: *Woe unto them that draw iniquity with cords of vanity, and sin as it were with a cart rope* (Is. v, 18). He said: 'Those who "draw iniquity" are the men who sin before their Master every day, and in whose eyes the sins they commit are like gossamer threads, which are of no account and are not noticed by God. And so they go on until they make their guilt as strong as a cart rope which cannot be broken. See now, when the time comes for God to pass sentence on sinners, although they have provoked Him every day, He is yet unwilling to destroy them, and though He sees their deeds, He is yet indulgent towards them because they are the work of His hands, and therefore He gives them a respite. When at last He does come to execute judgement upon them, He is, as it were, grieved, since they are the work of His hands, although it is written, "Honour and majesty are before him, strength and joy are in his place" (Ps. xcvi, 6).' R. Jose said: 'Observe that it says, "He was grieved to his heart". The seat of the grief was the heart and no other place, "heart" having here the same sense as in the verse, "according to that which is in mine heart and in my mind" (1 Sam. 11, 35).' R. Isaac said: 'The word "repented" here has the same sense as in the sentence, "And the Lord repented of the evil which he had said he would do unto his people" (Ex. xxxii, 14). R. Yesa says that the word *niham*, used of God, means "repent", as has been remarked, implying that God bethinks Himself that the sinners are the work of His hands, and therefore pities them and is grieved because they sin before Him. R. Hizkiah says that it means "is consoled", implying that when God resolves to destroy the wicked, He comforts Himself for their loss like one who resigns himself to the loss of some article, and once He has done so, justice takes its course and repentance no longer avails; for up to that point the decision may still be reversed. No only so, but judgement is executed with additional rigour, until the sinners are utterly destroyed. The text tells us as much; for the words "the Lord was comforted" indicate that God resigned Himself, and the words "he was grieved to his heart" that He allowed justice to take its course without mercy.' R. Hiya said: 'The words "God was comforted because he had made man" refer to the time when man was first created on the earth, in the supernal image, and God rejoiced because the angels praised Him saying, [57b] "Thou hast made him (man) little lower than God, and crownest him with glory and honour" (Ps. VIII, 6). But afterwards when man sinned, then God "was grieved", because now the angels could say that they had been right in protesting against his creation, saying: "What is man that thou art mindful of him and the son of man that thou visitest him?" (*Ibid.* 5).' R. Judah said: 'God was grieved because the execution of judgement is always displeasing to Him. Thus we read that Jehoshaphat when going out to war "appointed those that should sing.... Give thanks unto the Lord, for his mercy endureth for ever" (II Chron. XX, 21), and R. Isaac has explained that the reason why the words "for he is good" do not appear in this chant, as in other passages where it is given, is because He was about to destroy the works of His hands before Israel. Similarly, at the time when Israel crossed the Red Sea, when the angels came as usual to chant their praises before God on that night, God said to them: "The works of my hands are drowning in the sea, and will you chant praises?"; hence it says, "and this (angel) drew not near to that one all the night" (Ex. XIV, 20). Thus whenever destruction of the wicked takes place, there is grief for them above.' R. Abba said: 'God had already been grieved when Adam sinned before Him and transgressed His commandment. He said to him: "Woe to thee that thou hast weakened the heavenly power, for at this moment thou hast quenched a light"; and forthwith He banished him from the Garden of Eden, saying: "I put thee in the garden to bring offerings, but thou hast impaired the altar so that offerings cannot henceforth be brought on it; henceforth therefore it is thy doom to labour at the ground." '

God also decreed that he should die. Taking pity on him, however, God allowed him when he died to be buried near the Garden of Eden. For Adam had made a cave near the Garden, and had hidden himself there with his wife. He knew it was near the Garden, because he saw a faint ray of light enter it from there, and therefore he desired to be buried in it; and there he was buried, close to the gate of the Garden of Eden. So it is that when a man is about to depart from life, Adam, the first man, appears to him and asks him why and in what state he leaves the world. He says: "Woe to thee that through thee I have to die." To which Adam replies: "My son, I transgressed one commandment and was punished for so doing; see how many commandments of your Master, negative and positive, you have transgressed".' R. Hiya said: 'Adam exists to this day, and twice a day he sees the patriarchs and confesses his sins, and shows them the place where once he abode in heavenly glory. He also goes and looks at all the pious and righteous among his descendants who have attained to celestial glory in the Garden of Eden. All the patriarchs then praise God, saying: "How precious is thy lovingkindness, O God, and the children of men take refuge under the shadow of thy wings" (Ps. xxxvi, 8).' R. Yesa said: 'Adam appears to every man at the moment of his departure from life to testify that the man is dying on account of his own sins and not the sin of Adam, according to the dictum, "there is no death without sin". There are only three exceptions, namely, Amram, Levi, and Benjamin, who were deprived of life through the prompting of the primeval serpent; some add also, Jesse. These did not sin, and no ground could be assigned for their death save the prompting of the serpent, as we have said.

'All the generations contemporary with Noah committed their sins openly, in the sight of all. R. Simeon was one day walking through the gate of Tiberias when he saw some men drawing the bow tight over earthenware pots. He cried: "What! do these miscreants dare to provoke their Master thus openly?" He scowled at them, and they were thrown into the sea and drowned. Take note that every sin which is committed openly repels the Shekinah and causes her to remove her abode from this world. The contemporaries of Noah committed their sins openly and defiantly, and so they drove the Shekinah away from the world, in punishment for which God removed them from the world, in accordance with the maxim, "Take away the dross from the silver, and there cometh forth a vessel for the finer; take away the wicked from before the king, and his throne shall be established in righteousness" (Prov. xxv, 4 and 5).'

AND THE LORD SAID, MY SPIRIT SHALL NOT STRIVE WITH MAN FOR EVER, FOR THAT HE ALSO IS FLESH. R. Eleazar said: 'When God created the universe, He ordained that this world should be served [58a] from the world above. Hence when mankind are virtuous and walk in the right path, God puts in motion the spirit of life from above until it comes to the place where Jacob abides. From there the life descends further until the spirit reaches the world in which David is located; and from there blessings descend on all here below, who through the streaming of the spirit from above are able to maintain their existence. Now, however, that men sinned, the streaming ceased, so that the spirit of life no longer descended on this world for the benefit of its denizens. "For that he also is flesh": i.e. in order that, through being shed over this world, the spirit might not benefit the serpent, the lowest of the grades, which might also have grasped hold of it; and the holy spirit ought not to mix with the unclean spirit. The reference in "he also" is to the primeval serpent, as in the verse, "the end of all flesh comes before me" (Gen. VI, 13), which R. Simeon explains to mean the angel of death. HIS DAYS SHALL BE A HUNDRED AND TWENTY YEARS: a period of grace for the continued union (of body and soul). THE NEFILIM WERE IN THE EARTH. R. Jose says, following a tradition, that these were Uzza and Azael, whom, as already mentioned, God deprived of their supernal sanctity. How, it may be asked, can they exist in this world? R. Hiya answers, that they were of the class of spirits referred to in the words "And birds which fly on the earth" (Gen. I, 20), and these, as we have said, appear to men in the form of human beings. If it is asked, how can they transform themselves? The answer is, as has been said, that they do in fact transform themselves into all kinds of shapes, because when they come down from heaven they become as concrete as air and take human shape. These are Uzza and Azael, who rebelled in heaven, and were cast down by God, and became corporeal on the earth and remained on it, not being able to divest themselves of their earthly form. Subsequently they went astray after women, and up to this day they exist and teach men the arts of magic. They begat children whom they called *Anakim* (giants), while the Nefilim themselves were called "sons of God", as has been elsewhere explained.

AND THE LORD SAID, I WILL DESTROY MAN WHOM I HAVE CREATED FROM THE FACE OF THE GROUND. R. Jose quoted in this connection the verse, *For my thoughts are not your thoughts* (Is. LV, 8). He said: 'When a man wants to take vengeance on another, he keeps his counsel and says nothing, for fear that, if he discloses his intention, the other will be on his guard and escape him. Not so God. Before punishing the world, God proclaims His intention once, twice, and three times, because there is none who can stay His hand and say to Him, "what doest Thou ?", and in vain would one attempt to guard against Him. So now God said, "I will blot out man whom I have created from the face of the earth"; He proclaimed His intention to them by the hand of Noah, and warned them several times, but they would not listen. Then at last He executed judgement on them and exterminated them.

AND HE CALLED HIS NAME NOAH SAYING, THIS SHALL COMFORT US, ETC. How did Noah's father know this ? In this way. When God cursed the earth, Adam said to Him, [58b] "Sovereign of the Universe, how long shall the earth be subject to this curse ?" God replied: "Until a descendant of yours shall be born circumcised, like yourself." So they waited until at last a child was born circumcised and marked with the holy sign. When his father saw this, and observed the Shekinah hovering over him, he called him Noah,[1] in anticipation of his future career. For up to his time men did not know the proper way to sow or reap or plough, and they used to work the ground with their hands. But when Noah came, he taught them the arts of husbandry, and devised for them the necessary implements. Hence it is written: "This one shall comfort us for our work and for the toil of our

---

[1] lit. 'rest'.

hands." It was indeed Noah who liberated the earth from its curse; for up to his time they used to sow wheat and reap thorns and thistles; hence Noah is called "a man of the ground" (Gen. IX, 20).' R. Judah said: 'The word *ish* (man) is applied to him because he was righteous, and through the sacrifice which he brought he liberated the earth from its curse. We see, then, how he received his name in anticipation of the future.' R. Judah once expounded the text: *Come, behold the works of the Lord,*[1] *who hath made desolations in the earth* (Ps. XLVI, 9). 'If,' he said, 'it had been the works of *YHVH*, then they would have brought more life into the world, but being the works of *Elohim*, they made desolation in the world.' Said R. Hiya to him: 'As you have raised this point, I take leave to differ from you. In my opinion, whichever name is used the result is beneficial; and in this verse we should, as our colleagues have pointed out, read not *shammoth* (desolations), but *shemoth* (names).' R. Isaac said: 'You are both right. As R. Hiya says, if the world had been created through the name which connotes mercy (*YHVH*), it would have been indestructible; but since it has been created through the name which connotes justice (*Elohim*), "desolations have been placed in the earth", and rightly so, since otherwise the world would not be able to endure the sins of mankind. Consider also this. When Noah was born, they gave him a name which connoted consolation, in the hope that it would work out its own fulfilment for them. His relation to God, however, is expressed by the same letters in the reverse order, viz. *HeN* (favour), as it is written, "and Noah found favour in the eyes of the Lord".' Said R. Jose: 'The names of the righteous influence their destiny for good, and those of the wicked for evil. Thus the anagram of Noah's name is *hen* (favour), and we find it written of him, "and Noah found favour in the eyes of the Lord"; whereas the anagram of the name of Er the (wicked) son of Judah is *ra'* (evil), and of him it is written, "and Er was evil in the sight of the Lord" (Gen. XXXVIII, 7). When Noah grew up, and saw how mankind were sinning before God, he withdrew himself from

---

[1] So our texts (*Yhvh*). But it is obvious from what follows that the *Zohar* read *Elohim* (God).

their society and sought to serve his Master, so as not to be led astray by them. He was especially diligent in the study of the book of Adam and the book of Enoch which we have mentioned, and from them he learnt the proper forms in which to worship God. This explains how it is that he knew it was incumbent upon him to bring an offering; it was these books which revealed to him the basis on which the existence of the world depends, to wit, the sacrifices, without which neither the higher nor the lower world can endure.'

R. Simeon was once travelling in company with his son R. Eleazar and R. Jose and R. Hiya. As they were going along steadily, R. Eleazar said, 'This is a favourable opportunity for hearing some explanation of the Torah.' R. Simeon thereupon commenced a discourse on the text: *Also when the fool walketh by the way, his understanding faileth him, etc.* (Eccl. x, 3). He said: 'If a man desires that his journey should be agreeable in the sight of God, he should, before he starts, take counsel of God and offer the appropriate prayer, according to the Rabbinical dictum based on the verse, "When righteousness goeth before him, then he shall set his feet on the way" (Ps. LXXXV, 14), for then the Shekinah is not parted from him. But of him who does not believe in his Master it is written, [59a] "Also when the fool walketh in the way, his understanding (lit. heart) faileth him." By "heart" is here designated the Holy One, blessed be He, who will not accompany him on the way nor lend him His support, because he is a man who does not believe in his Master and did not seek His support before starting on the journey. Likewise on the journey itself he does not busy his thoughts with the Torah, and for this reason also it is said that "his heart faileth him", because he does not walk with his Master and is not found in His path. Further, "he saith to all, it is folly": that is, when he does hear a word of true doctrine, he says it is folly to pay attention to it; like the man who was asked about the sign of the covenant imprinted on the flesh, and replied that it was no article of faith, whereupon R. Yeba the Elder frowned on him and he became a heap of bones. We, therefore, being on this journey with the support of the Almighty, are beholden to discuss some point of Torah.' He thereupon took the text: *Teach me thy way, O Lord, I will walk in thy truth, unite my heart to fear thy name* (Ps. LXXXVI, 11). He said: 'This verse seems to conflict with the Rabbinical dictum that a man's whole career is in the hands of heaven, save his choice of virtue or vice. If this is so, how could David make such a request as this of God? What David really asked, however, was only that God should teach him His ways, that is, open his eyes to know the right and proper way; then he would himself be able to walk in the way of truth without turning aside right or left. As for the expression "my heart", this has the same significance as in the verse "the rock of my heart and my portion" (Ps. LXXIII, 26). All this I entreat, he said, in order to fear Thy name, to cleave to Thy fear and to keep to the straight path. The words "to fear thy name" refer to David's allotted place in which the fear of God is located. Consider this. Every man who fears God is secure in his faith, since he is whole-hearted in the service of his Master. But he who does not constantly fear his Master is not truly possessed of faith, nor is he accounted worthy of a share in the future world.' R. Simeon further discoursed on the text: *But the path of the righteous is as the shining light, that shineth more and more unto the perfect day* (Prov. IV, 18). He said: 'Happy are the righteous in this world and the world to come, since God desires to glorify them. For their path is as "the shining light", that is to say, that radiant light which God created at the beginning of things, and which He set aside for the righteous in the future world. This "shineth more and more", for its brightness continually augments. But of the wicked it is written, "The way of the wicked is as darkness, they know not at what they stumble" (*Ibid.* 19). In truth they do know; but they walk in a crooked path, and will not stop to reflect that one day God will judge them in the future world, and chastise them with the punishments of Gehinnom. Then they will bewail themselves every day, saying, "Woe to us that we did not incline our ears and listen." But as for the righteous, God will illumine them in the future world and will give them their due reward in a place which eye has never beheld, as it is written, "Eye hath not seen beside thee, O God, what thou wilt do for him that waits for thee" (Is. LXIV, 3). Also, "And they shall go forth and look upon the carcasses of the men that have transgressed against me" (Is. LXVI, 24); and again, "And ye shall tread down the wicked, for they shall be ashes under the soles of your feet" (Mal. III, 21). Happy are the righteous in this world and in the world to come; of them it is written, "the righteous shall for ever inherit the earth" (Is. LX, 21), and also, "verily the righteous shall praise thy name, the upright shall dwell in thy presence" (Ps. CXL, 14). Blessed is the Lord for ever, Amen and Amen.'

NOAH

Gen. VI, 9–XI, 32

THESE ARE THE GENERATIONS OF NOAH. R. Hiya opened with the text: *And thy people are all righteous, they will inherit the land for ever ; the branch of my planting, the work of my hands wherein I glory* (Is. LX, 21). He said: 'Happy are the people of Israel, who occupy themselves with the Torah and are familiar with its paths, through following which they will merit the world to come. For all Israelites have a portion in the world to come, for the reason that they observe the covenant on which the world is established, and of which it is said: "If my covenant be not (observed) day and night, it were as if I had not appointed the ordinances of heaven and earth" (Jer. XXXIII, 25). Hence Israel, who have accepted the covenant and observe it, have a portion in the world to come. Furthermore, they are therefore called righteous. We learn this from Joseph, who, by reason of his having observed the covenant, is known as "Joseph the righteous".'

R. Eleazar said: 'The term "These are", as we have learnt, always implies that something spoken of before in the text is now of no account. Now it is written above in the account of the Creation[1] that "A river went out from Eden to water the garden and from thence it was parted, etc." (Gen. II, 10). That stream which flows perennially entered the Garden to water it from the supernal waters, and brought gladness to it, making it produce fruit and seed for the universal content; and so the stream gladdened the Garden, as it is written, "And he rested on the seventh day" (*Ibid.* 3). Thus the words "these are the generations" imply that this brought forth products and no other. So it was with Noah in the lower world. Noah was the sacred covenant below corresponding to that above, and hence is called "Man of the earth". The inner meaning which we learn from this is that Noah had need of an ark with which to become united

---

[1] Where also we find the expression 'these are the generations' (Gen. II, 4).

in order thereby to preserve the seed of all species, as it is written, "To preserve seed". This ark is the Ark of the Covenant, and Noah with the ark below corresponded to a similar union above. The word "covenant" is used in connection with Noah, as it is written, "And I will establish my covenant with thee", and before the covenant was established with him he did not enter the ark, as it is written, "And I will establish my covenant with thee and thou shalt come into the ark." Thus his ark represented the Ark of the Covenant, and Noah and the ark together were a symbol of the supernal pattern. And since this covenant above brought forth products, so Noah below also bore generations. Hence it says. "These are the generations of Noah."

NOAH WAS A RIGHTEOUS MAN. Assuredly so, after the supernal pattern. It is written, "The Righteous one is the foundation of the world" (Prov. x, 25), and the earth is established thereon, for this is the pillar that upholds the world. So Noah was called *Zaddik* (righteous) below. All this is implied in the words NOAH WALKED WITH GOD, meaning that he never separated himself from Him, and acted so as to be a true copy of the supernal ideal, a "Zaddik the foundation of the world", an embodiment of the world's covenant of peace. And it is thus that NOAH FOUND FAVOUR IN THE EYES OF GOD. PERFECT HE WAS IN HIS GENERATIONS: this refers to his descendants; he perfected them all, and he was more virtuous than all of them. Again, the words "He was perfect" indicate that he was born circumcised (cf. of Abraham, "Walk before me and *be perfect*, i.e. circumcised" Gen. XVII, 1). IN HIS GENERATIONS: and not in those of his contemporaries, for all future generations issued from him only. Consider this. From the day that the world was created, Noah was the first man fitted to be joined in union with the ark and to enter it, and until they were joined the world had not yet reached a stable condition. But once this had happened we read "From these all the earth was overspread" (Gen. x, 32). These words are analogous to the expression "And from thence the river parted" (*Ibid.* II, 10), of the Garden of Eden, which indicate that from this point there was a parting and diffusion of progeny into all quarters of the world. The two cases are analogous in every way. Hence it says: "*These* are the generations"; assuredly "these", as it was he who was the foundation of the world that brought forth [60a] generations to abide on the earth.' R. Abba then approached and kissed him, saying: 'The lion in his might has pierced through the rock and broken it asunder. Your exposition is certainly the right one, as can also be deduced from the measurements of the ark.'

THESE ARE THE GENERATIONS OF NOAH. R. Judah discoursed on the text: *The good man is gracious and lendeth, he ordereth his affairs according to justice* (Ps. CXII, 5). ' "The good man" refers to the Holy One, Blessed be He, since He is called "good" (as well as "Man"), as it is written, "The Lord is good to all" (*Ibid.* CXLV, 9), as well as "The Lord is a man of war" (Exod. XV, 3). Thus God is gracious and lends to that quarter which has no possession of its own, but derives its sustenance from Him. This idea is further developed in the sentence "He ordereth his affairs according to justice", indicating that that quarter is granted sustenance only according to justice, as it is written, "Righteousness and justice are the foundation of thy throne" (Ps. LXXXIX, 15). According to another explanation, the "good man" refers to the Righteous one (*Zaddik*), as it is written, "Say ye of the righteous one that he is good" (Is. III, 10). R. Jose said that it refers to Noah, as it is written, "Noah was a righteous man." R. Isaac said that it refers to the Sabbath, since the psalm in praise of the Sabbath commences with the words "It is a good thing to give thanks unto the Lord" (Ps. XCII, 2).' R. Hiya said: 'It is the *Zaddik* who produces offspring in the world. Who constitute this offspring? The souls of the righteous, these being the fruit of the handiwork of the Holy One, blessed be He.' R. Simeon said: 'When the Holy One, blessed be He, puts on his crowns, he receives them from above and from below: above, from the region of absolute remoteness; below, he is crowned by the souls of the righteous. The result is an increment of life-energy from above and below, embracing the place of the sanctuary on all sides, and causing the cisterns to become full and the sea to be replenished, and providing sufficiency for all. It is written: "Drink water out of thine own cistern, and running water out of thine own well" (Prov. v, 15). Why speak first of a cistern (*bor*), which is naturally waterless, and then of a well (*beer*), which is a fountain bubbling with water? In truth, both are one: this first refers to a certain region which is beset by poverty, and is thus called "cistern", as not possessing anything of its own save what is given to it: that region is called *daleth* (poverty, also the fourth letter of the alphabet). In time, however, it becomes a well, filled on all sides with bubbling water; it then typifies the letter *hé*, being filled from on high [60b] and bubbling up from below. It is filled from above in the way already explained, while its bubbling from below is from the souls of the righteous. (According to another interpretation, "drink water out of thine own cistern" refers to King David, who said, "Oh that one would give me water to drink of the cistern of Bethlehem" (II Sam. XXIII, 15); and "running waters" refers to Abraham; "out of the midst" refers to Jacob, he representing the centre; "thine own well" signifies Isaac, who is called "well of living waters". Thus in this verse is a reference to the sacred and honoured team of the three patriarchs with King David associated with them.) As the desire of the female towards the male only awakes when a certain spirit enters into her and the flow ascends to meet that of the male, so the congregation of Israel only conceives a longing for the Holy One, blessed be He, when it is permeated with the spirit of the righteous. It is then that its energy rises from below to meet the energy from above so as to form a perfect union. There flows from this a universal content, and it is then that the Holy One, blessed be He, walks familiarly among the souls of the righteous. See now, all the offspring of the Garden of Eden did not issue from the Righteous one until he entered into that ark of which we have spoken and became one with it—that ark which contained all in embryo. Similarly Noah the righteous man did not beget offspring to populate the world until he entered the ark in which all (life) was gathered and safely stored and from which it afterwards emerged to multiply in the world and to have an abiding existence on earth. Had not these creatures been through the ark they would not have endured in the world. And all this was planned after the supernal pattern. As they emerged from the Ark there on high, so they emerged from the ark here below. And thus the world then obtained the character of permanency which it had not possessed before. Hence the expression "And running waters out of the midst of thy well", which is echoed by the verse "And Noah begat three sons." '

AND THE EARTH WAS CORRUPTED BEFORE GOD. Said R. Judah: 'What does the phrase "before God" signify?' It signifies that they perpetrated their crimes openly in the eyes of all.' Said R. Jose: 'I interpret it in a reverse sense, namely, that at first "the earth was corrupted before God", that is, that they committed their sins secretly, so as to be known only to God but not to man. They finished, however, by coming out into the open, as it is written, AND THE EARTH WAS FILLED WITH VIOLENCE, indicating that there was not a place in the whole earth which did not witness their sins.' R. Abba said: 'From the time that Adam transgressed the command of his Master, all the succeeding generations were called "sons of Adam" in a derogatory sense, as much as to say, "the sons of the man who transgressed his Master's commands". But when Noah appeared, mankind were called by his name, to wit, "the generations of Noah", in an honourable sense, since he secured for them permanent existence in the world, and not "the generations of Adam", since he had caused them to be driven from the world and brought death to all.' Said R. Jose to him: 'But in a later passage (Gen. XI, 5) it is written, "and the Lord came down to see the city and the tower which the *children of Adam* had built"—Adam and not Noah.' R. Abba replied: 'It was because he was the first sinner. Better had it been for him that he should not have been created, so as not to be mentioned in this verse. See now, it is written: "A wise son causeth his father to rejoice" (Prov. x, 1). When a son is good, people mention his father's name with praise; but if he is bad, they mention his father with reproach. So it was with Adam. He transgressed the command of his Master, and therefore when later men arose who rebelled against their Master, they were designated by the Scripture "the sons of Adam", that is, the sons of the first man who rebelled against his Master and transgressed His commands. Hence "these are the generations of Noah"—these and not the former ones; these who entered into and emerged from the ark and brought forth generations to people the world; but they are not the generations of Adam, who emerged from the Garden of Eden without bringing any progeny forth from thence. For indeed, if Adam had brought offspring with him out of the Garden of Eden, these would never have been destroyed, the light of the moon would never have been darkened, and all would have lived for ever; and not even the angels would have equalled them in illumination and wisdom, as we read, "In the image of God he created him" (Gen. 1, 27). But since, [61a] through his sin, he left the Garden by himself and bore offspring outside it, these did not endure in the world, and this ideal was, therefore, not realised.' Said R. Hizkiah: 'How could they have begotten children there, seeing that, had the evil inclination not enticed him to sin, Adam would have dwelt for ever in the world by himself and would not have begotten children? In the same way, if Israel had not sinned by making the golden calf, they would not have borne children and no new generations would have come into the world.' R. Abba replied: 'If Adam had not sinned, he would not have begotten children from the side of the evil inclination, but he would have borne offspring from the side of the holy spirit. But now, since all the children of men are born from the side of the evil inclination, they have no permanence and are but short-lived, because there is in them an element of the "other side". But if Adam had not sinned and had not been driven from the Garden of Eden, he would have begotten progeny from the side of the holy spirit—a progeny holy as the celestial angels, who would have endured to eternity, after the supernal pattern. Since, however, he sinned and begat children outside the Garden of Eden, these did not take root, even in this world, until Noah arose, who was a righteous man and entered the ark, so that from the ark there went forth all the future generations of mankind, who spread thence into the four quarters of the earth.'

AND GOD SAW THE EARTH AND BEHOLD IT WAS CORRUPT. It was corrupt because "all flesh had corrupted its way", in the sense we have explained. R. Hiya adduced the following text: *And God saw their works that they turned from their evil way* (Jonah III, 10). 'See now,' he said, 'when the sons of men are righteous and observe the commands of the Torah, the earth becomes invigorated, and a fullness of joy pervades it, because then the Shekinah rests upon the earth, and there is thus gladness above as well as below. But when mankind corrupt their way and do not observe the commands of the Torah, and sin before their Master, they, as it were, thrust the Shekinah out of the world, and the earth is thus left in a corrupt state. For the Shekinah being thrust out, another spirit comes and hovers over the world, bringing with it corruption. It is in this sense that we say that Israel "gives strength unto Elohim", that is, to the Shekinah, and thereby makes the world more secure. Should, however, Israel—God forbid—prove sinful, then, in the words of the Scripture, "God withdraws himself above the heavens" (Ps. LVII, 6). Why ? Because "they have prepared a net for my footsteps, my soul is bent down", through their violence and causeless hatreds, "they have digged a pit before me" (*Ibid.* 7). The same thing happened with the generation of the Flood, whose violent acts led to mutual hatred and contention among them. We might think that the same applies to the Land of Israel. Our teachers, however, have laid down that no other spirit rests upon the Land of Israel, nor has it any guardian angel save God alone. There was, however, one occasion when another spirit did rest upon it in order to destroy the people. That was in the time of David, when, as it is written, "David saw the angel of the Lord . . . having a drawn sword in his hand stretched out over Jerusalem" (1 Chron. XXI, 16), and thus destruction came upon the land.'
R. Eleazar said: 'Even then it was the Holy One, blessed be He, Himself, the term "angel" here having the same meaning, as in the passages "the angel who redeemed me" (Gen.

XLVIII, 16), and "the angel of God removed" (Ex. XIV, 19). Be it for good or for ill, the Holy One, blessed be He, always has sway over it personally. For good, so that it should not be delivered into the hands of the "higher chieftains", and so that all the inhabitants of the world should be ashamed of their wicked deeds; for ill, so that the nations should not have the gratification of ruling over it. It is true, the Scripture says in one place, "For she hath seen that the heathen are entered into her sanctuary" (Lam. I, 10), and have destroyed the House, from which it may be inferred that if those alien chiefs had not had sway, the Temple would not have been destroyed. This, however, must not be stressed; for the Scripture also says, "For thou hast done it" (*Ibid.* I, 21), and "The Lord hath done what he hath devised" (*Ibid.* II, 17).' R. Hiya continued: 'It is written here, in connection with Noah, "And God saw the earth and behold it was corrupt." Contrast with this the verse "And God saw their deeds, and they had repented of their evil ways" (Jonah III, 10). There the earth called to God, reaching out towards heaven, and beautifying her face, as it were, like a woman trying to please her husband; so the earth tried to please God by raising up for Him righteous children. But here, when the generation of the Flood did not repent of their sins, it is written, "And God saw the earth, and behold it was corrupt", like a faithless wife who hides her face from before her husband. But when mankind committed sin upon sin openly and flagrantly, then the earth became brazen-faced like an abandoned female without any sense of shame, as it is said on another occasion, "And the earth was defiled under its inhabitants" (Is. XXIV, 5). Hence this is the connection here: "God saw that the earth was corrupted", why? "Because all [61*b*] flesh had corrupted their way upon the earth".'

R. Eleazar went to see R. Jose, the son of R. Simeon, the son of Lakunia, his father-in-law. The latter, as soon as he saw him, spread out for him a carpet under a canopy, on which they sat down. He asked his son-in-law, 'Did you happen to hear from your father the interpretation of the verse: *The Lord hath done that which he devised, he hath performed his word that he commanded in the days of old*

(Lam. II, 17)?' He answered, 'Our colleagues have interpreted it thus. They take the words *bitza imratho* ("He hath performed his word") to mean "He rent his purple cloak"—that cloak which "he commanded from days of old", that is, which He had appointed from the beginning of things. On the day the Temple was destroyed He rent that purple cloak which was His glory and ornament.' Said R. Jose: 'What of the words "the Lord hath done that which he (had already) devised"? Does a king devise evil against his sons before they sin?' R. Eleazar replied: 'Imagine a king who possessed a precious vase, and who, being constantly apprehensive lest it should be broken, had it ever under his eyes, and never lost sight of it for a moment. One day his son came and provoked him to anger, so that in his rage he took up the vase and broke it in pieces. In this way the Lord "hath done that which he had already devised". From the day when the Temple was built, the Holy One, blessed be He, used to contemplate it fondly, and every time He came to the sanctuary, He used to put on the purple cloak we have mentioned. But when Israel sinned, and provoked their King, the Temple was destroyed, and the mantle was rent. Only on that occasion did God mourn the destruction of the wicked, but at any other time the Holy One, blessed be He, takes joy in nothing so much as in the destruction of the world's sinners, and of those who have provoked Him to anger, as it is written, "And when the wicked perish there is joy" (Prov. XI, 10). So throughout the generations, whenever justice is executed on sinners, there is joy and thanksgiving before the Holy One, blessed be He. But, you may say, is there not a dictum of the Rabbis that the Holy One, blessed be He, does not rejoice when he executes judgement on sinners? The truth is that He does take joy in the destruction of the wicked, but only when He has been long-suffering with them and they have still remained unrepentant. But if He exacts punishment from them before that time, before the measure of their sins has been completed (cf. "For the iniquity of the Amorite is not yet full", Gen. XV, 16), then there is no joy before Him, but, on the contrary, He is grieved at their destruction. Another difficulty here arises:

if their time has not come, why should punishment be at all inflicted on them? But, indeed, they themselves are to blame for this. For the Holy One, blessed be He, never inflicts punishment on the wicked before the full time, except when they interfere with Israel in order to do them harm. It is then that He inflicts punishment upon them before the full time, and it is then that their destruction grieves Him. It was for this reason that He drowned the Egyptians in the Red Sea, and destroyed the enemies of Israel in the days of Jehoshaphat, and inflicted punishment on others; they were all destroyed before the full time on account of Israel. But if the time of respite expires without their showing any sign of repentance, then their destruction is a cause of joy and glory before Him. Nevertheless, it was not so with the destruction of the Temple; for on that occasion, although Israel had filled up the cup of provocation, there was no joy before Him, and since that time there has been no joy, neither above nor below.'

FOR YET SEVEN DAYS, AND I WILL CAUSE IT TO RAIN UPON THE EARTH FORTY DAYS AND FORTY NIGHTS. R. Judah said: 'What is the point of mentioning the exact period? The answer is that forty is the appropriate number for the punishment of sinners, in accordance with the ordinance, "Forty stripes he may give him, he shall not exceed" (Deut. xxv, 3). Further, this number corresponds to the four quarters of the world, so that there were ten for each quarter. For since man was created from the four quarters of the world, and the decree went forth, "And I will blot out every living substance that I have made from the face of the earth", forty were required for this purpose.' R. Isaac studied regularly with R. Simeon. One day he asked him: 'With reference to the passage "And the earth was corrupt", [62a] if men sinned, why should the earth be called corrupt?' R. Simeon replied: 'We find a parallel in the passage, "And the land was defiled, therefore I did visit the iniquity thereof upon it" (Lev. XVIII, 25), where the same problem arises. The explanation is that mankind constitute the essence of the earth, so that they infect the earth with their own corruption. This is made clear by the language of the Scripture in the passage, "And God saw the earth, and behold it was corrupt, *for* all flesh had corrupted their way upon the earth." For indeed all the other sins of man, involving but his own corruption, admit of repentance. But the sin of onanism is one by which man corrupts both himself and the earth; and of such a one it is written, "The stain of thine iniquity remains before me" (Jer. II, 22), also "For thou art not a God that hath pleasure in wickedness, evil shall not sojourn with thee" (Ps. v, 5), and it is further written, "And Er, Judah's firstborn, was wicked in the sight of the Lord, and the Lord slew him" (Gen. XXXVIII, 7), as explained elsewhere.' R. Judah further asked, "Why did the Holy One, blessed be He, punish the world with water, and not with fire or any other element?" R. Simeon replied: 'There is a mystical reason, based on the fact that they "corrupted their ways". As their sin consisted in not allowing the upper and lower waters to meet in conjunction, as they ought, so were they punished with water. Further, the waters of the Deluge were burning hot, and caused their skins to peel off, this being a meet punishment for the sin they committed in wasting the warm fluid. It was all measure for measure. The words in the text, "All the fountains of the great deep were broken open" refer to the lower waters, and the words "And the windows of Heaven were opened" refer to the upper waters. Thus were the two waters combined as a fit punishment for their sins.'

R. Hiya and R. Judah, while once going on their travels, came to some huge mountains, in the ravines of which they found human bones left over from the generation of the Flood. They measured a bone and found to their amazement that it was three hundred paces long. They said: 'This bears out what our colleagues have said, that the men of the time of the Flood did not fear the vengeance of the Holy One, blessed be He, as it is written, "They said unto God, Depart from us, for we desire not the knowledge of thy ways" (Job XXI, 14), and that one of the things they did was to stop up with their feet the fountains of the deep, until the waters which bubbled up became too hot for them to endure, so that they finally succumbed and fell to the ground and died.'

AND NOAH BEGAT THREE SONS.[1] Said R. Hiya to R. Judah: 'Let me tell you what I have heard regarding this text. A man once entered the recesses of a cavern, and there issued two or three children together, who differed from one another in their character and conduct: one was virtuous, a second vicious, and a third average. Similarly we find three strands of spirit which flit about and are taken up into three different worlds. The *neshamah* (spiritual soul) emerges and enters between the gorges of the mountains, where it is joined by the *ruah* (intellectual spirit). It descends then below where the *nefesh* (vital spirit) joins the *ruah*, and all three form a unity.' R. Judah said: 'The *nefesh* and the *ruah* are intertwined together, whereas the *neshamah* resides in a man's character—an abode which cannot be discovered or located. Should a man strive towards purity of life, he is aided thereto by a holy *neshamah*, whereby he is purified and sanctified and attains the title of "saint". But should he not strive for righteousness and purity of life, he is animated only by the two grades, *nefesh* and *ruah*, and is devoid of a holy *neshamah*. What is more, he who commences to defile himself is led further into defilement, and heavenly help is withdrawn from him. Thus each is led along the path which he chooses.' [62b]

AND GOD SAID TO NOAH, THE END OF ALL FLESH IS COME BEFORE ME. R. Judah illustrated this passage from the verse: *Lord, make me know mine end, and the measure of my days what it is; let me know how short lived I am* (Ps. XXXIX, 5). He said: 'David said before the Holy One, blessed be He, "There are two 'ends', one on the right and one on the left, these being the two paths by which men proceed towards the other world." The end on the right is referred to in the words "at the end of the right" (Daniel XII, 13); and the end on the left in the words "He setteth an end to darkness, and the ending of all things does he search out" (Job XXVIII, 3). "End" here is the angel of destruction, who is also the serpent, and who is called "End of all flesh". When the doom of destruction is hanging over the world,

---

[1] This paragraph is out of place. It should properly follow 'begat three sons', on p. 196.

this "searches out" and explores every avenue through which it can bring accusations against the world so as to reduce men to despair. [63a] The term "end of the right", as already said, is based on the phrase "at the end of the right" in the book of Daniel. The Holy One, blessed be He, said to Daniel, "Thou shalt go towards the end, and wilt rest" (Dan. XII, 13). Daniel asked: "Rest in this world or in the next world?" "Rest in the next world", was the answer (cf. "They will rest in their beds", Is. LVII, 2), "and thou shalt stand up to thy lot at the end of days". Daniel asked, "Shall I be among the resurrected or not?" God answered, "And thou wilt stand up." Daniel then said, "I know full well that the dead will rise up in various classes, some righteous and some wicked, but I do not know among whom I shall be found." God answered, "To thy lot." Daniel then said, "As there is a right end and a left end, I do not know whether I shall go to the right end (*l'qets hayamin*) or to the end of days (*l'qets hayamim*)." The answer was, "To the end of the right (*l'qets hayamin*)." Similarly, David said to the Holy One, blessed be He, "make me to know my end", that is, he wished to know to which end he was allotted, and his mind was not at rest till the good tidings reached him, "Sit at my right hand" (Ps. CX, 1). So to Noah also the Holy One, blessed be He, said, "The end of all flesh is come before me." The term "end", as we have seen, alludes to the angel of death, who reduces men to despair, and who is indeed the end of all flesh. "Is come before me": from this we learn that though the wicked go half-way to meet him and draw him to themselves, yet only after he receives authorisation does he take a man's soul: he cannot take it before. Hence we read "is come before me", to wit, to obtain permission to darken the faces of mankind, and so "I will destroy them with the earth". Hence the command given to Noah, MAKE THEE AN ARK OF GOPHER WOOD, to save thyself therein and so that he should not have power over thee. There was also another reason. We have a dictum that when death rages in a town or in the world at large, no man should show himself in the street, because the destroying angel is then authorised to kill indiscriminately. Hence the Holy One, blessed be He, said to Noah, "It behoves thee to take heed to thyself and not show thyself before the destroyer, so that he may have no power over thee." You may perhaps say that there was not here any destroying angel, but only the onrush of the overwhelming waters. This is not so; no doom is ever executed on the world, whether of annihilation or any other chastisement, but the destroying angel is in the midst of the visitation. So here there was indeed a flood, but this was only an embodiment of the destroyer who assumed its name. Hence the command given to Noah to hide himself and not to show himself abroad. But, you may object further, the ark was exposed to full view in the midst of the world through which the destroyer was roaming. The answer is that this made no difference, since, as long as the face of a man is not seen by the destroyer, he has no power over him. We learn this from the precept given at the time of the Exodus, "and none of you shall go out of the door of his house until the morning" (Ex. XII, 22), the reason being that the destroyer was then abroad with power to destroy anyone who showed himself. For the same reason Noah withdrew himself and all under his charge into the ark, so that the destroyer had no power over him.'

R. Hiya and R. Jose in the course of their travels came to the mountains of Kurdistan, and observed there some deep ravines which had been left from the Flood. Said R. Hiya: 'These ravines are vestiges of the days of the Flood, and the Holy One, blessed be He, has left them throughout the generations so that the sins of the wicked should not be blotted out from before Him. For just as God causes the memory of those who do His will to endure on high and here below from generation to generation, so He ordains that the evil memory of the sins of the wicked who have not obeyed Him shall not pass away but remain for all generations, as it is written, "The stain of thine iniquity remains before me" (Jer. II, 22).'

R. Jose discoursed on the text: *Cry thou with a shrill voice, oh daughter of Gallim! Hearken, oh Laish! Oh thou poor Anathoth!* (Is. x, 30). He said: 'Our companions have already interpreted this verse in their own way, but in truth it refers to the Community of Israel, called "the daughter of springs" (*Gallim*), on the analogy of the expression, "A spring (*gal*) shut up" (S. S. IV, 12). The term "spring" has special reference to those streams that converge and flow into the Garden, as it is written, "Thy shoots are a garden (*pardes*) of pomegranates" (*Ibid.* 13). The term *laisha* is akin to the term *laish* in "the lion (*laish*) perisheth for lack of prey" (Job IV, 11). Why is the Community of Israel called "lion"? It might be in allusion to "the lion which is mighty among beasts" (Prov. XXX, 30), or again to "the lion perisheth for lack of prey". But indeed, the two aspects are combined in it. At one time it is *laish* (he lion), filled with the lower-world energy emanating from the higher-world energy; and then again it is reduced to the state of "a lion perishing for lack of prey", when the rivers dry up and do not come to replenish her, at which time she is rather called *laisha* (lioness). [63b] The name *laisha* is further explained by the words which immediately follow, *aniah anathoth*, which properly mean 'poorest of the poor". The word *anathoth* is found with a similar meaning in the passage "of the priests that were in Anathoth" (Jer. I, 1). Another example of the word used in this sense is in the verse "Anathoth, get thee unto thine own fields" (I Kings II, 26). The meaning of this verse is as follows. So long as King David was alive, Abiathar was wealthy and prosperous; but after David died, Solomon ordered him to get to his own fields, calling him "Anathoth". Why did he give him this name? It cannot be because this was the name of the town he came from, since it is written, "and one of the sons of Ahimelech the son of Ahitub, named Abiathar, escaped" (I Sam. XXII, 20), which proves that he belonged to Nob, the city of the priests. Some, indeed, are of opinion that Anathoth and Nob are two names of the same place, the name "Anathoth" having been given to it on account of the poverty and destitution to which it had been reduced by Saul through the slaughter of all its priestly inhabitants. This, however, is incorrect, as Anathoth was distinct from Nob. The real reason why Solomon called Abiathar "Anathoth" is to be found in the words "and because thou wast afflicted (*hithanitha*) in all wherein my father was afflicted" (1 Kings II, 26); thus the name "Anathoth" alludes to the poverty and affliction which he underwent in the time of David.'

R. Hiya said: 'The world was in a state of poverty and misery from the time Adam transgressed the command of the Almighty until Noah came and offered up a sacrifice, when its prosperity returned.' R. Jose said: 'The world was not properly settled, nor was the earth purged from the defilement of the serpent, until Israel stood before Mount Sinai, where they laid fast hold of the Tree of Life, and so established the world firmly. Had not Israel backslided and sinned before the Holy One, blessed be He, they would never have died, since the scum of the serpent had been purged out of them. But as soon as they sinned, the first tablets of the Law were broken—those tablets which spelt complete freedom, freedom from the serpent who is the "end of all flesh". When the Levites rose up to slay the guilty, the evil serpent went in front of them, but he had no power over Israel, because they were girt with a certain armour which protected them against his attacks. When, however, God said to Moses, "Therefore now put off thy ornaments from thee" (Ex. XXXIII, 5), this was the signal that they were placed in the power of the serpent (this is indicated by the form *vayithnaselu*, which shows that they were stripped by the hand of another). The ornaments referred to are those which they received at Mount Horeb at the time when the Torah was given to Israel.' R. Hiva said: 'Why did not Noah, being a righteous man, cause death to vanish from the world? The reason is that the scum of the serpent had not yet been removed from the world, and further, that his generation did not believe in the Holy One, blessed be He, and all of them clung to the "lower leaves of the tree", and were clothed with an unclean spirit. Furthermore, they persisted in their sins, and followed their evil inclination as before, and the holy Torah, which is the Tree of Life, had not yet been brought down to the earth. Moreover, Noah himself drew death into the world, through his own sin, of which it is written, "And he drank of the wine and was drunken, and he was uncovered within his tent" (Gen. IX, 21), as elsewhere explained.'

As they were going along they saw a man coming towards them. Said R. Jose: 'This man is a Jew.' When he came up to them they asked him who he was. He said: 'I am on a religious errand from the village of Ramin, where I live. As it is near the Feast of Tabernacles, we require a palm branch with its accessories. I am therefore on my way to pluck them.' They all then walked on together. The Judean said to them: 'In regard to these four plants which we take in order to propitiate the Almighty, have you heard why we require them precisely on the Feast of Tabernacles?' Said R. Jose to him: 'Our colleagues have already discussed this question. But if you have any explanation of your own, tell us.' He replied: 'The place where we live is indeed only a little hamlet, but all its inhabitants diligently study the Torah under the guidance of a learned teacher, R. Isaac the son of Jose by name, of Mehozah, who every day gives us some fresh explanation of points in the Torah. Regarding this festival, he explained that this is the fitting period for Israel to obtain dominion over the chiefs who have charge of the nations of the Gentiles, and who are called by them "the proud waters" (Ps. CXXIV, 6). In order to obtain dominion over them, we come with a symbolic representation of the Divine name by means of the four plants, which we also take for the purpose of placating the Almighty [64a] so as to procure for ourselves a plenitude of sacred waters with which to pour a libation on the altar. He further told us that on the New Year there is in the world "a first stirring". What is meant by "a first stirring"? This is the lower-world tribunal which bestirs itself to bring the world to judgement, as God then sits in judgement over the world. This tribunal continues in session until the Day of Atonement, when the face of the moon is bright, and the slanderous serpent leaves the world alone, being occupied with the he-goat which has been offered to him—an appropriate offering, as the goat is from the "impure region". Being occupied with that goat, he does not come near the sanctuary. This goat performs the same function as the goat offered up on the New Moon, with which also the serpent occupies himself, allowing the moon to grow bright. In consequence, all Israel find favour in the eyes of the Almighty, and their guilt is removed. He further discoursed to us on another mystery which it is not permitted to disclose save to those of excelling wisdom, saintliness, and piety.' 'What is it?' asked R. Jose. 'I cannot say unless I first test you,' replied the Jew. They then proceeded on their way, and after a time he said: 'When the moon approaches the sun, the Holy One, blessed be He, stirs up the northern side, and it grasps the moon lovingly and draws her towards itself. Then the South awakens from the other side, and the moon rises and joins the East. She thus draws sustenance from two sides, and noiselessly receives blessings; and thus it is that the moon is blessed and attains her fullness. Now as there is a symbolical attribution of members to the (supernal) Adam, so there is to the (supernal) Female, and so, too, there is the symbolism of another Adam under the moon, and also of a Female. As the Left Arm above grasps the Female and lovingly draws her to him, so below the serpent, which is the left arm of the unclean spirit, and joined with it he that rides on it, draw near to the moon and draw her tightly to them, so that she becomes defiled. Israel, therefore, here below offer up a goat, to which the serpent is drawn away. The moon then purges herself, ascends on high, and unites herself to the higher sphere to receive blessing, and her lower face, which was darkened, becomes bright. So here on the Day of Atonement, since the evil serpent is occupied with the he-goat, the moon breaks loose from him, and earnestly pleads the cause of Israel, and watches over them like a mother over her children, so that the Holy One, blessed be He, blesses them from above and forgives their sins. Afterwards, when Israel celebrate the Feast of Tabernacles, the "right side" is awakened on high, so that the moon may attach herself to it and her face may become completely bright. She then shares out blessings to all those presiding chiefs of the lower world, so that they may be fully occupied with their own portions, and not attempt to draw sustenance from the side from which Israel obtained their portion. The same thing happens here below. When all the other nations receive their blessings, they are fully occupied with their own portions, and so do not come and meddle with Israel or covet the portion of their heritage. Israel for this reason cause blessings to flow to all those presiding chiefs, in order that they may be absorbed with their own portions and not meddle with that of Israel. And when the moon obtains her due fill of blessings, Israel come and draw sustenance from her all by themselves; and of this it is written, "on the eighth day there shall be to you a solemn gathering" (*atsereth*, Num. XXIX, 35). This "gathering" indicates the gathering of all the blessings from above, from which no other nation draws sustenance save Israel; hence "there shall be to *you* a gathering", to you, and not to the other nations and presiding chiefs. And for this reason Israel entreats Heaven to grant a plenitude of rain, so as to accord the nations their share of blessings, that they may be fully occupied therewith, and not meddle in the festivity of Israel, who imbibe the superior blessings. Concerning this day it is written, "My beloved is mine and I am his" (S. S. II, 16), and there is no third one with us. The following parable will make this clearer. A king once invited his favourite to a special feast on an appointed day, thus making known to him [64b] that he stood high in the favour of the king. The king, however, was apprehensive lest in the midst of the feast all the governors of his provinces might put in an appearance, sit down to table, and partake of the repast intended for his beloved friend. What did he do ? He first treated his governors and ministers to a repast of meat and vegetables. Afterwards he sat down with his favourite to that special banquet where all the finest delicacies of the world were spread before them ; and whilst alone with the king the favourite laid before him all his petitions and requests, which the king granted. Thus the king enjoyed the company of his friend alone and undisturbed. So it is with Israel in their relation to the Holy One, blessed be He, and hence it is written, "the eighth day shall be to you a gathering".' Said R. Hiya and R. Jose: 'The Holy One, blessed be He, has led our footsteps in the right path. Happy those who occupy themselves with the Torah.' With these words they came up to him and embraced him. R. Jose applied to him the verse, "And all thy children shall be taught of the Lord, and great shall be the peace of thy children" (Is. LIV, 13).

When they came to a certain field, the stranger discoursed thus. 'In the account of the destruction of Sodom and Gomorrah it is written, "And the Lord (*YHVH*) caused to rain, etc." (Gen. XIX, 24), whereas throughout the narrative of the Flood the term Elohim (God) is used exclusively. What is the reason for this difference? We have been taught that the term *V-YHVH* (and the Lord), wherever written indicates the Deity presiding over his Court of Justice, whereas the term Elohim (God) is used when the Deity judges alone. Now the destruction of Sodom was limited to one locality, and did not involve the whole world, hence it was decreed in open court, as indicated by the term *V-YHVH* (and the Lord); whereas the Flood overwhelmed the whole world, and therefore had to be decreed by the Deity alone, in concealment, as it were; hence the term Elohim. (As for Noah and his companions, they were only saved through being carefully concealed from sight.) In this light we explain the verse "The Lord sat at the Flood" (Ps. XXIX, 10), that is, He sat as it were all by Himself, on the analogy of the expression "He shall sit alone" (Lev. XIII, 46). Now it is because Noah was completely hidden from sight that, after the world had suffered its doom and the wrath of the Deity had been appeased, we read AND GOD (ELOHIM) REMEMBERED NOAH, for Noah having been so long out of sight had to be specially brought to mind. From this passage we derive the mystical doctrine that the Holy One, blessed be He, is sometimes discoverable and sometimes undiscoverable. He is discoverable when presiding over the lower Court. He remains undiscoverable in the spot whence all blessings flow. Hence those possessions of a man which are hidden from sight are receptive of the heavenly blessing; whereas things which are exposed to view attract the notice of the accuser, and are subject to the influence of him who is named "Evil of eye". There is a deep mystery which connects all this with the supernal pattern.' R. Jose, with tears in his eyes, said: 'Happy is the generation in which R. Simeon flourishes, for it is through his merit that we have been privileged to hear so sublime a discourse as this.' R. Jose said further, 'God must have sent that man on this road to impart to us these ideas.' When they came to R. Simeon and repeated to him all they had heard, he said, 'Of a truth he spoke well.'

R. Eleazar, studying one day with his father, R. Simeon, asked him, 'Did the "End of all flesh" derive nourishment from the sacrifices which Israel used to offer on the altar?' His father replied: 'All alike derived sustenance from them, both above and below. Consider this. The priests, the Levites, and the Israelites are called Adam (Man), through the unison of the holy liturgies which proceed from them. Whenever a sheep or a lamb, or any animal, was brought as an offering, it was required of those who brought it, before it was offered on the altar, to recite over it all sins and evil intentions and thoughts, and to make confession of them, and it is thus that the creature is designated a *b'hemah* (animal) throughout, in that it carries these sins and evil thoughts. As in the case of the *Azazel* (scapegoat) offering it is written, "And he shall confess over him all the iniquities of the children of Israel, etc." (Lev. XVI, 21), so it is here: the one offering brought on the altar bears a twofold burden. Consequently each part goes to its fitting place, the one *qua* "man" and the other *qua* "beast", as we read, "Man and beast thou dost save, O Lord" (Ps. XXXVI, 7). Baked meal-offering or other meal-offerings are the means of invoking the Holy Spirit on the service of the priests, the song of the Levites, and the prayer of the Israelites; and from the smoke that rises up from the oil and the flour all the accusers replenish themselves, [65a] so that they are powerless to pursue the indictment which has been delivered into their hands. Thus we see that things have been so arranged in the mystery of faith that the adversary should have his share in the holy things, and that the requisite portion should ascend even to the Limitless.'

R. Simeon said: 'When praying, I raise my hand on high, that when my mind is concentrated on the highest, there is higher still that which can never be known or grasped, the starting-point that is absolutely concealed, that produced what it produced while remaining unknowable, and irradiated what it irradiated while remaining undisclosed. It is the desire of the upward-striving thought to pursue after this and to be illumined by it. In the process a certain fragment is detached, and from that fragment, through the pursuit of the upward-striving thought, which reaches and yet does not reach it, there is a certain illumination. The upward-striving thought is thus illumined by a light undisclosed and unknowable even to that thought. That unknowable light of Thought impinges on the light of the detached fragment which radiates from the unknowable and undisclosed, so that they are fused into one light, from which are formed nine Palaces (*Hekaloth*). These Palaces are neither lights nor spirits nor souls, neither is there anyone who can grasp them. The longing of the nine illuminations which are all centred in the Thought—the latter being indeed counted as one of them—is to pursue these Palaces at the time when they are stationed in the thought, though they are not (even then) grasped or known, nor are they attained by the highest effort of the mind or the thought. All the mysteries of faith are contained in those Palaces, and all those lights which proceed from the mystic supreme Thought are called *EN-SOF* (Limitless). Up to this point the lights reach and yet do not reach: this is beyond the attainment of mind and thought. When Thought illumines, though from what source is not known, it is clothed and enveloped in *Binah* (understanding), and then further lights appear and one is embraced with the other until all are intertwined. The symbolism of the sacrifices consists, then, in this. When the whole ascends one part is knit with the other and its elements shine through one another, so that all ascend and the thought is embraced in the limitless. The light from which the upward-striving thought is illumined is called *En-Sof*, and from it all radiation proceeds and on it is based the whole of existence. Happy the portion of the righteous in this world and in the world to come. In regard, then, to the "end of all flesh", just as there is unison above with joy (at the time of the sacrifice), so also below there is joy and appeasement. There is thus satisfaction both above and below, and the Mother of Israel watches lovingly over her children. Consider this. At every New Moon the "End of all flesh" is given a portion over and above that of the daily offering, so as to divert his attention from Israel, who are thus left entirely to themselves and in full freedom to commune with their King.

This extra portion comes from the he-goat (*sa'ir*), being the portion of Esau, who is also called *sa'ir*, as it is written, "Behold Esau my brother is a hairy (*sa'ir*) man" (Gen. XXVII, 11). Esau thus has his portion and Israel their portion. Hence it is written, "For the Lord hath chosen Jacob unto himself, and Israel for his own treasure" (Ps. CXXXV, 4). Consider this point. The whole desire of this "End of all flesh" is for flesh only, and the tendency of flesh is ever towards him; it is for this reason that he is called "End of all flesh". Such power, however, as he does obtain is only over the body and not over the soul. The soul ascends to her place, and the body is given over to its place, in the same way as in an offering the devotion of him who offers ascends to one place, and the flesh to another. Hence the righteous man is, of a truth, himself an offering of atonement. But he who is not righteous is disqualified as an offering, for the reason that he suffers from a blemish, and is therefore like the defective animals of which it is written, "they shall not be accepted for you" (Lev. XXII, 25). Hence it is that the righteous are an atonement and a sacrifice for the world.' [65*b*]

AND NOAH WAS SIX HUNDRED YEARS OLD. Why is Noah's age specified here ? The reason is that if he had not reached this age, he would not yet have been qualified to enter the ark and become united with it. Hence, after the measure of the world's sins had been completed, God respited them until Noah, having lived to the age of six hundred years, reached his full development and attained the condition of "a man righteous and perfect". Then it was that he entered the ark, and reproduced the supernal pattern.

AND I, BEHOLD I DO BRING THE FLOOD OF WATERS. Note the repetition of the term "behold I" after "I". The explanation is as follows: Wherever the term *ani* (I) is used of the Deity, it signifies, as it were, the relation of a body to a soul which inspires it. For this reason it is figuratively called "the sign of the covenant" in the passage "I (*ani*) behold (am) my covenant with thee" (Gen. XVII, 4), i.e. "I" who am manifest and in course of becoming known; "I" the throne to the Essence on high; "I" who exact vengeance from generation to generation. The word *va'ani* (and I) embodies male and female in conjunction; afterwards the male is noted separately, as being held in readiness to execute judgement, in the word "behold I" (*hineni*). I DO BRING THE FLOOD OF WATERS. If "flood", why also "waters"? The truth is that the term "flood" here indicates the angel of death, who was the chief agent of destruction, although he used the waters as his instrument. With reference to the word *ani*, our teachers have explained that the expression "I am (*ani*) the Lord" is equivalent to "I am faithful to recompense the righteous and to punish the wicked"; hence Scripture always uses the term *ani* (I) in recording God's promise to the righteous to reward them and His threat to the wicked to punish them in the world to come. TO DESTROY ALL FLESH: to wit, through the world's destroying angel, as already explained; the same that is referred to in the verse "And he will not suffer the destroyer to come into your houses to smite you" (Ex. XII, 23). Hence "to destroy all flesh" means, from the side of "the end of all flesh". For as soon as the time of grace expired which God granted them till Noah should reach the age of six hundred years, then the moment arrived to "destroy all flesh".

R. Simeon discoursed on the text: *I said, I shall not see the Lord, even the Lord in the land of the living; I shall behold man no more with the inhabitants of the world* (Is. XXXVIII, 11). 'How obtuse,' he said, 'are the sons of men who do not know nor pay heed to the words of the Torah, but think only of worldly matters, so that the spirit of wisdom is forgotten of them. For when a man departs from this world, and goes to give an account to his Master of all his actions in this world while body and soul were still joined together, he sees many strange things on his way, and at length meets Adam, the first man, sitting at the gate of the Garden of Eden, ready to welcome with joy all those who have observed the commands of their Master. Round him are many righteous men, those who in this life have kept clear of the path to Gehinnom and followed the path to the Garden of Eden. It is these who are here called "inhabitants of the world". The word used for "world" here is not the usual *ḥoled*, but *ḥadel*. The reason is that *ḥoled* is akin to *ḥuldah* (mole), a creature whose characteristic it is laboriously to heap up provision and leave it to it knows not whom. The term *ḥodel*, on the other hand, is derived from a root signifying "avoidance", and thus is a description of the righteous who avoid and keep far from the ways of Gehinnom and cling to those leading to the Garden of Eden. According to another interpretation, the expression "inhabitants of *ḥodel*" designates penitents who have resolutely kept clear of their former sins, and since Adam was the first penitent, he was given charge of all penitents, those who are called "sons of hodel" (avoidance), and he therefore sits at the gate of the Garden of Eden, welcoming with joy and gladness the righteous who take the path to the Garden of Eden. It says further in the same passage: "I will not see God". Naturally one cannot see God, but the expression is explained by the concluding words, "God in the land of the living". When souls ascend to the place of the "bundle of life" (v. 1 Sam. xxv, 29), they feast their eyes on the beams of the "refulgent mirror" which radiates [66a] from the most sublime region. And were the soul not clothed in the resplendency of another (i.e. nonfleshly) garment, it would not be able to approach that effulgence. The esoteric doctrine is that in the same way as the soul has to be clothed in a bodily garment in order to exist in this world, so is she given an ethereal supernal garment wherewith to exist in the other world, and to be enabled to gaze at the effulgence of life radiating from that "land of the living". Hence it is that Moses was not able to draw near to the place of God and to fix his gaze on what was to be seen there until he was first enveloped in another garment, as we read: "And Moses entered into the midst of the cloud, and went up into the mount" (Ex. XXIV, 18), that is, he enveloped himself in the cloud, as in a garment, and then he "drew near into the thick darkness where God was" (Ex. xx, 18), and "was in the mount forty days and forty nights" (*Ibid*. XXIV, 18), and was able to see what he did see. In similar fashion the souls of the righteous in the other world clothe themselves in garments belonging to that world, so that they can endure to gaze on the light which is diffused in that "land of the living". This is what Hezekiah meant when he said "God, God in the land of the living" (Is. XXXVIII, 11). He was afraid that he would be found unworthy to gaze on that light because he had allowed the life-giving stream to cease with him, through not begetting children. In his further words, "I shall behold Adam no more" (*Ibid.*), there is a reference to Adam the first man, as has already been explained. He spoke in this strain because the prophet had told him, "for thou shalt die and not live" (*Ibid.* 1), "die", that is, in this world, and "not live" in the other world. For he who does not beget children in this world is denied all the blissfulness we have mentioned, and he is not privileged to contemplate the glorious effulgence. If this was the case with Hezekiah, who came of pious ancestors, and was himself worthy, righteous and pious, how much more so must it be the case with one who has no such ancestral merit to support him, and has himself sinned before his Master? That garment of which we have spoken is the same which the companions call "the robe of the sages", with which they are clothed in the other world. Happy the portion of the righteous, for whom the Holy One, blessed be He, has treasured up blessings and delights in the other world! Of them it is written, "Eye hath not seen besides thee, O God, what thou shalt do for him that waiteth for thee" (Is. LXIV, 3).'

AND I, BEHOLD I, DO BRING THE FLOOD OF WATERS UPON THE EARTH. R. Judah discoursed on the text: *These are the waters of strife, wherein the children of Israel strove with the Lord and he was sanctified in them* (Num. XX, 13). He said: 'As this was not the only occasion when the children of Israel strove with the Lord, why is the epithet of "strife" attached to these waters in particular? The reason is that these waters gave added strength and confidence to the accusers. For there are sweet waters and bitter waters, clear waters and turbid waters, waters of peace and waters of strife. These were waters of strife, because through them Israel drew upon themselves the unwelcome visitor through whom they became defiled; this is indicated in the word *vayiqadesh.*' Said R. Hizkiah:

'If this is so, we should have the plural *vayiqadeshu* (and they were defiled). The truth is that the singular refers not to the Israelites but to the moon, and the word *vayiqadesh* is not used here in a good sense.' R. Jose said: 'Woe to the wicked who will not repent of their sins before the Almighty while they are still in this world. For when a man repents of his sins and feels remorse for them, the Holy One, blessed be He, forgives them. But those who cling to their sins and refuse to repent of them will in the end descend to Gehinnom and never come up again. Thus because the generation of Noah were stubborn of heart and flaunted their sins openly and defiantly, the Holy One, blessed be He, punished them as here described.' Said R. Isaac: 'When a man sins in secret, if he repents, the Holy One, blessed be He, being merciful, relents and forgives him; but if not, He then publishes his sins before the world. We learn this from the treatment of the faithless wife (*Sotah*).[1] Similarly here, the wicked were exterminated in sight of all. The manner of their death was as follows: scalding water spurted up from the abyss, and as it reached them it first burnt the skin from the flesh, and then the flesh from the bones; the bones then came asunder, no two remaining together, and thus they were completely blotted out.' R. Isaac said: 'The words "they were *blotted out* from the earth" is analogous to the expression "let them be *blotted out* of the book of the living" (Ps. LXIX, 29), thus indicating that they will not participate in the resurrection and will not rise in the Day of Judgement.' [66b]

AND I WILL ESTABLISH MY COVENANT WITH THEE, R. Eleazar said: 'From this we learn that there is an establishment of the covenant on high co-ordinate with the establishment of the covenant here below. This we deduce from the expression "with thee".' R. Eleazar further said: 'We also learn from here that when there are righteous men in this world, the universe is more firmly established both above and below.' R. Simeon said: 'A recondite principle is here enshrined. As the desire of the male towards the female is intensified by jealousy, so is the desire of the Most

[1] v. Numbers v.

High towards the Shekinah. Thus, when there is a righteous man in the world, the Shekinah attaches herself to him and never leaves him. This creates, as it were, jealousy on high, which provokes love towards her in the same way as the male is incited to love the female through jealousy; this is implied in the expression "And I will establish my covenant with thee", as much as to say: "Desire hath awakened through you." The same idea is contained in the words "but my covenant will I establish with Isaac" (Gen. XVII, 21). AND I WILL ESTABLISH MY COVENANT WITH THEE: in other words: "Thou shalt be the embodiment of my covenant in the world." and then: AND THOU SHALT COME INTO THE ARK. For had not Noah been righteous, he could not have entered the ark, as only the Righteous one (*Zaddik*) can become united with the ark, as has been explained.'
R. Eleazar said: 'As long as men remain attached to that ark and do not loosen their hold of it, there is no nation or language in the world that can harm them. Noah too kept fast hold of the covenant and observed it, and therefore the Holy One, blessed be He, preserved him; but all his contemporaries who did not keep the covenant were destroyed.' As has already been stated, the manner of their destruction corresponded exactly to the character of their crimes.

R. Judah studied regularly with R. Simeon. On one occasion they discussed the verse: *And he repaired* (lit. healed) *the altar of the Lord that was thrown down* (I Kings XVIII, 30). 'What', they asked, 'is meant by the term *vayrappe* (and he healed)?' 'The answer is this. In the days of Elijah, all Israel forsook the Holy One, blessed be He, and neglected the holy covenant. When Elijah became aware that the children of Israel had entirely neglected the covenant, he set himself to rectify the evil and to restore the covenant to its former vogue. Hence the expression, "And he healed the altar of the Lord that was thrown down", to wit, the established covenant that was utterly neglected. It is further written: "And Elijah took twelve stones according to the number of the tribes of the sons of Jacob" (this being the appropriate means of repairing the altar of the Lord), "unto whom the word of the Lord came saying, Israel shall be thy name" (*Ibid.* 31), implying that Israel was to be the name by which he could ascend on high and restore the covenant in its place. It is for this reason that Elijah said expressly, "for the children of *Israel* have forsaken thy covenant" (*Ibid.* XIX, 10), and, as a consequence, "thrown down thine altars" (*Ibid.*). Take note that as long as Israel observe the holy covenant, they thereby effect the stabilisation of the world above and below, as it is written: "If my covenant be not (observed) day and night, the ordinances of heaven and earth were as if I had not appointed them." (Jer. XXXIII, 25). The repairing, then, of the shattered altar was truly a healing, as it had for its purpose the reintegration of the spot to which faith attaches itself. Similarly with Phineas at the time when he was filled with zeal to punish the crime of Zimri: he also re-established the covenant in its place, and hence God said to him, "Behold, I give unto him my covenant of peace" (Num. XXV, 12). This does not mean that the covenant was on account of Phineas, or that he was in conflict with the covenant, but that now it was firmly attached to its place. This is shown by the combination of the words "covenant" and "peace", as if to say, "Behold I give to him the peaceful confirmation of the covenant in its place", from which it had been torn by the transgressors. Hence, too, "and it shall be unto him and to his seed after him the covenant of an everlasting priesthood, because he was jealous for his God".' (*Ibid.* 13). R. Simeon said: 'There is no sin in the world which so much provokes the anger of the Almighty as the sin of neglecting the covenant, as we read, "a sword that shall execute the vengeance of the covenant" (Lev. XXVI, 25). The proof is that in the generation of the Flood the measure of sin was not filled up until mankind became (sexually) perverted and destroyed their seed. And although they defrauded each other, as it is written, [67a] "And the earth was filled with violence",[1] and again "for the earth is filled with violence through them", yet it was because "the earth was corrupt before God" that the doom was finally pronounced, "behold I will destroy (lit. corrupt) them". Thus they suffered measure for measure:

---

[1] lit. 'fraud', 'overreaching'.

they were doomed to corruption for having corrupted and perverted their ways. According to another view, it was the sin of violence which finally completed the measure of their guilt, as they used to overreach one another and were thus wicked both towards Heaven and towards their fellow men. For many are the guardians on high charged to lend ear to those who cry out for justice against their oppressors. Hence the words FOR THE EARTH IS FILLED WITH VIOLENCE THROUGH THEM are immediately followed by the words AND BEHOLD I WILL DESTROY THEM WITH THE EARTH.

AND THE LORD SAID UNTO NOAH, COME THOU AND ALL THY HOUSE. Said R. Simeon: 'How is it that throughout this passage God is always designated *Elohim* save in this place, where we find the name *Jehovah*, significant of the attribute of mercy? There is here an inner meaning which is at the same time a lesson. The lesson is that a woman should not admit a guest into her house without the consent of her husband. So here, when Noah wished to enter the ark, and to become united with her, it was not becoming for her to admit him before her Master gave his permission to enter and said: "Come thou and all thy house into the ark." Hence the name Jehovah is used here, to designate what we call the husband of the ark. Similarly we learn that neither may the guest enter the house save with the consent of the husband, who is the master of the house, and hence it was only later that NOAH WENT IN. Note again the words: FOR THEE I HAVE SEEN RIGHTEOUS BEFORE ME IN THIS GENERATION. We learn from this the lesson that a man should not admit into his house any guest whom he suspects of wrong-doing, but only such a one as is above all suspicion in his eyes. It was in accordance with this principle that God said unto Noah, "Come thou and all thy house into the ark, for thee have I seen righteous before me in this generation." We further learn that special permission must be obtained for the guest's household, as it is written: "Come thou and thy house".'

R. Judah discoursed on the verse: *Of David a psalm. The earth is the Lord's and the fulness thereof* (Ps. XXIV, 1). He said: 'We have been taught that the heading "Of David a psalm" in the Book of Psalms implies that David began to compose of himself and thereby induced the Holy Spirit to rest on him, whereas the heading "A psalm of David" implies the opposite, viz. that the Holy Spirit rested on him first, and under its inspiration he was moved to song. "The earth" here refers to the holy land of Israel, and by the words "and the fulness thereof" is meant the Shekinah, which is associated with fulness in the verses "for the glory of the Lord filled the house of the Lord" (1 Kings VIII, 2), and again, "and the glory of the Lord filled the tabernacle" (Ex. XL, 35). This last passage means literally "the glory of the Lord was full" (*malé*), i.e. full to overflowing, full from all sides both from the sun and the moon like a storehouse filled with all kinds of good things. Similar is the sense of the words "and the fulness thereof" here. The words "the world and they that dwell therein" refer to the rest of the world. According to another view, the words "the earth and the fulness thereof" refer to the supernal Holy Land in which is the delight of the Holy One, blessed be He, and the words "the fulness thereof" refer to the souls of the righteous who fill this earth. What is meant by "the righteous filling the earth" is this. When the righteous multiply in the world, then the earth is truly productive and filled with goodness. But when the wicked multiply in the world, then it may be said that "the waters cease from the sea, and the river is drained dry" (Job XIV, 11), the "sea" being the Holy Land, which is watered by the supernal stream.'

R. Judah further said: 'When the sinners were destroyed in the time of Noah, God was very anxious for the preservation of the world, but could see no one who might save it from His wrath; for the whole efforts of Noah were required to save himself and to repeople the world. So it is written: FOR THEE HAVE I SEEN RIGHTEOUS BEFORE ME IN THIS GENERATION, i.e. he was righteous only by comparison with his contemporaries.' R. Jose said: [67*b*] "The words "in this generation" are a tribute to Noah, as much as to say, surrounded as he was by that wicked generation, he yet remained as righteous and perfect a man as if he had lived in the generation of Moses. But he could not save the world, for the reason that there were not to be found ten righteous men in it (similarly we read of Sodom, "peradventure ten shall be found there", Gen. XVIII, 32), but only Noah and his three sons with their womenfolk.' R. Eleazar asked R. Simeon, his father: 'We have been taught that when the world becomes full of sin and is doomed to destruction, woe is then to the righteous man who is found in it, for he is first made answerable for its sins. How, then, was Noah able to escape the general doom?' His father replied: 'It has already been said that the Holy One, blessed be He, desired to people the world anew through him when he should issue from the ark. And further, the general doom could not reach him because he was securely stored away in the ark and concealed from sight, thus fulfilling the verse, "Seek righteousness, seek humility, it may be ye shall be hid in the day of the Lord's anger" (Zeph. II, 3). Because Noah sought righteousness, he was permitted to enter the ark, and thus "was hid in the day of the Lord's anger", and was placed beyond the reach of the Adversary.' The word *vayimahu* (and they were blotted out) contains a hint to the "saints of the Most High"[1] of the secret power of the sacred letters of the alphabet, and their destructive potency when used in the reverse order.

R. Isaac expounded here the verse: *He who caused his glorious arm to go at the right hand of Moses, that divided the water before him to make himself an everlasting name* (Is. LXIII, 12). 'In these words', he said, 'is a reference to the merit of Abraham, which was the "right hand" and the "glory" of Moses and divided the water before him, in order that he might "make himself an everlasting name". Observe the difference between Moses and other men. When God said to Moses, "now therefore let me alone . . . and I will make of thee a great nation, etc." (Ex. XXXII, 10), Moses said immediately, "Shall I abandon Israel for my own advantage? The world will say that I killed Israel and did to them as Noah did to his generation. For when God bade Noah save himself and his household in the ark from the universal destruction at the time of the Flood, he did not intercede on

---

[1] *v*. Daniel VII, 18.

behalf of his generation, but let them perish." It is for this reason that the waters of the Flood are named after him, as it is written, "for this is as the waters of Noah unto me" (Is. LIV, 9). Moses thus said: "Everyone will think that I killed them because the Lord promised to make me a great nation. It is therefore better that I should die and that Israel should not be destroyed." Immediately, therefore, he besought mercy for his people, and mercy was indeed vouchsafed to them.' R. Isaac said further: 'How come Moses to begin his intercession with the words, "Why, O Lord, doth thy wrath wax hot against thy people?" (Ex. XXXII, 11) How could Moses ask such a question, knowing as he did that they had worshipped a strange god, as we read "they have made them a molten calf and have worshipped it, etc." (*Ibid.* 8)? In truth we are taught here that when endeavouring to appease a man who is angry with his neighbour for an offence committed against him, one should not magnify the offence, but, on the contrary, should seek to minimise it: whereas subsequently, when speaking to the offending person himself, one should emphasise the enormity of the offence, as Moses did when he said to Israel, "Ye have sinned a great sin" (*Ibid.* 30). Moses went so far in his intercession as to offer his own life, as it is written, "and if not, blot me, I pray thee, out of thy book which thou hast written" (*Ibid.* 32), with the result that the Holy One, blessed be He, forgave them, as it is written, "and the Lord repented of the evil" (*Ibid.* 14). But Noah did not do so, but was intent on saving himself only, leaving the world to its fate. Thus, whenever the world is called to strict account, the Holy One, blessed be He, says, "Alas that there is no one to be found like Moses, as it is written, 'and his people remember ... the days of Moses; where is he that brought us up out of the sea, etc.?'" (Is. LXIII, 11). Moses is called "he that brought them up out of the sea" because their deliverance at that time was due to his prayer, as we read, "and the Lord said to Moses, Wherefore criest thou unto me?" (Ex. XIV, 15). So, too, the words which follow, "where is he that put his holy spirit in the midst of them?" refer to Moses who planted [68a] the Shekinah in the midst of Israel. So, too, the words, "Who led them through the deeps", when the waters were cleft, and they went through the deeps on dry land. The whole achievement is ascribed to Moses because he risked his life for Israel.'

Said R. Judah: 'Although Noah was a righteous man, he was not so pious that God should think fit to save the world for his sake. Observe that Moses pleaded not his own merit, but that of the ancient patriarchs. Noah, however, did not possess this resource. Nevertheless, after God had said to him "and I will establish my covenant with thee", he should have entreated mercy for his fellow men, and should then have offered up the sacrifice which he brought later, in order to appease God's anger against the world.' Said R. Judah: 'What could he do? He was in fear for his own life, lest he should perish along with the wicked, whose iniquities and provocations he had observed for so long.' R. Isaac said: 'When the wicked spread, it is the righteous man in their midst who first suffers for their sins, as it is written, "and from my sanctuary ye should commence" (Ez. IX, 6), where the word *mimiqdashi* (my sanctuary) may be read—so tradition tells us—as *mimqudashai* (my saintly ones). How is it, then, that God saved Noah from the midst of the sinners? It was in order to people the world anew through him, as he was a righteous man, meet for this purpose; and further, he daily warned the people, who, however, disregarded his warning, so that to him may be applied the words, "yet if thou warn the wicked ... but thou hast delivered thy soul" (Ezek. III, 19). From this we learn that he who warns the wicked, even if his warning is disregarded, saves himself and is not involved in the punishment which befalls them. If it is asked, how long should one go on warning, the answer is, till he is peremptorily forbidden. This is the point fixed by the colleagues.'

When R. Jose was studying regularly with R. Simeon, he one day said to him: 'What was the motive of the Almighty in extirpating all the animals of the field and the birds of the air along with the wicked among men? If men sinned, what wrong had the animals and birds and other creatures committed?' R. Simeon answered: 'The reason is given in the words, "For all flesh had corrupted their way upon the earth." This indicates that the whole of the animal world had become corrupted and had confounded their species. Observe that it was the wicked among mankind who brought about the unnatural intercourse in the animal world, and who sought thereby to undo the work of creation: they made the rest of creation pervert their ways in imitation of themselves. Said God to them: "You seek to undo the work of my hands; your wish shall be fully granted, for every living thing that I have made will I blot out from the face of the earth. I will reduce the world to water, to its primitive state, and then I will form other creatures more worthy to endure." '

AND NOAH WENT IN AND HIS SONS AND HIS WIFE AND HIS SONS' WIVES WITH HIM. R. Hiya quoted in this connection the verse: *Can any hide himself in secret places that I shall not see him? saith the Lord* (Jer. XXIII, 24). 'How blind and obtuse are the sons of men who regard not and know not the honour of their Master, of whom it is written, "Do not I fill heaven and earth?" (*Ibid.*). And yet men imagine that they can hide their sins, saying, "Who seeth us? And who knoweth us?" (Is. XXIX, 15). Where, indeed, can they hide themselves? There was once a king who built a palace and constructed underneath it secret subterranean chambers. One day the courtiers rose in revolt against the king, who thereupon laid siege to the palace with his army. The rebels sought safety by hiding in the subterranean passages and chambers. Said the king: "It is I who constructed these secret places, and do you think to escape from me by hiding there?" So God says to the wicked, "Can anyone hide himself in secret places that I shall not see him?" As much as to say, "I have created all chasms and caverns, I have made darkness and light; how, then, can you think to hide yourselves from Me?" Observe this. When a man sins before his Master and uses all devices to conceal himself, the Holy One, blessed be He, chastises him openly. Should, however, the man purify himself of his sins, God will then shield him so that he shall not be visible in the day of the fierce wrath of the Lord. For assuredly a man should take care [68b] not to make himself visible to the destroying angel when he swoops down upon the world, and not to attract his notice, since he is authorised to destroy whosoever comes within his view. This accords with a remark of R. Simeon, that a man possessed of an evil eye carries with him the eye of the destroying angel; hence he is called " destroyer of the world", and people should be on their guard against him and not come near him, so that they should not be injured by him; it is actually forbidden to come near him in the open. If, therefore, it is necessary to beware of a man with an evil eye, how much more should one beware of the angel of death ? An example of a man with an evil eye was Balaam, of whom it is written, "thus saith the man whose eye is closed"[1] (Num. XXIV, 3); this means that he was possessed of an evil eye, and on whatsoever he fixed his gaze he drew thereon the destroying spirit. Knowing this, he sought to fix his gaze on Israel, in order that he might destroy everything upon which his look should fall. Thus it is written, "And Balaam lifted up his eye" (*Ibid.* 2), indicating that he raised one eye and lowered the other, so that his evil eye should fall upon Israel. Israel, however, were immune; for it is written, "and he saw Israel dwelling tribe by tribe" (*Ibid.*), that is, he saw the Shekinah hovering over them and kept in position by the twelve tribes beneath, and his eye had no more power over them. "How," he said, "can I prevail against them, seeing that the holy spirit from on high rests on them and shields them with her wings ?" This is indicated in the words, "He couched, he lay down as a lion, who shall rouse him up ?" (*Ibid.* 9); that is, who shall raise Him from over them so that they shall be exposed to the influence of the evil eye ? In the same manner the Holy One, blessed be He, sought to shield Noah, and to hide him from the evil eye, so that the impure spirit should have no power over him, and do him no harm.'

AND NOAH WENT IN, as has already been said, to hide himself from all eyes, BECAUSE OF THE WATERS OF THE FLOOD, which were already pressing him hard. Said R. Jose: He saw the angel of death coming, and so he went into

---

[1] So the Rabbinical interpretation of the word *sh'thum*.

hiding for a twelvemonth.' Why for a twelvemonth? On this point R. Isaac and R. Judah differed. One said it was because a twelvemonth is the fixed term of punishment in Gehinnom for the guilty. The other said that it was in order that the righteous Noah might complete his twelve degrees and the other degrees which it was fitting that he should bring with him out of the ark. R. Judah asked: 'Seeing that for six months the wicked (in Gehinnom) are punished by water and another six months by fire, why did the waters prevail for twelve months?' R. Jose answered: 'The punishments of Gehinnom, water and fire, were here let loose together. Rain descended upon them from above, and at the same time scalding waters, hot as fire, gushed up from below. Their punishment was thus the same as that in Gehinnom, which consists of fire and water, and it continued until they were utterly destroyed. Meanwhile Noah was hidden in the ark, concealed from sight, so that the destroyer could not come near him, while the ark floated on the face of the waters, as we read: AND THEY BORE UP THE ARK, AND IT WAS LIFTED ABOVE THE EARTH. For forty days they suffered punishment, as it is written, AND THE FLOOD WAS FORTY DAYS UPON THE EARTH, and for the rest of the time they were gradually being exterminated, as it is written, AND THEY WERE BLOTTED OUT FROM THE EARTH. Woe to those sinners, since they will not rise from the dead on the day of the last judgement. This is indicated by the expression "and they were blotted out", which contains the same idea as the verse "Thou hast blotted out their name for ever and ever" (Ps. IX, 6).'

AND THEY BORE UP THE ARK, AND IT WAS LIFTED UP ABOVE THE EARTH. R. Abba connected this text with the verse: *Be thou raised above the heavens, O Elohim, thy glory be above all the earth* (Ps. LVII, 6). 'Woe,' he said, 'to the sinners who daily provoke their Master, and through their sins repel the Shekinah and cause it to disappear from the world, wherefore the Scripture says: "Be thou raised above the heavens, O Elohim" (the Shekinah being called Elohim). So here, the words, "and they bore up the ark" indicate that they thrust her forth, and the words, "it was lifted up above the earth", that she found no more rest in the world, and so departed altogether from it. And in the absence of the Shekinah there is no one to take thought for the world, with the result that divine justice is exercised upon it with rigour. But when the wicked are blotted out and removed from the world, the Shekinah again takes up her abode therein.' R. Jose put to R. Abba the question: 'Why, after the sinners in the land of Israel were wiped out, did the Shekinah not return to her former habitation?' R. Abba replied: 'It is because the remnant of the righteous did not remain there, for wherever these went the Shekinah descended and made [69a] her habitation with them. We thus see that in a strange land she does not separate from them; how much more would she cling to them had they remained in the Holy Land! All sins of mankind repel the Shekinah, particularly the sin of him who corrupts his way upon the earth. Therefore such a one will not see the face of the Shekinah, and will not gain entrance to the celestial Palace. For when the day comes on which the Holy One, blessed be He, will raise the dead to life, He will physically re-create all those dead who have been buried in strange lands. For if but one bone of them is left in the earth, this will be like the lump of leaven which causes the dough to rise, and on it the Holy One, blessed be He, will build up the whole body. But God will not restore their souls[1] to them save in the land of Israel, as it is written, "Behold I will open your graves, and cause you to come up out of your graves, O my people, and I will bring you into the land of Israel" (to which they will roll through subterranean passages), and then "I will put my spirit in you and you shall live" (Ezek. xxxvii, 12, 14). We see thus that only in the land of Israel will souls be provided for the resurrected. But those will be excluded who defile themselves and defile the earth, and of them it is written, "and they were blotted out of the earth". The word "earth" we take to mean here "the land of the living" (although some of the ancient sages question this), and the whole expression is analogous to the verse, "let them be

---

[1] The *neshamah* (v. pp. 203, 278).

blotted out of the book of the living" (Ps. LXIX, 29).' R. Simeon said to him: 'Undoubtedly they will have no portion in the world to come, since the expression "and they were blotted out of the earth" is the exact opposite of the expression "they shall inherit the land for ever" (Is. LX, 21); but they will be called up for judgement, as it is with reference to them that the Scripture says, "and many of them that sleep in the dust of the earth shall awake, some to everlasting life, and some to reproaches and everlasting abhorrence" (Dan. XII, 2).'

AND HE BLOTTED OUT EVERY (*eth-kol*) LIVING SUB-STANCE WHICH WAS UPON THE FACE OF THE EARTH. Said R. Abba: 'The particle *eth* signifies the inclusion of all those higher chieftains who control and superintend the earth: these are "the substance which was upon the face of the earth". For whenever the Holy One, blessed be He, executes judgement on the earth, those higher chieftains are brought to justice first, and only in the next place those who abide beneath the shelter of their wings. This is illustrated in the passage, " the Lord will punish the host of the high heavens on high", and then "and the kings of the earth upon the earth" (Is. XXIV, 21). The punishment of these chieftains is, to be driven through burning fire, as it is written, "for the Lord thy God is a devouring fire, a jealous God" (Deut. IV, 24); that is, fire consuming fire. The "living substance" of the upper regions were thus passed through fire, and those under their control through water ; and so, first, HE BLOTTED OUT EVERY LIVING SUBSTANCE WHICH WAS UPON THE FACE OF THE GROUND, and then, BOTH MAN AND CATTLE AND FOWL OF THE HEAVEN, AND THEY WERE BLOTTED OUT FROM THE EARTH—to wit, all those beneath. AND NOAH ONLY WAS LEFT; the particle *ach* (only) shows that absolutely nothing was left save what was in the ark'. R. Jose said: 'It indicates that even Noah was not left intact, as he was injured by a blow from a lion, as elsewhere explained.'

AND GOD REMEMBERED NOAH AND EVERY LIVING THING AND ALL THE CATTLE THAT WERE WITH HIM

IN THE ARK. R. Hiya quoted in this connection the verse: *A prudent man seeth evil and hideth himself* (Prov. XXII, 3). 'This verse,' he said, 'refers to Noah, who went into the ark and hid himself there, not, however, before the waters forced him in. It has already been said that before he entered the ark he caught sight of the angel of death going among the people and encircling them. As soon as he espied him, he went into the ark and hid himself there. Thus, "the prudent man saw evil and hid himself", i.e. Noah saw the angel of death and hid himself from him, going into the ark, as the Scripture says, "because of the waters of the flood".' R. Jose said that the reference of the verse is to what has been said above, viz. that when death is raging in the world the prudent man goes into hiding and does not venture abroad, so as not to be seen by the destroying angel, who, once he has obtained leave, will destroy whomsoever he meets at large, and whoever passes before him in the open, as the latter part of the verse expresses it, "but the thoughtless pass on and are punished". According to another interpretation, the word *abroo* (pass on) means here "transgress", i.e. they transgress the precept of self-preservation and are therefore punished. According to yet another interpretation, while the first half of the verse refers to Noah, the second half refers to his contemporaries. When he had remained a sufficient time under cover, [69b] the Scripture says that GOD REMEMBERED NOAH. Said R. Simeon: 'Observe that all the time that judgement was being executed there was no remembering, but only after the chastisement had been completed and the wicked had been exterminated do we find mention of remembering. For as long as judgement hangs over the world, there is no communion of man with God, and the destroying angel is rampant. But as soon as judgement has run its course and wrath has been allayed, everything returns to its previous state. Hence we read "and God remembered Noah", remembrance being centred in him since he was entitled "righteous".'

It is written:[1] *Thou rulest the proud swelling of the sea, when the waves thereof arise, thou stillest them* (Ps. LXXXIX, 10). When

[1] Here, apparently, there should be a text-heading: AND GOD MADE A WIND PASS OVER THE EARTH, AND THE WATERS WERE ASSUAGED.

the stormy waves of the sea mount on high, and beneath them yawn the chasms of the deep, the Holy One, blessed be He, sends down a thread from the "right side" which in some mysterious way restrains the mounting waves and calms the rage of the sea. How is it that when Jonah was cast into the sea, and had been swallowed by a fish, his soul did not at once leave his body? The reason is that the Holy One, blessed be He, has dominion over the swelling of the sea, which is a certain thread from the "left" that causes the sea to heave, and rises with it. And if not for the thread of the "right side" it would never be removed, for as soon as this thread descends into the sea, and is fairly grasped by it, then the waves of the sea are stirred up, and begin to roar for prey, until the Holy One, blessed be He, thrusts them back to their own place, as it says ,"when the waves thereof arise, thou stillest them". (According to another interpretation, the term *teshabhem* (thou stillest them), is related to the word *shabah* (praise), and signifies here, "thou praisest them", because they mount to the top in their eagerness to see the outer world. The lesson to be learnt from this is that he who manifests an eagerness to examine things and to acquire new knowledge, although he lacks talent, merits praise and receives praise from all around him.) R. Judah said: 'While Noah was in the Ark, he was apprehensive lest God should never more remember him. He was, however, wrong, for after judgement had been executed, and the wicked had perished from the world, the Scripture tells us that GOD REMEMBERED NOAH.' Said R. Eleazar: 'When the world is being called to account, it is not advisable that a man should have his name mentioned on high, for the mention of his name will be a reminder of his sins, and will cause him to be brought under scrutiny. This we learn from the words of the Shunammitess. It was on New Year's day, when God sits in judgement on the world, that Elisha asked her, "Wouldst thou be spoken for to the king?" (II Kings IV, 13), i.e. to the Holy One, blessed be He, for on that day He is, in a special sense, King, Holy King, King of Judgement. She answered, "I dwell among my own people" (*Ibid.*), as much as to say, "I do not wish to be remembered and to have attention drawn to me, save among my own people." He who keeps himself in the midst of his own people does not draw attention upon himself, and so escapes criticism. In the same way, as long as the heavenly wrath was raging in the world, Noah was not remembered; but as soon as judgement had been executed, then, as we read, "God remembered Noah".'

R. Hizkiah was going from Cappadocia to Lud, when R. Yesa met him. Said the latter to him, 'I am surprised at your walking all alone, seeing that we have been taught that no man should proceed on a journey unaccompanied.' R. Hizkiah replied, 'There is a youth accompanying me, and he is following on.' Said R. Yesa, 'I am still more surprised to find that you have for a companion one with whom you could not discuss points of the Torah, since we have been taught that he who makes a journey unaccompanied by discussions on the Torah exposes himself to danger.' R. Hizkiah replied, 'It is certainly so.' Meanwhile the youth came up with them. Said R. Yesa to him, 'My son, where do you come from?' The lad answered, 'From the town of Lud, and when I heard that this learned man was proceeding thither, I offered him my service and company.' 'My son,' said R. Yesa, 'do you know any Torah-exposition?' 'I do,' was the reply, 'as my father used to teach me the section of the sacrifices, and I also used to listen attentively to the expositions he gave to my elder brother.' At the invitation of R. Yesa, he then commenced to discourse as follows.

AND NOAH BUILDED AN ALTAR UNTO THE LORD; AND TOOK OF EVERY CLEAN BEAST, AND OF EVERY CLEAN FOWL, AND OFFERED BURNT OFFERINGS ON THE ALTAR. The altar that Noah made was the very same on which Adam, the first man, offered up sacrifice. Why did Noah bring burnt offerings, [70a] seeing that a burnt offering is brought only to counteract wrongful thoughts? Was, then, Noah guilty of such? In truth, Noah did harbour wrongful thoughts, since he said to himself, "Behold, the Holy One, blessed be He, has decreed the destruction of the world, and who knows but that through my being saved I have used up all the merit which I had accumulated?" He therefore hastened to build an altar unto the Lord. The altar was the very same on which Adam, the first man, offered up sacrifice, but as the wicked had wrenched it from its place, Noah had to rebuild it. AND OFFERED BURNT OFFERINGS. It is written *olath* (burnt offering) defectively, which would indicate only one. This is explained by reference to the verse, "it is a burnt offering, a fire offering for sweet savour to the Lord" (Lev. I, 17). A burnt offering has to be male, not female, as it says: "he shall offer it a male, without blemish" (Lev. 1, 3). The word "fire offering" (*isheh*) seems to be superfluous, as we know there was fire on the altar. We should therefore read *ishah* (lit. woman), and we learn from this that the female element must not be parted from the male, which is offered through it, so that the two are united. It was right for Noah to bring a burnt offering, since God had set him in the place of a male in relation to the ark. "The burnt offering is *isheh*", to wit, *esh hé* (fire of *hé*), indicating that the Left is joined with the Female (since the female is from the left and the male from the right) through the clinging of one to the other. Hence the female is called *isheh*, indicating the bond of love in which the Left is joined to her, so as to mount with her on high and be united with her there. Hence the words "a burnt offering, a fire offering", indicate the bond of the male and female.

'AND THE LORD SMELLED THE SAVOUR OF APPEASEMENT. It is also written "a fire offering, a savour of appeasement" (Lev. 1, 13). With reference to the term "fire offering" we have heard the following. Fire and smoke are joined together, there being no smoke without fire, as it is written: "Now Mount Sinai was altogether on smoke, because the Lord descended upon it in fire" (Ex. XIX, 18). It is in this way. Fire, being very tenuous, issues from an inmost part, and then takes hold of some substance outside which is less tenuous, and by the junction of the two smoke is engendered: the reason being that fire has taken hold of something catching. An example is the warm breath that issues from the nostrils. Hence it is written, "They shall put incense in thy nose" (Deut. XXXIII, 10), i.e. they shall act so as to cause the fire to recede to its place, since through the smell of the incense the nose contracts inwardly, till the whole odour is drawn in and brought near to the thought, producing a pleasing sensation. Hence there results "a savour of appeasement", when the anger is appeased and calm is restored, since the smoke has been gathered in and condensed in the fire, and the fire has seized the smoke and both have been drawn further and further back until the anger is assuaged and a reunion is formed, called "appeasement": an appeasement of the spirit, a universal rejoicing, a radiance of lamps, a brightening of faces, and thus, AND THE LORD SMELT THE SAVOUR OF APPEASEMENT as one who smells and draws in the savour to the innermost spot.'

R. Yesa then approached the lad and kissed him, saying, 'To think that all these precious goods were in thy possession and I was unaware of it.' He further said, 'I will go out of my way to remain in thy company.' Whilst they proceeded R. Hizkiah said, 'On this road we are accompanied by the Shekinah. Let us, then, go forward confidently, since no harm can befall us on the way.' He then took hold of the lad's hand and they went along. They then said to him, 'Repeat to us one of those Scriptural expositions you have heard from your father.' The lad then began a discourse on the text: *Let him kiss me with the kisses of his mouth* (S. S. 1, 2). 'This,' he said, 'is a more burning desire, in which affection issues from the mouth with a fire unlike that which issues from the nostrils. For when mouth is joined with mouth to kiss, fire issues from the strength of affection, accompanied by radiance of the countenance, by rejoicing on both sides and by gladsome union. "For thy love is better than wine" (*Ibid.*), to wit, than that wine which exhilarates and brightens the countenance, which makes the eyes sparkle and induces good feeling; not the wine that intoxicates, induces rage, beclouds the countenance, and inflames the eyes, the wine of rage. It is because this wine is exhilarating and cheering and induces love and affection that a libation of it is offered every day on the altar, of just such a quantity [70b] as would induce in him who drinks it a cheerful mood and a spirit of contentment, as it is written, "And the drink offering thereof shall be a fourth part of a hin" (Num. XXVIII, 7). "For thy love is better than wine" alludes thus to the wine that induces love and desire. And as here below, so is love awakened on high. For there are two lamps, and when the light of the one on high is extinguished, by the smoke that rises from the one below it is relit.' Said R. Hizkiah: 'Assuredly it is so, the lower and the upper world are interdependent; and since the destruction of the Temple there are no blessings, either on high or below, which proves their interdependence.' R. Jose said: 'Not only are there no blessings, but there are everywhere curses, as the supply of sustenance is now drawn from the "sinister side". Why so? Because Israel do not dwell now in the land, and thus do not perform the holy service which is required for lighting the (celestial) lamps and so obtaining blessings. Hence they are to be found neither on high nor here below, and the world is out of gear.'

I WILL NOT AGAIN CURSE THE GROUND ANY MORE FOR MAN'S SAKE. R. Hizkiah asked, 'What does this verse mean?' R. Yesa replied: 'I have heard from R. Simeon the following. So long as the supernal fire is gathering force, the smoke, which is the execution of judgement here below, rages more and more fiercely and is more and more destructive; for once the fire starts, there is no keeping it back until the judgement has been fully executed. But when punishment below is not intensified by punishment from above, it burns itself out without bringing the world to ruin. Hence it is written, *lo osif* (I will not add) as much as to say, "I will not lend any additional force and volume to the punishment below".'

Said the young lad, 'I have heard that the expression "for man's sake" alludes to the utterance, "cursed is the ground for thy sake" (Gen. III, 17). For at the time when the earth was cursed for the sin of Adam, full dominion over her was granted to that evil serpent, the destroyer and exterminator of the world and its inhabitants. From the day, however, that Noah offered up sacrifices, and the Holy One, blessed be He, smelt their sweet savour, the earth was liberated from the dominion of the serpent and threw off his defilement. It is for this same reason that Israel bring offerings, so as to keep bright the countenance of the earth.' Said R. Hizkiah, 'This is correct, but nevertheless this liberation remained in suspense until Israel stood at Mount Sinai.' R. Yesa said: 'The Holy One, blessed be He, had already diminished the moon and allowed the serpent to obtain sway, but on account of the sin of Adam she was actually cursed in order that the whole world might be cursed. But on that day the earth was freed of that curse, whilst the moon remained in her diminished state, save during the time when offerings are brought and Israel dwell in their own land.' R. Yesa asked the child, 'What is your name?' He replied, 'Abba'. He said to him, 'Abba (=father, chief) you shall be in everything, in wisdom and in years.' He further applied to him the verse. "Thy father and thy mother will be glad, and she that bore thee will rejoice" (Prov. XXIII, 25). R. Hizkiah said: 'The Holy One, blessed be He, will one day sweep away the unclean spirit, as it is written, "And the unclean spirit I will cause to pass out of the land" (Zech. XIII, 2), and further, "He will swallow up death for ever, and the Lord God will wipe away tears from all faces, and the reproach of his people will he take away from off all the earth, for the Lord hath spoken it" (Is. XXV, 8). The Holy One, blessed be He, will also one day restore the moon to its full light, and dissipate the darkness brought on her by the evil serpent, as it is written, "And the light of the moon shall be as the light of the sun, and the light of the sun shall be sevenfold, as the light of the seven days" (*Ibid.* XXX, 26), the reference here being to the primordial light which the Holy One, blessed be He, stored away during the period of the creation.'

AND GOD (*Elohim*) BLESSED NOAH AND HIS SONS, AND SAID UNTO THEM: BE FRUITFUL AND MULTIPLY, ETC. R. Abba began his discourse with the text: *The blessing of the Lord, it maketh rich, and no pain shall be added thereto* (Prov. X, 22). ' "The blessing of the Lord" is bound up with the Shekinah, as she is in charge of the blessings of the world, and from her flow blessings for all. Observe that at first (Gen. VII, 1) it was written, AND YHVH SAID TO NOAH, COME THOU AND ALL THY HOUSE INTO THE ARK, which conforms with what was said before, that the master of the house gave him permission to enter; whereas afterwards it was the wife who speeded him out of the ark, as it is written, AND ELOHIM (=Shekinah) SPOKE UNTO NOAH, SAYING: GO FORTH FROM THE ARK. From here we learn that it is the master [71a] of the house that takes in the guest and it is the wife that speeds him forth, but that she may not herself bid him enter. We learn further from here that it is proper for the guest on departing to leave presents for the mistress of the house, as she is always in the house and supervises it. It is fitting to give her those presents, not in her own hand directly, but through the agency of her husband, so as to enhance their mutual affection. This we deduce from the text: AND HE TOOK OF EVERY CLEAN BEAST AND HE OFFERED BURNT OFFERINGS ON THE ALTAR. These were the presents for her which he gave, as it were, into the hands of the husband in order to enhance his love for his consort. Noah then received a blessing, as it is written, "And God blessed Noah and his sons, and said unto them, Be fruitful and multiply, etc." All this is illustrated by the text, "The blessing of the Lord, it maketh rich." As for the words "and no pain shall be added thereto", these allude to the pain mentioned in the passage "in pain shalt thou eat of it" (Gen. III, 17), that is, in pain and perturbation, with sad and gloomy looks, since the moon was darkened, and so blessings were no more. Again "in pain" refers to the side of the impure spirit who kept back blessings from the world. But now "No pain will be added thereto"; the word "add" (*yosif*) here shows the inner meaning of the words, "I will not again (*osif*, lit. add) curse the earth any more."

AND THE FEAR OF YOU AND THE DREAD OF YOU SHALL BE UPON EVERY BEAST OF THE EARTH: as much as to say, "Henceforward you will assume the facial impress of man"; for up to that time their facial impress was not that of human beings. For at first: "in the image of God created he him" (Gen. I, 27), also "in the likeness of God made he him" (*Ibid.* v, 1); but when they sinned, their facial impress was changed from the supernal prototype, and through this transformation they became afraid of the beasts of the field. Whereas formerly all the creatures of the world, when looking up towards man, encountered the supernal sacred impress and thus were filled with fear and trembling, now after they sinned their appearances were transformed, and it was men who feared and dreaded the rest of the animal world. Thus it is that all who are mindful of their Master, who keep themselves from sin and do not transgress the precepts of the Torah, retain their visage unaltered from the supernal prototype, and hence all the creatures of the world fear them and tremble before them. But when men transgress the precepts of the Torah, their visages change, and they fear the other creatures and tremble before them; the beasts of the field obtain dominion over men because they do not see any more in them the true supernal image. Hence, now that the world was reinstated in its former position, He bestowed on them His blessing and granted them dominion over all the creatures, as we read: AND UPON ALL THE FISHES OF THE SEA: INTO YOUR HAND ARE THEY DELIVERED; that is, all, even to the fishes of the sea.' R. Hiya said: ' It is written "into your hand *were* they delivered" (*nithanu*), i.e. originally, for when the Holy One, blessed be He, created the world, He delivered all in man's hand, as it is written, "and have dominion over the fish of the sea, and over the fowl of the air, etc." (Gen. 1, 28).' In reference to the words "And God blessed Noah", R. Hizkiah discoursed on the text: *Of David, Maskil. Happy is he whose transgression is forgiven, whose sin is covered* (Ps. XXXII, 1). He said: 'This verse contains deep mysteries of wisdom. For we have been taught that David, in offering praise to the Holy One, blessed be He, made use of ten varieties of praise, one of which was *Maskil*, which is one of the ten grades (of illumination), and the word here implies that David qualified himself to attain that grade. The verse proceeds: "Happy is he whose transgression is forgiven, whose sin is covered." The words *nesui pesha* mean literally "whose transgression is uplifted". That is to say, when the Holy One, blessed be He, weighs the sins and the merits of men in the balance, happy then is he whose sins rise and mount in the one scale whilst his merits sink down in the other. "Whose sin is covered": i.e. when the world is being chastised, that man will be concealed so that the destroyer will have no power over him, in the same way that Noah was concealed by the Holy One, blessed be He, so that he escaped the consequences that Adam's sin drew upon the world. For that sin transferred dominion from man to the other creatures, making him fear them, and thus reversing the true order of things. Therefore when Noah went forth from the ark, the Holy One, blessed be He, blessed him, as it is written, "And God blessed Noah and his sons, etc."

AND YOU, BE YE FRUITFUL AND MULTIPLY. The women do not seem to have been included in this blessing, as it was only addressed to Noah and his sons. R. Simeon, however, said that the term *ve-athem* (and you) includes both male [71*b*] and female. And further, the particle *eth* preceding "his sons" signifies the inclusion of their spouses. It is because the women were included that God said: "Do you be fruitful and multiply", to propagate your kind. On this occasion the Holy One, blessed be He, gave them seven precepts of the Torah—to them and to all their successors, until Israel stood at Mount Sinai, when they received all the precepts of the Torah in one code.'

AND GOD SAID TO NOAH . . . THIS IS THE TOKEN OF THE COVENANT WHICH I MAKE BETWEEN ME AND YOU . . . I HAVE SET MY RAINBOW IN THE CLOUD. The past tense "I have set" shows that the bow had already been there. In connection with this passage R. Simeon discoursed on the verse: *And above the firmament that was over their heads was the likeness of a throne, as the appearance of a sapphire stone* (Ezek. 1, 26). 'Before this verse,' he said, 'we find the words, "And when they went I heard the noise of their wings like the noise of great waters, like the voice of the Almighty" (*Ibid.* 24). These are the four sacred and mighty beings called *Hayyoth* (animals), by whom the firmament is upheld, and whose wings are usually joined together to cover their bodies. When, however, they spread out their wings, a volume of sound swells forth, and they break out into songs of praise, "as the voice of the Almighty", which never becomes silent, as it is written, "so that my glory may sing praise to thee, and not be silent" (Ps. xxx, 13). The tenour of their praises is, "The Lord hath made known his salvation, his righteousness hath he revealed in the sight of the nations" (Ps. xcviii, 2). It says further: "A noise of tumult like the noise of a host" (Ezek. i, 24), i.e. like the sound of the holy camps when all the supernal armies assemble on high. What is it they declaim? "Holy, holy, holy, is the Lord of Hosts, the whole earth is full of his glory" (Is. vi, 3). They turn to the south and say "holy", they turn to the north and say "holy", they turn to the east and say "holy", they turn to the west and say "blessed". And that firmament rests upon their heads, and in whatever direction it turns, their faces turn also. They turn their faces to the four cardinal points, and all revolve in a circle. The firmament is imprinted, at the four corners of a square, with four figures, of a lion, an eagle, an ox, and a man; and the face of a man is traced in all of them, so that the face of Lion is of Man, the face of Eagle is of Man, and the face of Ox is of Man, all being comprehended in him. Hence it is written: "As for the likeness of their faces, they had the face of a man" (Ezek. i, 10). Further, the firmament with its enclosed square contains the gamut of all the colours. Outstanding are four colours, each engraved with four translucent signs, both higher and lower. These when decomposed become twelve. They are green, red, white, and sapphire, which is made up of all these colours. Hence it is written, "As the appearance of the bow that is in the cloud in the day of rain, so was the appearance of the brightness round about. This was the appearance of the likeness of the glory of the Lord" (*Ibid.* i, 28): containing, that is to say, all shades of all colours. The same is referred to in the text I HAVE SET MY BOW IN THE CLOUD. The "bow" here has a parallel in the text, "But his bow abode firm" (Gen. xlix, 24), i.e. the covenant of Joseph, because he was a righteous man, had for its symbol the bow, since the bow is linked with the covenant, and the covenant and the righteous are integral in one another. And because Noah was righteous, the sign of his covenant was the bow. (The word *vayophozu*, mentioned in connection with Joseph, is akin to the term *paz* (fine gold) in the passage, "More to be desired are they than gold, yea, than much fine gold" (Ps. XIX, 11), and it means that his arms shone with the lustre of the most desirable substance, they shone with the light supernal, since he had observed the covenant; hence he is named "Joseph the righteous".) And the rainbow is therefore called "covenant" because they embrace one another. Like the firmament it is a supernal resplendent glory, a sight of all sights, resembling the hidden one (the Shekinah), containing colours undisclosed and unrevealable. Hence it is not permitted to gaze at the rainbow when it appears in the heavens, as that would be disrespectful to the Shekinah, the hues of the rainbow here below being a replica of the vision of the supernal splendour, which is not for man's gaze. Hence when the earth saw the rainbow as a holy covenant, it was once more firmly established, and therefore God said, AND IT SHALL BE FOR A TOKEN OF A COVENANT BETWEEN GOD, ETC. The three primary colours and the one compounded of them, which we mentioned before, are all one symbol, and they all show themselves in the cloud. "And above the firmament that was over their heads was the likeness of a throne, as the appearance of a sapphire stone" (Ezek. I, 26). This alludes to the "foundation stone" (*eben shethiah*), which is the central point of the universe and on which stands the Holy of Holies. "The likeness of a throne", i.e. the supernal holy throne, possessing four supports, and which is symbolic of the Oral Law. "And upon the likeness of the throne was the likeness as the appearance of a man upon it above" (*Ibid.*); this symbolises the Written Law. From here we learn that copies of the Written Law should rest [72a] on copies of the Oral Law (and not *vice versa*), because the latter is the throne to the former. "As the appearance of a man" refers to the image of Jacob, who sits on it.'

R. Judah one night, whilst staying at an inn in Matha-Mehasia, rose at midnight to study the Torah. At the time there happened to be there a certain Judean traveller who had with him two sacks of clothes. R. Judah began to expound the verse, "And this stone which I have set up for a pillar shall be God's house" (Gen. XXVIII, 22). 'That stone', he said, 'was the foundation stone out of which the world evolved, and on which the Temple was built.' The Judean raised his head and said, 'How is this possible? This foundation stone was created before the world, to be the point from which the world evolved, and yet you say that it is referred to in the verse, "and this stone which I have set up for a pillar", which indicates that Jacob put it there, this being the same stone of which it is said, "and he took the stone that he had put under his head" (*Ibid.* 18). A further difficulty is that Jacob was in Bethel, whereas the foundation stone is in Jerusalem.' R. Judah, without turning his head, recited the verse, "Prepare to meet thy God, O Israel" (Amos IV, 12), and also "Be attentive and hearken, O Israel" (Deut. XXVII, 9). 'We learn from here, he said, 'that the study of the Torah must be approached with proper preparation, not only of the mind but also of the body.' The Judean then arose and put on his garments, and seating himself beside R. Judah, said, 'Happy are ye righteous who give yourselves up to the study of the Torah day and night.' Said R. Judah to him, 'Now that you have properly attired yourself, say what you have to say, so that we may join together, as the study of the Torah requires a seemly garb as well as an attentive mind. Otherwise I could just as well lie in my bed and meditate. But we have been taught that even a single person who sits and studies the Torah has for his companion the Shekinah; and how could the Shekinah be here whilst I am in bed ? Furthermore, the words of the Torah must be clearly articulated. Moreover, when a man gets up to study at midnight, at the time when the Holy One, blessed be He, comes to disport Himself with the righteous in the Garden of Eden, He and all the righteous in the Garden are listening to the words that issue from his mouth. Since that is so, that the Holy One, blessed be He, and all the righteous feel delight in listening to the words of the Torah at this time, should I remain lying in bed ?' He then said to him, 'Now say what you have to say.'

The Judean then said, 'Regarding your remark that Jacob's stone was the foundation stone, I have asked you, first, how can that be, seeing that the foundation stone preceded the creation of the world, and was the one from which the world evolved, whereas Jacob's stone was put by him in its place, as it is written, "and the stone which I have put", also, "And he took the stone that he had put under his head." And secondly, how can the two be identified, seeing that Jacob was in Bethel and that the stone was in Jerusalem?'

R. Judah answered, 'The whole land of Israel was folded up beneath him, so that that stone was underneath him.' The Judean repeated his question, quoting again the expressions 'that he put'—'the stone which I had put'. Said R. Judah to him, 'If you know a better answer, say it.' The Judean then discoursed as follows.

'It is written, *As for me, I shall behold thy face in righteousness; I shall be satisfied when I awake with thy likeness* (Ps. XVII, 15). King David felt great affection and attachment for this stone: it was of it that he said, "The stone which the builders rejected is become the corner stone" (*Ibid.* CXVIII, 22). And whenever he desired to gaze at the reflection of the glory of his Master, he first took that stone in his hand and then he entered, as whoever wishes to appear before his Master can only do so through that stone, as it is written, "Herewith shall Aaron come into the holy place" (Lev. XVI, 3). It was David's boast that "As for me, I shall behold thy face in righteousness", and he exerted himself in every way to appear before Him on high in proper guise by means of that stone. Now, Abraham instituted morning prayer and taught the world the character of his Master, and made that hour a propitious one for prayer. Isaac instituted afternoon prayer (*minhah*) and taught the world that there is a supreme Judge who can either pardon or condemn the world. Jacob instituted evening prayer. And it was in reference to this prayer, which he instituted for the first time as a proper method of propitiation, that he said in his own praise, [72b] "And this stone which I had put for a pillar", as up to that time no one had erected one like it. This is implied in the expression, "and he put it as a *matsebah*" (erection, upstanding), implying that he set up again something which had been prostrate. He also "poured oil on its head", thus doing more than anyone else to restore it.'

R. Judah thereupon embraced the Judean, saying, 'You have all this knowledge, and yet you occupy yourself with commerce and neglect that which gives life eternal!' He answered, 'Times are pressing, and I have two sons at school, and I have to work to provide their food and payment for their tuition, so that they may continue diligently to study the Torah.' He then resumed his discourse, taking the text: "And Solomon sat upon the throne of David his father, and his kingdom was established firmly" (1 Kings 11, 12). He said: 'What great achievement, it may be asked, is here ascribed to Solomon? The truth is that he prepared the foundation stone and set over it the Holy of Holies, and for this his kingdom was established firmly.'

The stranger further said: 'It is written: "And I will look upon it (the rainbow) that I may remember the everlasting covenant." This means that God's desire is constantly for the bow, and that he who is not visible therein will not enter into the presence of his Master. The inner meaning of the words, "And I will look upon it", is to be found in the words, "and set a mark upon the foreheads, etc." (Ezek. IX, 4), so as to be clearly visible.' (According to others, the mark was symbolic of the holy mark in the flesh.) R. Judah said, 'This is assuredly so, but the rainbow that appears in the sky has a profound mystic significance, and when Israel will go forth from exile that rainbow is destined to be decked out in all the finery of its colours, like a bride who adorns herself for her husband.' The Judean said to him, 'This is what my father said to me when he was on the point of departing this world: "Do not expect the coming of the Messiah until the rainbow will appear decked out in resplendent colours which will illumine the world. Only then expect the Messiah." We learn this from the words, "And I will look upon it, that I may remember the everlasting covenant" (Gen. IX, 16). That is, at present the bow appears in dull colours, since it is only designed as a reminder that there shall be no return of the Flood; but at that time it will appear in its full panoply of colours as a bride does for her husband, and that will be "to remember the everlasting covenant". The Holy One, blessed be He, will remember the covenant which is in exile and He will raise her from the dust, as it is written, "and they will seek the Lord their God and David their king" (Hos. III, 4); also, "But they shall serve the Lord their God, and David their king, whom I will raise unto them" (Jer. XXX, 9), i.e. raise from the dust, in accordance with the text: "I will raise up the tabernacle of David that is fallen" (Amos IX, 11). The "everlasting covenant" will thus be remembered to be raised from the dust. My father also said that it is for that reason that in Scripture the redemption of Israel and the remembrance of the rainbow are mentioned together, as it is written: "For as I have sworn that the waters of Noah should no more go over the earth, so have I sworn that I would not be wroth with thee, nor rebuke thee" (Is. LIV, 9).'

AND THE SONS OF NOAH THAT WENT FORTH FROM THE ARK WERE SHEM, AND HAM, AND JAPHETH. R. Eleazar asked why the Scripture inserts the words "who went forth from the ark". Did, then, Noah have other sons who did not go forth from the ark? R. Abba said: "Yes: the children whom his sons bore afterwards; and the Scripture points out that these did not go forth from the ark.' R. Simeon said: 'Had I been alive when the Holy One, blessed be He, gave mankind the book of Enoch and the book of Adam, I would have endeavoured to prevent their dissemination, because not all wise men read them with proper attention, and thus extract from them perverted ideas, such as lead men astray from the Most High to the worship of strange powers. Now, however, the wise who understand these things keep them secret, and thereby fortify themselves in the service of their Master.' [73a] Of the three sons of Noah that went forth from the ark, Shem, Ham, and Japheth, Shem is symbolic of the right side, Ham of the left side, whilst Japheth represents the "purple", which is a mixture of the two. AND HAM WAS THE FATHER OF CANAAN. Ham represents the refuse and dross of the gold, the stirring and rousing of the unclean spirit of the ancient serpent. It is for that reason that he is designated the "father of Canaan", namely, of Canaan who brought curses on the world, of Canaan who was cursed, of Canaan who darkened the faces of mankind.

For this reason, too, Ham is given a special mention in the words, "Ham, the father of Canaan", that is, the notorious world-darkener, whereas we are not told that Shem was the father of such-a-one, or that Japheth was the father of such-a-one. No sooner is Ham mentioned, than he is pointed to as the father of Canaan. Hence when Abraham came on the scene, it is written, "And Abraham passed through the land" (Gen. XII, 6), for this was before the establishment of the patriarchs and before the seed of Israel existed in the world, so that the land could not yet be designated by this honoured and holy name. Observe that when Israel were virtuous the land was called by their name, the Land of Israel; but when they were not worthy it was called by another name, to wit, the Land of Canaan. Hence it is written: AND HE SAID, CURSED BE CANAAN, A SERVANT OF SERVANTS SHALL HE BE UNTO HIS BRETHREN, for the reason that he brought curses on the world, in the same way as the serpent, against whom was pronounced the doom, "Cursed art thou among all cattle" (Gen. III, 14).

THESE THREE WERE THE SONS OF NOAH. By these was established the whole world, and also the higher symbolism. AND OF THESE WAS THE WHOLE EARTH OVERSPREAD. Herein is a mystical allusion to the three supernal colours. For when that river that flows perennially watered the Garden by the power of those three supernal influences, there spread forth those terrestrial colours here below, each combined with the others, which show that the glory of the Holy One, blessed be He, extends through all the heights and the depths, and that He is one above and below. R. Eleazar said: "These three colours are themselves displayed in all those who issue from the side of holiness, and their reflection falls upon all those who issue from the side of the other spirit. And if you ponder the mystery of grades, you will find how the colours radiate to all sides until they enter the lower sphere through those twenty-seven mystic channels which are the sides of the doors that stop up the abyss. All this is known to the adepts in mystic lore. Happy the portion of the righteous whom the Holy One delights to honour and to whom He reveals the sublime mysteries of wisdom. Of them it is written: "The counsel of the Lord is with them that fear Him" (Ps. xxv, 14).' R. Eleazar here quoted the verse: "O Lord, thou art my God, I will exalt thee, I will praise thy name, for thou hast done wonderful things, even counsels of old, in faithfulness and truth" (Is. xxv, 1). 'How greatly', he said, 'it behoves men to reflect on the glory of the Holy One, blessed be He, and to offer up songs of praise to His glory, for when one knows how to offer praise to his Master in the manner appropriate, the Holy One, blessed be He, accomplishes his will. Such a man, furthermore, causes an increase of blessings on high and below. He, therefore, who knows how to offer praise to his Master and to proclaim His unity is held in affection on high and is beloved below; the Holy One, blessed be He, is proud of him, and of him it is written: "And he said unto me, thou art my servant, Israel, in whom I will be glorified" (Is. XLIX, 3).'

AND NOAH THE HUSBANDMAN BEGAN AND PLANTED A VINEYARD. R. Judah and R. Jose differed as to the origin of this vine. One said that it came from the Garden of Eden and Noah now planted it here. The other said that it had been on the earth before the Flood and Noah had plucked it and now replanted it. On the same day it blossomed, ripened, and brought forth grapes. Noah then pressed out from them wine, drank of it and became drunken. R. Simeon said: 'There is a mystical allusion in this verse. When Noah began to probe into the sin of Adam, not for purpose of practising it but in order to understand it, and so warn the world against it, he pressed grapes in order to make researches into that vineyard. But when he reached that point he was "drunken and uncovered"—he lost his (mental) balance and uncovered the breach of the world which hitherto had been closed up. WITHIN HIS TENT. It is written *oholoh* (lit. her tent), an allusion to the idea contained in the passage, "And come not nigh the door of her house" (Prov. v, 8), "her tent" implying the tent of that vineyard. The same explanation applies to the case of the sons of Aaron, who, we have been taught, were drunk from wine (when they sinned). Who then, gave them wine at that place to drink? And is it conceivable that they would dare to get drunk at such a time? But in reality the wine which made them drunk was this same wine of Noah, as it is written, "and they offered strange fire before the Lord" (Lev. x, 1), an analogous term to which is found in the passage, "That they may keep thee from the strange woman" (Prov. VII, 5): all these terms allude to one and the same thing. The same sense, then, underlies the verse, "And he drank of the wine and was drunken, and he was uncovered within his tent." This, as explained, was observed by Ham, the father of Canaan, and Canaan seized the opportunity to work his will by removing from that righteous man the mystical symbol of the covenant; for this, according to tradition, is what he did. Therefore Noah said, CURSED BE CANAAN, since through him the curse returned to the world. A SLAVE OF SLAVES HE SHALL BE: these words correspond to those addressed to the serpent: "cursed art thou from all cattle, etc." (Gen. III, 14). Hence, while all others will be saved in the world to come, he will not be saved; all others will obtain their freedom, but not he. This is a mystery known to the adepts in the ways and paths of the Torah.'

R. Simeon further discoursed, beginning with the verse: *For I know my transgressions, and my sin is ever before me* (Ps. LI, 5). He said: 'How much must a man be on his guard against sinning before the Holy One, blessed be He, for each sin committed by man is recorded on high, and is not blotted out save by much repentance, as it is said, "For though thou wash thee with nitre, and take thee much soap, yet thine iniquity is marked before me" (Jer. II, 22). For when a man commits a sin once before God, it leaves a mark, and when he repeats the same sin that mark is deepened, and after a third time it becomes a stain spreading from one side to the other, as expressed in the words, "thine iniquity is become a stain before me" (*Ibid.*). When David committed his great sin in taking Bath-Sheba, he thought that it would leave its mark forever, but the message came to him, "The Lord also hath put away thy sin, thou shalt not die" (II Sam. XII, 13); i.e. the stain has been removed.' R. Abba put this question to R. Simeon: 'Since we have been taught that Bath-Sheba was destined for King David from the day of the creation, how comes it that the Holy One, blessed be He, first gave her to Uriah the Hittite?' R. Simeon replied: 'Such is the way of the Holy One, blessed be He; although a woman is destined for a certain man, He first allows her to be the wife of another man until his time arrives. As soon as that time arrives, he departs from the world to make way for the other, although the Holy One, blessed be He, is loth to remove him from the world to make way for the other man before his time arrives. This is the inner reason why Bath-Sheba was given to Uriah first. Now reflect and you will find the reason for the Holy Land having been given to Canaan before Israel came there. You will find that the inner reason underlying the two is the same. Observe, further, that David, although he confessed his sin and repented, could not obliterate from his heart and mind the memory of the sins that he had committed, especially of that concerning Bath-Sheba, and was always apprehensive lest one of them would prove a stumbling-block to him in the hour of danger. Hence he never removed them from his thoughts. According to another interpretation, the words "For I know my transgressions" indicate his knowledge of the diverse grades to which the various sins of men are to be referred, while the words "and my sin" (*hatathi* = my failing) refer to the defect of the moon, which did not emerge from her impurity until the time of Solomon, when her light once more became whole, so that the world became firmly established and Israel dwelt secure, as it is written: "And Judah and Israel dwelt safely, every man under his vine and under his fig tree" (1 Kings v, 5). Nevertheless, as David said, "My deficiency is ever before me", and that will not be obliterated from the world until the Messiah will come, as it is said: "And the unclean spirit I will cause to pass out from the earth" (Zech. XIII, 2).'

HE WAS A MIGHTY HUNTER BEFORE THE LORD; WHEREFORE IT IS SAID: LIKE NIMROD A MIGHTY HUNTER BEFORE THE LORD. Truly he was a man of might, because he was clad in the garments of Adam, and was able by means of them to lay snares for mankind and beguile them. R. Eleazar said: 'Nimrod used to entice people into idolatrous worship by means of those garments, which enabled him to conquer the world and proclaim himself its ruler, so that mankind offered him worship. He was called "Nimrod", for the reason that he rebelled (*marad*=rebel) against the most high King above, against the higher angels and against the lower angels.' [74a] R. Simeon said: 'Our colleagues are acquainted with a profound mystery concerning these garments.'

AND THE WHOLE EARTH WAS OF ONE LANGUAGE AND OF ONE SPEECH. R. Simeon began his discourse with the verse: *And the house in its being built, was built of stone made ready at the quarry ; and there was neither hammer nor axe nor any tool of iron heard in the house in its being built* (1 Kings VI,7). He said: The phrase "in its being built" (*behibbonotho*) implies self-building, as though without the hands of artisans. Were not, then, Solomon with all his workpeople engaged in the work of building? It was here as with the candlestick, in regard to which we read, "And thou shalt make . . . of beaten work will the candlestick be made" (Ex. xxv, 31). If the candlestick was to be made of itself, why say "thou shalt make it"? In reality it was made of itself, by a miracle. So soon as the artisans set their hands to the work, it showed them how to proceed in a manner quite novel to them, the reason being that the blessing of the Almighty rested on their hands; and similarly here, in the building of the Sanctuary. It was built of its own accord, though seemingly by the hands of the labourers; it showed the workers a design which guided their hands and from which they did not turn their eyes until the whole building of the house was completed. Further it says: "Of stone made ready at the quarry" (1 Kings VI, 7). The word *sh'lemah* (made ready, complete) is written defectively, as though *sh'lomoh* (Solomon), for truly it was of Solomon; while *massa* (lit. transporting) implies that the hands of the workers were moved involuntarily, so that they did they knew not what. "And there was neither hammer nor axe nor any tool of iron heard in the house in its being built" (*Ibid.*), because the *shamir* (stone-cutting insect) performed all the splitting without any sound being heard. No cutting-tools were thus required, the whole work being accomplished by a miracle.' Said R. Simeon, 'How precious are the words of the Torah ! Happy is the portion of him who occupies himself with them and knows how to follow the path of truth ! The Scripture says, "And the house in its being built." When the Holy One, blessed be He, wills that His glory should be glorified, there issues from His thought a determination that it should spread forth; whereupon it spreads from the undiscoverable region of thought until it rests in *garon* (throat), a spot through which perennially flows the mystic force of the "spirit of life". When the thought, after its expansion, comes to rest in that place, it is called *Elohim hayyim* (living God). It then seeks to spread and disclose itself still further, and there issue from that spot fire, air, and water, all compounded together. There also emerges "Jacob, the perfect man", symbolic of a certain voice that issues and becomes audible. Thus the thought that was hitherto undisclosed and withdrawn in itself is now revealed through sound. In the further extension and disclosure of the thought, the voice strikes against the lips, and thus comes forth speech which is the culmination of the whole and in which the thought is completely disclosed. It is thus clear that all is composed of that undisclosed thought which was withdrawn into itself, and that the whole is one essence. When the expansion has reached that stage, and speech has been generated by the force of that voice, then "the house in its being built", i.e. throughout the whole process of its construction, "is of complete stones", as has been explained. The word "transported" means that the thought issues from within and commences to transport itself outside; it issues from above and commences to transport itself below. "And there was neither hammer nor axe nor any tool of iron": this alludes to the lower grades, which all depend upon the Thought, and which are not heard or admitted inside when the Thought ascends on high to draw fresh sustenance. When she does so, all of them rejoice and draw sustenance and are filled with blessings. At that time all worlds are sustained as one unity without any division whatever. After they have taken their several portions they all disperse, each to its side and to its assigned function. [74b] Hence it says: "And the whole earth was of one language", and afterwards, "and it came to pass as they journeyed *miquedem*" (lit. from before), i.e. from that which is the starting-point of the world, "that they found a valley in the land of Shin'ar", for from there they spread out in all directions, and that spot is the starting-point of differentiation. It may be objected that differentiation started later, as we read, "a river went forth from Eden to water the garden, and from *there* it parted". The truth is that when they move from the first spot there is separation, and when they gather together to draw sustenance there is no separation, and when they journey again there is separation. Hence it is written, "And it came to pass when they journeyed from the East that they found a valley", as has been explained.'

AND THE WHOLE EARTH WAS OF ONE LANGUAGE AND ONE SPEECH, i.e. the world was still a unity with one single faith in the Holy One, blessed be He. BUT AFTERWARDS THEY JOURNEYED AWAY *miquedem* (lit. from before), that is, from the One who is before all, from the foot of the world, who was the object of universal faith. AND THEY FOUND A PLAIN, that is, they made a discovery, by means of which they shook off their faith in the Most High. So it is written of Nimrod: AND THE BEGINNING OF HIS KINGDOM WAS BABEL, this being the starting-point from which he commenced to attach himself to other powers. Similarly here, "they found a plain in the land of Shin'ar", a place in which they conceived the idea of forsaking the Supernal Power for another power.

AND THEY SAID: COME, LET US BUILD US A CITY, AND A TOWER, WITH ITS TOP IN HEAVEN, AND LET US MAKE US A NAME. R. Hiya began his discourse with the text: *And the wicked are like the driven sea* (Is. LVII, 20). 'When can the sea be said to be "driven"? When it becomes violently disturbed and sways this way and that and is driven from its bed; it is then like a drunken man, reeling and staggering and heaving up and down. "For it cannot rest, and its waters cast up mire and dirt" (*Ibid.*), i.e. it throws up all the dirt and foul matter of the sea on to the shore. So it is with the wicked who leave the straight path and reel and stagger in the crooked roads they have taken, like a man drunk with wine. And what is more, with every word which they utter in their rage there issues from their mouth filth and abomination so that they are utterly defiled. [75*a*] See now, they said: "Come let us build a city, and a tower, with its top in heaven." Underlying these words there was a plan of rebellion against the Holy One, blessed be He. It was a foolish scheme, born out of the stupidity of their heart.' R. Abba said, 'Foolish they certainly were, but at the same time they had a crafty design to rid themselves of the Supreme Power and to transfer His glory to another. Throughout, there is an allusion to the mysteries of religion. Thus, the words "Come, let us build a city and a tower" mean that when they reached that plain, which signifies the "strange power", and there was revealed to them the place of its dominion, which extends particularly over "the fishes of the sea", they said, "Here is a place where the beings of the lower world can abide in comfort." At once they said: "Come, let us build a city, and a tower, and let us make us a name." This place, they said, shall be to us a centre of worship, and no other; so "let us build a city and a tower"; what need is there for us to go up to the regions on high where we cannot derive any enjoyment ? Behold, here is a place all made ready for us. Further they said: AND LET US MAKE A NAME, that is, an object of worship, LEST WE BE SCATTERED ABROAD, i.e. to other grades and different quarters of the world.

AND THE LORD CAME DOWN TO SEE THE CITY AND THE TOWER. This is one of the ten occasions on which the Shekinah descended to earth. "To see" here means "to consider methods of punishment", as in the verse, "May the Lord see and judge" (Gen. XVI, 5). It is not written, "to see the *people*", but "to see the *city* and the *tower*". Why so ?

Because when the Holy One, blessed be He, sets out to execute judgement, He first surveys the upper ranks and then the lower ranks, and since this action of mankind affected also the regions on high, the first consideration was directed to those on high. This is implied in the words, "to see the city and the tower which the sons of man (Adam) built". Mankind are here called "sons of Adam", because it was Adam, the first man, who rebelled against his Master and brought death into the world. R. Simeon began his discourse with the verse: *Thus [75b] saith the Lord God : The gate of the inner court that looketh towards the east shall be shut the six working days ; but on the Sabbath day it shall be opened, and in the day of the new moon it shall be opened* (Ezek. XLVI, 1). He said: 'If this verse is attentively considered, it is found to contain an allusion with which we are familiar. The reason why the gate is to be shut on the six working days is in order that the profane should not make use of the sacred; "but on the Sabbath day it shall be opened and on the day of the new moon it shall be opened", since in this case the sacred makes use of the sacred, and so the moon comes then to form a junction with the sun. The reason why that gate is not to be opened on the six working days is because from them this lower world draws sustenance, and they have control of the whole world with the exception of the Land of Israel: that land cannot be touched by them because the gate is shut. But on the Sabbath day and on the day of the new moon they are removed from control because the gate is open, and the world is in festivity and derives its sustenance from there, and is not under any other power. But think not that the six days have the sole dominion, even when they are in control, for we are told that that gate "looketh towards the east", i.e. the Eternal; for the Eternal, even before they assumed control, had the world under His observation, only the gate is not to be opened, so that the world should not receive sustenance from the sacred source save on Sabbath and new moons. Indeed, all the days are attached to the Sabbath day, from which they draw their sustenance, and on which all the gates are opened, and rest is vouchsafed to all on high and below. Similarly here, THE LORD CAME

DOWN TO SEE, i.e. He descended from the sacred to the profane, in order to survey what they had built and what steps they had taken to establish an idolatrous worship.'

R. Isaac was once studying with R. Simeon and put to him the question: 'How could these people have been so foolish as to raise a rebellion against the Holy One, blessed be He, and what is more, with such unanimity?' R. Simeon replied: "That has already been explained, and the answer is indicated in the words, "And it came to pass when they journeyed *miqedem*" (from the Eternal), which means that they proceeded downwards, from above to below, from the Land of Israel to Babel. They said that that was just the right place to which to attach themselves, since there the divine chastisement could be successfully resisted. There, too, the whole world could obtain nourishment in abundance, for from the higher realm sustenance could only be procured with difficulty. And furthermore, they said, we will ascend into heaven and make war against it so as to prevent it bringing a flood on the world as before.'

AND THE LORD SAID: BEHOLD, THEY ARE ONE PEOPLE, AND THEY HAVE ALL ONE LANGUAGE, i.e. being united they may indeed succeed in their undertaking. Let, therefore, all the grades be dispersed, each in its own direction, and in this way mankind below will also be dispersed. Hence it it written: AND THE LORD SCATTERED THEM ABROAD FROM THENCE. Why was their language confounded? Because they all spoke the holy tongue, and this was of help to them. For in the utterance of prayer, it is Hebrew words which fully express the purpose of the heart, and thus help to the attainment of the desired goal; hence their tongue was confounded in order that they might not be able to express their desires in the holy tongue. Since the angels on high do not understand any language save the sacred language, therefore as soon as the language of the rebels was confounded they lost the source of their power. For whatever men utter below in the holy tongue all the hosts of heaven understand and take heed of, but any other language they do not understand. Hence as soon as the language of the builders was confounded THEY LEFT OFF TO BUILD THE CITY, since their strength was broken and they were unable to achieve their purpose. We read, "Blessed be the name of God from everlasting even unto everlasting; for wisdom and might are his" (Dan. II, 20). Truly His: for whenever the Holy One, blessed be He, allowed the deep mysteries of wisdom to be brought down into the world, mankind were corrupted by them and attempted to declare war on God. He gave supernal wisdom to Adam, but Adam utilised the wisdom disclosed to him [76a] to familiarise himself with the lower grades also, until in the end he attached himself to the *yetzer-hara* (evil tempter), and the fountains of wisdom were closed to him. After he repented before his Master, parts of that wisdom were again revealed to him, in that same book, but through that same knowledge people came later on to provoke God. He gave wisdom to Noah, who, indeed, worshipped by means of it the Holy One, blessed be He, but afterwards "he drank of the wine and was drunken and uncovered", as already explained. He gave wisdom to Abraham, who by means of it served the Holy One, blessed be He, but then he gave birth to Ishmael, who provoked the Holy One, blessed be He. The same with Isaac, from whom Esau was born. As for Jacob, he married two sisters. He gave wisdom to Moses, of whom it is written: "He is trusted in all my house" (Num. XII, 7). There was none like Moses, a faithful servant, who was cognisant of all the grades, but whose heart was not seduced by any one of them from firm faith in the highest. He gave profound wisdom to Solomon, who called himself *l'ithiel, l'ithiel v'ukhal* (Prov. XXX, 1), as much as to say: "God is with me, and since wisdom is His, *v'ukhal*, I am able to do my own will." But afterwards "the Lord raised up an adversary for Solomon" (I Kings XI, 14). Thus we see that in virtue of the fragments which those people retained from that wisdom of the ancients, they provoked the Holy One, blessed be He, built a tower, and did various kinds of mischief, until they were scattered over the face of the earth, and there was no wisdom left with them for any purpose at all. But in the future the Holy One, blessed be He, will cause wisdom to be disseminated in the world, and the peoples will worship Him, as it is written:

"And I will set my spirit within you" (Ezek. XXXVI, 27), but—in contrast with the generations of old, who used it for the ruin of the world—"I will cause you", the verse continues, "to walk in my statutes and ye shall keep mine ordinances, and do them" (*Ibid.*).

As R. Jose and R. Hiya were once walking together, R. Jose said: 'Let us begin some discourse on the Torah, and evolve some new idea.' R. Jose thereupon began with the verse: *For the Lord thy God walketh in the midst of thy camp, to deliver thee, and to give up thine enemies before thee; therefore shall thy camp be holy, that he see no unseemly thing in thee, and turn away from thee* (Deut. XXIII, 15). He said: 'The term for "walketh" is here *mithhalekh*, as in the passage, "walking (*mithhalekh*) in the garden towards the cool of the day" (Gen. III, 8) (in connection with Adam's eating of the forbidden tree). *Mithhalekh* is the term for the female, and corresponding to it for the male is the term *mehalech*. This is the same power that went in front of Israel whilst they were going through the wilderness, as it is written: "And the Lord went before them by day" (Ex. XIII, 21). It is this same power that goes in front of a man when he is on a journey, as it is written: "Righteousness shall go before him, and shall make his footsteps a way" (Ps. LXXXV, 14). It walks in front of a man when he is virtuous in order "to deliver thee and to give up thine enemies before thee", to wit, to rescue a man when journeying from the power of "the other one". Hence it is incumbent on a man to guard himself against sin and to purify himself. How purify himself? In the manner indicated in the words, "therefore shall thy camp be holy". The word *qadosh* (holy) here is singular, which shows that by the word "camp" we may understand the members of which the body is composed; these are "thy camp" which is to be "holy". By the term "unseemly thing" is indicated indecency, which is a thing most hateful to the Holy One, blessed be He. Further, the term *dabar* (thing, lit. word) alludes to the obscene word by which sinners besmirch and befoul themselves. Why all this? Because "He walketh before thee". If thou be remiss in regard to this, He will immediately "turn away from thee". Now, since we are walking along before

Him in the road, let us occupy ourselves with words of the Torah. For when the Torah forms a crown over a man's head, the Shekinah does not depart from him.'

R. Hiya then discoursed as follows: 'It is written: "And the Lord said: Behold they are one people, and they have all one language." After this we read: "And it came to pass as they journeyed *miqedem*." The term *miqedem* signifies "away from the Ancient One (*qadmon*) of the world". "That they found." We should have expected "saw"; but the word "found" is used to indicate that they found remnants of the secret wisdom that had been left there by the generation of the Flood, and with that they made their attempt to provoke the Holy One, blessed be He. As they said, [76b] so they did. Note what is written, "Behold, they are one people and they have all one language." Being of one mind, of one will, and speaking one language, "nothing will be withholden from them which they purpose to do". But, said God, I know what to do; I will confound for them the grades on high and their language below, and thus their work will stop. Now, seeing that, because they were all of one mind and one will and spoke the holy tongue, it is written of them "nothing will be withholden from them which they purpose to do", and the supernal judgement was powerless against them, how much more must this apply to us or any other of the companions who are occupied in the study of the Torah !' R. Jose said: 'From here we learn that quarrelsome folk soon come to grief. For we see here that as long as the peoples of the world lived in harmony, being of one mind and one will, although they rebelled against the Holy One, blessed be He, the supernal judgement could not touch them; but as soon as they were divided, "the Lord scattered them abroad". Of the world to come, however, it is written: "For then will I turn to the peoples a pure language, that they may all call upon the name of the Lord, to serve him with one consent" (Zeph. III, 9); also: "And the Lord shall be King over all the earth; in that day shall the Lord be one, and his name one" (Zech. XIV, 9). Blessed be the Lord for ever. Amen and Amen !'

LECH LECHA
Gen. XII, 1–XVII, 27

R. Abba introduced this portion with a discourse on the text: *Hearken to me, ye obstinate of heart who are far from righteousness* (Is. XLVI, 12). He said: 'How obstinate is the heart of sinners who see the paths and ways of the Torah and pay no heed to them, but harden their hearts and do not return in repentance to their Master, wherefore they are called "obstinate of heart". Also "far from righteousness", because they keep themselves far from the Torah. R. Hizkiah says, that it is because they keep themselves far from God; they refuse to draw near to God and therefore they are far from righteousness. And because they are far from righteousness, therefore they are far from peace, and they have no peace, as it is written. "There is no peace, saith the Lord, unto the wicked" (Is. XLVIII, 22). The reason is that they are far from righteousness. See now, Abraham sought to draw near to God, and he succeeded. So it is written, "Thou didst love righteouness and hate wickedness" (Ps. XLV, 8), and it is further written, "Abraham who loves me" (Is. XLI, 8), i.e. Abram is said to have "loved God" because he loved righteousness; this was Abram's love of God, in which he excelled [77a] all his contemporaries, who were obstinate of heart and far from righteousness, as has been said.'

R. Jose opened with the text: *How amiable are thy tabernacles, O Lord of Hosts* (Ps. LXXXIV, 2). He said: 'It behoves men to consider well the importance of the service of the Holy One, blessed be He. For the mass of mankind do not know or reflect what it is that keeps the world or themselves in existence. For when God created the world, He made the heavens of fire and water mingled together but not compact, and afterwards they were made compact and firm by a divine spirit. From there God planted forth the world to rest upon supports, which themselves are kept up only by that spirit. When that spirit departs they all quiver and shake and the world trembles, as it is written, "Who shaketh the earth out of her place and the pillars thereof tremble" (Job IX, 6). The whole is based upon the Torah. Thus when Israel devotes itself to the Torah the world is firmly established and they are secure and the supports are firmly fixed in their places. See now, at the moment when midnight arrives and the Holy One, blessed be He, enters the Garden of Eden to disport Himself with the righteous, all the trees in the Garden sing praises before Him, as it is written, "Then sing the trees of the wood for joy before the Lord" (1 Chron. XVI, 33). A herald proclaimeth lustily: "To you we speak, exalted holy ones; who is there among you whose ears are quick to hear and whose eyes are open to see and whose heart is alert to perceive, what time the spirit of all spirits culls the sweet effluence of the inner soul, and a voice goes forth from there saying, Disperse, ye hosts, to the four corners of the world?" Then

1. One mounts to one side.
2. One descends on that side.
3. One enters between the two.
4. Two crown themselves with a third.
5. Three enter into one.
6. One produces various colours.
7. Six of them descend on one side and six of them on the other.
8. Six enter into twelve.
9. Twelve bestir themselves to form twenty-two.
10. Six are comprised in ten.
11. Ten are fixed in one.

Woe to those that sleep with eyes fast closed and do not know or consider how they will arise in the Day of Judgement; for reckoning is exacted [77b] when the body is defiled, and the soul flits over the face of the transparent ether, now up and now down, and if the gates are not opened it is tossed about like a stone from the sling. Woe to them! Who shall plead for them? For they shall not be admitted to this joyaunce, among the delightful habitations of the righteous their places shall be missing, they shall be delivered into the hands of Duma, they shall descend and not ascend. Of them it is written, "As the cloud is consumed and vanisheth away, so he that goeth down to Sheol shall come up no more" (Job VII, 9). At that moment a certain flash springs forth from the side of the North and strikes the four quarters of the world and comes down and alights between the wings of the cock, which is thereby awakened and begins to crow. But none are stirred save those truly pious ones who rise and remain awake and study the Torah, and then the Holy One, blessed be He, and all the righteous in the Garden of Eden listen to their voices, as it is written, "Thou that dwellest in the gardens, the companions hearken for thy voice, cause me to hear it" (S. S. VIII, 13).

AND THE LORD SAID TO ABRAM. Just before this it is written, "And Haran died in the presence of Terah his father" (Gen. XI, 28). The connection is as follows. Up to that time no one had ever died in the lifetime of his father. Haran, however, was killed at the time when Abram was cast into the furnace. Then it says, "And Terah took Abram his son and Lot the son of Haran, etc. . . . and they went forth with them from Ur of the Chaldees." We should expect "and they went forth with *him*", referring to Terah; why, then, does it say "with them"? The reason is that Terah and Lot went forth with Abram and Sara, who led the way in departing from that sinful district; for when Terah saw that Abram was rescued from the fire, he began to be guided by Abram, and therefore we read, "and they went forth with them", i.e. Terah and Lot with Abram and Sara. Also it was "to go into the land of Canaan", where *they* wanted to go. We learn further from this text that whoever makes an effort to purify himself receives assistance from above. For no sooner is it written, "to go to the land of Canaan" than we read "and God said to Abram, Get thee forth"; this message was not given to him until he made the first move himself. For the upper world is not stirred to act until an impulse is given from the lower world. The prototype of this process is that the blackish light is not caught up by the white light until it has first itself begun to mount;[1] but when it does so, forthwith the white

---
[1] v. p. 163.

light rests upon it, and therefore it is written, "O Lord, keep not thou silence, hold not thy peace and be not still, O God" (Ps. LXXXIII, 2), in order that the white light may never be withheld from the world. So, too, it says, "Ye that are the Lord's remembrancers, keep not silence" (Is. LXII, 6), in order to give the impulse from below for the influence to descend from the upper world. Similarly the prophetic spirit rests upon man only when he has first bestirred himself to receive it. So here, too, when once Abram and his family had left Ur of the Chaldees, then God said to him, "Get thee forth"; the word "thee" here, says R. Eleazar, means "for thine own advantage, to prepare thyself, to perfect thy degree". "Get thee forth": that is, it is not fitting for thee to remain here among these sinners. The real truth of the matter is this. [78a] God inspired Abram with a spirit of wisdom so that he was able to discover by means of certain tests the characters of all the inhabited countries of the world. He surveyed them and weighed them in the balance, and discovered the (heavenly) powers to which each is entrusted. When he came to the central point of the inhabited world he tried to weigh it, but obtained no response. He tried to find the power to which it was entrusted, but could not grasp it, though he weighed again and again. He noted that from that point the whole world was planted out, and he once more tested and weighed and found that the upper power in charge of it was one which could not be gauged, that it was recondite and hidden, and not like the (powers in charge of) the outlying parts of the inhabited world. He once more reflected, and came to the conclusion that as the whole world had been planted out in all directions from that point in the centre, so the power in charge of it was the one from which issued all the powers in charge of the other quarters of the world and to which they were all attached: hence "they went forth with them from Ur of the Chaldees to go to the land of Canaan". He then once more reflected and weighed in the balance and tested to find out the real truth about that place, but he could not get to the root of it. He felt himself baffled by the obscurity which surrounded it, and therefore "they came to Haran and abode there". The reason, as we have seen, is that Abraham was able to test all the upper powers that rule the world in all the quarters of the inhabited section, and did actually test them and find out which of the guiding powers among the stars and constellations had sway over which, and he weighed successfully all the inhabited parts of the globe. But when he came to this place he was met with a baffling obscurity which he could not penetrate. When God, however, perceived his efforts and his desire, He straightway revealed Himself to him and said: GET THEE FORTH, so as to know thyself and prepare thyself, FROM THY LAND: from that side of the inhabited world to which thou wast hitherto attached, AND FROM THY KINDRED, from that wisdom wherewith thou didst cast thy horoscope, noting the hour and second of thy birth and the star that was then in the ascendant, AND FROM THY FATHER'S HOUSE, that thou shouldst not heed thy father's house, even if thou couldst hope in virtue of thy father's house for some prosperity in this world; therefore get thee gone from *this* wisdom and from *this* consideration. That this explanation is right may be proved thus. They had left Ur of the Chaldees and were in Haran. Why, then, should God say to Abram, "Get thee forth from thy land and from thy kindred"? It must therefore be as we have explained. TO THE LAND WHICH I SHALL SHOW THEE: i.e. I shall show thee that which thou wast not able to discover, the power of that land so recondite and obscure.

AND I SHALL MAKE THEE A GREAT NATION, ETC. "I shall make thee", in compensation for "get thee gone"; AND I SHALL BLESS THEE, in compensation for "from my land"; AND I WILL MAKE GREAT THY NAME, in compensation for "and from thy kindred"; AND BE A BLESSING, in compensation for "and from thy father's house". R. Simeon said: "I shall make thee a great nation"; from the side of the Right; "and I shall bless thee", from the side of the Left; "and I shall make great thy name", from the realm of the Centre; "and be thou a blessing", from the side of the Land of Israel. Here we have an allusion to the throne resting on four supports, all of which were comprised in Abram. From this point blessings are transmitted to others also, who are sustained from here, as it is written, I SHALL BLESS THEM THAT BLESS THEE, [78b] AND CURSE THEM THAT CURSE THEE, AND ALL THE FAMILIES OF THE EARTH SHALL BE BLESSED IN THEE. R. Eleazar was sitting one day before his father, R. Simeon, and with him were R. Judah and R. Isaac and R. Hizkiah. Said R. Eleazar to R. Simeon: In reference to this verse, GET THEE FORTH FROM THY LAND AND FROM THY KINDRED, since they all went forth, why was not Abram told that they should go? For though Terah was an idolater, yet since he had the good impulse to go forth with Abram, and since, as we know, God delights in the repentance of sinners, and Terah actually began the journey, why is it not written "get *ye* forth"? Why was it said to Abram alone "get *thee* forth"? R. Simeon replied: If you think that Terah left Ur of the Chaldees in order to repent of his past life, you are mistaken. The truth is that he was running away for his life, as his fellow-countrymen wanted to kill him. For when they saw that Abram was delivered (from the fiery furnace) they said to Terah, "It is you who misled us with those idols of yours", and it was through fear of them that Terah left. When he reached Haran he did not go any further, as it is written, "And Abram went as the Lord had said to him, and Lot went with him", but Terah is not mentioned. R. Simeon expounded in this connection the text, "And from the wicked their light is withholden, and the high arm is broken" (Job XXXVIII, 15). The words "and from the wicked their light is withholden", he said, can be referred to Nimrod and his contemporaries, from whom Abram, who was their light, departed. Or we may refer them to Terah and his household, whose light was Abram. It does not say "light", but "*their* light", viz. the light that was with them. "The high arm is broken" refers to Nimrod, who led astray the whole of mankind. Therefore it is written *lech lecha* (lit. go for thyself), to give light to thyself and to all that shall follow thee from now onwards. R. Simeon further discoursed on the text, "Now they see not the light; it is bright in the skies, and a wind passeth and cleanseth them" (Job XXXVII, 21). "Now they see not the light", i.e. Abram's family saw not the light when God said to Abram, "Get thee forth from thy land and from thy kindred and from thy father's house". "It is bright in the skies" means that God willed to make Abram cleave to that supernal light and to shine there. "A wind passeth and cleanseth them": because subsequently Terah and all his household repented, as it is said, "and the souls which they had saved (lit. made) in Haran", referring to Terah's household, and further, "and thou shalt come to thy fathers in peace" (Gen. xv, 15), which shows that Terah joined Abram.

So ABRAM WENT AS THE LORD HAD SPOKEN TO HIM, ETC. Said R. Eleazar: 'It is not written "and Abram *went forth*", but simply "Abram *went*"; the first step was "going forth", as it is written, "and they went forth (*vayez'u*) from Ur of the Chaldees" (Gen. xi, 31), but the second step was "going", corresponding to God's command "Go (*lech*) thou" (*Ibid.* xii, 1). AS THE LORD HAD SPOKEN TO HIM: i.e. because he had received all those promises. AND LOT WENT WITH HIM: i.e. he attached himself to him to learn his ways, and in spite of this he did not learn them too well.' Said R. Eleazar: 'Happy are the righteous who learn the ways of the Holy One, blessed be He, to walk in them and to go in fear of that Day of Judgement when man will be called to account before God.' To illustrate this, R. Eleazar expounded the text: "By his hand every man sealeth, that all men may acknowledge their works" (Job. xxxvii, 7). He said: [79a] 'On the day when man's time arrives to depart from the world, when the body is broken and the soul seeks to leave it, on that day man is privileged to see things that he was not permitted to see before, when the body was in full vigour. Three messengers stand over him and take an account of his life and of all that he has done in this world, and he admits all with his mouth and signs the account with his hand as it is written, "every man sealeth with his hand": the whole account is signed with his hand so that he should be judged in the next world for all his actions, former and later, old and new, not one of them is forgotten (as it is written, "that every man should acknowledge his works");

and for all the deeds which he committed with his body and his spirit in this world he gives an account with his body and spirit before he leaves the world. For just as sinners are stiff-necked in this world, so they are stiff-necked even at the moment when they are on the point of departing from the world. Happy, therefore, is the man who learns in this world the ways of God to walk in them. But sinners, even though they observe the righteous, are too stiff-necked to learn from them. Therefore it behoves the righteous to importune them and, even though the sinner be stiff-necked, not to relax his hold of him, for if he let him go, he may depart and destroy the world. We see this from the case of Gehazi when driven out by Elisha. So, too, with Lot: as long as Abram was with him, he did not associate with the wicked, but as soon as he left him, what do we find ? "So Lot chose him all the plain of Jordan"; and further, "and he moved his tent as far as Sodom", the inhabitants of which "were wicked and sinners against the Lord exceedingly". Said R. Abba to R. Eleazar, 'With reference to your observation that the text says "Abraham went", and not "went forth", what do you make of the end of the verse which says "when he went forth from Haran" ?' Said R. Eleazar: 'The words "from Haran" are important; the journey was in the first instance a "going forth" from the land of his kindred. AND ABRAM TOOK SARAI HIS WIFE. The word "took" signifies that he pleaded with her and persuaded her. For a man is not permitted to take his wife with him to another country without her consent. The word "take" is used in a similar sense in the texts "Take Aaron" (Num. XX, 25), and "Take the Levites" (*Ibid.* III, 45). So Abram spoke persuasively to Sarai, pointing out to her how wicked were the ways of their contemporaries. Further, Abram took LOT HIS BROTHER'S SON. Abram's reason for taking Lot with him was that he foresaw through the Holy Spirit that David was destined to issue from him. AND THE SOULS THAT THEY HAD GOTTEN IN HARAN: these were the male and female proselytes whose souls they had saved. Abram converted the men and Sarai the women, and therefore they are spoken of as if they had made them.' Said R. Abba: 'If so, they must have been a great crowd, if you say that they all went with him.' Said R. Eleazar: 'That is so; and therefore the whole company that went with him were called [79b] "the people of the God of Abraham", and he travelled through the land without fear, as it is written, "And Abram passed through the land".' Said R. Abba to him: 'I interpret differently, viz. that the particle *eth* here signifies the augmentation of his merit by that of the souls that went with him, since one who puts another in the path of righteousness ever reaps benefit from his merit also. So it was the merit of those souls which were "made" in Haran that accompanied Abram.'

GET THEE FORTH. R. Simeon said: 'What is the reason that the first communion which God held with Abraham commenced with the words "Get thee forth" (*lech lecha*)? It is that the numerical value of the letters of the words *lech lecha* is a hundred, and hence they contained a hint to him that he would beget a son at the age of a hundred. See now, whatever God does upon the earth has some inner and recondite purpose. Abram was not cleaving to God as closely as he should have done, and therefore God said to him, "Get thee forth", alluding thereby to the place where he would be able to draw near to God, which was the first grade for entering before God; hence "get thee forth". Abram could not attain to this grade until he had entered the promised land; but there he was destined to attain it. Similarly with David, of whom it is written, "And David inquired of the Lord saying, Shall I go up into any of the cities of Judah? And the Lord said unto him, Go up. And David said, Whither shall I go up? And he said, Unto Hebron." (II Sam. II, 1). Seeing that Saul was dead and the kingship belonged of right to David, why was he not at once declared king over all Israel? Here again there was an inner purpose: David was not qualified to become king until he had attached himself to the patriarchs who were buried in Hebron, and therefore he stayed there seven years in order to qualify himself completely for the kingship. Thus all was done with an inner purpose, and in order that there should be no flaw in his kingship. Similarly Abram did not enter into the covenant of God until he entered the land. Observe that the text says "And Abram passed through the land", where we should have expected "went through". We have here an allusion to the holy name of seventy-two letters with which the world is sealed, all of which are in this name. We read here "and he *passed*", and in another place we find "And the Lord *passed* by before him and proclaimed" (Ex. xxxiv, 6). In the book of the venerable R. Yesa we find: It is written here "And Abram *passed* through the land", and in another place it says "I will make all my goodness *pass* before thee" (Ex. xxxiii, 19), this being an allusion to the holiness of the land which emanates from a heavenly source.

UNTO THE PLACE OF SHECHEM, UNTO THE OAK OF MORETH, i.e. from one sphere to the other, as befitted. AND THE CANAANITE WAS THEN IN THE LAND. This confirms what has previously been said, that up to that time the wicked serpent that was cursed and brought curses on the world held sway over the land, as it is written, "Cursed is Canaan, a servant of servants shall he be unto his brethren" (Gen. ix, 25), and of the serpent, "Cursed art thou above all cattle" (Gen. iii, 14). It was in that land that Abram drew near to God. For it is written here AND THE LORD APPEARED UNTO ABRAM: here was revealed to him what [80*a*] he could not previously find out, the hidden force that ruled over the (holy) land, and so HE BUILT THERE AN ALTAR TO THE LORD WHO APPEARED TO HIM. The words "who appeared to him", which seem to be superfluous, indicate that here was revealed to him that grade which rules over the land, and that he entered into it and was confirmed in it.

AND HE REMOVED FROM THENCE UNTO THE MOUNTAIN: The word *ha-harah* (to the mountain) can be rendered "to the mountain of *hé*", implying that he now became acquainted with this and with all the grades planted there. AND PITCHED HIS TENT: here, again, the letter *hé* in the word *aholoh* (his tent) indicates that he purified himself and acknowledged the kingship of heaven in all the grades attached to it. He acquired the certainty that God rules over all, and so he built an altar. There were, in fact, two altars, because here it was revealed to him that God is ruler over all, and he became acquainted with the higher wisdom, which he had not known previously. He therefore built two altars, one for the grade (of the Godhead) which was already known to him, and one for the grade which was still concealed. This can be seen from the text: it first says "And he built there an altar to the Lord who appeared to him", and afterwards it says "and he built an altar to the Lord", simply—with an allusion to the higher wisdom. Thus Abram proceeded from grade to grade until he reached his own rightful grade, as it is written, "And Abram journeyed, going on still toward the South", the South (typifying wisdom) being the allotted portion of Abram, and there he finally fixed himself.

AND THERE WAS A FAMINE IN THE LAND: because up to now the power in charge of the land had not endowed the land with strength to produce food, since as yet it (the land) had not attained its complete development. So, seeing that the power in charge of the land was not endowing it with its rightful force and energy, ABRAM WENT DOWN TO EGYPT TO SOJOURN THERE. How did Abram know that the land was still defective? Because it was said to him, UNTO THY SEED WILL I GIVE THIS LAND. From this Abram knew that the land would not be invested with its appropriate holiness save through the grades of holiness which would be exhibited by his offspring. [81b]

AND ABRAM WENT DOWN TO EGYPT TO SOJOURN THERE. Why to Egypt? Because it is compared to the Garden of the Lord, as it is written, "Like the garden of the Lord, like the land of Egypt". For there a certain stream (from the Garden) which is on the right descends and flows, as it is written, "The name of the one was Pishon, that it is which compasseth the whole land of Havilah where there is gold" (Gen. II, 11). When Abram knew God and became perfect in faith, he sought to acquaint himself with all those grades (of wisdom) which are attached to the lower world, and since Egypt derived from the Right, he went down to Egypt. (We remark here that famine comes only when mercy ceases to temper justice.)

NOW IT CAME TO PASS THAT WHEN HE WAS COME NEAR TO ENTER INTO EGYPT. The word *hikrib* (came near) literally means "*brought* near"; as much as to say that he brought himself fittingly near to God. TO ENTER INTO EGYPT: i.e. to examine those other (worldly) grades so as to know how to avoid them and to shun the ways of the Egyptians. R. Judah said: 'Consider this. Because Abram went down to Egypt without first obtaining God's consent (for nowhere is it written that God told Abram to go down to Egypt), therefore his descendants were enslaved to the Egyptians four hundred years.' All that night he was filled with anxiety concerning Sarai, AND HE SAID TO SARAI HIS WIFE, BEHOLD NOW I KNOW THAT THOU ART A FAIR WOMAN TO LOOK UPON. Did he then not know it before? This confirms what we have learnt, that up to that time Abram had never looked closely at the features of Sarai on account of the excessive modesty which ruled their intercourse, but when he approached Egypt they were disclosed, and he saw how fair she was. According to another explanation, he knew it through the fact that, contrary to the usual experience, she looked as beautiful as ever after the fatigues of the journey. Another explanation is that Abram said so because he saw with her the Shekinah. It was on this account that Abram made bold to say subsequently, "she is my sister", with a double meaning: one the literal, the other figurative, as in the words "say to Wisdom, thou art my sister" (Prov. VII, 4). SAY NOW THOU ART MY SISTER. R. Yesa said: 'Abram knew that all the Egyptians were full of lewdness. It may therefore [82a] seem surprising that he was not apprehensive for his wife and that he did not turn back without entering the country. But the truth is that he saw with her the Shekinah and was therefore confident. THAT IT MAY BE WELL WITH ME FOR THY SAKE: these words were addressed to the Shekinah, as if to say: "that God may entreat me well for thy sake". AND THAT MY SOUL MAY LIVE

BECAUSE OF THEE: because through this (the Shekinah) man ascends and becomes privileged to enter on the path of life.'

NOW IT CAME TO PASS THAT WHEN ABRAM WAS COME TO EGYPT THE EGYPTIANS BEHELD THE WOMAN THAT SHE WAS VERY FAIR. R. Judah said: 'He brought her in a box, and they opened it to levy duty. When it was opened a light like that of the sun shone forth, as it says "that she was very fair". The word "very" indicates that they saw in the box another figure; for when they took her out, they saw a figure in the box as before. Hence the Scripture repeats, AND THE PRINCES OF PHARAOH SAW HER, and on this account THEY PRAISED HER TO PHARAOH.' R. Isaac said: 'Woe to the sinners of the world who do not know and do not observe the work of the Holy One, blessed be He, nor do they reflect that all which takes place in the world is from God, who knows from the outset what will be at the end, as it is written, "declaring the end from the beginning" (Is. XLVI, 10). He looks ahead and lays a train now for developments in the distant future. Thus had not Sarai been taken to Pharaoh, he would not have been plagued, and it was his castigation which caused the subsequent castigation of the Egyptians. The word "great" is applied here to the plagues inflicted on Pharaoh and also to the "signs and wonders which God showed upon Egypt" (Deut. VI, 22), to indicate that here, as there, were ten plagues, and that just as God performed wonders for Israel by night, so He performed wonders for Sarai by night.'

R. Jose expounded the text: *Thou, O Lord, art a shield about me, my glory and the lifter up of mine head* (Ps. III, 4). He said: 'What David meant was: "though the whole world should come to make war on me, thou, O Lord, art a shield about me". David further said to God: "Sovereign of the Universe, wherefore do not the Israelites conclude one of their blessings with my name as they do with the name of Abraham,[1] of whom it is written 'I am thy shield' (Gen. XV, 1)?" God replied: "Abraham I have already tried and tested

---

[1] The first blessing of the *Amidah*.

and found to be wholly stedfast." Said David: "If so, 'examine me, O Lord, and prove me, try my reins and my heart' (Ps. XXVI, 2)." When he sinned in the matter of Bathsheba, David remembered what he had said, and he exclaimed " 'Thou hast proved mine heart, thou hast visited me in the night, thou hast tried me and hast not found, my thoughts should not have passed my mouth' (Ps. XVII, 3). I said, Examine me, O Lord, and prove me, and thou hast proved my heart; I said, Try my reins, and thou hast tried me; but thou hast not found me as I should be; would that what was in my mind had not passed my lips." (And with all this the Israelites do conclude a blessing with his name.[1]) Therefore David said: " 'Thou, O Lord, art a shield about me, my glory and the lifter up of my head': this grade assuredly is my glory with which I am crowned." '

AND PHARAOH GAVE MEN CHARGE CONCERNING HIM, AND THEY SENT HIM ON HIS WAY. Assuredly God is a shield to the righteous to save them from falling into the power of men, and so God shielded Abram that the Egyptians should not have power to harm him and his wife. For the Shekinah did not leave Sarai all that night. When Pharaoh tried to approach her, the angel came and smote him. Whenever Sarai said "smite", he smote, and meanwhile Abram firmly trusted in God that He would allow no harm to come to Sarai, as it is written, "the righteous are bold as a lion" (Prov. XXVIII, 1). This is one of the trials which Abram endured without complaining against God. R. Isaac said that God purposely refrained from telling Abram to go down to Egypt, and allowed him to go of his own accord, in order that people might not be able to say that after making him go there He brought trouble on him through his wife. R. Isaac here expounded the text *The righteous shall flourish like the palm tree, he shall grow like the cedar in Lebanon* (Ps. XCII, 13). 'Why is the righteous man compared to a palm tree? Because just as, if a palm tree is cut down, it takes a long time for one to grow again, so if the world loses a righteous man, it is a long time before another arises in his

---

[1] The third blessing after the *Haftarah*.

place. Further, just as a palm tree does not grow unless the male be accompanied by the female, so the righteous cannot flourish save when they are male and female together, like Abram and Sarai. Again, "he shall grow like a cedar in Lebanon": just as a cedar is pre-eminent and all can sit under it, so the righteous man is pre-eminent and all sit under him. The world is supported upon one righteous one, as it is written, "the righteous is the foundation of the world" (Prov. x, 25).' Said R. Judah, 'Is it not a dictum of the Rabbis that the world rests on seven supports, as it is written, "Wisdom hath hewn out her seven pillars" (Prov. IX, 1)?' R. Jose replied: 'That is so, but those others depend on one [82b] who is the real support of the world. This is the *Zaddik* who waters and refreshes the world and feedeth all, and of whom it is written, "Say of the Zaddik that he is good, for (through him) they eat of the fruit of their works" (Is. III, 10), and again, "The Lord is good to all and his tender mercies are over all his works" (Ps. CXLV, 9).'

R. Isaac said: 'The Scripture tells us that "a river went forth from Eden to water the garden" (Gen. II, 10). It is this river which is the support upon which the world rests. It waters the Garden and causes it to bear fruits which spring up and blossom in the world, and which uphold the world and make possible the study of the Torah. What are these fruits? They are the souls of the righteous which are the fruit of God's handiwork. Therefore every night the souls of the righteous mount on high, and at the hour of midnight the Holy One, blessed be He, comes to the Garden of Eden to disport Himself with them. With which of them? R. Jose said, with all: both with those whose abode is in the other world and with those who are still in their dwellings in this world—with all of them God disports Himself at midnight. For the world on high requires to be stirred by the impulse of the lower world, and so when the souls of the righteous leave this world and mount on high, they all clothe themselves with a supernal light, with a resplendent figure, and God disports Himself with them and delights in them, since they are the fruit of His handiwork, and for this reason Israel who are possessed of holy souls are called sons to the Holy One, blessed be He, as it is written, "Ye are sons to the Lord your God" (Deut. XIV, 1), that is, the fruit of His handiwork.' Said R. Yesa, 'You say that God disports Himself also with the souls in this world: how is this?' He answered, 'At midnight all the truly righteous arise to read the Torah and to sing psalms, and we have learnt that the Holy One, blessed be He, and all the righteous in the Garden of Eden listen to their voices, and in consequence a certain grace is imparted to them by day; so it is written, "The Lord will command his grace in the day-time, and in the night his song shall be with me" (Ps. XLII, 9). Hence it is that the praises which are sung at night constitute the most perfect praise. So when God was slaying the first-born in Egypt, the Israelites in their houses were singing praises and psalms to Him. See now, King David too used to get up in the middle of the night, as it is written, "At midnight I will rise to give thanks to thee" (Ps. CXIX, 62). He did not remain sitting or lying in his bed, but he literally rose and stood up to compose psalms and praises. Therefore it is that King David lives for ever, and even in the days of the King Messiah he will be king, according to the dictum: "If the King Messiah will be from the living, David will be his name, and if he will be from the dead, David will be his name." He, as it were, awoke the dawn, as it is written, "Awake, my glory, awake, psaltery and harp; I myself will awake right early" (Ps. LVII, 9).

In the night when Sarai was with Pharaoh, the angels came to sing praises before God, but God said to them, "Go all of you, and deal heavy blows on Egypt, in anticipation of what I intend to do subsequently"; hence it is written, "And the Lord smote Pharaoh with great plagues." Then, PHARAOH CALLED ABRAM, ETC. What gave him this idea, seeing that God did not say anything to him as He did later to Abimelech, as when He said, "And now restore the man's wife, for he is a prophet", etc. (Gen. XX, 7)?' Said R. Isaac, 'The answer is contained in the words BECAUSE OF SARAI ABRAM'S WIFE: the angels as they smote him said "this blow is because of Sarai Abram's wife" and no more, and then he knew that she was Abram's wife, and straightway "Pharaoh called Abram and said, etc." AND

PHARAOH GAVE MEN CHARGE CONCERNING HIM: why so? In order that no man should come near to hurt them. AND THEY BROUGHT HIM ON THE WAY: i.e. they conducted him through the land of Egypt. Said God to him: So art thou destined to do to his descendants: thou shalt conduct them from thy land, as it is written, "And it came to pass when Pharaoh let go (*beshallach*, lit. escorted) the people" (Ex. XIII, 17).' R. Abba said: 'All this happened to Abram and he had to go through all this only in order that he and Sarai might acquire a great name in the world. [83a] For even in Egypt, a country of magicians from whom no man could escape, Abram distinguished himself, and he raised himself there to a higher eminence, as it is written, AND ABRAM WENT UP OUT OF EGYPT. To where did he ascend? INTO THE SOUTH.' Said R. Simeon: 'Observe that these words have an inner meaning, and indicate to us that Abram went down to the "lower degrees" in Egypt, and probed them to the bottom, but clave not to them and returned unto his Master. He was not like Adam, who, when he descended to a certain grade, was enticed by the serpent and brought death upon the world; nor was he like Noah, who, when he descended to a certain grade, was enticed and "drank of the wine and became drunk and was uncovered in the midst of his tent" (Gen. IX, 21). Unlike them, Abram came up again and returned to his place, to the upper grade to which he had been attached previously. This whole incident is related in order to show that he was stedfast in his attachment to Wisdom, and was not seduced, and returned to his former condition. "Into the South": this is the higher grade to which he was attached at first, as it is written, "going on still to the South". The inner significance of this narrative is that if Abram had not gone down to Egypt and been tested there, his portion would not have been in the Lord. Similarly with his descendants, whom God desired to make a unique and perfect people and to bring near to Himself: if they had not first gone down to Egypt and been tested there, they would not have been God's chosen people. Similarly, too, if the Holy Land had not been first given to Canaan to rule over, it would not have become the lot and portion of the Holy

One, blessed be He. In all these facts the same mystical purpose is to be observed.'

R. Simeon was once on a journey in company with his son R. Eleazar and R. Abba and R. Judah. As they were going along, R. Simeon said: 'I marvel how indifferent men are to the words of the Torah and the problem of their own existence!' He proceeded to discourse on the text: *With my soul have I desired thee in the night, yea, with my spirit within me will I seek thee early* (Is. XXVI, 9). He said: 'The inner meaning of this verse is as follows. When a man lies down in bed, his vital spirit (*nefesh*) leaves him and begins to mount on high, leaving with the body only the impression of a receptacle which contains the heart-beat. The rest of it tries to soar from grade to grade, and in doing so it encounters certain bright but unclean essences. If it is pure and has not defiled itself by day, it rises above them, but if not, it becomes defiled among them and cleaves to them and does not rise any further. There they show her certain things which are going to happen in the near future: and sometimes they delude her and show her false things. Thus she goes about the whole night until the man wakes up, when she returns to her place. Happy are the righteous to whom God reveals His secrets in dreams, so that they may be on their guard against sin! Woe to the sinners who defile their bodies and their souls! As for those who have not defiled themselves during the day, when they fall asleep at night their souls begin to ascend, and first enter those grades which we have mentioned, but they do not cleave to them and continue to mount further. The soul which is privileged thus to rise finally appears before the gate of the celestial palace, and yearns with all its might to behold the beauty of the King and to visit His sanctuary. This is the man who ever hath a portion in the world to come, and this is the soul whose yearning when she ascends is for the Holy One, blessed be He, and who does not cleave to those other bright essences, but seeks out the holy essence in the place from which she (originally) issued. Therefore it is written, "With my soul have I desired thee in the night", to pursue after thee and not to be enticed away after false powers. Again, the words

"With my soul have I desired thee [83*b*] in the night" refer to the soul (*nefesh*) which has sway by night, while the words "with my spirit within me will I seek thee early" refer to the spirit (*ruaḥ*) which has sway by day. "Soul" (*nefesh*) and "spirit" (*ruaḥ*) are not two separate grades, but one grade with two aspects. There is still a third aspect which should dominate these two and cleave to them as they to it, and which is called "higher spirit" (*neshamah*). (All these grades are arranged in wisdom, and contemplation of them throws light on the higher Wisdom.) This spirit enters into them and they cleave to it, and when it dominates, such a man is called holy, perfect, wholly devoted to God. "Soul" (*nefesh*) is the lowest stirring, it supports and feeds the body and is closely connected with it. When it sufficiently qualifies itself, it becomes the throne on which rests the lower spirit (*ruaḥ*), as it is written, "until the spirit be poured on us from on high" (Is. XXXII, 15). When both have prepared themselves sufficiently, they are qualified to receive the higher spirit (*neshamah*), to which the lower spirit (*ruaḥ*) becomes a throne, and which is undiscoverable, supreme over all. Thus there is throne resting on throne, and a throne for the highest. From observing these grades of the soul, one obtains an insight into the higher Wisdom, and it is wholly through Wisdom that in this way certain mysteries are connected together. For *nefesh* is the lowest stirring to which the body cleaves, like the dark light at the bottom of the candle-flame which clings to the wick and exists only through it. When fully kindled it becomes a throne for the white light above it. When both are fully kindled, the white light becomes a throne for a light which cannot be fully discerned, an unknown something resting on that white light, and so there is formed a complete light. So with the man who attains perfection and is called "holy", as in the verse "for the holy ones that are in the earth". And so also in the upper world. Hence at the time when Abram entered the land God appeared to him and he received there a *nefesh*, and built an altar to the corresponding grade (of divinity). Then "he journeyed to the South", receiving a *ruaḥ*. Finally he rose to the height of cleaving to God through the medium of the *neshamah*, whereupon he "built an altar to the Lord", indicating the most recondite grade corresponding to the *neshamah*. He then found that it was requisite for him to test himself and endow himself with grades, so he went down to Egypt. There he preserved himself from being seduced by those bright essences, and after testing himself he returned to his place: he "went up" from Egypt literally, strengthened and confirmed in faith, and reached the highest grade of faith. Thenceforth Abram was acquainted with the higher Wisdom and clung to God and became the right hand of the world. Hence it says AND ABRAM WAS VERY RICH IN CATTLE, IN SILVER, AND IN GOLD: "very rich", from the side of the East; "in cattle", from the side of the West; "in silver", from the side of the South; "in gold", from the side of the North.' R. Eleazar and R. Abba and all the companions thereupon came and kissed his hands. R. Abba wept and said, 'Alas, alas, when thou departest from the world, who shall cause the light of the Torah to shine forth ? Happy the lot of the companions who hear these words of the Torah from thy mouth,' Said R. Simeon, Let us proceed.

AND HE WENT ON HIS JOURNEYS, i.e. to revisit his place and his grades, until he reached the first grade where the first revelation had taken place. "On his journeys": all those grades, grade after grade, as has been said. [84*a*] EVEN TO BETHEL: to prepare his place and to combine "the South" and "Bethel" in a complete unity, since from the South to Bethel comprised the whole gamut of Wisdom. UNTO THE PLACE WHERE HIS TENT HAD BEEN AT THE BEGINNING, to wit, Bethel, the "perfect stone". The spot is further defined as THE PLACE OF THE ALTAR WHICH HE HAD MADE THERE AT THE FIRST, as it was said, "to the Lord who appeared unto him", and therefore now ABRAM CALLED ON THE NAME OF THE LORD, in proof that he had attained to perfect faith. Note this. At first Abram proceeded from the lower to the higher, as it is written, "And the Lord appeared to Abram", and again, "to the Lord who appeared to him", and then "going on his journeys to the South"—grade after grade until he was endowed with the

South which was his rightful portion. From thence he began to reverse the process and descended from the higher to the lower, so as to fix all in its proper place. On the return journey, too, the mention of his stages contains an allusion to the higher Wisdom. It is written, "And he went on his journeys from the South", i.e. from the side of the Right, from the very beginning of the upper world, the mysterious and recondite, reaching to the Limitless (*En Sof*), and then descended stage by stage "from the South to Bethel", where "Abram called on the name of the Lord", i.e. he affixed the unity to its proper place, viz. "the place of the altar which he had made there at the first": i.e. he had taken it from the lower to the upper grade, and now he brought it down by stages from the upper to the lower in order that it should not depart from those upper grades nor they from it and the whole should constitute an indissoluble unity. Then was Abram fully endowed, and he became the lot and the portion of God in real truth. Happy are the righteous who are crowned in God as God in them! Happy in this world and happy in the world to come! Of them it is written, "Thy people shall be all righteous, they shall inherit the earth for ever" (Is. LX, 21); and again, "The path of the righteous is as the shining light, that shineth more and more unto the perfect day" (Prov. IV, 18).

The travellers went on until they came to a field, where they sat down. R. Simeon then discoursed on the text: *Turn unto me and have mercy upon me* (Ps. LXXXVI, 16). He said: 'This verse deserves careful study, for although we have already explained it more than once, yet it has still an inner meaning. How could David say to God, "Turn to me"? The truth is that he was referring to the grade with which he was endowed. Similarly he said *Give thy strength to thy servant* (*Ibid.*). The word "strength" refers to the supernal Force (*Geburah*), as in the verse "And he gave strength to his king" (Is. II, 19). The word "king", used thus without qualification, refers to the Messiah, as also does the word "servant" in this passage. *And save the son of thy handmaid.* Why does he call himself the son of his mother and not of his father Jesse? This bears out what we have laid down, that when a man comes to ask something of heaven, he should only say that of which he is certain; hence he mentioned his mother and not his father. And further, tradition refers this verse to the Messiah, as we have said.' R. Simeon proceeded:

AND THERE WAS A STRIFE BETWEEN THE HERDMEN OF ABRAM'S CATTLE. The omission of the letter *Yod* from the word *rib* (strife) indicates that Lot desired to revert to the idolatry of the inhabitants of the country; this is confirmed by the end of the verse AND THE CANAANITE AND THE PERIZZITE DWELT THEN IN THE LAND. That Lot actually did revert to idolatry we know from the words AND LOT JOURNEYED FROM THE EAST: the word *mi-qedem* (from the East) is equivalent to *mi-qadmono* (from the Ancient One) of the world (similarly it says of the men who built the Tower of Babel that they journeyed "from the East", Gen. XI, 1). As soon as Abram saw that this was in Lot's mind, straightway HE SAID TO LOT . . . SEPARATE THYSELF, I PRAY THEE, FROM ME; as if to say, thou art not worthy to associate with me. So Abram separated from him and refused to accompany or join him, since whoever associates with a sinner eventually follows in his footsteps and so brings punishment [84*b*] upon himself. We know this from Jehoshaphat, who through joining with Ahab would have brought punishment on himself had he not been saved by the merit of his ancestors. Therefore Abram refused to accompany Lot; and for all that Lot did not turn from his evil course, but CHOSE HIM ALL THE PLAIN OF THE JORDAN and journeyed *mi-qedem*, i.e. departed from the Ancient One of the world, and did not seek to perfect himself in faith like Abram. So ABRAM DWELLED IN THE LAND OF CANAAN, to cleave to the place where faith could be strengthened and to learn wisdom in order to cleave to his Master, whereas LOT DWELLED IN THE CITIES OF THE PLAIN and MOVED HIS TENT AS FAR AS SODOM, with those godless sinners who had abandoned faith, as it is written, NOW THE MEN OF SODOM WERE WICKED AND SINNERS AGAINST THE LORD EXCEEDINGLY. Thus each went his own way. Happy are the companions who devote themselves to the

Torah day and night and seek converse with God; of them it is written, "Ye that cleave unto the Lord your God are alive every one of you this day" (Deut. IV, 4).'

AND THE LORD SAID TO ABRAM AFTER THAT LOT WAS SEPARATED FROM HIM. In connection with this verse R. Abba discoursed on the following text: *Jonah rose up to flee to Tarshish from the presence of the Lord* (Jonah, I, 3). He said: 'Woe to the man who seeks to hide himself from God, of whom it is written, "Do I not fill heaven and earth, saith the Lord?" (Jer. XXIII, 24). Why, then, did Jonah seek to flee from Him? The reason is to be found in the verse "My dove that art in the clefts of the rock, in the coverts of the steep place" (S. S. II, 14). "My dove" refers to the community of Israel; "the clefts of the rock" refers to Jerusalem, which is firm and eminent like a rock; "the coverts of the steep place" refer to the place which is called "holy of holies", the heart of the world. It is called "coverts" because there the Shekinah is concealed like a woman who converses only with her husband and never goes out. The community of Israel does not dwell outside its own place save in the time of exile, and because it is in exile, therefore other nations enjoy greater prosperity. When Israel were in their own land everything was as it should be, the heavenly throne was fully spread over them, and the liturgy which they performed pierced through the ether and ascended on high to its place. For Israel alone was qualified to serve God in that land, and therefore the Gentiles kept aloof, since they did not rule over it as now, but were nourished only by the "residue". You may say, How do you reconcile this with the fact that a number of (foreign) kings ruled over it at the time when the Temple still existed. The answer is that in the time of the first Temple, before Israel defiled the land, the Gentiles did not rule over it but were nourished from the "residue". But when Israel sinned and defiled the land, they, as it were, drove the Shekinah from its place, and it went to another place, and therefore other nations were allowed to rule over the land. For no angel has control of the land of Israel, but only God. When Israel sinned and burned incense to other gods in the Holy Land, the Shekinah was driven from its place, and other gods were associated with it, and so other nations obtained dominion and the prophets died out, and all the higher grades ceased to rule, and dominion was not withdrawn from other nations, because they drew the Shekinah to themselves. Hence in the time of the second Temple the rule of the other nations did not cease, and even less so in the period of the Exile, when the Shekinah found herself among other nations where other chieftains exercise dominion, deriving their sustenance from the Shekinah, which has consorted with them. Thus we see that [85a] when Israel dwelt in their own land and maintained the Temple service, the Shekinah remained among them in privacy, and did not issue from her house openly. Therefore all the prophets who lived in those times drew their inspiration only from her place, as we have said. That was the reason why Jonah fled from the Holy Land, namely, that the prophetic inspiration should not come to him, and he should not have to take the Lord's message. But, you may say, did not the Shekinah reveal itself (to Ezekiel) in Babylon, which is outside the Holy Land? The answer is that, according to an authentic tradition, the words "came expressly" used at the beginning of Ezekiel's prophecy indicate that this was without precedent from the day when the Temple was built, and this prophecy was for a special emergency. Further, the incident took place on the river Khebar (*khebar*=of old), so called because it was qualified for this from the beginning of the world, and the Shekinah had been constantly revealed on it, as it is written, "And a river went out from Eden to water the garden and from there it parted, etc." (Gen. II, 10). This was one of the four rivers, and there the Shekinah was revealed exceptionally to relieve Israel in their emergency; but at other times it did not appear there. Therefore Jonah left the Holy Land in order that the Shekinah might not rest upon him or appear to him, and hence it says "from the presence of the Lord", and again, "for the men knew that he fled from the presence of the Lord" (Jon. I, 10). What is the point of all this? It is that just as, in the case of Jonah, the Shekinah did not reveal itself save in the fitting place, so in the case of Abram it did not reveal itself save when he was in fitting company. For from the day when Lot made up his mind to become a renegade, the Holy Spirit departed from Abram; but when Lot left him, straightway the Holy Spirit rested upon him: so it is written, AND THE LORD SAID UNTO ABRAM AFTER THAT LOT WAS SEPARATED FROM HIM. Furthermore, when Abram saw that Lot had reverted to his sinful ways, he was afraid and said to himself, "Perhaps through associating with this man I have lost the holy heritage with which God has endowed me"; hence, when Lot left him, God said to him, LIFT UP NOW THINE EYES AND LOOK FROM THE PLACE WHERE THOU ART. "The place where thou art" means "the place to which thou didst cleave before, and in which thou wast endowed with perfect faith". NORTHWARD AND SOUTHWARD AND EASTWARD AND WESTWARD: These are the same as the "journeys" referred to in verse 3, indicating, like them, the "higher degrees". Abram now received tidings that that perfect faith which he had acquired on his first passage through the land would not depart from him and his descendants for ever; hence it is written, FOR THE LAND WHICH THOU SEEST, TO THEE WILL I GIVE IT AND TO THY SEED FOR EVER: the words "which thou seest" indicate the first grade which he had acquired originally, and which now included and exhibited all the other grades.'

R. Eleazar was once at an inn at Lud, where R. Hizkiah also happened to be. In the course of the night he got up to study the Torah, as did also R. Hizkiah. On seeing him, he said, 'An inn like this is always a meeting-place for the companions.' He then began to discourse on the text: *As the apple tree among the trees of the wood, so is my beloved among the sons* (S. S. II, 3). 'The apple tree,' he said, 'indicates the Holy One, blessed be He, being more delightful than all the other trees, and distinguished among them by its colours. So none can compare with Him; therefore "I delighted in his shadow"—in his shadow and not in that of the other guardian-angels, even from the time when Abram was in the world, Abram, who was attached to God in love, as it is written, "Abraham my friend" (Is. XLI, 8). *His fruit was sweet to my taste* refers to Isaac, who was a holy fruit. The words " In his shadow I delighted and sat down" may also be referred to Jacob, and the words "and his fruit was sweet to my taste" to Joseph, who produced holy fruit in the world. [85*b*] It is also possible to understand the words "Like an apple tree among the trees of the wood" of Abraham, who smelt sweetly like an apple tree, who was distinguished in faith above all his contemporaries, and who was marked out as unique both above and below, as it is written, "Abraham was one" (Ezek. XXXIII, 24). He was so called because no one else of his contemporaries attained to the virtue of faith in God.' Said R. Hizkiah to him: 'What of the words "And the souls which they made in Haran"?' He replied: 'These did not reach the higher grades which Abraham acquired.' Later on he said to him: 'Another thing I have been told is that Abraham was not called "one" until he had associated with himself Isaac and Jacob. When he had done this and when all three were patriarchs, then Abraham was called "one", and then he became the apple tree distinguished above all the rest of the world.' He said: 'Your explanation is good. According to another explanation, the words "the apple tree", "my beloved", and "in his shadow" all equally indicate the Holy One, blessed be He. "I delighted and sat": to wit, on the day when God revealed Himself on Mount Sinai and Israel received the Torah and said, "We will do and we will hearken" (Ex. XXIV, 7). "His fruit is sweet to my taste" refers to the words of the Torah which are called "sweeter than honey and the honeycomb" (Ps. XIX, 11). Another explanation refers the "fruit" to the souls of the righteous, who are the fruit of the handiwork of the Almighty and abide with Him above. Listen to this. All the souls in the world, which are the fruit of the handiwork of the Almighty, are all mystically one, but when they descend to this world they are separated into male and female, though these are still conjoined. When they first issue forth, they issue as male and female together. Subsequently, when they descend (to this world) they separate, one to one side and the other to the other, and God afterwards mates them—God and no other, He alone knowing the mate proper to each. Happy the man who is upright in his works and walks in the way of truth, so that his soul may find its original mate, for then he becomes indeed perfect, and through his perfection the whole world is blessed.' Said R. Hizkiah: 'I have heard the following explanation of the verse "From me is thy fruit found" (Hos. xiv, 9). The Holy One, blessed be He, said to the Community of Israel, "From me assuredly is thy fruit found"—not my fruit, but thy fruit: the desire of the female produces a vital spirit and is embraced in the vehemence of the male, so that soul is joined with soul and they are made one, each embraced in the other. Afterwards they become two in this world, and thus through the force of the male is produced the fruit of the female. According to another explanation, the fruit of the male is produced through the desire of the female, since if not for the desire of the female for the male no fruit would ever be produced.'

NOW IT CAME TO PASS IN THE DAYS OF AMRAFEL KING OF SHINAR. R. Jose expounded in this connection the text: *Who hath raised up one from the East, whom Righteousness calleth to follow him?* (Is. XLI, 2). He said: 'This verse has been explained in various ways, but it also contains an esoteric allusion. God, we have learnt, has made seven firmaments on high, all of which acknowledge the glory of the Almighty and are capable of pointing the lesson of true faith. Now there is above these seven a hidden firmament which guides and illumines them. Of this one we cannot discover the true nature, however much we inquire, and therefore it is designated by the interrogative particle *Mi* (Who), as has been pointed out: hence the Scripture says: "From the womb of Whom (*Mi*) came forth the ice" (Job XXXVIII, 29), which has been explained to refer to the highest firmament [86a] over the other seven. At the bottom again there is a firmament, the lowest of all, which has no light; and on that account the highest firmament joins with it in such a way as to insert in it the two letters of its own name, so that it is called *Yam* (sea), being, as it were, the sea of that highest firmament, because all the other firmaments serve as streams (to convey its light), and flow into this lowest one as into a sea; and it thereupon produces fruits and fishes after their kind, and in reference to this David said; "Lo, the sea great and wide, wherein are things creeping innumerable, both small and great beasts" (Ps. CIV, 25). We now see what is meant by the words "Who raised up from the East". The one raised up was Abraham. The words "Righteousness calleth him to follow him" refer to the lowest firmament, which has become "sea". It is this which "giveth nations before him", which executes vengeance and overthrows the enemy. "He giveth nations before him": these are the peoples of the earth. "And maketh him to rule over kings": these are the guardian-angels of the nations above, for when God executes judgement on a people, He does so both below and above. "He pursueth them and passeth on safely" (Is. XLI, 3): this is Abram who pursued them while God passed before him and slew them, as it says, "Peace passeth on" (*Ibid.*), "Peace" referring to God. "Even by a way that he had not gone by his feet": if not with his feet, how then did Abram go—on the clouds or with horses and chariots? No: what it means is that it was not an angel or a messenger, but God Himself, that went before Abram, the word "feet" here referring to the angels, who are subject to God, as in the verse "And his feet shall stand in that day" (Zech. XIV, 4). Another explanation of the verse is as follows. When God "awoke" the world to bring Abram and to draw him near to Himself, this was because Jacob was destined to issue from him and to establish twelve tribes who should all be righteous in the sight of God. "Whom he calleth in righteousness": because God was calling him constantly from the day that the world was created, as it is written, "calling the generations from the beginning" (Is. XLI, 4). "To his foot": i.e. to attach him to His service and to bring him near to Himself. R. Judah says: "Who aroused from the East" this refers to Abraham, who received his first impulse to seek God from the East. For when he saw the sun issuing in the morning from the East, he was first moved to think that that was God, and said "this is the King that created me", and worshipped it the whole day. In the evening when the sun went down and the moon commenced to shine, he said, "Verily this rules over the orb which I worshipped the whole day, since the latter is darkened before it and does not shine any more." So he served the moon all that night. In the morning when he saw the darkness depart and the East grow light, he said, "Of a surety there is a king who rules over all these orbs and orders them." So when God saw Abram's longing to find Him, He revealed Himself unto him and spoke with him, as it is written, "Righteousness called to him to follow him." '

R. Isaac explained in connection with Abraham the verse: *I am the Lord speaking righteousness, declaring what is right* (Is. XLV, 19). [86b] He said: 'All God's words are truth and His acts are righteousness. For when God first created the world it was unstable and rocked to and fro. Said God to the world, Wherefore rockest thou? It answered: Sovereign of the Universe, I cannot be firm, because I have no foundation on which to rest. God thereupon said: Behold, I intend to raise up in thee a righteous man, Abraham, who will love Me. Hearing this, the world straightway became firmly established; therefore it is written, "these are the generations of the heavens and the earth *behibaream* (when they were created), which by a transposition of letters becomes *beabraham* (for the sake of Abraham).' R. Hiya enlarged upon the words "declaring what is right". He said: 'The world continued to remonstrate with God, saying, "From this Abraham will issue descendants[1] who will destroy the Temple and burn the Law." God replied: "He will also have one descendant, namely Jacob, who will be the father of twelve tribes who will all be righteous." Forthwith the world was established for his sake, and therefore God is said to be "declaring (the advent of) things that are right".' R. Eleazar said: 'It has been noted that there is a difference between "speaking" (*dober*) and "declaring" (*maggid*). "Speaking" is from a revealed source, an outer grade, not of the highest; therefore it is applied here to "righteousness" (*zedek*). But "declaring" indicates the inner grade which controls that belonging to "speaking"; hence it says here "declaring things that are right" (*mesharim*), these referring to the higher grade in which is that of Jacob.' Said R. Isaac to him, 'Is there not a

[1] The peoples of Ishmael and Esau.

text "he declares to you his covenant" (Deut. IV, 13) ?' He replied: 'The "covenant" also is a grade superior to that referred to in the expression "speaking righteousness". One must be careful too to note that although "speaking" is lower than "declaring", it still actually designates a high grade and is very pregnant in signification.'

R. Eleazar was once on the way to visit his father-in-law along with R. Hiya and R. Jose and R. Hizkiah. Said R. Eleazar, 'It is borne in upon me that stirring above is produced only in response to an impulse from below, and depends upon the longing of that below.' He illustrated this from the text: *O God, keep thou not silence, hold not thy peace, and be not still, O God* (Ps. LXXXIII, 2), which he expounded thus. 'David said: "O God, keep thou not silence." These words represent an impulse to *Elohim* to exert His sway. David said in effect: "*Elohim*, cease not to rouse the Highest and to associate thyself with the Right." Wherefore so? Because "thine enemies make a tumult, etc.", they have consulted together with one consent, against Thee do they make a covenant. "Therefore, O God, be not silent," as explained. For when *Elohim* is joined with the Right, then the enemies are crushed, as it is written, "Thy right hand, O Lord, is glorious in power, thy right hand, O Lord, dasheth in pieces the enemy." Note that, when all those kings joined together to make war on Abram, they designed to make away with him. But so soon as they got possession of Lot, his brother's son, they went off (as it is written, AND THEY TOOK LOT, ABRAM'S BROTHER'S SON, AND HIS GOODS AND DEPARTED), the reason being that Lot closely resembled Abram, so that thinking they had Abram, they went off. The reason of their enmity to Abram was that Abram weaned men from idolatry and taught them to worship God. Also God incited them to make their invasion in order to aggrandise Abram and to attract him to his service. Esoterically speaking, when Abram started to pursue them, then God "did not keep silent" until the whole was linked up with Abram; then when the whole was linked up with Abram, then all those kings were crushed before him, as we have said.'

AND MELCHIZEDEK KING OF SALEM BROUGHT FORTH BREAD AND WINE. R. Simeon adduced here the text "In Salem also is his tabernacle" (Ps. LXXVI, 3). He said: 'When God decided to create the world, He first produced a flame of a scintillating lamp. He blew spark against spark, causing darkness and fire, and produced from the recesses [87a] of the abyss a certain drop which He joined with the flame, and from the two He created the world. The flame ascended and encircled itself with the Left, and the drop ascended and encircled itself with the Right. They then crossed and changed places, going up and down alternately until they were closely interlocked, and there issued from between them a full wind. Then those two sides were made one, and the wind was set between them and they were entwined with one another, and so there was harmony above and harmony below; the grade was firmly established, the letter *hé* was crowned with *vau* and *vau* with *hé*, and so *hé* ascended and was joined in a perfect bond. This is alluded to in the words "Melchizedek (lit. king of righteousness) king of Salem" (lit. completeness), i.e. the king who rules with complete sovereignty. When is he completely king? On the Day of Atonement, when all faces are illumined. According to another explanation, "Melchizedek" alludes to the lower world, and "king of Salem" to the upper world; and the verse indicates that both are intertwined inseparably, two worlds like one, so that the lower world also is the whole, and the whole is one. "Brought forth bread and wine": signifying that both of these are in it. AND HE WAS PRIEST OF GOD MOST HIGH: i.e. one world ministers to the other. "Priest" refers to the Right, and "Most High God" to the upper world; and hence a priest is required to bless the world. For this lower world receives blessings when it is associated with a High Priest; hence there is a special force in the words "and he blessed him and said, Blessed is Abram to the Most High God". After this model it behoves the priest on earth to intertwine his fingers when blessing in the synagogue in order that he may be linked with the Right and that the two worlds may be linked together. BLESSED IS ABRAM. The words of the text are a prototype of the formula of blessing (used by the Israelites). "Blessed is Abram" (in the sense we have given to it) corresponds to "blessed art Thou". "To the Most High God" corresponds to "O Lord our God". "Possessor of heaven and earth" corresponds to "king of the universe". Further, AND HE BLESSED HIM indicates the course of blessing from below to above; BLESSED IS THE MOST HIGH GOD indicates from above to below. AND HE GAVE HIM A TENTH OF ALL: so that he should cleave to the place where the link was formed with the lower world.'

As they were going along they came across R. Yesa and a certain Judean with him who was explaining the text "To David: Unto thee, O Lord, do I lift up my soul" (Ps. xxv, 1). He said: 'Why is the inscription of this psalm simply "to David" and not "A Psalm of David"? It is because the real meaning is "for the sake of David", i.e. of his grade. "Unto thee, O Lord", i.e. upward-striving; "my soul", i.e. David himself, his original grade; "I lift up": to wit, I cause to ascend, since David was ever striving to rise to a higher grade and to link himself to it firmly. Similarly it was for the sake of his grade that David uttered the words "To David: Bless the Lord, O my soul" (where the word *eth* indicates his desire to be linked above) "and all that is within me bless his holy name" (Ps. CIII, 1), referring to the "beasts of the field" which are called "inwards".' Said R. Eleazar to R. Yesa, 'I see that you have come in company with the Shekinah.' He said, "Assuredly it is so. I have been walking with him three parasangs, and he has told me ever so many excellent things. I hired him as a porter, not knowing that he was the shining light which I have discovered him to be.' R. Eleazar then said to the man, 'What is your name?' He said: 'Joezer'. Whereupon he said: 'Let Joezer and Eleazar sit together.' So they sat down on a rock [87b] in that field. The Judean then commenced to discourse on the text *I, even I, am he that blotteth out thy transgressions, for mine own sake, and thy sins I will not remember* (Is. XLIII, 25). He said: 'The word "I" occurs here twice: once in reference to Sinai (cf. "I am the Lord thy God", Ex. xx, 2), and the other in reference to the creation of the world (cf. "I have made the earth and created man upon it", Is. XLV, 12), to show that there is no division between the upper and lower worlds. "That *blotteth out* thy transgressions": not merely removing them, so that they shall never be seen more. "For mine own sake": i.e. for the sake of the mercy which I dispense, as it is written, "For the Lord thy God is a merciful God" (Deut. IV, 31). Another explanation of the words "that blotteth out thy transgressions for mine own sake" is as follows. Sinners in this world impair the influence of the upper world, for when they sin, mercy and the supernal light depart, and the stream of blessing does not descend to this world, and this grade (of mercy) does not take up the blessings from above in order to convey them to the lower world. Hence God acts "for His own sake", in order that the stream of blessing should not be withheld. Similarly it is written, "See now that I, I am he" (Deut. XXXII, 39), to show that there is no division between the upper and the lower. See now, in this way, when there are righteous men in the world, blessings are sent to all worlds. When Abram came, blessings were sent to the world, as it is written, "And I shall bless thee, and be thou a blessing, i.e. that blessing should be found both above and below for his sake. When Isaac came he taught the world that there is a judge executing judgement above to punish the wicked, and he invoked justice upon the world in order that its inhabitants might fear God. When Jacob came he obtained mercy for the world and perfected men's faith in God. Hence in the days of Abram MELCHIZEDEK KING OF SALEM (salem=completeness), i.e. God whose throne was then established in its place and whose sovereignty therefore became complete, BROUGHT OUT BREAD AND WINE, i.e. produced the appropriate food for the whole world, and did not withhold blessing from all the worlds; from the upper grades He brought forth food and blessings for all the worlds. AND HE WAS A PRIEST TO THE MOST HIGH GOD, the whole thus being in the most perfect order; to show that as the wicked upset the world and cause blessing to be withheld, so the righteous bring blessing to the world and for their sakes all its inhabitants are blessed. AND HE GAVE HIM A TENTH OF ALL, to wit, of those blessings which issue from "all", the source of all the blessings which descend upon the world.

According to another explanation, God gave Abram a tenth, namely, the grade[1] in which all the sources of faith and blessing are established, and which is the tenth, one out of ten and ten out of a hundred; and from this point onwards Abram was fully confirmed from above.' Said R. Eleazar to him: 'What you say is right.' R. Eleazar further asked him what his business was. He said: 'I was a teacher of children in my town till R. Jose came, when they left me and went to him. Nevertheless the townsfolk used to pay me my salary as before. Not wishing, however, to take money for nothing, I entered into the service of this Sage.' Said R. Eleazar: 'This is a case where my father's blessings are required.' They went to R. Simeon, and the Judean used to study all day before him. One day he was studying the subject of washing the hands, and said: 'Whoever does not wash his hands as required, although he is punished in the next world is also punished in this world, because he endangers his health. And similarly, he who washes his hands as required procures for himself blessings above which rest upon his hands, and is also blessed with wealth.' [88a] Afterwards R. Simeon caught sight of him washing his hands and using a great quantity of water, and he exclaimed: 'Fill his hands with thy blessings.' And so it came to pass, since he found a treasure and grew rich, and he used to study the Torah and give sustenance to the poor every day and smile upon them benignantly, so that R. Simeon applied to him the verse "And thou shalt rejoice in the Lord and glory in the Holy One of Israel." '

AFTER THESE THINGS. R. Judah discoursed on the text: *I am my beloved's and his desire is towards me* (S. S. VII, 11). He said: 'The inner meaning of this verse is that the stirring below is accompanied by a stirring above, for there is no stirring above till there is a stirring below. Further, blessings from above descend only where there is some substance and not mere emptiness. We learn this from the wife of Obadiah, to whom Elisha said, "Tell me, what hast thou in the house" (II Kings, IV, 2), meaning that blessings from above would not descend on an empty table or an empty place. When she

---

[1] *Malkuth.*

said: "Thy handmaid hath nothing in the house save a cruse of oil"—only enough to smear her little finger—he said to her: "You have relieved me, for I did not see how blessings were to descend from above on to an empty place, but since you have some oil, this will provide a place sufficient for the purpose." (The connection of "oil" with "blessing" is found in Psalm cxxxiii, where it says "like the good oil," etc., and then "for there the Lord commanded the blessing, life for evermore". It is true, the immediate comparison in the passage is with dew, not oil, but the two mean the same thing, as this dew was distilled by God from the supernal oil. Wine and oil belong respectively to the Left and the Right sides, and from the Right side blessings descend on the world, and from there the holy kingdom is anointed. Thus because it was fixed upon below, oil was first prepared above as the source of blessings. From the stirring [88b] of this supernal oil the lower oil was poured on David and Solomon to bring blessings on their descendants. This is derived from a collation of the text "and the oil *stood*", in II Kings IV, 6, with the text "the root of Jesse which *standeth* for an ensign of the nations", Is. XI, 10.) We derive the same lesson from the fact that the table of shew-bread, from which issued blessings, was not to be left empty a single moment; and on that account we do not say grace over an empty table, since blessings from above do not rest on an empty table. To resume, then, the verse "I am my beloved's and towards me is his desire" indicates that "first of all I am my beloved's, and then, in consequence, his desire is towards me; first I prepare for him a place, and then his desire is towards me". The verse may also be explained by reference to the dictum that the Shekinah is not found in the company of sinners, but when a man exerts himself to purify himself and to draw near to God, then the Shekinah rests on him. So "I am my beloved's" to begin with, and then "his desire is towards me".'

AFTER THESE THINGS, i.e. after Abram pursued the kings and God slew them, Abram felt some qualms lest he had perchance forfeited some of his reward for converting men to the service of God, seeing that now some of his fellow creatures had been killed through him. Therefore God said to him: FEAR NOT, ABRAM, I AM THY SHIELD, THY REWARD IS EXCEEDING GREAT: you have received a reward for them, for none of them shall ever be accounted innocent. THE WORD OF THE LORD CAME UNTO ABRAM IN A VISION SAYING. "Vision" is the grade in which all figures are beheld. R. Simeon said: 'Up to the time when Abram was circumcised, only one grade spoke with him, namely Vision, which is also mentioned in the verse "who seeth the vision of Shaddai" (Num. XXIV, 4). After his circumcision, all grades combined with this grade, and in this way God spoke with him. [89a] It may be objected that according to our interpretation the verses "and the Lord appeared to Abram", "and Abram journeyed to the South", "and he built there an altar", indicate that he had attained to these higher grades; how, then, can you say that before he was circumcised these grades did not combine with this one to speak with him? The answer is that previously God gave wisdom to Abraham to cleave to Him and to know the true meaning of faith, but only this lower grade actually spoke with him; but when he was circumcised, all the higher grades joined this lower grade to speak with him, and thus Abraham reached the summit of perfection. See now, before a man is circumcised he is not attached to the name of God, but when he is circumcised he enters into the name and is attached to it. Abram, it is true, was attached to the name before he was circumcised, but not in the proper manner, but only through God's extreme love for him; subsequently He commanded him to circumcise himself, and then he was vouchsafed the covenant which links all the supernal grades, a covenant of union which links the whole together so that every part is intertwined. Hence, till Abram was circumcised, God's word with him was only in a vision, as has been said.'

Consider this. When God created the world, it was created only through a covenant, as it is written, "*Bereshith* (*b'rith esh*, covenant of fire), God created"; and it is further written, "If my covenant of day and night stand not, if I have not appointed the ordinances of heaven and earth" (Jer. XXXIII, 25), since there is a covenant of union that day and night shall not be separated. R. Eleazar said: 'When God created the world, it was on condition that if Israel when they came into the world should accept the Torah, it would be well, but if not, then the world should revert to chaos. Nor was the world firmly established until Israel stood before Mount Sinai and accepted the Torah. From that day God has been creating fresh worlds, to wit, the marriages of human beings, for from that time God has been making matches and proclaiming "the daughter of so-and-so for so-and-so"; these are the worlds which He creates.'

I AM A SHIELD TO THEE: this "I" is the first grade to which he was attached at the start. [90b] AND ABRAM SAID, O LORD GOD: the two names indicate the union of the upper and the lower world. WHAT WILT THOU GIVE TO ME, SEEING THAT I GO CHILDLESS? i.e. not having a son, and we have learnt that he who has no son is called childless. The words "What wilt thou give to me" would seem to indicate some want of faith on the part of Abraham, but this is not so. God said to him: "I am thy shield," to wit, in this world, "thy reward is very great", to wit, in the next world. Abram, however, knew from the wisdom which he had acquired that a man who has not begotten a son is not rewarded with the future world, and he therefore said, "How canst thou give me (such a reward), seeing that I have not merited it?" (Hence we learn that a man who is not vouchsafed sons in this world is not granted in the future world the privilege of entering within the curtain.) Abram saw from his horoscope that he was fated not to have children; therefore HE BROUGHT HIM FORTH ABROAD; that is, God said to him: "Take no notice of that, for through my name thou shalt have a son"; hence it says SO (*Koh*) SHALL THY SEED BE. The word *Koh* indicates the Holy Name, which was now linked to him from that side. It is the gateway of prayer through which a man obtains his request; it is the side which comes from the side of *Geburah* (might), from which Isaac also came. The side of *Geburah* is called *Koh*, because from it come fruit and produce to the world, and not from the side of the stars and constellations. AND HE

BELIEVED IN THE LORD: he clave to the higher and not the lower; he believed in the Lord and not in stars and constellations: in the Lord who had promised to give him great recompense in the future world. "He believed in the Lord": namely in the grade which was vouchsafed him, that from there seed would come to him to bear children in the world. AND HE COUNTED IT TO HIMSELF FOR KINDNESS: i.e. although this *koh* was pure justice, Abram counted it as mercy. Another explanation is that he linked the upper with the lower to join them together, in this way. According to tradition, God told Abram that he would not beget till his name had been changed to Abraham. The question has been asked, did he not beget Ishmael while he was still Abram? The answer is that he did not beget the son who was promised him while he was still Abram. Then he only bore for the lower world, but when he obtained the name Abraham and entered into the covenant he bore for the upper world. Hence Abram did not bear for the upper union, but Abraham did, as we have said, and he was linked above through Isaac.'

NOW WHEN ABRAM WAS NINETY-NINE YEARS OLD, ETC. In connection with this verse R. Abba discoursed on the text: *For who is God save the Lord, and who is a rock save our God?* (II Sam. XXII, 32). He said: 'These words of King David may be paraphrased: What (heavenly) ruler or chieftain is there who can do anything without the Lord, anything save what he has been commanded by the Holy One, blessed be He, since all are subject to Him and cannot do anything of themselves? And what mighty power is there that has any force in himself save what he derives from our God? Another explanation is that a vision shown by the stars is not like a vision shown by God, for they show a thing and God changes it. And again, "Who is a rock (*tsur*) save our God?" i.e. there is no fashioner (*tsayar*) who fashions form within form and finishes it in all its details and inserts in it the heavenly soul which bears likeness to the Deity. See now, when desire brings man and woman together, there issues from their union a son in whom both their forms are combined, because God has fashioned him in a mould partaking of both. Therefore a man should sanctify himself at such time, in order that the form may be as perfect as possible.' Said R. Hiya, 'How great are the works of the Holy One, blessed be He, for man is fashioned as a microcosm of the world, and every day God creates a world by bringing the proper couples together, and He fashions the forms of the offspring before they are born. See now what R. Simeon has told us, in explanation of the verse "This is the book of the generations of Adam", that God showed Adam every generation and its students, etc. This does not simply mean that he saw through the spirit of prophecy that they were destined to come into the world, like one who in wisdom foresees the future, but it means that he literally saw with his eyes the form in which they were destined to exist in the world. He was able to do this because from the day on which the world was created all the souls which were destined to come to life among mankind were existing before God in that very form which they were destined to assume [91a] on earth (in the same way that the righteous after death are clothed in a form similar to that which they wore in this world), and so Adam saw them with his eyes. Nor can it be thought that after he saw them they disappeared, for all God's creations exist before Him permanently until they descend below. Similarly when Moses said "with him that standeth here this day with us, etc." (Deut. XXIX, 14), we understand him to have indicated that all who were yet to be born were there. (This point demands a little more consideration. The words of the text are, "him that standeth here ... and him that is not here with us this day". The word "standeth" is omitted from the second half of the clause to show that the future generations were in fact standing there, but they were not visible. It may be asked, why were they not visible here in the same way that they were visible to Adam, seeing that here there was more reason. The reason is that when the Torah was given to Israel, they beheld and gazed upon other sights and other grades, and they yearned to contemplate the glory of their Master, and therefore they had no eyes but for that.) The same idea is expressed in the words of the Psalmist, "Thine eyes did see mine unperfect substance" (Ps. CXXXIX, 16); viz. the other celestial form resembling the one on earth. Thus we understand the words "Who is a *tsur* like our God", i.e. who is so excellent a fashioner (*tsayar*) as God who fashioned all. It is also possible to explain the words "For who is God besides the Lord, etc." in a more esoteric way. The word for "God" here is *El*, which signifies the union of all grades. Now there is a text "El hath indignation every day" (Ps. VII, 12), which might lead us to suppose that it designates a separate grade. Hence it says here "Who is El without Jehovah", indicating that *El* is never alone disjoined from Jehovah; and similarly there is no "Rock" (signifying the attribute of justice) "without our God".'

Until Abram was circumcised, God spoke to him only in a vision, as it says above, "The word of the Lord came unto Abram in a vision" (Gen. XV, 1). By "vision" we understand the grade in which all figures are apparent, and which symbolises the covenant. This seems to contradict what was said before, that till Abram was circumcised he was addressed only by that grade to which the other grades are not attached. The truth is that this grade is indeed the reflection of all the higher grades, and was rendered possible through that reflection; it reflects all the colours (symbolic of the divine attributes)—white at the right, red at the left, and a further colour compounded of all colours. In this reflection God stood over Abram and spoke with him, although he was not circumcised. Of Balaam it is said that he saw "the vision of Shaddai" (Num. XXIV, 4), and of Abraham that God spoke to him "in a vision", simply. The difference is that Balaam saw only those (angels) below the Almighty, whereas Abram saw the *Hé* in which all the celestial figures are reflected. Till Abram was circumcised, he was addressed only by that degree which we have mentioned; after he was circumcised, then THE LORD APPEARED UNTO ABRAM, i.e. all the other grades appeared over this grade, and this grade addressed him without reserve. Thus when Abram was circumcised he emerged from the unripe state and entered into the holy covenant, and was crowned with the sacred crown, and entered into the covenant on which the world is based, and thus the world was firmly established for his sake. For it is written, "But for my covenant, I had not set the ordinances of heaven and earth", and also "There are the generations of heaven and earth when they were created"—the word *behibaream* (when they were created) can be read anagrammatically both *beabraham* (for the sake of Abraham) and *b'hé b'raam* (he created them with *Hé*), and both come to the same thing.

When God showed Adam all future generations, he saw them all in the Garden of Eden in the form which they were destined to assume in this world. When he saw David—so we have been told—with no span of life at all apportioned to him, he was grieved, and gave him seventy years of his own; that is why Adam lived seventy years short of the thousand, the rest being given to David. The fact of David's only having seventy years from Adam, the first man, symbolises something in the higher world, as does everything here below.

Note that all the figures of souls that are to be born stand before God in pairs, and afterwards when they come to this world God mates them. R. Isaac says: 'God announces, The daughter of so-and-so for so-and-so.' R. Jose said: 'How can that be, seeing that, as the Scripture tells us, "there is nothing new under the sun"?' R. Judah said: 'It is true that God creates nothing new under the sun; but this is done above.' R. Jose further asked: 'Why is there a proclamation, seeing that, as we have been told by R. Hizkiah in the name of R. Hiya, a man's wife is assigned to him at the very moment when he is born?' Said R. Abba: 'Happy are the righteous whose souls are beatified before the Holy King before they come into this world. For we have learnt that when God sends souls into the world they are formed into pairs of male and female, and thus united are placed in the hands of an emissary who has charge of conception, and whose name is Night. After that they are separated, and subsequently taken down among mankind (not always both at the same time). When their time of marriage arrives, God, who knows each spirit and soul, joins them as at first, and proclaims their union. Thus when they are joined they become one body and one soul, right and left in unison, and in this way "there is nothing new under the sun". You may object that there is also a dictum that "a man only obtains the wife he deserves". This is so, the meaning being that if he leads a virtuous life he is privileged to marry his own true mate, whose soul emerged at the same time as his.' R. Hiya asked: 'Where should a man of good character look for his soul-mate?' He replied: 'There is a dictum that a man should sell all his property in order to obtain in marriage a daughter of a scholar, for the special treasure of God is deposited with the learned in the Torah. We have also learnt in the esoteric Mishnah that one whose soul is a second time on earth can through prayer anticipate another in marrying a woman who is really destined for him; this is the meaning of the warning of the colleagues, "it is permissible to affiance a woman on the festival, lest another through prayer anticipate him"; and they were right. The word "another" is used significantly; and it is for this reason that marriages constitute a difficult task for the Almighty, for in all cases "the ways of the Lord are right" (Hos. xiv, 10).' R. Judah sent a question to R. Eleazar. 'I know', he said, 'about marriages in heaven, but I would like to ask, from where do those whose souls are a second time on earth obtain their mates?' The reply R. Eleazar sent him was this: 'It is written: "How shall we do for wives for them that remain?" (Jud. xxi, 7), and again, "and you shall catch every man his wife, etc." (*Ibid.* 21). This story of the Benjaminites shows us how it can be done, and hence the dictum "lest another anticipate him through his prayers".' [92a] Said R. Judah: 'No wonder we say that marriages constitute a difficult problem for the Almighty! Happy the lot of Israel who learn from the Torah the ways of God and all hidden things, and even the most secret of His mysteries! "The Law of the Lord is perfect", says the Scripture. Happy the lot of him who occupies himself with the Torah without cessation, for if a man abandons the Torah for one moment, it is as if he abandoned eternal life, as it says, "For it is thy life and the length of thy days" (Deut. xxx, 20), and again, "For length of days and years of life and peace shall they add to thee" (Prov. iii, 2).'

NOW ABRAM WAS NINETY YEARS OLD, ETC. R. Jose discoursed on the text: *Thy people are all righteous, they shall inherit the land for ever* (Is. LX, 21). He said: 'Happy are Israel above all peoples, in that the Holy One, blessed be He, has called them righteous. For so we have learnt from tradition that there are a hundred and twenty-eight thousand winged creatures who flit about over the world ready to catch up any voice that they hear; for, as tradition tells us, there is nothing done in the world which does not produce a certain sound, and this soars to the firmament and is caught up by those winged creatures, who carry it aloft to be judged, whether for good or ill, as it is written, "For a bird of the heaven shall carry the voice and that which hath wings shall tell the matter" (Eccl. x, 20).' At what time do they judge the voice? R. Hiya said: 'At the time when a man is asleep in his bed, when his soul leaves him and testifies against him; it is then that the voice is judged, for so it says, "from her that lieth in thy bosom keep the doors of thy mouth" (Mich. VII, 5), because it is she who testifies against a man.' R. Judah said: 'Whatever a man does in the day his soul testifies against him at night.' We have learnt as follows: R. Eleazar says: 'At the beginning of the first hour of the night, when the day is expiring and the sun going down, the keeper of the keys of the sun finishes his process through the twelve gates that were open in the day, and they are all closed. A herald then proclaims to the guardians of the gates, "Each one to his place to lock the gates." When the herald has finished, all of them come together and go aloft without uttering a sound. Then the accusing angels below begin to stir and to fly about the world, and the moon begins to shine and the trumpeters sound a blast. At the second blast, the angels of song start up and chant before their Lord. Emissaries of chastisement also start up, and punishment commences in the world. Then the souls of men who are sleeping give their testimony and are declared guilty, but the Holy One, blessed be He, deals kindly with men and allows the soul to return to its place. At midnight, when the cock crows, a wind blows from the North, but at the same time a current from the South arises and strikes against it, causing it to subside. Then the Holy One, blessed be He, rises as is His wont to disport himself with the righteous in the Garden of Eden. Happy the portion of the man who rises at that hour to study with zest the Torah, for the Holy One, blessed be He, and all the righteous listen to his voice; for so it is written, "Thou that dwellest in the gardens, the companions hearken for thy voice, cause me to hear it" (S. S. VIII, 13). Nay more, God draws round him a certain thread of grace which secures him the protection both of the higher and the lower angels, as it is written, "By day the Lord will command his grace, and at night I shall chant his song" (Ps. XLII, 9).' R. Hizkiah said: 'Whoever studies the Torah at that hour has constantly a portion in the future world.' Said R. Jose to him: 'What do you mean by "constantly"?' He replied: 'I have learnt that at midnight, when the Holy One, blessed be He, enters the Garden of Eden, all the plants of the Garden are watered more plenteously by the stream which is called [92b] "the ancient stream" and "the stream of delight", the waters of which never cease to flow. When a man rises and studies the Torah at this hour, the water of that stream is, as it were, poured on his head and he is watered by it along with the other plants of the Garden of Eden. Moreover, because all the righteous in the Garden listen to him, he is given a right to be watered by that stream, and in this way he has a portion constantly in the future world.'

R. Abba was journeying from Tiberias to meet other learned scholars at the house of his father-in-law. He was accompanied by his son, R. Jacob. Coming to Kfar Tarsha, they decide to spend the night there. Said R. Abba to his host, 'Have you a cock here?' He said, 'Why?' 'Because,' he said, 'I want to get up precisely at midnight.' He answered, 'You have no need of a cock for that. I have a water-clock by my bed from which the water issues drop by drop till exactly midnight, when all the water is emptied and the wheel swings back with a great noise which wakens the whole house. I made it for the sake of a certain old man who used to get up every night at midnight to study the Torah.' Said R. Abba, 'Blessed be God for sending me here.' At midnight the wheel of the water-clock swung back, and R. Abba and

R. Jacob got up. They heard the voice of their host, who was sitting in the lower part of the house with his two sons and saying: 'It is written: *Midnight I will rise to give thanks to thee because of thy righteous judgments* (Ps. CXIX, 62). Since the word "at" is omitted, we may take "Midnight" as an appellation of the Holy One, blessed be He, who is addressed thus by David because He is to be found with His retinue at midnight, that being the hour when He enters the Garden of Eden to converse with the righteous.' Said R. Abba to R. Jacob: 'Truly we have now an opportunity to associate with the Shekinah.' So they went and sat by him, and said to him, 'Repeat what you just said, for it is excellent. Where did you get it from?' He replied: 'I learnt it from my grandfather.[1] He told me that during the first three hours of the night the accusing angels below are actively going about the world, but at midnight precisely God enters the Garden of Eden and the accusations below cease. These nightly ceremonies above take place only at midnight precisely; we know this from what it says of Abraham, that "the night was divided for them" (Gen. XIV, 15); also from the words "and it came to pass at the middle of the night" in the account of the Exodus (Ex. XII, 29), and from many other places in the Scripture. David knew this, because—so the old man told me—his kingship depended on this; and therefore he used to rise at this hour and chant praises, and for this reason he addressed God as "Midnight". He also said, "I rise to give thanks to Thee for Thy righteous judgements", because this is the fount of justice, and the judgements of earthly kings derive from here; therefore David never neglected to rise and sing praises at this hour.' R. Abba came and kissed him, saying, 'Of a surety it is so. Blessed be God who has sent me here! For night is the time of judgement in every place, as we have fully established, and as has been discussed in the presence of R. Simeon.' The young son of the inn-keeper thereupon asked: 'If so, why does it say "midnight"?' He replied: 'It is laid down that the heavenly Majesty rises at midnight.' Said the boy: 'I can give another explanation.' Said R. Abba: 'Speak, my child; for the voice

---

[1] Al. 'Old visitor'.

of the Lamp[1] will speak through thy mouth.' He thereupon said: 'What I have heard is this. Night is in truth the time of the royal judgement, and that judgement extends to all parts alike. Midnight, however, is fed from two sides, from justice and from clemency; only the first half of the night is the time of judgement, but the second half is illumined from the side of clemency (*hesed*). Therefore David said "Midnight".' R. Abba rose and placed his hands on his head and blessed him. He said: 'I thought indeed that wisdom was to be found only in a few favoured pious ones. Now I see that even children in the generation of R. Simeon are endowed with heavenly wisdom. Happy art thou, R. Simeon! Woe to the generation when thou departest from it!'

So they sat till [93a] morning studying the Torah. R. Abba then discoursed on the text: *Thy people are all righteous, they shall for ever inherit the earth, a branch of my planting, etc.* (Is. LX, 21). He said: 'Our colleagues have pointed out that these words cannot be taken literally, seeing how many sinners there are in Israel who transgress the precepts of the Law. The meaning is, as we have learnt in the esoteric teaching of our Mishnah: "Happy are Israel who bring an acceptable offering to the Almighty by circumcising their sons on the eighth day. They thereby become the portion of the 'Zaddik (Righteous One) who is the foundation of the world', and are called righteous; and therefore 'they shall for ever inherit the earth'. They are 'the branch of my planting': that is, a branch of those shoots which God planted in the Garden of Eden, and of which the 'earth' mentioned here is one; hence Israel have a goodly portion in the future world, as it is written 'the righteous shall inherit the earth' (Ps. XXXVII, 29)." We have further learnt: "The reason why the name Abraham occurs for the first time in connection with the circumcision is that when he was circumcised he became associated with the letter *Hé*, and the Shekinah rested on him."' Said R. Abba: 'Happy are Israel in that God has chosen them from all peoples and has given them this sign of the covenant; for whoever has this sign of the covenant will not descend to Gehinnom if he guards it properly, not

[1] R. Simeon.

subjecting it to another power or playing false with the name of the King; for to betray this sign is to betray the name of God, as it is written, "they have dealt treacherously against the Lord in that they have born strange children" (Hos. v, 7).'
Said R. Abba further: 'When a man takes up his son to initiate him in this covenant, God calls to the ministering angels and says, "See what a creature I have made in the world." At that moment Elijah traverses the world in four sweeps and presents himself there; and for this reason we have been taught that it behoves the father to prepare an extra chair for his honour, and to say "this is the chair of Elijah"; and if he neglects to do so, Elijah does not visit him nor go up and testify before the Almighty that the circumcision has taken place. Why has Elijah to testify? For this reason. When God said to him "What dost thou here, Elijah?" (1 Kings XIX, 9), he answered, "I have been very jealous for the Lord, the God of Hosts, for the children of Israel have forsaken thy covenant." Said God to him: "As thou livest, wherever my sons imprint this sign upon their flesh, thou shalt be there, and the mouth which charged Israel with forsaking the covenant shall testify that they are observing it." Our teachers have also taught that the reason why Elijah was punished was because he brought false charges against God's children.'

By this time it was full daylight and they rose to go, but the host came to them and said: 'Will you not finish the subject on which you were engaged to-night?' They said to him: 'What do you mean?' He said: 'To-morrow you have a chance of seeing the sponsor of the covenant,[1] for to-morrow is the celebration of the circumcision of my son, and my wife begs you to stay.' Said R. Abba: 'We are invited to a pious act, and if we stay, it will be to behold the divine presence.' They accordingly stayed the whole of that day. [93b] When night came the host brought together all his friends and they studied the Torah all that night and not one of them slept. Said the host to them, 'May it please you that each one should give an exposition of the Torah.'

Then one began on the text: *For that there was an uncovering*

---
[1] Elijah.

of flesh in Israel, for that the people offered themselves willingly, bless ye the Lord (Jud. v, 2). He said: 'The reason why Deborah and Barak commenced their song with these words was as follows. The world, as we have been taught, rests only upon this covenant of circumcision, according to the verse in Jeremiah (XXXIII, 25), "If not for my covenant day and night, I had not set the ordinances of heaven and earth." Hence as long as Israel observe this covenant, the heaven and earth go on in their appointed course. But if Israel neglect this covenant, then heaven and earth are disturbed, and blessing is not vouchsafed to the world. Now in the time of the Judges the Gentiles gained power over Israel only because they neglected this covenant, to this extent, that they did not uncover the flesh after circumcision: this is indicated by the words "And the children of Israel forsook the Lord." Hence God delivered them into the hand of Sisera, until Deborah came and made all Israel vow to circumcise properly; then their enemies fell before them. Similarly, as we have learnt, God said to Joshua, "Do you not know that the Israelites are not circumcised properly, as the flesh has not been uncovered; how then can you expect to lead them into the land and subdue their enemies?" Hence God said to him, "Circumcise again the children of Israel a second time" (Josh. v, 2); and until the uncovering was performed, they did not enter the land and their enemies were not subdued. So here, when Israel vowed to observe this sign, their enemies were overcome and blessing returned to the land.'

Another one then discoursed on the text: *And it came to pass on the way at the lodging place that the Lord met him and sought to kill him.* He said: 'By "him" is here meant Moses. Said God to him: "How can you think to bring Israel out of Egypt and to humble a great king, when you have forgotten my covenant, since your son is not circumcised?" Forthwith "he sought to slay him": that is, as we have learnt, Gabriel came down in a flame of fire to destroy him, having the appearance of a burning serpent which sought to swallow him. The form of a serpent was chosen as emblematical of the king of Egypt, who is compared to a serpent (Ezek. XXIX, 3). Zipporah, however, saw in time and circumcised her son, so that Moses was released; so it is written, "And Zipporah took a flint and cut off the foreskin of her son", being guided by a sudden inspiration.'

Another then discoursed on the text: *And Joseph said to his brethren, Come near to me, I pray you, and they came near* (Gen. XLV, 4). He said: 'Seeing that they were already standing by him, why did he tell them to come near? The reason was that when he said to them "I am Joseph your brother", they were dumbfounded, seeing his royal state, so he showed them the sign of the covenant and said to them: "It is through this that I have attained to this estate, through keeping this intact." From this we learn that whoever keeps intact this sign of the covenant is destined for kingship. Another example is Boaz, who said to Ruth, "As the Lord liveth, lie down until the morning" (Ruth III, 13). By this adjuration he exorcised his passion, and because he guarded the covenant he became the progenitor of the greatest lineage of kings, and of the Messiah, whose name is linked with that of God.'

Another then discoursed on the text: *Though an host should encamp against me, ... in this* (zoth) *will I be confident* (Ps. XXVII, 3). He said: 'We have learnt that the word *zoth* (this) alludes to the sign of the covenant, which is always on a man's person and also has its counterpart above. If so, it may be said, why should David alone be confident in it and not everyone else? The answer is that this *zoth* was attached to him in a peculiar degree, being the crown of the kingdom.[1] It was because David did not guard it properly that the kingship [94a] was taken from him for so long a time. For this *zoth* symbolises also the supernal Kingdom and Jerusalem the holy city, and when David sinned a voice went forth and said: "David, thou shalt now be disjoined from that with which thou wast united; thou art banished from Jerusalem and the kingship is taken from thee"; thus he was punished in that wherein he had sinned. And if David could be so punished, how much more so other men?'

[1] i.e. of the Sefirah *Malkuth*, of which David's throne was the counterpart below.

Another then discoursed on the text: *Unless the Lord had been my help, my soul had soon dwelt in silence* (duma) (Ps. XCIV, 17). He said: 'We have learnt that that which saves Israel from descending to Gehinnom and being delivered into the hands of Duma like other nations is this same covenant. For so we have learnt, that when a man leaves this world, numbers of angels swoop down to seize him, but when they behold this sign of the holy covenant they leave him and he is not delivered into the hands of Duma, so as to be sent down to Gehinnom. Both upper and lower (angels) are afraid of this sign, and no torture is inflicted on the man who has been able to guard this sign, because thereby he is attached to the name of the Holy One, blessed be He. So with David, when he was dethroned and driven from Jerusalem, he was afraid that he would be delivered into the hands of Duma and die in the future world, until the message came to him, "The Lord also hath put away thy sin, thou shalt not die" (II Sam. XII, 13). Then it was that he exclaimed "Unless the Lord had been my help, etc." '

Another one then discoursed as follows: 'What did David mean by saying (when fleeing from before Absalom): *and he shall show me both himself* (otho) *and his habitation* (II Sam. XV, 25) ?' He said: 'Who is there that can see God ? In truth the word *otho* here means not "him" but "his sign", and it is as we have learnt, that when David's punishment was decreed, and he knew that it was for not having guarded properly this sign (which is the sum and substance of all, and without the due observance of which no one can be called righteous), he prayed that God should show him this sign, fearing that it had parted from him, because on it depended both his throne and Jerusalem; hence he joined the sign and the habitation, meaning that the kingdom conferred by this sign should be restored to its place.'

Another then discoursed on the text: *From my flesh shall I see God* (Job XIX, 26). He said: 'The words "my flesh" are to be literally taken as the place where the covenant is imprinted, as we have learnt: "Whenever a man is stamped with this holy imprint, through it he sees God", because the soul (*neshamah*) is attached to this spot. So if he does not guard it, then of him it is written, "they lose the soul (*neshamah*) given by God" (Job IV, 9). If, however, he guards it, then the Shekinah does not depart from him. He cannot be sure of it till he is married, when at last the sign enters into its place. When the man and wife are joined together and are called by one name, then the celestial favour rests upon them, the favour (*Hesed*) which issues from the supernal Wisdom and is embraced in the male, so that the female also is firmly established. Further, it has been pointed out that the word for "God" in this passage, viz. *Eloah*, may be divided into *El*, signifying the radiance of Wisdom, the letter *Vau*, signifying the male, and the letter *Hé*, signifying the female; when they are joined, the name *Eloah* is used, and the holy *neshamah* is united to this spot. And since all depends on this sign, therefore it is written, "and from my flesh I shall see Eloah". Happy are Israel, the holy ones, who are linked to the Holy One, blessed be He, happy in this world and happy in the next: of them it is written, "Ye that cleave unto the Lord your God, are alive every one of you this day" (Deut. IV, 4).'

Said R. Abba: 'I marvel that with so much learning you are still living in this village.' They said to him: 'If birds are driven from their homes, [94b] they do not know where to fly, as it is written, "As a bird that wandereth from her nest, so is a man that wandereth from his place" (Prov. XXVII, 8). It is in this place that we have learnt the Torah, because it is our habit to sleep half the night and to study the other half. And when we rise in the morning the smell of the fields and the sound of the rivers seem to instil the Torah into us, and so it becomes fixed in our minds. Once this place was visited with punishment for neglect of the Torah, and a number of doughty scholars were carried off. Therefore we study it day and night, and the place itself helps us, and whoever quits this place is like one who quits eternal life.' R. Abba thereupon lifted up his hands and blessed them. So they sat through the night, until at last they said to some boys who were with them: 'Go outside and see if it is day, and when you come back let each one of you say some piece of Torah to our distinguished guest.' So they went out and saw that it was day. One of them said: 'On this day there will be a fire from above.' 'And on this house,' said another. Said a third: 'There is an elder here who this day will be burnt with fire.' 'God forbid,' said R. Abba, who was greatly perturbed, and did not know what to say. 'A cord of the (divine) will has been grasped on earth,' he exclaimed. And it was indeed so; for on that day the companions beheld the face of the Shekinah, and were surrounded with fire. As for R. Abba, his countenance was aflame with the intoxication of the Torah. It is recorded that all that day they did not leave the house, which was enveloped in smoke, and they propounded new ideas as if they had on that day received the Torah on Mount Sinai. When they rose they did not know whether it was day or night. Said R. Abba: 'While we are here, let each one of us say some new word of wisdom in order to make a fitting return to the master of the house, who is making the celebration.'

Thereupon one opened with the text: *Blessed is the man whom thou choosest and causest to approach unto thee, that he may dwell in thy courts; we shall be satisfied with the goodness of thy house, the holy place of thy temple* (Ps. LXV, 5). 'This verse', he said, 'speaks first of *courts*, then of *house*, then of *temple*. These are three grades, one within the other and one above the other. At first a man "dwells in thy courts", and of him it may be said "he that is left in Zion and he that remaineth in Jerusalem shall be called holy" (Is. IV, 3). As a next step "we are satisfied with the goodness of thy house", which is explained by the text "a house shall be built through Wisdom". (Note that it does not say "Wisdom shall be built as a house", which would imply that Wisdom itself is called "house", but "by Wisdom", with allusion to the verse "a river went forth from Eden to water the Garden".) Lastly, "the holy place of thy temple" (*hekal*) is the culmination of all, as we have been taught: the word *hekal* (temple) may be divided into *hé* and *kol* (all), implying that both are in it in complete union. The opening words of the verse, "Blessed is the man whom thou choosest and causest to approach thee", indicate that whoever brings his son as an offering before God pleases God therewith, so that God draws him near and places his abode in two courts, which He joins so as to form one (hence the plural "courts"). Hence when the pious men who lived in this place in former times made this offering of their children, they used to begin by exclaiming, "Blessed he whom thou choosest and bringest near, he shall dwell in thy courts", while the company present replied, "We shall be satisfied with the goodness of thy house, the holy place of thy temple." Afterwards the celebrant said the blessing, "who sanctified us with his commandments and commanded us to initiate the child in the covenant of our father Abraham", while those present responded, "As thou hast initiated him into the covenant, etc." This ritual is in accordance with the dictum: "A man should first pray for himself and then for his neighbour," as it is written, "and (the High Priest) shall make atonement for himself and for all the congregation of Israel"—for himself first and then for the congregation. To this custom we adhere, for so we think proper.' Said R. Abba: 'Assuredly it is so, and he who does not recite these words excludes himself from the ten canopies which God intends to raise for the righteous in the future world, and which all depend upon this. Hence it is that there are ten words in this verse, out of each of which, if recited with proper faith, is made a canopy. Happy your lot in this world and in the world to come, for the Torah is fixed in your hearts as if you had yourselves stood [95a] at Mount Sinai when the Law was given to Israel.'

Another then discoursed on the text: *An altar of earth thou shalt make unto me, and shalt sacrifice thereon thy burnt offerings and thy peace offerings, etc.* (Ex. xx, 24). He said: 'We have learnt that whoever makes this offering of his son is esteemed no less worthy than if he had offered to God all the sacrifices in the world, and had built an altar before Him. Therefore it is fitting that he should make a kind of altar in the shape of a vessel full of earth over which the circumcision may be performed, that so God may reckon it to him as if he had sacrificed on it burnt offerings and peace offerings, sheep and oxen, and be even better pleased therewith; for so it is written in the latter half of the text: "in every place where I record my name I will come to thee and bless thee", where the words "I will record my name" refer to the circumcision, of which it is written, "The secret of the Lord is with them that fear him, and he will show them his covenant" (Ps. xxv, 14). So much for the altar of earth. In the next verse we read: "And if thou make me an altar of stone." This alludes to the proselyte who comes from a stubborn and stony-hearted people. The text proceeds: "thou shalt not build it of hewn stones". This means that the proselyte must enter into the service of God, and that he must not be circumcised until he puts out of his mind the alien worship which he practised hitherto, and removes the stoniness of his heart. For if he is circumcised before he does this, then he is like a statue which, though hewn into shape, still remains stone. Hence "thou shalt not build it of hewn stones", since if he is still obdurate, "thou hast lifted up thy tool upon it and hast polluted it"; i.e. the act of circumcision is of no use to him. Wherefore happy is the lot of him who brings this offering with gladness and pleases God thereby; and it is fitting that he should rejoice in this boon the whole of the day, as it is written, "For all those that put their trust in thee shall rejoice, they shall ever shout with joy, and they that love thy name shall exult in thee" (Ps. v, 12).'

Another then discoursed on the text: *Now when Abram was ninety years* (lit. year) *and nine years old, the Lord appeared . . . and said unto him, I am God Almighty, walk before me, etc.* (Gen. XVII, 1). 'This verse presents a number of difficulties. In the first place, it seems to imply that God only now appeared to Abram when he had attained this age, whereas God had already spoken to Abram on various occasions (*v.* Gen. XII, 1; XIII, 14; XV, 13). Again, the word "years" is mentioned twice, first in the singular (*shanah*) and then in the plural (*shanim*). The answer is, as our teachers have stated, that as long as Abram was closed in body, and therefore in heart, God did not fully reveal Himself to him, and hence it is not stated hitherto that God *appeared* to Abram. Now, however, God *appeared* to him because He was now about to expose in him this sign and holy crown, and further because God desired to bring forth from him holy seed, and this could not be so long as his flesh was closed; now, however, that he was ninety-nine years old and

the time was drawing near for holy seed to issue from him, it was fitting that he himself should be holy first. Hence his age is stated on this occasion, and not on all the others when God spoke to him. Further, the expression "ninety *year*", instead of "ninety *years*", indicates that all his previous years counted for no more than one year, and that his life had been no life; but now that he had come to this point, his years were really years. Further we may ask, why is the term "God Almighty" (*El Shaddai*) used here for the first time? The reason is, as we have learnt, that God has made lower crowns which are not holy, and which, in fact, pollute, and with these are marked all who are not circumcised. The mark consists of the letters *Shin* and *Daleth*,[1] and therefore they are polluted with the demons and cling to them. After circumcision, however, they escape from them and enter under the wings of the Shekinah, as they display the letter *Yod*, the holy mark and the sign of the perfect covenant, [95b] and there is stamped upon them the name *Shaddai* (Almighty), complete in all its letters. Hence we find written in this connection, "I am *El Shaddai*." It says further: "Walk before me and be perfect", as much as to say: "Hitherto thou hast been defective, being stamped only with *Shin Daleth:* therefore circumcise thyself and become complete through the sign of *Yod*." And whoever is so marked is ready to be blessed through this name, as it is written, "And God Almighty (*El Shaddai*) shall bless thee" (Gen. XXVIII, 3), to wit, the source of blessings, that dominates the "lower crowns" and inspires fear and trembling in them all. Hence all that are not holy keep afar from one who is circumcised, and have no power over him. Moreover, he is never sent down to Gehinnom, as it is written, "Thy people are all righteous, they shall for ever inherit the earth" (Is. LX, 21).'
Said R. Abba: 'Happy are ye in this world and in the world to come! Happy am I that I am come to hear these words from your mouths! Ye are all holy, all the sons of the Holy God; of you it is written, "One shall say, I am the Lord's, and another shall call himself by the name of Jacob, and another shall subscribe with his hand unto the Lord and

---

[1] Forming the word *Shed* (demon).

surname himself by the name of Israel" (*Ibid.* XLIV, 5). Everyone of you is closely attached to the holy King on high: ye are the mighty chieftains of that land which is called "the land of the living", the princes of which feed on the manna of holy dew.'

Another then discoursed on the text: *Happy art thou, O land, when thy king is a son of freedom and thy princes eat in due season* (Eccl. X, 17). 'Just before this it is written: "Woe to thee, O land, when thy king is a child, and thy princes eat in the morning." There is an apparent but not a real contradiction between these verses. The reference in the verse "happy art thou, O land," is to the supernal realm which has control over all the life above, and is therefore called "land of the living". Of this it is written, "a land which the Lord thy God careth for continually" (Deut. XI, 12), and again "a land where thou shalt eat bread without scarceness, thou shalt not lack anything in it" (*Ibid.* VIII, 9). Why so? Because "thy king is a son of freedom". By this is meant the Holy One, blessed be He, who is called a "son of freedom" because of the Jubilee, which is the source of freedom. It is true that, according to this explanation, we should expect to have in our text the word *ḥeruth* (freedom) and not, as we actually find written, *ḥorin* (free ones). The reason is, as we have learnt in our secret Mishnah, that when the *Yod* is united with the Hé, they produce "the river which issues from Eden to water the Garden" (Gen. II, 10). It is, in fact, misleading to say "*when* they unite", for they are indeed united, and therefore it is written *ben ḥorin*. Hence "happy art thou, O land, when thy king is a *ben ḥorin*, and thy princes eat in due season", with joy, with sanctity, and with God's blessing. On the other hand, "Woe to thee, O land, when thy prince is a child." This is the land of the lower world; for so we have learnt: "All the lands of the Gentiles have been committed to great chieftains who are appointed over them, and above all is he of whom it is written, 'I was a lad and am now old'" (Ps. XXXVII, 25), words which, according to tradition, were pronounced by the "Prince of the Globe". Hence, "Woe to thee, O land, when thy king is a lad": i.e. woe to the world which derives sustenance from this side; for when Israel are in captivity, they, as it were, derive their sustenance from an alien power. Further, "when thy princes eat in the morning"; i.e. in the morning only and not the whole day, or any other time of the day. For so we have learnt, that at sunrise when men go forth and bow down to the sun, wrath is suspended over the world, and at the time of the afternoon prayer also wrath is suspended over the world. Why is this? Because "thy king is a lad", viz. he who is called "lad". But you, truly pious ones, sainted to those above, do not derive sustenance from that side, but from that holy place above. Of you it is written: "Ye who cleave to the Lord are alive all of you this day" (Deut. IV, 4).'

R. Abba then discoursed on the text: *Let me sing for my wellbeloved a song of my beloved touching his vineyard, etc.* (Is. V, 1). He said: 'This passage presents many difficulties. In the first place it should rather be called a "reproof" than a "song". Then again why first "wellbeloved" and then "beloved"? Also, we find nowhere else mention of a place called "Keren Ben Shemen" (horn of the son of oil). Our colleagues have expounded these verses in many ways, and all of them are good, but I explain them in this way. The word "wellbeloved" contains an allusion to Isaac, who was called so before he was born. For so we have learnt, that God showed great love for him in not allowing him to be born until Abraham his father had been circumcised and called perfect and had been completed by the addition to his name of the letter *hé*. To Sarah, too, a *hé* had been given. Here arises a question. We understand *hé* for Sarah, but for Abram the added letter should have been not *hé* but *yod*, he being a male. The reason is in truth a somewhat deep and recondite one. Abraham rose to the highest stage, and took as his additional letter the higher *hé*, which symbolises the sphere of the male. For there are two symbolic *hé*'s, one higher and one lower, one associated with the male and the other with the female. Hence Abraham ascended with the *hé* of the higher sphere, and Sarai descended with the *hé* of the lower sphere. Further it is written, "thus (*koh*) shall be thy seed", and the word "seed" here, as we have learnt, is to be taken exactly (of Isaac). For it was he who entered into this covenant from his birth, and whoever enters from his birth really enters. It is for this reason that a proselyte who is circumcised is called "a proselyte of righteousness", because he does not come from the holy stock who have been circumcised; and therefore one who enters in this way is called by the name of the first pioneer "Abraham". Thus the letter *hé*, too, was given to him; and if it had not also been given to Sarah, Abraham would of necessity have begotten on a lower level, in the same way as *Koh*, which begets on a lower level. But when *hé* was given to Sarah, the two *hé*'s were joined together, and brought forth on a higher level, that which issued from them being *yod*; hence *yod* is the first letter of the name of Isaac, symbolising the male. From this point the male principle began to extend, and therefore it is written, "For in Isaac shall thy seed be called", and not in thee. Isaac bore on the higher level, as it is written, "Thou givest truth to Jacob" (Micah VII, 20), showing that Jacob completed the edifice. It may be asked: "Was Abraham attached only to this grade and no more?" If so, why does it say, "kindness (*hesed*) to Abraham"? (*Ibid.*) The answer is that *hesed* was his portion because he dealt kindly with mankind, but for bearing children, it was here that he was attached and here that he began. Hence it was that Abraham was not circumcised till he was ninety-nine years old; the inner reason for this is well known and has been explained in our Mishnah. For this reason, too, Isaac typifies stern justice, which was his portion, but for begetting he was called "kindness" (*hesed*). Hence Jacob crowned the edifice on this side and on that. In respect of the strivings of Abraham and Isaac for portions above he was the culmination; and in respect of the privilege which was granted to them to bear sons better than themselves he was also the culmination. Hence the Scripture says of him, "Israel in whom I glory" (Is. XLIX, 3). In him were united attributes both from the higher and the lower. Hence the word "song" is used in this passage. According to some, the word "wellbeloved" here refers to Abraham, who transmitted this inheritance; but it is more correct to refer it to Isaac, as I do. To proceed: "the song of my beloved to his vineyard" refers to the Holy One, blessed be He, who is commonly called "beloved" (*dod*), as in the verse, "My beloved is white and ruddy" (S. S. v, 10). Thus, my well-beloved unites with my beloved, who is male, and from him springs forth a vineyard, as it is written, "My wellbeloved had a vineyard." The Scripture further says that this vineyard sprang forth in "Keren-Ben-Shemen". This "Keren" is the same as the "horn" (*keren*) of the Jubilee, and it is united with the male that is called *ben shemen* (son of oil), which is the same as *ben horin* (son of freedom). "Shemen" is mentioned because it is the source of the oil for lighting the lamps (of understanding). This oil makes faces shine and kindles lamps until it is gathered in a horn, which is then called "the horn of the Jubilee". For this reason Royalty is always anointed from a horn; and the reason why the kingdom of David endured was because he was anointed from a horn and was true to it. The next words are, "he put a fence round it and stoned it": [96*b*] i.e. he removed from himself and from his portion all the celestial chieftains and champions, and all the "lower crowns", and chose this vineyard for his portion, as it is written, "For the Lord's portion is his people, Jacob is the lot of his inheritance" (Deut. XXXII, 9). Further, "He planted it with the choicest vine", as it says elsewhere, "I planted thee a noble vine, wholly a right seed" (Jer. II, 21). (The word *kuloh* (wholly) in this sentence is written with *hé*, to point the same lesson as the text "thus (*koh*) shall be thy seed".) Our text closes with the words: "He built a tower in the midst of it"—the "tower" is that mentioned in the verse, "The name of the Lord is a strong tower, the righteous runneth into it and is safe" (Prov. XVIII, 10) "and also hewed out a wine press therein": this is the "gate of righteousness" mentioned in the verse, "Open to me the gates of righteousness" (Ps. CXVIII, 19). We learn from this that every Israelite who is circumcised has the entry into both the tower and the gate. He who makes this offering of his son brings him under the ægis of the Holy Name. On this sign, too, are based the heaven and earth, as it is written, "But for my covenant day and night, I had not set the ordinances of heaven and earth" (Jer. XXXIII, 25). Our host of to-day has been privileged to see the Holy One, blessed be He, face to face this day. Happy we that we have lived to see this day, and happy thy portion with us. To this son that is born to thee I apply the words of the Scripture, "Every one that is called by my name . . . I have formed him, yea I have made him" (Is. XLIII, 7); also the verse, "and all thy children shall be taught of the Lord, etc." (*Ibid.* LIV, 13).'

They then rose and escorted R. Abba on his way for three miles. They said to him: 'Your host who made the ceremony deserves all the honour he has received, because his act was a doubly pious one.' He said: 'What do you mean?' They answered: 'This man's wife was formerly the wife of his brother, who died without children, and so he married her, and this being the first son, he calls him after the name of his dead brother.'[1] Said R. Abba: 'From now onwards his name shall be Iddi'; and in fact he grew up to be the well-known Iddi bar Jacob. R. Abba then gave them his blessing and continued his journey. When he reached home, he informed R. Eleazar of all that had happened, but was afraid to tell R. Simeon. One day as he was studying with R. Simeon, the latter said: 'It is written: "And Abraham fell on his face and God spoke with him saying, As for me, behold my covenant is with thee." This shows that until he was circumcised, he used to fall on his face when God spoke with him, but after he was circumcised he stood upright without fear. Further, the words "behold, my covenant is with thee" show that he found himself circumcised.' Said R. Abba to him: 'Perhaps your honour will permit me to relate some excellent ideas which I have heard on this subject.' 'Speak,' he said. 'But I am afraid,' continued R. Abba, 'that the people who told me may suffer through my telling.' 'God forbid!' said R. Simeon. 'Remember the verse: "He shall not be afraid of evil tidings, his heart is fixed trusting in the Lord".' He then told him what had happened, and related to him all that he had heard. Said R. Simeon: 'You mean to say that you knew all this and did not say a word to me? I order you during the next thirty days to do your very utmost to forget it. Does not the Scripture say: "Withhold

---

[1] *v.* Deut. XXV, 5–10.

not good from them to whom it is due, when it is in the power of thine hand to do it"?' And so it came to pass. R. Simeon further said: 'I order that with these explanations they shall be banished to Babylon, I mean to say, among our colleagues in Babylon.' R. Abba was sorely grieved at this. One day R. Simeon, seeing him, said: 'Your looks betray some inward sorrow.' He replied: 'I am not grieving for myself, but for them.' He answered: 'God forbid they should be punished for anything except for speaking too openly. For this let them go into exile among the colleagues and learn from them how to keep things to themselves; for these matters are not to be divulged save among ourselves, since the Holy One, blessed be He, has confirmed our ideas, and made us the instruments for disclosing them.' R. Jose said: 'It is written, "Then shall thy light break forth as the morning, etc." (Is. LVIII, 8). This means that the Holy One, blessed be He, will one day proclaim with regard to his sons: "Then shall thy light break forth as the morning, and thy healing shall spring forth speedily, and thy righteousness shall go before thee and the glory of the Lord shall be thy rereward".' [97a]

VAYERA

Gen. XVIII, 1–XXII, 24

AND THE LORD APPEARED UNTO HIM. R. Hiya commenced to discourse on the verse: *The flowers appear on the earth, the time of song is come, and the voice of the turtle is heard in our land* (S. S. II, 12). He said: 'When God created the world, He endowed the earth with all the energy requisite for it, but it did not put forth produce until man appeared. When, however, man was created, all the products that were latent in the earth appeared above ground. Similarly, the heaven did not impart strength to the earth until man came. So it is written, "All the plants of the earth were not yet on the earth, and the herbs of the field had not yet sprung up, for the Lord God had not caused it to rain upon the earth, and there was not a man to till the ground" (Gen. II, 5), that is to say, all the products of the earth were still hidden in its bosom and had not yet shown themselves, and the heavens refrained from pouring rain upon the earth, because man had not yet been created. When, however, man appeared, forthwith "the flowers appeared on the earth", all its latent powers being revealed; "the time of song was come", the earth being now ripe to offer up praises to the Almighty, which it could not do before man was created. "And the voice of the turtle is heard in our land": this is the word of God, which was not in the world till man was created. Thus when man was there, everything was there. When man sinned, the earth was cursed, and all these good things left it, as it is written, "cursed is the earth for thy sake" (Gen. III, 17), and again, "when thou tillest the ground it shall not give its strength to thee" (*Ibid*. IV, 12), and again, "thorns and thistles it shall bring forth to thee" (*Ibid*. III, 18). When Noah came, he invented spades and hoes, but afterwards he sinned through drunkenness, and the rest of the world also sinned before God, and the strength of the earth deserted it. So matters continued until Abraham came. Then once more "the blossoms appeared in the earth", and all the powers of the earth were restored and displayed themselves. "The time of pruning (*zamir*) came", i.e. God told Abraham to circumcise himself. When at length the covenant existed in Abraham through the circumcision, then all this verse was fulfilled in him, the world was firmly established, and the word of the Lord came to him openly: hence it is written, AND THE LORD APPEARED UNTO HIM.' Said R. Eleazar: 'Until Abraham was circumcised, God did not speak with him save from a lower grade, whereon, too, the higher grades were not resting. But when he was circumcised, straightway "the blossoms appeared in the earth", to wit, the lower grades which the earth put forth, thereby establishing that lower grade we have mentioned; further, "the time of pruning came", to wit, the pruning of the boughs of *orlah;* and to crown all, "the voice of the turtle was heard in the land", to wit, the voice which issues from the innermost [98a] recess. This voice was now heard, and shaped the spoken words and gave them their perfect form. This is implied in the words here used, "and the Lord appeared to him". Already, before Abraham was circumcised, we are told that "the Lord appeared unto Abram" (Gen. XVII, 1), and if the word "him" in this sentence refers to Abraham, we may well ask, what advance had he made (in prophecy) by being circumcised? The answer is that the word "him" here has an inner meaning: it refers to the grade which now spoke with him. Now for the first time "the Lord appeared" to that grade; that is to say, the Voice was revealed, and associated itself with the Speech (*dibbur*) in conversing with him. Similarly in the words, AS HE SAT IN THE TENT DOOR IN THE HEAT OF THE DAY, the word "he" has an inner meaning, indicating that all the grades rested on this lower grade after Abraham was circumcised. Thus the words "And the Lord appeared unto him" contain a mystic allusion to that audible Voice which is united to Speech, and manifests itself therein. "As he sat in the tent door" refers to the supernal world which was at hand to illumine him. "In the heat of the day." That is, it was the right side, to which Abraham clave, that illumined. According to another exposition, "in the heat of the day" indicates the time when the grades approach each other, impelled by mutual desire.' [98b]

AND THERE APPEARED UNTO HIM. R. Abba said: 'Before Abraham was circumcised he was, as it were, covered over, but as soon as he was circumcised he became completely exposed to the influence of the Shekinah, which thereupon rested on him in full and perfect measure. The words "as he sat in the tent door" picture the supernal world hovering over this lower world. When is this? "In the heat of the day", that is, at a period when a certain *Zaddik* (righteous one) feels a desire to repose therein. Straightway "it lifts up its eyes and looks, and lo, three men stand over against it". Who are these three men? They are Abraham, Isaac, and Jacob, who stand over this lower grade, and from whom it [99a] draws sustenance and nourishment. Thereupon "it sees and runs to meet them", since it is the desire of this lower grade to attach itself to them, and its joy is to be drawn after them. "And it bows down to the ground", to prepare a throne near them. Observe that the Almighty made King David one of the under-pillars of the supernal throne, the patriarchs being the other three. For he was a pedestal to them, yet when he is joined with them he becomes one of the pillars upholding the supernal throne; and on that account he reigned in Hebron for seven years, namely, in order that he might be closely associated with them, as explained elsewhere.'

R. Abba opened a discourse with the verse: *Who shall ascend into the mountain of the Lord? And who shall stand in his holy place?* (Ps. XXIV, 3). 'Mankind', he said, 'little realise on what it is that they are standing whilst in this world. For the days as they pass ascend and range themselves before the Almighty—namely, all the days of men's existence in this world. For all these have been created, and they all present themselves on high. That they have been created we know from the words of Scripture, "The days were fashioned" (Ps. CXXXIX, 16). And when the time comes for the days to depart from this world, they all approach the Most High King, as it is written, "And the days of David drew nigh that he should die" (1 Kings II, 1), and again, "And the days of Israel drew nigh that he should die" (Gen. XLVII, 29). Man, however, whilst in this world, considers not and reflects not what it is he is standing on, and each day as it passes he regards as though it has vanished into nothingness. When the soul departs this world she knows not by what path she will be made to travel; for it is not granted to all souls to ascend by the way that leads to the realm of radiance where the choicest souls shine forth. [99b] For it is the path taken by man in this world that determines the path of the soul on her departure. Thus, if a man is drawn towards the Holy One, and is filled with longing towards Him in this world, the soul in departing from him is carried upward towards the higher realms by the impetus given her each day in this world.' R. Abba continued: 'I once found myself in a town inhabited by descendants of the "children of the East", and they imparted to me some of the Wisdom of antiquity with which they were acquainted. They also possessed some books of their Wisdom, and they showed me one in which it was written that, according to the goal which a man sets himself in this world, so does he draw to himself a spirit from on high. If he strives to attain some holy and lofty object, he draws that object from on high to himself below. But if his desire is to cleave to the other side, and he makes this his whole intent, then he draws to himself from above the other influence. They said, further, that all depends on the kind of speech, action, and intention to which a man habituates himself, for he draws to himself here below from on high that side to which he habitually cleaves. I found also in the same book the rites and ceremonies pertaining to the worship of the stars, with the requisite formulas and the directions for concentrating the thought upon them, so [100a] as to draw them near the worshipper. The same principle applies to him who seeks to be attached to the sacred spirit on high. For it is by his acts, by his words, and by his fervency and devotion that he can draw to himself that spirit from on high. They further said that if a man follows a certain direction in this world, he will be led further in the same direction when he departs this world; as that to which he attaches himself in this world, so is that to which he will find himself attached in the other world: if holy, holy, and if defiled, defiled. If he cleaves to holiness he will on high be drawn to that side and be made a servant to minister before the Holy One among the angels, and will stand among those holy beings who are referred to in the words, "then I will give thee free access among these that stand by" (Zech. III, 7). Similarly if he clings here to uncleanness, he will be drawn there towards that side and be made one of the unclean company and be attached to them. These are called "pests of mankind", and when a man leaves this world they take him up and cast him into Gehinnom, in that region where judgement is meted out to those who have sullied themselves and soiled their spirits. After that he is made a companion of the unclean spirits and becomes a "pest of mankind" like one of them. I then said to them: My children, all this is similar to what we learn in our Torah, nevertheless you should keep away from these books so that your hearts should not [100b] be led astray after those idolatrous services and after those "sides" mentioned here. Be on your guard lest, God forbid, you be led astray from the worship of the Holy One, since all these books mislead mankind. For the ancient children of the East were possessed of a wisdom which they inherited from Abraham, who transmitted it to the sons of the concubines, as it is written, "But unto the sons of the concubines that Abraham had, Abraham gave gifts, and he sent them away from Isaac his son, while he yet lived, eastward, unto the country of the children of the East" (Gen. XXV, 6). In course of time they followed the track of that wisdom into many (wrong) directions. Not so with the seed of Isaac, with the portion of Jacob. For it is written, "And Abraham gave all that he had unto Isaac" (*Ibid.* 5), this being the holy heritage of faith to which Abraham clave, and from the sphere of which issued Jacob, of whom it is written, "And, behold, the Lord stood beside him" (Gen. XXVIII, 13), and also, "And thou, Israel, my servant, etc." (Is. XLI, 8). Hence it behoves a man to follow the Holy One and to cleave to Him continually, as it is written, "and to him shalt thou cleave" (Deut. X, 20). It is written, "Who shall ascend into the mountain of the Lord ?" and the answer is given, "He that hath clean hands and a pure heart" (Ps. XXIV, 3-4), that is, he that has not made with his hands vain shapes nor grasped with them wrongful objects, nor has he defiled himself through them like those who defile their bodies wilfully.

"And pure of heart": that is, he that averts his heart and mind from the "other side" and directs them towards the service of the Holy One. It says further: "Who hath not lifted up his soul unto falsehood ... he shall receive a blessing from the Lord" (*Ibid.* 4-5); [101a] that is to say, when he leaves this world his soul ascends furnished with good works which will enable him to obtain entry among the holy celestial beings, in accordance with the verse, "I shall walk before the Lord in the lands of the living" (Ps. CXVI, 9), for since "he hath not lifted his soul unto falsehood, he shall receive a blessing from the Lord, etc."'

When Abraham was still suffering from the effects of the circumcision, the Holy One sent him three angels, in visible shape, to enquire of his well-being. You may, perhaps, wonder how angels can ever be visible, since it is written, "Who makes his angels spirits" (Ps. CIV, 4). Abraham, however, assuredly did see them, as they descended to earth in the form of men. And, indeed, whenever the celestial spirits descend to earth, they clothe themselves in corporeal elements and appear to men in human shape. Now Abraham, although he was in great pain from his wound, ran forward to meet them so as not to be remiss in his wonted hospitality. R. Simeon said: 'Assuredly he saw them in their angelic forms, since it is written, AND HE SAID, ADONAI (my Lord), which shows that the Shekinah (one appellative of which is *Adonai*) had come with them, and that the angels accompanied her as her throne and pillars, because they are the three colours below her, and Abraham, now that he was circumcised, saw what he could not see before.' [101b] At first he took them for men, but afterwards he became aware that they were holy angels who had been sent on a mission to him. This was when they asked him, WHERE IS SARAH THY WIFE? and announced to him the coming birth of Isaac. AND THEY SAID TO HIM: in the word *elau* (to him) there are dots over the letters *aleph*, *yod*, and *vau*, which spell out the word *ayo* (where is he?). This is a reference to the Holy One who is above. Again, the word thus formed *ayo* is followed by the word *ayeh* (where?), which is a feminine form of the same, to emphasise the bond of union between the male and the female, which is the secret of true faith. Where is that bond of union complete? The answer is, BEHOLD IN THE TENT: there it is found, and there is the all-in-all union. WHERE IS SARAH THY WIFE? Did not the celestial angels know that she was in the tent? The fact is that angels do not know of happenings in this world save what is necessary for their mission. This is borne out by the text, "For I will pass through the land of Egypt ... I am the Lord" (Ex. XII, 12), which indicates that although the Holy One had many messengers and angels to perform His work, yet they would not have been able to distinguish between the germ of the first-born and of the later born—only the Almighty Himself could do this. Another example is the verse, "and set a mark upon the foreheads of the men etc." (Ezek. IX, 4), which proves that the angels require a mark, as otherwise they only know what is specially communicated to them, as, for instance, the sufferings which the Holy One is about to bring upon the world as a whole and which He proclaims throughout the seven heavens. Thus when the destroying angel is at large [102a] in the world, a man should take shelter in his house, remain under cover and not show himself in the open, so that no hurt may befall him, as the Israelites were bidden in Egypt, "and none of you shall go out of the door of his house until the morning" (Ex. XII, 22). From the angels one can hide oneself, but not from God, of whom it is written, "Can any hide himself in secret places that I shall not see him? saith the Lord" (Jer. XXIII, 24). The angel asked: "Where is Sarah thy wife?" for the reason that he did not want to deliver the message in her presence; but as soon as Abraham said, "Behold, she is in the tent", he said: I WILL CERTAINLY RETURN UNTO THEE WHEN THE SEASON COMETH ROUND, AND, LO, SARAH THY WIFE SHALL HAVE A SON. Note the delicacy of the angels in not announcing anything to Abraham before he invited them to eat, so as not to make it appear that the invitation was a repayment for their good tidings. We thus read first, "and they did eat", and then, "and they said unto him". AND THEY DID EAT: how so? Do celestial angels eat? The truth is that they only simulated eating in honour of Abraham. R. Eleazar said:

'They certainly did eat, in the sense of fire consuming fire invisibly; of a truth what Abraham offered them they ate, as it is from the side of Abraham that they obtain sustenance on high.'

Note that Abraham kept all his food in a state of ritual cleanliness, and therefore he personally waited on them whilst they were eating. He observed so strictly the laws regarding clean and unclean that no man in a state of ritual impurity was allowed to serve in his house until he had duly cleansed himself by bathing before nightfall or by abstention for [102b] seven days, according to the degree of his defilement. And as Abraham prepared the means of purification for men in such a state, so did Sarah for women. The reason why Abraham did this was because he was himself pure and is designated "pure" (as it is written, "Who can bring forth a pure one from one impure?" (Job XIV, 4), which is a reference to Abraham, who was born of Terah). R. Simeon said that it was in order to confirm Abraham in his special grade, which is symbolised by water, that he set out to keep the world pure by means of water. The same symbolic meaning underlies the words uttered by him when he invited the angels to partake of food, to wit, "Let a little water be fetched", he wishing thereby to confirm himself in the degree symbolised by water. He therefore endeavoured to purify people in all respects—to cleanse them from idolatry and to cleanse them from ritual impurity. In the same way Sarah purified the women. The result was that all in their house were in a state of ritual purity. Wherever Abraham took up his residence he used to plant a certain tree, but in no place did it flourish properly save in the land of Canaan. By means of this tree he was able to distinguish between the man who adhered to the Almighty and the man who worshipped idols. For the man who worshipped the true God the tree spread out its branches, and formed an agreeable shade over his head; whereas in the presence of one who clung to the side of idolatry the tree shrank within itself and its branches stood upright. Abraham thus recognised the erring man, admonished him, and did not desist until he had succeeded in making him embrace the true faith. Similarly the tree received under its shade those who were clean, and not those who were unclean; and when

Abraham recognised the latter, he purified them by means of water. Moreover, there was a spring of water under that very tree, and when a man came who required immediate immersion, the waters rose and also the branches of the tree: and that was a sign for Abraham that that man needed immersion forthwith. On other occasions the water dried up: this was a sign to Abraham that that man could not be purified before the lapse of seven days. Note that Abraham, in offering his invitation to the angels, said, "and recline yourselves under the tree": this was for the purpose of testing them, in the same way as he tested by the same tree any wayfarer who came. By the word "tree", he also referred to the Holy One, blessed be He, who is the tree of life for all, as though to say, "recline yourselves under His shade, and not under the shelter of strange gods". Note that Adam transgressed through eating of the tree of knowledge of good and evil, and this brought death into the world. God then said, "and now, lest he put forth his hand, and take also the tree of life etc." (Gen. III, 22). But when Abraham came, he remedied the evil by means of that other tree, which is the tree of life, and by means of which he made known the true faith to the whole world.

AND HE SAID: I WILL CERTAINLY RETURN UNTO THEE WHEN THE SEASON COMETH ROUND, ETC. R. Isaac said: 'Instead of "I will return", we should have expected here "he will return", since the visitation of barren women is in the hand of the Almighty Himself and not in the hand of any messenger, according to the dictum: "Three keys there are which have not been entrusted to any messenger, namely, of child-birth, of the resurrection, and of rain." But the truth is that the words "I will return" were spoken by the Holy One, blessed be He, who was present there. This is corroborated by the use here of the term *vayomer* (and he said). For it is to be observed that wherever the verb *vayomer* (and he said), or *vayiqra* (and he called), occurs without a subject, then the implied subject is the Angel of the Covenant and no other. Examples are: "And he said, If thou wilt diligently hearken etc." (Ex. xv, 26); also: "And he called unto Moses" (Lev. I, 1); also: "And unto Moses he said" (Ex. XXIV, 1).

[103a] In all these passages, as well as in our present passage, the unspecified subject of the sentence is the Angel of the Covenant.

AND, LO, SARAH THY WIFE SHALL HAVE A SON. Why not "and *thou* shalt have a son"? In order that Abraham should not think that possibly he should be from Hagar, like the previous one. R. Simeon here discoursed on the text: *A son honoureth his father, and a servant his master* (Mal. 1, 6). He said: 'A conspicuous example of a son honouring his father is presented by Isaac at the time when Abraham bound him on the altar with the intent of offering him up as a sacrifice. He was then thirty-seven years old, whilst his father was an old man; and though he could easily, by a single kick, have liberated himself, he let himself be bound like a lamb in order to do the will of his father. A servant's honouring his master is illustrated by Eliezer's conduct on the occasion when he was sent by Abraham to Haran; he there followed out all the wishes of his master and paid him great respect, as it is written, "And he said, I am Abraham's servant; and the Lord blessed my master Abraham" (Gen. XXIV, 34-35). Here was a man who had with him silver and gold and precious stones and camels and was himself of a goodly presence; yet he did not present himself as a friend of Abraham or one of his kin, but openly declared, "I am the servant of Abraham", in order to extol his master and make him an object of honour in the eyes of his hearers. Hence the prophet proclaims: "A son honoureth his father, and a servant his master", as much as to say, "but ye Israel my children, ye feel ashamed to declare that I am your father or that ye are my servants". Hence the verse proceeds: "If then I be a father, where is my honour?" (Mal. 1, 6). So when it says of Isaac, "And lo, a son", it means, "truly a son, a son proper, not an Ishmael, but a son who will pay due respect and honour to his father". Further it is said, "And Sarah thy wife shall have a son", because Isaac was indeed a son to Sarah, since it was on his account that she died, on his account she suffered anguish of soul until her life departed, and, further, on his account she is exalted at the time when the Holy One sits in judgement on the world, for on that day the Israelites read the portion: "And the Lord remembered Sarah as he had said" (Gen. XXI, 1), mentioning Sarah for the sake of Isaac. Truly he was "a son to Sarah". AND SARAH HEARD IN THE TENT DOOR, AND IT WAS BEHIND HIM. We should have expected "and *she* was behind him". But the inner meaning of the whole verse is that Sarah heard the "Door of the Tent", which is identical with the Holy One in the lower grade, making the declaration, and that "He", to wit, the Holy One in the supernal grade, "was behind him" (the door), confirming the declaration. During the whole of her lifetime Sarah never heard any utterance from the Holy One save on that occasion. According to another interpretation, the expression "and he was behind him" refers to Abraham, who was behind the Shekinah.'

NOW ABRAHAM AND SARAH WERE OLD, THEY HAD ARRIVED IN REGARD TO DAYS. The expression "they had arrived (*ba'u*) in regard to days" is equivalent to "their days had approached their allotted term", Abraham being a hundred years old and Sarah ninety. We may compare the expression "for the day arrived" (*ba*), i.e. the day had declined towards evening. IT HAD CEASED TO BE WITH SARAH AFTER THE MANNER OF WOMEN: but at that moment she experienced a rejuvenation. Hence her remark AND MY LORD IS OLD, as much as to say that he was unfitted to beget children on account of age. R. Judah here began a discourse with the verse: *Her husband is known in the gates, when he sitteth among the elders of the land* (Prov. XXXI, 23). He said: 'The Holy One, blessed be He, is transcendent in His glory, He is hidden and removed far beyond all ken; there is no one in the world, nor has there ever been one, whom His wisdom and essence do not elude, since He is recondite and hidden and beyond all ken, so that neither the supernal nor the lower beings are able to commune with Him until they utter the words "Blessed be the glory of the Lord from his place" (Ezek. III, 12). The creatures of the earth think of Him as being on high, declaring, "His glory is above the heavens" (Ps. CXIII, 4), while the heavenly beings think of Him as being below, declaring, "His glory is over all the earth" (Ps. LVII, 12), until they both, in heaven and on earth, concur in declaring, "Blessed be the glory of the Lord from his place", because He is unknowable and no one can truly understand Him. This being so, how can you say, "Her husband is known in the gates"? [103b] But of a truth the Holy One makes Himself known to every one according to the measure of his understanding and his capacity to attach himself to the spirit of Divine wisdom; and thus "Her husband is known", not "in the gates" (*bishe'arim*), but, as we may also translate, "by measure", though a full knowledge is beyond the reach of any being.' R. Simeon said: 'The "gates" mentioned in this passage are the same as the gates in the passage, "Lift up your heads, O ye gates" (Ps. XXIV, 7), and refer to the supernal grades by and through which alone a knowledge of the Almighty is possible to man, and but for which man could not commune with God. Similarly, man's soul cannot be known directly, save through the members of the body, which are the grades forming the instruments of the soul. The soul is thus known and unknown. So it is with the Holy One, blessed be He, since He is the Soul of souls, the Spirit of spirits, covered and veiled from anyone; nevertheless, through those gates, which are doors for the soul, the Holy One makes Himself known. For there is door within door, grade behind grade, through which the glory of the Holy One is made known. Hence here "the tent door" is the door of righteousness, referred to in the words, "Open to me the gates of righteousness" (Ps. CXVIII, 19), and this is the first entrance door: through this door a view is opened to all the other supernal doors. He who succeeds in entering this door is privileged to know both it and all the other doors, since they all repose on this one. At the present time this door remains unknown because Israel is in exile; and therefore all the other doors are removed from them, so that they cannot know or commune; but when Israel return from exile, all the supernal grades are destined to rest harmoniously upon this one. Then men will obtain a knowledge of the precious supernal wisdom of which hitherto they wist not, as it is written, "And the spirit of the Lord shall rest upon him, the spirit of wisdom and understanding, the spirit of counsel and might, the spirit of knowledge and of the fear of the Lord" (Is. XI, 2). All these are destined to rest on this lower door which is the "tent door"; all too will rest upon the Messiah in order that he may judge the world, as it is written, "But with righteousness shall he judge the poor, etc." (*Ibid.* 4). Thus when the good tidings were brought to Abraham, it was that grade which brought them, as we have deduced from the fact that the word *vayomer* (and he said) is used without a specific subject in the passage "And he said, I will certainly return unto thee when the season cometh round."

'Observe how the great love of the Almighty towards Abraham was manifested in the fact that Isaac was not born to him until he was circumcised. In this way it was made certain that his seed should be holy, according to the words of the Scripture, "wherein is the seed thereof after its kind" (Gen. I, 12). For had Abraham begotten before he was circumcised, his seed would not have been holy, as it would have issued from the state of *orlah*, and thus would have clung to that state here below; but after Abraham's circumcision the seed issued from the state of holiness and became attached to supernal holiness, and he begat children in the higher plane and thus became attached to his grade in the manner fitting.'

R. Eleazar asked one day of his father, R. Simeon: 'In regard to the name Isaac, why did the Holy One give him that name before he came into the world, by commanding "And thou shalt call his name Isaac" (Gen. XVII, 19)?' R. Simeon answered: 'We have elsewhere stated that through Isaac fire supplanted water. For water comes from the side of *Geburah* (Force), and it is further required of the Levites that they should entertain that side with hymns and songs on divers instruments. Hence Isaac was joyousness, because he issued from that side and became attached to it. Observe that the word *Yitzhak* (Isaac) means "laughter", to wit, rejoicing because water was changed to fire and fire to water; hence he was called Isaac, and hence the Holy One called him [104a] so before he came into the world, and He announced that name to Abraham. You will see that in other cases the Holy One permitted the parents, even the mothers, to give names to their children. Here, however, the Holy One did not give permission to the mother to name the child, but only to Abraham, as it is written: "And thou shalt call his name Isaac"—thou and no other, so as to intermingle water with fire and fire with water and to range it on his side.'

Having related how Abraham was informed of the coming birth of Isaac, the Scripture proceeds: AND THE MEN ROSE UP FROM THENCE, AND LOOKED OUT TOWARD SODOM. Said R. Eleazar: 'Observe how merciful the Holy One, blessed be He, shows Himself towards all beings, and especially towards those who walk in His paths. For when He is about to execute judgement on the world, before doing so He puts in the way of His beloved the occasion of performing a good act. We have thus been taught that when the Holy One loves a man, He sends him a present in the shape of a poor man, so that he should perform some good deed to him, through the merit of which he shall draw to himself a cord of grace from the right side which shall wind round his head and imprint a mark on him, so that, when punishment falls on the world, the destroyer, raising his eyes and noticing the mark, will be careful to avoid him and leave him alone. So when the Holy One was about to execute judgement on Sodom, He first led Abraham to do a meritorious action by the present which He sent him, so as thereby to save Lot his brother's son from destruction. It is therefore written, "And God remembered Abraham, and sent Lot out of the midst of the overthrow" (Gen. XIX, 29). It does not say that God remembered Lot, since he was saved through the merit of Abraham. What God remembered was the kindness which Abraham had shown to those three angels. Similarly, the charitable deeds which a man performs are remembered by the Holy One at the time when punishment impends upon the world, for every meritorious action is recorded on high, and when chastisement impends over that man the Holy One remembers the kindness he had performed with other men, as we read: "but charity delivereth from death" (Prov. XI, 4). The Holy One thus afforded Abraham in advance the occasion of a good action, so that by his merit he should deliver Lot from destruction.'

AND THEY LOOKED OUT TOWARD SODOM. This was immediately after "the men rose up from thence", that is, from the feast that Abraham had prepared for them, so performing a meritorious act. For although they were angels, his hospitality to them was a good action, since of the whole of the food offered them they left nothing over, purposely that Abraham should acquire merit thereby, as it is written, "and they did eat", the food having been consumed by their fire. It may be objected that the three angels were one of fire, one of water, and the third of air. The answer to this, however, is that they all partook of each other's essences, and hence "they did eat". Analogous to this is the passage "and they beheld God, and did eat and drink" (Ex. XXIV, 11). There it was truly eating, for they feasted themselves on the Shekinah. So here, "and they did eat" implies that they feasted themselves on that side to which Abraham was attached, and for that reason nothing remained of what Abraham put before them. For just as it behoves a man to partake of the cup of blessing (after a meal), that he merit the blessing from on high, so the angels also ate from what Abraham prepared for them that they might be privileged to feast on that which proceeds from the side of Abraham, for it is from that side that sustenance issues for all the celestial angels. AND THEY LOOKED OUT: with an impulse of mercy for the delivery of Lot. The word *vayashqifu* (and they looked out) here is analogous with its kindred word in "Look forth (*hashqifah*) from thy holy habitation" (Deut. XXVI, 15), and as there the implication is an exercise of mercy, so here. AND ABRAHAM WENT WITH THEM TO BRING THEM ON THE WAY; that is, to escort them. R Yesa said: 'This shows that Abraham was not aware that they were angels; for if he was, what need had he to see them off?' 'No,' answered R. Eleazar; 'although he knew, he kept to his usual custom with them, and saw them off. For it is highly incumbent on a man to escort a departing guest, for this crowns the good act. So whilst he was walking with them, the Holy One appeared to Abraham, as it is written, "And the Lord said, Shall I hide from Abraham that which I am doing?" The term *V-Yhvh* (and the Lord) implies God with the attendance of the heavenly Court. [104b] Thus we see that, when a man escorts his departing friend, he draws the Shekinah to join him and to accompany him on the way as a protection.'

AND THE LORD SAID, SHALL I HIDE FROM ABRAHAM THAT WHICH I AM DOING? R. Hiya quoted here the verse: *For the Lord God will do nothing, but he revealeth his counsel unto his servants the prophets* (Amos III, 7). 'Happy,' he said, 'are those pious ones of the world in whom the Holy One finds delight, and whom He uses as His agents for all that He does in heaven or intends to do in this world, not hiding anything from them. For the Holy One desires to associate with Himself the righteous so that they may admonish and call the people to repentance in order that they may escape the punishment decreed by the judgement-seat on high, and, in any case, so that they should not be left with any loophole for complaining that the Holy One metes out punishment without justice.' R. Eleazar said: 'Woe to the guilty who are steeped in ignorance and refrain not from sin. Now, seeing that the Holy One, whose acts are truth and whose ways are justice, nevertheless does not execute His designs in the world before He reveals His intent to the righteous, so as not to give occasion to mankind for censuring His acts, how much more must the sons of men be on their guard so to act as not to leave any room for others to spread evil rumours against them. So it is written: "And ye shall be clean before the Lord and before Israel" (Num. XXXII, 22). It is thus incumbent on these righteous to act so that men shall not be able to complain against God, and to warn them betimes, if they are sinful, not to give an opening to the stern justice of God to descend upon them. And how are they to guard themselves? By repentance and good deeds.' R. Judah commented as follows: 'The Holy One, blessed be He, gave the whole land to Abraham [105a] as an everlasting heritage, as it is written: "For all the land which thou seest, to thee I give it, etc." (Gen. XIII, 15). That he saw the whole land is indicated in the words which precede: "lift up now thine eyes from the place where thou art, northward, etc." (*Ibid.* 14). And now the Holy One found it necessary to uproot those places. He therefore said to Himself: "I have already given over the land to Abraham, he thus being the father of all its inhabitants [so it is written: 'for the father of a multitude of nations have I made thee' (Gen. XVII, 5)], and so it is not fitting for me to inflict punishment on the children without first giving warning to their father, to 'Abraham my friend' (Is. XLI, 8)." Hence, AND THE LORD SAID, SHALL I HIDE FROM ABRAHAM, ETC. ?' R. Abba said: 'Notice the unselfishness of Abraham. For although the Almighty notified him of the coming calamity, announcing VERILY, THE CRY OF SODOM AND GOMORRAH IS GREAT, and so on, and thus gave him a breathing-space before the final catastrophe, Abraham, nevertheless, did not plead for Lot to be delivered from the punishment. Why so? In order that it should not appear that he was asking a reward for his good deeds. But just for this reason did the Holy One send Lot forth and deliver him: it was for the sake of Abraham, as it is written, "And God remembered Abraham, and sent Lot out of the midst of the overthrow" (Gen. XIX, 29). In the same place it mentions "the cities in which Lot dwelt" to indicate that they were all guilty, without any redeeming features, save Lot. We learn also from this that any place inhabited by wicked people is doomed to destruction. Lot dwelt only in one of these cities, not in all of them, but it was due only to his presence that they were not all destroyed before. And this, too, was not due to Lot's own merits, but to the merits of Abraham.' As to this point, R. Simeon said: 'Note that any service rendered to a righteous man procures protection for the doer. Nay more, even if he himself is sinful, yet by rendering service to a righteous man he is bound to learn some of his ways and practise them. So you see that Lot, by reason of having kept company with Abraham, although he had not adopted all his ways, had learnt to show kindness to people in imitation of Abraham, and this it was that enabled those cities to exist so many years after Lot settled among them.' [105b]

I WILL GO DOWN AND SEE: IF IT IS ACCORDING TO THE CRY OF IT, THEN MAKE YE AN EXTERMINATION. To whom was this command addressed? It cannot be to the angels, since that would mean that God was speaking to one party (Abraham) and giving command to another (the angels), which is not usual. The explanation is that it was really addressed to Abraham, in whose jurisdiction the cities were. But then why the plural, "make ye" (*'asu*) instead of the singular "make thou" (*'ase*)? The answer is that it was addressed both to Abraham and the Shekinah, which was all the time with him. According to another interpretation the command was given to the angels, who were standing there ready at hand to do execution. According to another interpretation, again, the proper reading is *'asu* (they have made), and this accords with the translation of Onqelos. It says: "I will go down and see." Are not all things revealed before the Almighty that there was need for Him to go down and see? The expression, however, "I will go down", implies descent from the grade of mercy to that of rigour, and by "and see" is meant the consideration of the kind of punishment to be meted out to them. "Seeing" in the Scriptures can be both for good and for ill. An example of the former use is: "And God saw the children of Israel, and God took cognizance of them" (Ex. II, 25); an example of the latter is "I will go down and see", i.e. to determine the mode of punishment. In regard to all this God said, "Shall I hide from Abraham, etc."

SEEING THAT ABRAHAM WILL SURELY BECOME A GREAT AND MIGHTY NATION. How comes this blessing to be inserted here? It is to teach us that the Holy One, even when He sits in judgement on the world, does not change His nature, since whilst sitting in judgement on one He is displaying mercy to others, and all at one and the same moment. R. Judah objected that it is written: "But as for me, let my prayer be to thee, O Lord, in an acceptable time" (Ps. LXIX, 14), which would seem to show that there are with God acceptable moments and unacceptable, that at one time He grants audience, at another time He does not, that the Almighty is now accessible, now inaccessible; and this is corroborated by the verse: "Seek ye the Lord while he may be found, call ye upon him while he is near" (Is. LV, 6). In reply to this, R. Eleazar said that the verses cited apply to the prayers of an individual, whilst the lesson of our text applies to communal prayer; the former to a single locality, the latter to the world as a whole. Hence God here blessed Abraham because he was on a par with the whole world, as it is written: "These are the generations of the heaven and the earth when they were created" (Gen. II, 4), where the term *behibaream* (when they were created), by a transposition of letters, appears as *beabraham* (in Abraham). The numerical value of the letters of *yihyah* (will become) is thirty, which points to the traditional dictum that the Holy One provides for the world thirty righteous men in each generation in the same manner as He did for the generation of Abraham. R. Eleazar supported this from the verse: "He was more honourable than the thirty, but he attained not to the three" (II Sam. XXIII, 23). 'The thirty', he said, 'refers to the thirty righteous whom the Holy One has provided for the world without intermission; and Benaiah the son of Jehoiada of whom it is written "He was the most honourable of the thirty" was one of them. "But he attained not to the three": i.e. he was not equal to those other three[1] on whom the world subsists, neither being counted among them nor being deemed worthy to be associated with them and to have an equal share with them. Now since there were thirty righteous in the time of Abraham, as the term *yihyah* indicates, therefore God blessed him in their company.'

God said to Abraham, "Verily, the cry of Sodom and Gomorrah is great", as much as to say: I have taken note of their behaviour towards their fellow-men, which causes all men to avoid setting foot in Sodom and Gomorrah. So it is written: "The stream made a chasm for strangers, so they are forgotten of the foot that passeth by; they are the poorest of men, they move away" (Job. XXVIII, 4). The stream divided to swallow up any stranger who ventured to enter Sodom; for if anyone was detected offering food or drink to a stranger, the people of the town would cast him into the deepest part of the river, as well as the recipient. Hence, "they are forgotten of the foot", i.e. men avoided it and never put foot

[1] The Patriarchs.

into it; and as for those who happened to enter it—"they are the poorest of men, they move away", i.e. as no food or drink was given to them, their bodies became so emaciated that they scarcely looked any more like human beings, and hence "they moved away", i.e. people passed it by on one side. Even the birds of heaven [106a] avoided it, as it is written, "that path no bird of prey knoweth" (*Ibid.* 7). A universal outcry therefore went up against Sodom and Gomorrah and all the other towns that behaved like them. It is written here: "According to the cry of *it*." Why not of *them*, since two cities are mentioned here? This is explained as follows. From the side underneath the Hail-Stone vapours ascend to the shoulder (of the Divine Throne), where they gather themselves into one drop, and then descend into the chasm of the great abyss. There five become merged into one. When the voices of all of them are clear they unite into one. Then a voice ascends from below and mingles with them, and the combined cry keeps on ascending and clamouring for justice, until at last the Holy One appears to investigate the accusation. Hence R. Simeon says that the "it" here refers to the sentence of judgement, which demands execution day by day. This conforms with the tradition that for many years the sentence of judgement continued to demand reparation for the sale of Joseph by his brethren. Hence here also her cry went up for justice, and therefore it is written, "according to the cry of her". The word which follows, *habbaah* (which is come), really means "which is coming", i.e. coming continually.

AND ABRAHAM DREW NEAR, AND SAID: WILT THOU INDEED SWEEP AWAY THE RIGHTEOUS WITH THE WICKED? R. Judah said: 'Was there ever seen such a merciful father as Abraham? Observe that in regard to Noah it is written, "And God said to Noah, The end of all flesh is come before me ... Make thee an ark of gopher wood" (Gen. VI, 13–14), but Noah remained silent: he said nothing, nor did he beseech for mercy (for his fellow-men). Abraham, on the contrary, as soon as the Holy One made announcement to him, "Verily, the cry of Sodom and Gomorrah is great, ... I will go down and see, etc.", immediately "drew near, and said: Wilt Thou indeed sweep away the righteous with the wicked?"' Said R. Eleazar: 'Even Abraham's action is not beyond cavil. He was, indeed, better than Noah, who did nothing, whereas he pleaded earnestly for the righteous that they should not perish with the guilty, beginning his plea with the number of fifty righteous and descending to ten; then, however, he stopped, without completing his prayer for mercy for all, saying, as it were, "I do not wish to draw upon the recompense due to me for my good deeds." The perfect example is given by Moses, who as soon as the Holy One said to him, "they have turned aside quickly out of the way . . . they have made them a molten calf, and have worshipped it" (Ex. XXXII, 8), straightway "besought the Lord his God, etc." (*Ibid.* 11), concluding with the words "and if not, blot me, I pray thee, out of thy book which thou hast written" (*Ibid.* 32). And although the whole people had sinned, he did not stir from his place until God said: "I have pardoned according to thy word." Abraham was inferior in that respect, since he only asked for mercy in the event that there should be found righteous men, but not otherwise. Thus there never was a man who was so sure a bulwark to his generation as Moses, the "faithful shepherd".'

AND ABRAHAM DREW NEAR, that is, he made ready to plead, AND SAID: PERADVENTURE THERE ARE FIFTY RIGHTEOUS WITHIN THE CITY. Abraham began with the number fifty, which is the entrance to understanding, and ended with ten, which number is the last of all the grades. R. Isaac said: 'Abraham stopped at ten as the number symbolic of the ten days of Penitence between New-Year and the Day of Atonement. Reaching that number, Abraham said, as it were, "After this there is no more room for penitence", and therefore he did not descend further.'

AND THE TWO ANGELS CAME TO SODOM AT EVEN, ETC. R. Jose pointed out that the preceding verse, "And the Lord went his way as soon as [106*b*] he had left off speaking to Abraham", indicates that only when the Shekinah departed from Abraham, and Abraham returned to his place, did "the two angels come to Sodom at eve". (It says "two", because one of the angels departed with the Shekinah, leaving only two.) As soon as Lot saw them he ran after them. Why so ? Did Lot, then, take into his house all wayfarers and offer them food and drink ? Would not the townspeople have killed him, and meted out to him the same treatment as they did to his daughter ? (For Lot's daughter once offered a piece of bread to a poor man, and when it was found out, the people of the town covered her body with honey, and left her thus exposed on the top of a roof until she was consumed by wasps.) The angels, however, came in the night, so that Lot thought that the townspeople would not notice it. Nevertheless, as soon as the visitors entered his house all the people assembled and surrounded the house.' R. Isaac put the question, "Why did Lot run after them ?" R. Hizkiah and R. Yesa each gave an answer. One said that it was because he observed in them a likeness to Abraham; and the other, because he noticed the Shekinah hovering over them. This view is supported by the fact that of Abraham also it is written, "And he ran to meet them from the tent door", and the words there are taken to mean that Abraham saw the Shekinah.

AND LOT SAW AND RAN TO MEET THEM . . . AND HE SAID, BEHOLD NOW, MY LORDS, TURN ASIDE, I PRAY YOU. The expression "turn aside", instead of "draw near", implies that he took them by a roundabout way, so that the people of the town should not see them. R. Hizkiah here discoursed on the verse: *For he looketh to the ends of the earth, and seeth under the whole heaven* (Job XXVIII, 24). 'How incumbent it is', he said, 'upon the sons of men to contemplate the works of the Almighty and to busy themselves in the study of the Torah day and night, for through him who thus busies himself the Almighty is glorified on high and below. The Torah indeed is a tree of life for all those who occupy themselves with it, affording them life in this world and [107a] in the world to come. "For he looketh to the end of the land", to give them food and to satisfy all their needs; for He continually holds it under His eye, as it is written, "The eyes of the Lord thy God are always upon it, from the beginning of the year even unto the end of the year" (Deut. XI, 12). This is, again, the land of which it is written, "she bringeth her food from afar" (Prov. XXXI, 14), and then she provides food and sustenance for all those "beasts of the field", for so it is written, "she riseth also while it is yet night, and giveth meat to her household and a portion to her maidens" (*Ibid.* 15). It is further written: "Thou openest thy hand, and satisfiest every living thing with favour" (Ps. CXLV, 16). According to another interpretation, "He looketh to the ends of the earth" so as to survey the works of each man and to examine the doings of mankind throughout the world: "and seeth under the whole heaven", i.e. He scans and scrutinises each individual. Thus when the Holy One saw the works of Sodom and Gomorrah, He sent upon them those angels to destroy them.' Thereupon, as it is written, "Lot saw," to wit, the Shekinah. Not that anyone can see the Shekinah really, but he saw a resplendent halo about their heads, and therefore we read: "And he said, Behold now, my lords (*Adonay*)", as has been already explained, and it was on account of the halo, the reflection of the Shekinah, that he said, "turn aside, I pray you, into your servant's house, and tarry all night, and wash your feet". This was not the way that Abraham acted. For he first said: "wash your feet", and then: "and I will fetch a morsel of bread, etc." Lot, however, first said, "turn aside, I pray you, into your servant's house, and tarry all night", and then he said, AND WASH YOUR FEET AND YE SHALL RISE UP EARLY, AND GO ON YOUR WAY. His object was that the people should not become aware of their presence. AND THEY SAID, NAY, BUT WE WILL ABIDE IN THE BROAD PLACE ALL NIGHT, that being the custom for visitors to those cities, as no one would take them into his house. The verse proceeds: AND HE URGED THEM GREATLY. When the Holy One is about to execute judgement in the world, He sends one messenger for this purpose. Why, then, have we here two messengers, where one would have sufficed? The truth is that of the two angels one came to rescue Lot, and so only one was left to overthrow the city and destroy the soil.

THEN THE LORD CAUSED TO RAIN UPON SODOM AND UPON GOMORRAH, ETC. R. Hiya opened his discourse on this with the verse: *Behold, the day of the Lord cometh, cruel, etc.* (Is. XIII, 9). He said: 'The words "Behold, the day of the Lord cometh" refer to the lower Court. The term "cometh" has thus the same force as in the passage, "according to her cry which is come upon me", both implying that the lower power cannot execute judgement until it comes and appears on high and receives authorisation. So, too, in the verse, "the end of all flesh is come before me". According to another interpretation, "behold the day of the Lord cometh" refers to the destroying angel here below when he comes to take the soul of man. Hence "cruel, and full of wrath and fierce anger, to make the earth a desolation", referring to Sodom and Gomorrah; "and to destroy the sinners thereof [107b] out of it" (*Ibid.*), referring to the inhabitants of those cities. Immediately after we read, "For the stars of heaven and the constellations thereof, etc.", for He caused to rain upon them fire from heaven and exterminated them. Further on it is written: "I will make man more rare than fine gold, etc." (*Ibid.* 12), referring to Abraham, whom the Holy One exalted over all the peoples of the world.' R. Judah interpreted these verses as referring to the day on which the Temple was destroyed, as on that day both men and angels were plunged into gloom and the supernal and the lower realms and the heaven and the stars were darkened. R. Eleazar, again, interpreted these verses as referring to the day when the Holy One will raise the community of Israel from the dust. That day will be a day of note both above and below, as it is written, "and there shall be one day, which shall be known as the Lord's" (Zech. XIV, 7); that day will be the day of vengeance, the day which the Holy One, blessed be He, has appointed for taking vengeance on the idolatrous nations. For whilst the Holy One is taking vengeance on the idolatrous nations, He "will make a man more precious than gold", to wit, the Messiah, who will be raised and glorified above all mankind, and to whom all mankind will pay homage and bow down, as it is written, "Before him those that dwell in the wilderness will bow down ... the Kings of Tarshish and of the isles shall render tribute" (Ps. LXXII, 9–10). Observe that although this prophecy (in the book of Isaiah) was primarily intended for Babylonia, yet it has a general application, since this section commences with the words, "When the Lord shall have mercy on Jacob", and it is also written, "And peoples shall take them and bring them to their place."

AND THE LORD CAUSED TO RAIN UPON SODOM. The term *V'-Yhvh* (and the Lord) signifies the grade of the lower Court which requires authorisation from on high. R. Isaac said that God showed mercy in the midst of punishment, as it is written, "from *Yhvh* (the Lord) out of heaven". The exercise of mercy is recorded in the words: AND IT CAME TO PASS, WHEN GOD DESTROYED THE CITIES OF THE PLAIN, THAT GOD REMEMBERED ABRAHAM, AND SENT LOT OUT, ETC., from whom in course of time issued two entire nations, and who was destined to have among his descendants King David and King Solomon. AND IT CAME TO PASS, WHEN THEY HAD BROUGHT THEM FORTH ABROAD, THAT HE SAID, ETC. This is another proof that when punishment overtakes the world a man should not—as has already been said—let himself be found abroad, since the executioner does not distinguish between the innocent and the guilty. For this reason, as has been explained, Noah shut himself in in the ark so as not to look out on the world at the time when judgement was executed. So also it is written, "And none of you shall go out of the door of his house until the morning" (Ex. XII, 22). Hence the angel said to Lot, ESCAPE FOR THY LIFE, LOOK NOT BEHIND THEE, ETC. R. Isaac and R. Judah were once walking on the road together. The latter remarked: 'Both the punishment of the Flood and the punishment of Sodom were of the kinds meted out in Gehinnom, where sinners are punished by water and by fire.' R. Isaac said: 'That Sodom suffered the punishment of Gehinnom is shown by the words of the Scripture, "And the Lord caused to rain upon Sodom and upon Gomorrah brimstone and fire from the Lord out of heaven", the former proceeding from the side of water and the latter from the side of fire, both being punishments of Gehinnom inflicted upon sinners there.' R. Judah then said to him: 'The punishment of sinners in Gehinnom lasts twelve months, after which the Holy One raises them out of Gehinnom, where they have undergone purification. They remain then sitting at the gate of Gehinnom, and when they see sinners enter there to be punished, they beseech mercy for them. In time the Holy One takes pity on them and causes them to be brought to a certain place reserved for them. From that day onward the body rests in the dust and the soul is accorded [108a] her proper place. Observe that, as has been stated, even the generation of the Flood were punished with nothing else but with fire and water: cold water descended from above, whilst seething water bubbled up from below mingled with fire. They thus underwent the two punishments regularly meted out from on high; and so was Sodom also punished, namely, by brimstone and fire.' R. Isaac asked him: 'Will the generation of the Flood arise on the Day of Judgement?' R. Judah said: 'That question has already been discussed elsewhere; as regards the people of Sodom and Gomorrah, we can say that they will not arise. This is proved from the words of the Scripture, "and the whole land thereof is brimstone, and salt, and a burning that is not sown, nor beareth, nor any grass groweth therein, like the overthrow of Sodom and Gomorrah . . . which the Lord overthrew in his anger, and in his wrath" (Deut. XXIX, 22), where the words "which the Lord overthrew" refer to this world, and the words "in his anger" to the world to come, while the words, "and in his wrath" refer to the time when the Holy One will bring the dead to life.' R. Isaac then said to him: 'Observe that just as the soil of their land was destroyed to all eternity, so were the inhabitants themselves destroyed to all eternity. And observe further how the justice of the Holy One metes out measure for measure: as they did not quicken the soul of the poor with food or drink, just so will the Holy One not restore them their souls in the world to come. And further, just as they neglected the exercise of charity which is called life, so has the Holy One withholden from them life in this world and in the world to come. And as they closed their roads and paths to their fellow-men, so has the Holy One closed to them the roads and paths of mercy in this world and in the world to come.' R. Abba said: 'All men will rise up from the dead and will appear for judgement. Of these it is written, "and some to reproaches and everlasting abhorrence" (Dan. XII, 2). God, however, is the fountain of mercy, and since He punished them in this world and they suffered for their sins, they have no longer to suffer all the punishments of the next world.'

R. Hiya said: 'It is written: "And he sent Lot out of the midst of the overthrow, when he overthrew the cities in which Lot dwelt." The expression "the cities in which Lot dwelt" indicates that he tried to settle in each of the cities in turn, but none would keep him save Sodom, the king of which allowed him residence [108b] for the sake of Abraham. This is borne out by the passage, "and Lot dwelt in the cities of the plain, and moved his tent as far as Sodom" (Gen. XIII, 12). BUT HIS WIFE LOOKED BACK FROM BEHIND HIM. We should have expected "from behind *her*". It means, however, "From behind the Shekinah". R. Jose said that it means "from behind Lot", as the destroying angel followed him. How, it may be asked, could he follow him, seeing that he had sent him away ? The fact is that the angel kept behind Lot, destroying on the way, but he did not touch any spot till Lot had passed it. Hence he said, "look not behind thee", implying "for behind thee I am doing my work of destruction". But his wife looked back from behind him, thus turning her face to the destroying angel, and she became a pillar of salt; for as long as the destroying angel does not see the face of a man he does not harm him; but as soon as Lot's wife turned her face to look at him she became a pillar of salt.'

R. Eleazar and R. Jose were one day studying the verse: "A land which in it thou shalt eat bread without scarceness, which in it thou shalt not lack anything" (Deut. VIII, 9). Said R. Eleazar: 'The repetition of the term *bah* (in it) is to be noted. The reason is, as has been stated, that the Holy One has assigned all nations and countries to (celestial) chieftains and envoys, with the exception of the Land of Israel, which is under the governance of no angel or chieftain, but only under that of God Himself. For this reason He brought the people who have no ruler save Him into the land which has no ruler save Him. For the Holy One provides sustenance there first, and only then to the rest of the world. All the idolatrous nations suffer scarceness, but not so the Land of Israel: the Land of Israel receives the first supply, the residue being left for the rest of the world. Hence "A land which in it thou shalt eat bread without scarceness", and in a rich abundance: "in it" but in no other place; in it is the home of true faith and on it rests the heavenly blessing. Hence it is said that Sodom and Gomorrah were "like the garden of the Lord, like the land of Egypt" (Gen. XIII, 10), [109a] that is, possessing luxurious abundance. So was Egypt also: as the garden of the Lord does not need to be watered by man, neither did Egypt, being amply supplied by the river Nile, which periodically rises and irrigates the whole land. The Scripture says in one place that "it shall be, that whoso of the families of the earth goes not unto Jerusalem . . . upon them there shall be no rain" (Zech. XIV, 17), i.e. as a punishment; but the passage continues: "And if the family of Egypt go not up, and come not . . . there shall be the plague wherewith the Lord will smite the nations" (*Ibid.* 18). Observe that it is not written "upon them there shall be no rain", for the reason, that it never rains in Egypt, nor is there any need of rain there: hence, their punishment will be "the plague wherewith the Lord will smite all the nations". Similarly of Sodom it is written that "it was well watered everywhere" (Gen. XIII, 10); it possessed all the luxuries of the world, and its inhabitants were unwilling that other people should share them.' R. Hiya said: 'They deserved punishment both for their immorality and their uncharitableness. For whoever grudges assistance to the poor does not deserve to exist in this world, and he also forfeits the life of the world to come. Contrariwise, whoever is generous towards the poor deserves to exist in the world, and it is for his sake that the world exists, and the fulness of life is reserved for him in the world to come.'

AND LOT WENT UP OUT OF ZOAR, AND DWELT IN THE MOUNTAIN, AND HIS TWO DAUGHTERS WITH HIM, ETC. For what reason? Because Zoar was too near Sodom:

hence he moved away further. R. Isaac discoursed on the verse: *And they are turned round about by his devices, according to their work, etc.* (Job XXXVII, 12). 'This means', he said, 'that the Holy One, blessed be He, constantly turns the wheel of events, bringing hidden things to the top, and then again giving another turn and shaping things differently; and thus "by his devices" He is ever scheming and planning how to effect the change, and make a new pattern. [109b] All is "according to their work", i.e. the variation takes place in accordance to the works and deeds of man. The verse continues: "according as he commandeth them upon the face of the habitable world", that is, it is in accordance with man's works that God shapes the course of events, in all that He ordains on the face of the world.' R. Eleazar interpreted the words "and they are turned round about by His devices", in the following manner. 'The Holy One guides the course of events so as to bring to pass a seemingly stable state of things; but when the sons of men imagine that all before them is fixed and firmly established, then the Holy One turns His works into something altogether different from their former state. Further,' he said, 'we may translate not "devices", but "device", i.e. "instrument", and compare God to a potter who, in turning his wheel, constantly fashions new vessels according to his fancy. So is the Holy One constantly reshaping His works, the instrument which constitutes His potter's wheel, so to speak, being the lower world Judgement Court. And all is done in accordance with man's works. If they are good, the wheel revolves to the right, making the course of events highly favourable to them; and however long the wheel revolves, punishment never settles on that side. Should men, however, turn to evil ways [110a] the Holy One imparts to His device a spin to the left, and all things now take a direction to the left, and the wheel gives to events a course unfavourable to the sons of men. So it goes on until they become penitent and retrace their evil ways. But the motive power of the wheel is centred in the works of man; hence the phrase, "by His device, according to their work", there being no permanency. In this case too God manipulated events so as to attain a certain end, and all that happened had its roots in the supernal sphere. God had brought Abraham near to Him, and there issued from him Ishmael. Ishmael was born before Abraham was circumcised, that is, before he was made perfect through the sign of the holy covenant. Then the Holy One, blessed be He, so devised that Abraham circumcised himself and entered the covenant and acquired his complete name of Abraham, and was crowned by the supernal *he* with the symbolical issuing of water from wind. As soon as the symbolism was completed and Abraham was circumcised, there issued from him Isaac, who was the holy seed and who was attached to the supernal spheres as symbolising fire from water, and who was not in any way linked to the "other side". From Lot, again, and from his daughters there came forth two disparate nations who became attached to the side appropriate to them. We see here, again, how the Almighty contrives [110b] the course of things, turning them about so that everything should fit into the general scheme and fall into its proper place. For observe that it would have been more fitting for Lot that the Holy One should have produced these two nations from his union with his wife. It was, however, necessary that these nations should be attached to their predestined place, and for this wine had to play its part; and wine, indeed, was found ready at hand in that cavern. The mystical part played by wine here is similar to that regarding which we read, "and he drank of the wine, and was drunken" (Gen. IX, 21), as has already been explained elsewhere.

In regard to the names Moab and Ammon, R. Jose made the following comment. 'The first-born daughter was bold-faced enough to call her son "Moab", thereby proclaiming that he was *meab*, i.e. the issue of her own father; whereas THE YOUNGER SHE ALSO BORE A SON, AND CALLED HIS NAME BEN-AMMI: the mother out of delicacy gave him that name which being interpreted simply means "a son of my people", without betraying who his father was. Further, the words AND HE KNEW NOT WHEN SHE LAY DOWN, NOR WHEN SHE AROSE, occur twice in this passage, first in reference to the younger daughter, and then in reference to the elder. In the former case the word *b'qumah* (when she arose) occurring in it is written *plene*, i.e. with the letter *vau*, which, moreover, is provided with a dot; this is to signify that heaven, as it were, was an accomplice to the act which ultimately was to bring about the birth of the Messiah. Contrariwise, the similar word in reference to the younger one is written defectively, without the letter *vau*, for the reason that none of her issue had any part in the Holy One, blessed be He.' R. Simeon said: 'The underlying meaning of the words "and he knew not" is that he was unaware that the Holy One intended to raise from her King David and Solomon and all the other kings and, finally, the Messiah.' R. Simeon said further: 'The expression "when she arose" has its counterpart in the words used by Ruth, "and she rose up before one could discern another" (Ruth III, 14). For it was on that day that Lot's daughter could be said to have risen to the height of her destiny in that [111a] Boaz became attached to one of her lineage in order "to raise up the name of the dead upon his inheritance", by means of which there were raised from her all those kings and the elect of Israel. Again, "And he knew not when she lay down" has its counterpart in the verse, "and she lay at his feet until the morning" (*Ibid.*).

'Observe the restraint of Abraham in not beseeching grace on behalf of Lot, even when the Holy One at first announced to him His determination to execute punishment on Sodom; nor after he BEHELD, AND, LO, THE SMOKE OF THE LAND WENT UP AS THE SMOKE OF A FURNACE did he intercede for Lot, or address to the Holy One any word about him. Neither did the Holy One mention this subject to Abraham, in order that the latter should not think that God had used up some of his merit in order to save Lot. It cannot be said that Lot was of no account in the eyes of Abraham, seeing that Abraham risked his life on his behalf in waging war against five powerful kings. But because of his love for the Almighty and, in addition, because he saw that Lot's conduct fell far short of the proper standard, Abraham did not plead that any indulgence should be shown to Lot for his sake. This is the reason why Abraham did not intercede on behalf of Lot either at the beginning or at the end.'

AND ABRAHAM JOURNEYED FROM THENCE TOWARD THE LAND OF THE SOUTH. All his journeyings were toward the side of the South, [111b] which he preferred to the other sides, in that it is the side of Wisdom. AND ABRAHAM SAID OF SARAH, HIS WIFE, SHE IS MY SISTER. It is a dictum of our teachers that a man should not rely on miracles, and even if the Holy One, blessed be He, has once performed a miracle for him he should not count on it another time, for miracles do not happen every day. And whoever runs into obvious danger may thereby exhaust all his merit previously accumulated. This has been made clear in explanation of the verse, "I am not worthy of all the mercies, and of all the truth, etc." (Gen. XXXII, 11). Now, seeing that Abraham had already had once a miraculous deliverance when he journeyed into Egypt, why did he put himself now again into a similar difficulty by saying "she is my sister"? The answer is that Abraham did in no way rely on himself, but he saw the Shekinah constantly in the abode of Sarah, and that emboldened him to declare "she is my sister", in the sense of the verse "Say unto wisdom, Thou art my sister" (Prov. VII, 4).

AND GOD CAME TO ABIMELECH, ETC. Can that be? Does, then, the Holy One, blessed be He, come to the wicked? The same question is raised by the words, "and God came unto Balaam" (Num. XXII, 9), and again, "and God came to Laban" (Gen. XXXI, 24). In all these cases, however, it was, in fact, only a heavenly messenger who was dispatched to them, and who in executing their message assumed that divine name (*Elohim*), since they were emissaries of justice. Hence: AND GOD CAME TO ABIMELECH IN A DREAM OF THE NIGHT, AND SAID TO HIM, BEHOLD, THOU SHALT DIE BECAUSE OF THE WOMAN WHOM THOU HAST TAKEN, ETC. R. Simeon here discoursed on the verse: *The lip of truth shall be established for ever; but a lying tongue is but for a moment* (Prov. XII, 19). 'The first part of the verse,' he said, 'alludes to Abraham, whose words on every occasion were truth; and the other part of the verse is an allusion to Abimelech. Twice Abraham said of Sarah, "she is my sister". On the first occasion he referred to the Shekinah, who was constantly with Sarah, and as Abraham [112a] was of the right side he could indeed say of the Shekinah "she is my sister", using the term in the same mystic sense as in the verse, "my sister, my love, my dove, my undefiled" (S. S. v, 2). Abraham always called her "sister" because he was attached to her inseparably. Later he said: "And moreover she is my sister, the daughter of my father, but not the daughter of my mother." Was it really so? In truth he was alluding all the time to the Shekinah. At first he said, "she is my sister" in conformity with the admonition, "Say to wisdom, Thou art my sister." Then he amplified this by saying "moreover she is my sister, the daughter of my father", i.e. the daughter of Supernal Wisdom, for which reason she is called "my sister" and also Wisdom—"but not the daughter of my mother"—i.e. from the place where is the origin of all, most hidden and recondite. "And so she became my wife", i.e. by way of fondness and affection, in the sense of the verse "and his right hand embrace me" (S. S. II, 6). Thus all his words contained mystic allusions. Observe that on the first occasion, when they went down to Egypt, he called her "my sister" in order to cleave all the more firmly to the true faith, and not to be led astray after outer grades; similarly now he continued to declare "she is my sister" because he had not deviated from the true faith. For Abimelech and all the inhabitants of the land followed strange worship, and therefore Abraham, entering there, made bold to say "my sister", claiming thereby the same indissoluble kinship as between brother and sister. For the marital bond can be dissolved, but not that between brother and sister. So whereas all the people of that land were addicted to the worship of the stars and constellations, Abraham, the true believer, avowed "she is my sister", as much as to say, "We two will never separate." We can apply here the words, "and for his sister a virgin" (Lev. XXI, 3), which were spoken of the priest, but esoterically signify the abode where Abraham reposes. It is written: *The Lord thy God thou shalt fear; him shalt thou serve; and to him shalt thou cleave, and by his name shalt thou swear* (Deut. x, 20). The accusative particle *eth* points to the first grade, the region of the fear of God, and hence "thou shalt fear", for there a man must fear his master, it being the Court of Justice. The words "him shalt thou serve" point to a higher grade which rests upon the lower grade, the two being inseparable. This is the place of the holy covenant, the object of service. "And to him shalt thou cleave" refers to the region of complete union, to wit, the body which rests in the centre; "and by his name shalt thou swear" refers to the seventh of the grades. Abraham, therefore, clave to the true faith when he went down into Egypt and also when he went to the land of the Philistines. He was like a man who wanted to go down into a deep pit but was afraid he would not be able to come up again. He therefore fastened a rope above the pit, and having thus assured his ascent, he went down. In the same way Abraham, when he was about to go down to Egypt, first secured his faith firmly, and thus having something to hold by he went down there; and he did the same when he went into the land of the Philistines. "The lip of truth", then, "is established for ever; but a lying tongue is but for a moment", the "lying tongue" referring to Abimelech, who said, IN THE SIMPLICITY OF MY HEART AND THE INNOCENCY OF MY HANDS HAVE I DONE THIS. But what was the reply he received? YEA, I KNOW THAT IN THE SIMPLICITY OF THY HEART THOU HAST DONE THIS, but no mention was made of innocency of hands. NOW THEREFORE RESTORE THE MAN'S WIFE, FOR HE IS A PROPHET.'

R. Judah discoursed on the verse: *He guardeth the feet of his pious ones, etc.* (I Sam. II, 9). ' "His pious one",' he said 'is Abraham, whom God constantly kept under watchful care, whilst the word "feet" is an allusion to his wife, with whom God sent the Shekinah to guard her. According to another interpretation, the Holy One continually accompanied Abraham so that no one should do him any harm. "But the wicked shall be put to silence by the darkness" (*Ibid.*). These are the kings whom the Holy One had slain on that night when Abraham pursued them; the night, as it were, united with darkness to slay them, so that while it was

Abraham who pursued, it was the darkness that killed. So it is written: "And he divided himself against them by night, he and his servants, and he smote them" (Gen. XIV, 15). By "dividing" is here meant that the Holy One separated His attribute of mercy from that of justice in order to avenge Abraham. Instead of "and *he* smote them" we should have expected "and *they* smote them". But this is again a reference to the Holy One, "for man prevaileth not by strength", seeing that only Abraham and Eliezer were there.' R. Isaac put the question: 'Have we not been taught that a man should not court danger, in reliance on a miracle? And was not Abraham putting himself into extreme danger in pursuing the five kings and engaging in battle against them?' R. Judah replied: 'Abraham did not set out with the intention of joining battle, nor did he count upon a miracle. What impelled him to leave his house was the distress of Lot, whom he resolved to ransom, taking money with him for this purpose, and being prepared, in case he should not succeed, to die with him in captivity. But as soon as he set out he saw the Shekinah illumining the way before him, and hosts of angels encompassing him. Then it was that he began to pursue them, whilst the Holy One slew them. Hence the verse: "and the wicked are put to silence in darkness" (I Sam. II, 9).' R. Simeon said: 'The mystical interpretation of the verse is as follows: "He guardeth the feet of his pious ones"; this refers to Abraham. But when Abraham set out Isaac joined him and so the enemies fell before him. But had not Isaac been associated with Abraham, they would not have been exterminated. So it is written: "But the wicked shall be put to silence in darkness, for man prevaileth not by strength", indicating that although strength resides always in the right side, if not for the help of the left side (darkness), the opponents could not be overcome.' According to another interpretation, "He guardeth the feet of his pious ones" signifies that when a man truly loves God, then God reciprocates his love in all his doings and guards him in all his ways, as it is written, "The Lord shall guard thy going out and thy coming in, from this time forth and for ever" (Ps. CXXI, 8). Observe how assiduous Abraham was in his love towards the

Holy One; for wherever he went he had no regard whatever for himself [113a] and sought only to cleave to the Almighty. Hence God guarded the feet of "his pious ones", the term "feet" referring to Abraham's wife, in regard to whom it is written, "Now Abimelech had not come near her", also "Therefore suffered I thee not to touch her." We find also written in the case of Pharaoh, "And the Lord plagued Pharaoh and his house with great plagues at the word of Sarai" (Gen. XII, 17), implying that she, as it were, gave out the order and the Holy One administered the blows. Thus "He guardeth the feet of his pious ones." "But the wicked shall be put to silence in darkness": these are Pharaoh and Abimelech, to whom the Holy One administered punishment by night, while the words "For not by strength shall man prevail" refer to Abraham, on whose behalf God said, "Now therefore restore the man's wife, etc." '

AND THE LORD REMEMBERED SARAH AS HE HAD SAID, ETC. R. Hiya discoursed on the verse: *And he showed me Joshua the high priest standing before the angel of the Lord, and Satan standing at his right hand to accuse him* (Zech. III, 1). 'This verse,' he said, 'must be carefully pondered. "Joshua the high priest" is Joshua the son of Jehozedek; "the angel of the Lord" before whom he was standing is the region of the "bundle of the souls" of the righteous, which is known as "the angel of the Lord"; "Satan standing at his right hand to accuse him" is the evil tempter who roams to and fro through the world to snatch up souls and to lure beings to perdition, angels as well as human beings. Joshua had been cast by Nebuchadnezzar into the fire, along with the false prophets; and that was the moment seized by Satan to bring accusations against him on high in order that he should be burnt along with them. For this is the way of the Satan, to reserve his indictment for the hour of danger, or for a time when the world is in distress. At such a time he has authority both to accuse and to punish even without justice, as it says: "But there is that is swept away without a just cause" (Prov. XIII, 23). Satan then was standing "to accuse him", to wit, to plead that either they should all be delivered or all burnt in the fire. For when the angel of destruction obtains authorisation to destroy, he does not discriminate between innocent and guilty. It is for this reason that when punishment falls upon a town a man should flee from thence before he is overtaken. Here it was all the easier for the Satan, as the three were already joined as one in the fiery furnace, and he could thus demand a single treatment for them all, either to be burnt or to be saved. For a miracle is not performed [113b] in halves, delivering half and leaving half to be destroyed, but the whole is either miraculously saved or left to its doom.' Said R. Jose to him: 'Is it really so ? Did not God divide the Red Sea for the Israelites so that they could pass on dry land, while the same waters swept round on the Egyptians and drowned them, so that here you have a miraculous deliverance and a divine punishment at one and the same point ?' R. Hiya replied: 'This was precisely why the miracle of the Red Sea presented such difficulties to the Almighty. For when God does punish and miraculously deliver at the same time, it is usually not in the same place or the same house. If that does happen it constitutes a heavy task for Him. On the same principle the Holy One does not punish the guilty until the measure of their guilt is full, as it is written, "for the iniquity of the Amorite is not yet full" (Gen. xv, 16), and again, "in full measure, when thou sendest her away, thou dost contend with her" (Is. xxvii, 8). Satan, therefore, demanded that Joshua should be burnt along with the others, until he said to him, "The Lord rebuke thee, O Satan" (Zech. iii, 2). Who said this ? It was the angel of the Lord. The text, it is true, runs: "The Lord said to Satan, The Lord rebuke thee, O Satan." But observe that regarding Moses at the bush it is also written: "And the angel of the Lord appeared unto him in a flame of fire" (Ex. iii, 2), whilst a little later it is written, "And when the Lord saw that he turned aside to see" (*Ibid*. 4). The truth is that sometimes the Scripture says "the angel of the Lord", sometimes simply "the angel", and sometimes again "the Lord". Hence here also it is written, "The Lord rebuke thee, O Satan," and not: "Behold, I rebuke thee." So whenever the Holy One sits on the Throne of Judgement to judge the world, Satan, the seducer of men and angels, is at hand to do mischief and to snatch up souls.'

R. Simeon was one day in the course of his studies examining the verse, "And the elders of that city shall take a heifer of the herd . . . and shall break the heifer's neck there in the valley" (Deut. XXI, 3-4). 'According to the law,' he said, 'the neck must be broken with a hatchet.' Said to him R. Eleazar: 'What is the need of all this?' R. Simeon then wept and said: 'Woe to the world which has been lured after this one. For from the day that the evil [114a] serpent, having enticed Adam, obtained dominion over man and over the world, he has ever been at work seducing people from the right path, nor will the world cease to suffer from his machinations until the Messiah shall come, when the Holy One will raise to life those who sleep in the dust in accordance with the verse, "He will swallow up death for ever, etc." (Is. xxv, 8), and the verse, "And I will cause the unclean spirit to pass out of the land" (Zech. XIII, 2). Meanwhile Satan dominates this world and snatches up the souls of the sons of men. Observe now the passage: "If one be found slain in the land, etc." (Deut. XXI, 1-9). Ordinarily it is through the angel of death that the souls of men pass out of their bodies, but with that man it was not so, but he that slew him made his soul depart from him before the time came for the angel of death to gather him in. Hence it is written: "And no expiation can be made for the land for the blood that is shed therein, but by the blood of him that shed it" (Num. xxxv, 33). Is it not enough for the world that Satan should be continually on the watch to lead men astray and to formulate accusations against them, that one must needs increase his fury by depriving him of what is his due? But the Holy One is merciful towards His children, and so provided the offering of a calf as reparation for the soul of which Satan was deprived and as a means of pacifying the world's accuser. Herein is involved a deep mystery. The offerings of the ox, the cow, the calf, the heifer have all a deep mystical significance, and therefore we make reparation to him in the way mentioned in the text. Hence the declaration, "Our hands have not shed this blood, etc." (Deut. XXI, 7)— they have not shed this blood, and we have not caused his death; and by this means the accuser is thereby kept at a distance. All this constitutes good counsel given by the Holy One to the world. Observe that the same applies to New Year Day and to the Day of Atonement. That is the time when the world is on trial and Satan brings his accusations. Hence it is needful for Israel to give a blast on the trumpet and to emit a sound which is a compound of fire, water, and air; that sound ascends to the place of the Throne of Judgement, where the Court of Justice is sitting, and impinges on it and ascends further. As soon as the sound arrives from beneath, the voice of Jacob is reinforced on high, and the Holy One, blessed be He, [114b] is stirred to mercy. For corresponding to the sound uniting fire, water, and air, which Israel emits here below, there goes forth a blast from on high. Through the two blasts, the one on high and the other below, the world is fortified and mercy prevails. The accuser then, who thought to prevail in judgement and to obtain sentence on the world, becomes confounded; his strength fails and he is unable to achieve anything. The Holy One then, sitting in judgement, joins mercy to justice, and so the world is judged by mercy, and not rigorously. Observe the verse: "Blow the horn at the new moon, at the time of its covering for our feast day" (Ps. LXXXI, 4). The word *ba-keseh* (at the covering) means the time when the moon is invisible. For at that time the evil serpent is in power and is able to do hurt to the world. But when mercy is aroused, the moon ascends and is removed from that place, and so the evil serpent is confounded, loses his power and is unable to approach there. Hence on New Year Day it is necessary to confound him, so that he should be like one awakening from sleep and still half-conscious. Again, on the Day of Atonement it is requisite to pacify and propitiate him by means of the scapegoat which is brought to him, whereby he is induced to undertake the defence of Israel. But on New Year Day he becomes confused, and is unable to do anything. He sees the stirring of mercy ascending from below, the awakening of mercy on high, and the moon between them, and he is thereby confounded, and remains bewildered and powerless, and so the Holy One dispenses His judgement to Israel in a spirit of mercy, and accords them as a time of grace those ten days between New Year Day and the Day of Atonement, for the acceptance of all those who repent of their sins and for forgiveness of their iniquities, by giving them a respite till the Day of Atonement. The Holy One had thus given Israel all these commandments to save them from falling into the wrong hands and from being judged with rigour, so that they should all come out innocent on earth, [115a] through His mercy which is like the mercy of a father towards his children. All depends on actions and words, as we have explained.'

AND THE LORD VISITED SARAH AS HE HAD SAID: thus fulfilling the words, "I will certainly return unto thee when the season cometh round; and, lo, Sarah thy wife shall have a son" (Gen. XVIII, 10). A tradition teaches us that the term *paqad* (visited) is written in connection with women, and the term *zakhar* (remembered) in connection with men. Hence here it is written "And the Lord *visited* Sarah as he had said." The expression "as he had said" proves that the words "and he said", in the passage in Gen. XVIII, 10, refer to the Lord Himself, and no messenger. AND THE LORD DID UNTO SARAH AS HE HAD SPOKEN. Since the text has already said, "and the Lord visited Sarah", what need is there to add, "and he did unto Sarah"? The reason is this. It is one of our doctrines that the "fruit of the handiwork" of the Almighty springs from that river which flows forth from Eden. This "fruit of God's handiwork" is the souls of the righteous, and it is also the allotment (*mazzal*)[1] from which flow all good fortune and rains of blessing, as it is written, "to water the garden" (Gen. II, 10), that is, to cause the stream to flow from on high and irrigate and fertilise the world below. For mankind depends on that allotment and not on any other source. Hence, besides "visiting" Sarah, God also "did" something in the region on high, since everything depends on that. Hence the two stages of "visiting" and "doing", with the name of "the Lord" mentioned with each, the whole forming one process.'

R. Eleazar discoursed on the verse: *Lo, children are a*

---

[1] Lit. 'luck'; also 'flowing'.

heritage of the Lord, the fruit of the womb is a reward (Ps. CXXVII, 3). 'The meaning', he said, 'is that children confer on a man the heritage of the Lord, by which he attaches himself to the Lord to all time. For the man who is privileged to have children in this world will through them be worthy to enter "behind the partition" in the world to come; and by leaving a son in this world a man's merits are enhanced in the world to come, and through him he enters into the "heritage of the Lord". What is the "heritage of the Lord"? It is the "land of the living", a name by which the Land of Israel is called, as is proved from the words of King David, "for they have driven me out this day that I should not cleave unto the heritage of the Lord, saying, Go serve other gods" (1 Sam. XXVI, 19). Hence: "Lo, children are a heritage of the Lord", [115b] that is, it is children who make a man worthy of the heritage of the Lord. "The fruit of the womb is a reward" refers to reward in the next world, for by the fruit of the womb a man merits the world to come. Again, "a heritage of the Lord are children", that is, the heritage of the fruit of the works of the Holy One is from above, from the tree of life, for it is from thence that a man is blessed with children, as we read, "From me is thy fruit found" (Hos. XIV, 9). "Happy is the man that hath his quiver full of them; they shall not be put to shame, etc." (Ps. CXXVII, 5): happy in this world and happy in the world to come. "They will not be put to shame when they speak with their enemies in the gate": who are the "enemies in the gate"? They are the accusing angels. For when a man departs from this world, there are numbers of such accusing angels who try to block his way and prevent him from reaching his place. But he passes through "the gate" because he has left hostages in this world by virtue of whom he is found worthy of a place in the next world. Thus, "they shall not be put to shame when they speak with their enemies in the gate".'

R. Judah and R. Jose were walking on the road. Said R. Judah to R. Jose: 'Open thy lips and say something in exposition of the Torah, since the Shekinah is accompanying thee. For whenever the Torah is studied earnestly, the Shekinah comes and joins, and all the more so on the road,

where the Shekinah comes in anticipation, preceding those who cleave to their faith in the Holy One, blessed be He.'
R. Jose then began to discourse on the verse: *Thy wife shall be as a fruitful vine in the innermost parts of thy house; thy children like olive plants, round about thy table* (Ps. CXXVIII, 3). 'So long', he said, 'as a woman abides in the innermost parts of the house, she remains chaste and is fit to bear worthy children. She is like a vine, for just as a vine is never grafted with another kind but only with its own, so the worthy woman does not bear offspring from a strange man but only from her husband. Her reward is [116a] to have "children like olive plants, round about thy table". Just as the leaves of olive trees do not fall off but remain firmly attached to the twigs all the year round, so shall "thy children be like olive plants, round about thy table." The text proceeds: "Behold, surely thus shall the man be blessed that feareth the Lord" (*Ibid.* 4). The term "surely" seems to be superfluous. It indicates, however, a further lesson, viz. that so long as the Shekinah stayed modestly in her own place, if one may be permitted the expression, then it could be said of her, "thy children like olive plants, round about thy table", referring to Israel during the time that they dwelt in the Land of Israel; "round about thy table" they were, eating and drinking and bringing offerings and feasting before the Holy One, blessed be He: both all those on high and all those below were blessed through them. But when the Shekinah departed, Israel were driven from the table of their father, and dispersed among the nations, and they continually cried out without anyone taking heed, excepting the Holy One, as it is written: "And yet for all that, when they are in the land of their enemies, etc." (Lev. XXVI, 44). We have seen how many saintly and holy men have perished through tyrannical decrees, all as part of Israel's punishment for not keeping the Law when they were in the Holy Land. It is written, "Because thou didst not serve the Lord thy God with joyfulness, and with gladness of heart, by reason of the abundance of all things" (Deut. XXVIII, 47). The words "because thou didst not serve with joyfulness" refer to the priests, who offered sacrifices and holocausts "with joyfulness"; "and

with gladness of heart" alludes to the Levites; "by reason of the abundance of all things" is an allusion to the lay Israelites whose position was in the middle, and who received blessings from all sides. Again it is written, "Thou hast multiplied the nation, thou hast made great their joy" (Is. IX, 2), in allusion to the priests; "they joy before thee according to the joy in harvest" (*Ibid.*) indicates the lay Israelites whom the Holy One blesses with a good harvest of the field, from all of which they give a tenth; "as men rejoice when they divide the spoil" (*Ibid.*) refers to the Levites, who take a tenth from the threshing floor. According to another explanation: "Thou hast multiplied the nation" indicates Israel, who have faith in the Holy One; "Thou hast made great his joy" alludes to the first and supernal grade, to which Abraham attached himself, this being great and filled with joy; "they joy before thee" [116b] at the time when they go up to attach themselves to Thee, "according to the joy in harvest", an allusion to the community of Israel, to which properly belongs the joy in harvest; "as men rejoice when they divide the spoil", a reference to the joy evinced by the rest of the lower powers and chariot-riders when they divide the spoil and fall upon their prey in the forefront of all.'

R. Judah discoursed on the verse: *It is a time to work for the Lord; they have made void thy law* (Ps. CXIX, 126). It has been laid down that the term '*eth* (time) is a designation of the community of Israel. Why is the community of Israel designated "time" ('*eth*) ? Because all things with her are regulated by times and periods, when to come near the Deity, when to receive light (from above), and when to commune, as we read, "But as for me, let my prayer be unto thee, O Lord, in an acceptable time" (Ps. LXIX, 14). Thus, "the community must be made unto the Lord", that is, it must be prepared and fitted to commune with God (so the word "made" is used in the verse "and David made himself a name" (II Sam. VIII, 13)), and this by means of those who labour in the study of the Torah. And why all this ? Because "they have made void thy law", for if "they had not made void thy law" there would never have been any estrangement between the Holy One and Israel.' R. Jose said: 'In this way is explained the verse: "I the Lord will in its time hasten it" (Is. LX, 22). The word *b'itah* (in its time) may be resolved into *b'eth hé* (in the time of the letter *Hé*), i.e. "when the time arrives for the *Hé* to rise up from the dust I will hasten it".' Said R. Jose further: 'Yet the community of Israel is to remain only one day in the dust and no more.' Said R. Judah: 'Tradition agrees with what you have said. But observe what we have learnt regarding this, namely, that when the community of Israel was exiled from its home, the letters of the Divine Name became, if one may say so, separated, the *Hé* flying apart from the *Vau*. We can thus understand the sentence, "I was dumb with silence" (Ps. XXXIX, 3), as through the separation of the *Vau* from the *Hé* there was no Voice, and thus Utterance was silenced. She therefore lies in the dust all the day of the *Hé*, that is, the whole of the fifth thousand (although they were already in exile before the beginning of the fifth thousand, which is symbolised by the *Hé*); and when the sixth thousand, which is symbolised [117a] by the *Vau*, begins, the *Vau* will resuscitate the *Hé* at six times ten (an allusion to the sixty souls), which means the *Vau* repeated ten times. The *Vau* will ascend to the *Yod* and redescend to the *Hé*. The *Vau* will be multiplied into the *Hé* ten times, making sixty, when it will raise the exiles from the dust. At every sixty years of the sixth thousand the *Hé* will mount a stage higher, acquiring greater strength. And after six hundred years of the sixth thousand there will be opened the gates of wisdom above and the fountains of wisdom below, and the world will make preparations to enter on the seventh thousand as man makes preparations on the sixth day of the week, when the sun is about to set. As a mnemonic to this we take the verse, "In the six hundredth year of Noah's life . . . all the fountains of the great deep were broken up" (Gen. VII, 11).' Said R. Jose to him: 'Your calculations lay down a much longer period than that arrived at by the companions, according to whom the exile of the community of Israel was only to last one day (i.e. a thousand years), as it says, "He hath made me desolate and faint all the day" (Lam. I, 13).' R. Judah said in reply: 'This is what I have learnt from my father concerning the mysteries of the letters of the Divine Name, and of the duration of the world as well as of the days of creation, all of which belongs to the same mystical doctrine. At that time the rainbow will appear in the cloud in radiant colours, like a woman that decks herself out for her husband, in fulfilment of the verse, "and I will look upon it, that I may remember the everlasting covenant" (Gen. IX, 16), a passage already explained elsewhere. "I will see it" with all its bright colours, and I will thus "remember the everlasting covenant". Who is the everlasting covenant ? It is the community of Israel. The *Vau* will join the *Hé*, and will resuscitate her from the dust. When the *Vau* shall move to join the *Hé*, heavenly signs will appear in the world, and the Reubenites will make war against all the world; and so the community of Israel will be raised from the dust, for the Holy One will remember her. In this way the Holy One will have dwelt with her in exile years to the number of *Vau* times *Yod*, that is, six times ten, after which she will be raised, and vengeance will be executed on the world, and the lowly will be exalted.' Said R. Jose to him: 'All you say is right, being [117b] mystically indicated by the letters, and we need not enter upon any other calculations regarding the end (*qets*). For in the book of the venerable R. Yeba we find the same calculation. The verse, "Then shall the land satisfy her Sabbaths" (Lev. XXVI, 34) is an allusion to the mystical implication of the *Vau*, as indicated in a subsequent verse, "And I will remember my covenant with Jacob"[1] (*Ibid.* 42), and then it says, "and I will remember the land" (*Ibid.*), indicating the community of Israel. The word "will satisfy" (*tirzeh*) signifies that the Holy One will be favourable to her. As for the "one day" of which the companions have spoken, it is assuredly all hidden with the Holy One, and it is all found in the mystery of the letters of the Divine Name; for R. Jose here has revealed the end of the exile by means of these letters.' Said R. Judah: 'Observe that also when Sarah was visited, it was the grade of the divine essence symbolised by the *Vau* that visited her, as it is written, "And (*Va*) the Lord visited Sarah", for all is

[1] The name Jacob is in this verse exceptionally spelt *plene*, i.e. with a *vau. v. infra*, p. 369.

contained in the mystery of the *Vau*, and through it all things are to be revealed.' Said R. Jose: 'We have still a long time to be in exile until the day arrives, but all depends on whether the people will repent of their sins, as appears from the passage, "I the Lord will hasten it in its time" (Is. LX, 22), i.e. if they will be worthy, "I will hasten it", and if not, then "in its time".' The two then proceeded on their way. Suddenly R. Jose said: 'It comes to my memory that in this place I was once sitting with my father and he said to me: "When you will reach the age of sixty years you are destined to find in this place a treasure of sublime wisdom." I have lived to reach that age, and I have not found the treasure, but I wonder if the words spoken by us just now are not the wisdom that he meant. He further said to me: "When the celestial flame reaches the spaces between your fingers, it will escape from you." I asked him: "How do you know this?" He replied: "I know it by the two birds that passed over your head."' At this point R. Jose left him and entered a cavern, [118a] at the farther end of which he found a book hidden in the cleft of a rock. He brought it out and caught sight of seventy-two tracings of letters which had been given to Adam the first man, and by means of which he knew all the wisdom of the supernal holy beings, and all those beings that abide behind the mill with turns behind the veil among the supernal ethereal essences, as well as all that is destined to happen in the world until the day when a cloud will arise on the side of the West and darken the world. R. Jose then called R. Judah and the two began to examine the book. No sooner had they studied two or three of the letters than they found themselves contemplating that supernal wisdom. But as soon as they began to go into the book more deeply and to discuss it, a fiery flame driven by a tempestuous wind struck their hands, and the book vanished from them. R. Jose wept, saying, 'Can it be, Heaven forefend, that we are tainted with some sin? Or are we unworthy to possess the knowledge contained therein?' When they came to R. Simeon they told him what had occurred. He said to them: 'Were you, perhaps, scrutinising those letters which dealt with the coming of the Messiah?' They answered: 'We cannot tell, as we have forgotten everything.' R. Simeon continued: 'The Holy One, blessed be He, does not desire that so much should be revealed to the world, but when the days of the Messiah will be near at hand, even children will discover the secrets of wisdom and thereby be able to calculate the millennium; at that time it will be revealed to all, as it is written, "For then will I turn to the peoples a pure language, etc." (Zeph. III, 9), the term *az* (then) referring to the time when the community of Israel will be raised from the dust and the Holy One will make her stand upright; then "will I turn to the peoples a pure language, that they may all call upon the Lord, to serve him with one consent" (*Ibid.*).'

Observe that although it is said of Abraham that he "journeyed still toward the South" (Gen. XII, 9), he did not attain to his rightful grade until Isaac was born. But as soon as Isaac was born, he attained this grade, through the close association and union [118b] of the two. For that reason he, and no other, called him Isaac, in order that water and fire should be merged together. Hence: AND ABRAHAM CALLED THE NAME OF HIS SON THAT WAS BORN UNTO HIM, WHOM SARAH BORE TO HIM, ISAAC: to wit, the son that was born to him as fire born from water.

AND SARAH SAW THE SON OF HAGAR THE EGYPTIAN, WHOM SHE HAD BORN UNTO ABRAHAM, MAKING SPORT. R. Hiya said: 'After recording the birth of Isaac, the Scripture never mentions Ishmael by name so long as he was still in the house of Abraham: dross cannot be mentioned in the presence of gold. Hence Ishmael is referred to here as "the son of Hagar the Egyptian", as it was not fitting that his name should be mentioned in the presence of Isaac.' Said R. Isaac: 'The words "and Sarah saw" imply that she looked at him disdainfully, as being the son not of Abraham but of Hagar the Egyptian, and, furthermore, only Sarah regarded him so, but not Abraham, as we read that THE THING WAS VERY GRIEVOUS IN ABRAHAM'S SIGHT ON ACCOUNT OF HIS SON—not the son of Hagar, but his son.' R. Simeon said: 'The Scripture really speaks in praise of Sarah. For what she saw was that he was indulging in idolatrous practices. Hence she said: Surely, this is not the son of Abraham, who follows in the footsteps of Abraham, but the son of Hagar the Egyptian, who is reverting to the type of his mother. Hence: AND SHE SAID UNTO ABRAHAM: CAST OUT THIS BONDWOMAN AND HER SON; FOR THE SON OF THIS BONDWOMAN SHALL NOT BE HEIR WITH MY SON, EVEN WITH ISAAC.' It cannot be supposed that Sarah was moved by jealousy of her or her son. For if so, the Holy One would not have supported her by saying, IN ALL THAT SARAH SAITH UNTO THEE, HEARKEN UNTO HER VOICE. The truth, therefore, is that she observed him worshipping idols, and performing the practices which his mother had taught him. Hence the words of Sarah, "For the son of this bondwoman shall not be heir", as much as to say: "I know that he will never enter the fold of the true faith and that he will have no portion with my son either in this world or in the world to come." Therefore God supported her, since He wished to keep the holy seed carefully separated, for that was the end for which He created the world, as Israel was already in His thought before the creation of the world. It was therefore that Abraham appeared in the world, so that the world could be sustained for his sake. Abraham and Isaac together upheld the world, yet they were not firmly established until Jacob came into the world. When Jacob appeared, both Abraham and Isaac became firmly established and the whole world with them. From Jacob the holy people gradually emerged into the world, and so the whole of existence became duly established according to the holy pattern. Hence God said, "In all that Sarah saith unto thee, hearken unto her voice; for in Isaac shall seed be called to thee", i.e. in Isaac and not in Ishmael.

The text proceeds: AND SHE DEPARTED AND STRAYED IN THE WILDERNESS OF BEERSHEBA. The term *vatetha'* (and she strayed) indicates idolatry, like the kindred term in the verse, "They are vanity, work of delusion (*tha'athuim*, lit. "goings astray") (Jer. x, 15). Thus it was only for the sake of Abraham that the Holy One did not abandon her or her son. Observe that on the previous occasion when she fled from Sarah, it was said to her: "The Lord hath heard thy affliction" (Gen. XVI, 11); but now since she went astray after idols, although she lifted up her voice and wept, yet it says, FOR GOD HATH HEARD THE VOICE OF THE LAD WHERE HE IS. The expression "where he is" we interpret to imply that he was still a minor in the eyes of the heavenly court. For whereas in the human court, here below, the age of liability is reached at thirteen years, in the heavenly court it is reached only at twenty years; before that age, even if one is guilty, he is not punishable. Hence the phrase "where he is". Said R. Eleazar: 'If that be so, why should anyone be punished by dying before twenty? Before thirteen, it is true, he may die for the sins of his father, but why after thirteen?' R. Hiya replied: 'The Holy One has mercy on such a one so that he should die whilst still innocent, and obtain a reward in the other world, instead of dying in guilt and receiving punishment in that world.' R. Eleazar rejoined: 'But if he is already guilty before he reaches the age of [119a] twenty years, what are we to say? Since he has died (before reaching the age of punishment), how will he be punished?' R. Simeon replied: 'It is of such that it is written, "But there is that is swept away without judgement" (Prov. XIII, 23). For when chastisement descends on the world, then such a one is struck down by the destroying angel without express sentence pronounced either by the heavenly or the earthly tribunal, while Providence is not keeping watch over him. It is also written of such a one: "His own iniquities shall ensnare (*eth*) the wicked, and he shall be holden with the cords of his sin" (*Ibid.* v. 22). The accusative particle *eth* amplifies the term "the wicked" so as to make it include one who has not yet come of legal age; of him, then, it is said, "His own iniquities shall ensnare the wicked", but not the heavenly tribunal, "and he shall be holden with the cords of his sin", but not by the earthly tribunal. Hence it says here: "For God hath heard the voice of the lad where he is."'

R. Simeon discoursed on the verse: *And I will remember my covenant with Jacob, etc.* (Lev. XXVI, 42). 'The name Jacob', he said, 'is here written in full, with the letter *vau*. For what reason? In the first place as an allusion to the grade of Wisdom, the realm where Jacob dwells. But the chief reason is because the passage speaks of the exile of Israel, intimating that the redemption of Israel will come about through the mystic force of the letter *vau*, namely, in the sixth millennium, and, more precisely, after six seconds and a half a time. When the sixtieth year shall have passed over the threshold of the sixth millennium, the God of heaven will visit the daughter of Jacob with a preliminary remembrance (*p'qidah*). Another six and a half years will then elapse, and there will be a full remembrance of her; then another six years, making together seventy-two years and a half. In the year sixty-six the Messiah will appear in the land of Galilee. A star in the east will swallow seven stars in the north, and a flame of black fire will hang in the heaven for sixty days, and there shall be wars towards the north in which two kings shall perish. Then all the nations shall combine together against the daughter of Jacob in order to drive her from the world. It is of that time that it is written: "And it is a time of trouble unto Jacob, but out of it he shall be saved" (Jer. xxx, 7). At that time all the souls in *Guph* will have been used up, and will need to be re-created. As a mnemonic of this we may use the verse: "All the souls of the house of Jacob that came into Egypt ... all the souls were threescore and six" (Gen. XLVI, 26). In the year seventy-three all the kings of the world will assemble in the great city of Rome, and the Holy One will shower on them fire and hail and meteoric stones until they are all destroyed, with the exception of those who will not yet have arrived there. These will commence anew to make other wars. From that time the Messiah will begin to declare himself, and round him there will be gathered many nations and many hosts from the uttermost ends of the earth. And all the children of Israel will assemble in their various places until the completion of the century. The *Vau* will then join the *Hé*, and then "they shall bring all your brethren out of all the nations for an offering unto the Lord" (Is. LXVI, 20). The children of Ishmael will at the same time rouse all the peoples of the world to come up to war against Jerusalem, as it is written, "For I will gather all nations against Jerusalem to battle, etc." (Zech. XIV, 2), also, "The kings of the earth stand up, and the rulers take counsel together, against the Lord, and against his anointed" (Ps. II, 2); and further, "He that sitteth in heaven laugheth, the Lord hath them in derision" (*Ibid.* II, 4). Then the lesser *Vau* will rouse itself to unite (with the *Hé*) and renew the souls that had become old, so as to rejuvenate the world, as it is written, "May the glory of the Lord endure for ever, let the Lord rejoice in his works" (Ps. CIV, 31). The first part of this verse signifies that God's glory will attach itself to the world, and the latter half that He will cause souls to descend into the world and make them into new beings, so as to join the world into one. Happy are those who will be left alive at the end of the sixth millennium to enter on the Sabbath. For that is the day set apart by the Holy One on which to effect the union of souls and to cull new souls to join those that are still on earth, as it is written, "And it shall come to pass, that he that is left in Zion, and he that remaineth in Jerusalem, shall be called holy, even every one that is written unto life in Jerusalem" (Is. IV, 3).'

AND IT CAME TO PASS AFTER THESE THINGS, THAT GOD DID PROVE ABRAHAM, AND SAID UNTO HIM: ABRAHAM, AND HE SAID: HERE AM I. R. Judah discoursed on the verse: *Thou art my King, O God* (Ps. XLIV, 5). 'This allocution', he said, 'signifies the complete union of all grades. "Command the salvation of Jacob" (*Ibid.*), to wit, the emissaries who perform God's behests [119b] in the world, that they may be all from the side of mercy and not from the side of stern justice; since there are messengers from the side of mercy and others from the side of justice. Those belonging to the side of mercy never execute a mission of punishment in the world. It may be asked, how can we reconcile with this the case of the angel who appeared to Balaam, and of whom we have been taught that he was first a messenger of mercy and then was changed into one of severity. In reality the character of his mission was not changed, as he was throughout a messenger of mercy on behalf of Israel, to protect them and plead for them, but this meant punishment to Balaam. For this is the way of the Holy One, that when He confers kindness on one, the same kindness may result in punishment for another. Similarly here, the same messenger who was one of mercy for Israel turned into one of punishment for Balaam. Hence David prayed, "Command the salvation of Jacob", as much as to say: "When messengers are sent into the world, order such as are of the side of mercy."' R. Abba said: 'The words "command the salvation of Jacob" allude to those in exile, for whose redemption David prayed. Further, Jacob was the crown of the patriarchs, but if not for Isaac he would not have appeared in the world; hence the request "command the salvation of Jacob" refers primarily to Isaac, since the saving of his life was the salvation of Jacob.'

AND IT CAME TO PASS. Said R. Simeon: 'We have been taught that the expression "and it came to pass in the days" indicates that some trouble is about to be narrated, while the expression "and it came to pass", even without the addition of "in the days", presages a certain tinge of distress. AFTER THESE WORDS: this means, after the lowest grade of all the supernal grades, which is called "words" (*d'barim*), as in the passage, "I am not a man of words" (Ex. IV, 10). THAT ELOHIM PROVED ABRAHAM, i.e. the evil tempter came to accuse him before the Holy One, blessed be He. The text here is rather surprising, for instead of Abraham we should have expected here to read, "God proved Isaac", seeing that he was already thirty-seven years of age, and no longer under his father's jurisdiction. He could thus easily have refused without rendering his father liable to punishment. The truth, however, is that it was requisite, in order that Abraham might attain to perfection, that he should be invested with the attribute of rigour, which he had not exhibited up to that time. Now, however, water was united with fire and fire with water, and it was possible for him to dispense rigorous justice and make it part of his character. The evil tempter thus came to accuse Abraham on the ground that he could not be said to have perfected himself until he should have exercised rigour against Isaac. But observe that although only Abraham is explicitly mentioned as being proved, Isaac, nevertheless, was also included in the trial, as is implied by the amplifying particle *eth* before "Abraham", which indicates Isaac. For Isaac was at that time in the grade of the lower *Geburah* (Force, Rigour); but after he had been bound and made ready to undergo the rigorous trial at the hand of Abraham, he was equipped in his own place together with Abraham, and so fire and water were joined and rose to a higher grade, and the discord was appeased. For who ever saw a father's heart turn from compassion to cruelty? But the object here was to assuage the discord between fire and water so that they should be settled in their places until Jacob appeared, when all was put in order, and the triad of the patriarchs was completed, and higher and lower creations were firmly established.

AND HE SAID, TAKE NOW THY SON. The word "take" does not mean "take forcibly", since Abraham was too old for that, but it has the same sense as in "take Aaron and Eleazar his son" (Num. XX, 25), signifying that he should use persuasion and gently lead him on to do the will of God. THY SON, THINE ONLY SON, WHOM THOU LOVEST. This [120a] has been explained elsewhere. AND GET THEE INTO THE LAND OF MORIAH: the meaning is similar to that of the passage, "I will get me to the mountain of myrrh" (S. S. IV, 6), i.e. to become invigorated in the appropriate place.

ON THE THIRD DAY ABRAHAM LIFTED UP HIS EYES, AND SAW THE PLACE AFAR OFF. As we have already been told that Abraham went to the place, all this seems superfluous. But the truth is that "the third day" means the third generation, i.e. Jacob, and the words "he saw the place from afar" are parallel to the expression "from afar the Lord appeared unto me" (Jer. XXXI, 3). Or again, "the place" alludes to Jacob, of whom it is written, "and he took one of the stones of the place" (Gen. XXVIII, 11). For Abraham scrutinised the "third day", which is the third grade, and he beheld Jacob, who was destined to descend from him. "Afar off", to wit, at some distant time, and not soon. R. Eleazar said to R. Judah: 'What credit is herein ascribed to Abraham, if whilst about to bind Isaac he saw that Jacob was destined to descend from him?' R. Judah replied: 'Indeed Abraham did see Jacob, since even before that Abraham was endowed with the higher Wisdom; and now he scrutinised the third day, which is the third grade, in order to make sure. And indeed he did see him, but now only "from afar", for the reason that he was going to bind Isaac, and he did not wish to question the ways of the Holy One. "Afar off", that is, he saw him through a "dim glass" only, and therefore only partially; for if the "clear glass" had been resting upon the "dim glass", Abraham would have seen him properly. The "clear glass" did not function on this occasion, because this is the grade of Jacob, who, not yet being born, had not reached that grade; and also in order that Abraham's reward might be all the greater. AND THEY CAME TO THE PLACE WHICH GOD HAD TOLD HIM OF, ETC. Here it is intimated that although Abraham had some vision of Jacob, yet he said to himself, "Assuredly the Holy One knows another way which will serve." Forthwith, therefore, ABRAHAM BUILT THE ALTAR THERE. Before this it is written: AND ISAAC SPOKE UNTO ABRAHAM HIS FATHER, AND SAID, MY FATHER. As explained elsewhere, the reason why Abraham did not respond to him immediately was because the normal compassion of a father towards a son left him, and hence he simply said: 'Here I am, my son", implying that the quality of mercy in him had been transmuted into rigour. AND ABRAHAM SAID. It is not written: "and his father said", which shows again that he was regarding him not as his father but as his adversary. GOD WILL PROVIDE FOR HIMSELF THE LAMB FOR A BURNT OFFERING, MY SON. He should have said: "provide for us", but what he meant was, "God will provide for Himself when necessary, but for the present it is going to be my son and nothing else." Forthwith, AND THEY WENT BOTH OF THEM TOGETHER. R. Simeon discoursed here on the verse: *Behold, angels cry abroad, the angels of peace weep bitterly* (Is. XXXIII, 7). 'These angels', he said, 'are superior angels who "cried abroad" because they no longer knew what to make of God's promise to Abraham at the time when "He brought him forth abroad"

(Gen. XV, 5). The "angels of peace" are those other angels who were destined to go forth to meet Jacob, for whose sake the Holy One promised them peace, as it is written, "And Jacob went on his way, and the angels of God met him" (*Ibid.* XXXII, 2), and these are called "angels of peace". All these wept when they saw Abraham binding Isaac, the upper and the lower beings trembled and shook, and all on account of Isaac.

AND THE ANGEL OF THE LORD CALLED UNTO HIM . . . ABRAHAM, ABRAHAM. There is in the text a disjunctive mark between the two Abrahams, to show that the latter was not like the former; the latter [120b] was the perfected Abraham, while the former was still incomplete. Similarly, in the passage where the name Samuel is repeated with a disjunctive line between (I Sam. III, 10), the second is the perfected Samuel, whilst the first was not yet so. The second Samuel was a prophet, but not the first. But when we come to "Moses, Moses" (Ex. III, 4), we do not find any pausal sign between, for the reason that from the day Moses was born the Shekinah never departed from him. R. Hiya said that the angel repeated Abraham's name in order to animate him with a new spirit, and spur him to a new activity with a new heart. R. Judah said: 'Isaac purified himself and in intention offered himself up to God, was at that moment etherealised and, as it were, he ascended to the throne of God like the odour of the incense of spices which the priests offered before Him twice a day; and so the sacrifice was complete. For Abraham felt distressed when the angel said to him, "Lay not thy hand upon the lad", thinking that his offering was not complete and that his labour, his preparations and the building of the altar had all been in vain. Straightway, however, ABRAHAM LIFTED UP HIS EYES AND LOOKED AND BEHELD BEHIND HIM A RAM, ETC. We have been taught that that ram was created at twilight (on the sixth day of Creation), and he was of the first year, as it is written, "one he-lamb of the first year" (Num. VII, 63), thus being according to requirement. But if so, how could he have been created at twilight ? The truth is that from that time it was pre-ordained that that ram should be at hand at the moment when Abraham should require it. The same applies to all those things said to have come into being "at twilight", which in reality means that they were then predestined to appear at the requisite moment.

R. Judah further discoursed on the verse: *In all their affliction he was afflicted, and the angel of his presence saved them* (Is. LXIII, 9). He said: 'This is the translation of the *k'ri*, but according to the *k'thib* we should translate, "He was not afflicted." The lesson to be derived from this variation is that Israel's affliction reaches the Holy One even in the place above which is beyond affliction or perturbation. "And the angel of his presence saved them." If He is together with them in their affliction, how can it be said that He saves them? Observe, however, that it is not written, "He saves them", but "he saved them", that is, He determined in advance to partake in their sufferings. For whenever Israel is in exile the Shekinah accompanies them, as it is written, "Then the Lord thy God will return (*v'-shab*) with thy captivity" (Deut. XXX, 3). According to another explanation, "The angel of his presence" signifies the Shekinah, which accompanies them in exile. Hence in the Scripture the words "and I have remembered my covenant" (Ex. VI, 5) are immediately followed by "and now, behold, the cry of the children of Israel is come unto me; moreover, I have seen" (Ex. III, 9). It is also written, "And God remembered his covenant" (*Ibid.* II, 24), referring to the Shekinah, "with Abraham" (*Ibid.*), symbolic of South-west, "with Isaac" (*Ibid.*), symbolic of North-west, "and with Jacob" (*Ibid.*), symbolising the complete and perfect union. The Holy One, blessed be He, will one day send forth a voice to proclaim to the world the words, "For he said, Surely, they are my people, children that will not deal falsely; so he was their saviour" (Is. LXIII, 8). Blessed be the Lord for evermore, Amen and Amen.'

APPENDICES AND GLOSSARY

APPENDIX I

ON THE ZOHARIC EXPOSITION OF THE FIRST CHAPTER OF GENESIS

From page 15a onwards the *Zohar* consists mainly of a verse-by-verse exposition of the Pentateuch of the type known in Hebrew literature as *Midrash*. The discursive style of the work, and the amount of extraneous matter which has been intercalated in the original text, render this fact liable to be overlooked; and it has therefore been one of the objects of the translation to keep it clearly before the reader's eye.

The Zoharic expositions of the Scripture are frequently, if not usually, difficult to follow, on account partly of their far-fetched character, partly of their technical language, partly of the abrupt and even uncouth manner in which they are expressed. The point which the *Zohar* desires to make is often highly elusive, and not to be grasped without close and attentive scrutiny. Particularly can we apply this remark to the expositions of the first chapter of Genesis contained in pages 15a–22a and 29a–31a of the original text. On these passages there rests a special and exceptional obscurity which, it is to be feared, the translation has done little to dispel. It seems, therefore, advisable to add some observations setting forth the views by which the translators have sought to guide themselves through the intricacies of these pages, and which have determined their version of many obscure passages. An endeavour to understand these pages is all the more necessary as we may surmise *a priori* that they contain some of the most important teaching of the *Zohar;* and we do indeed find on examination that they are capable of yielding light on two of the most fundamental tenets of the *Zohar*—the distinction of the divine grades and the potency of the sacred Name—and so of providing the key to the whole of its esoteric doctrine.

1. One of the most characteristic ideas of the *Zohar* is that God, while essentially one, is yet found in various grades or

degrees. These 'grades' turn out on examination to be degrees of creative power, arranged in descending or ascending order according to the sphere in which each one functions and the stage of development which it postulates in the created universe, and which thus constitutes, so to speak, its 'opposite number'. Thus the highest grade corresponds to sheer nothingness, and the lowest grade to the conscious soul of man (the *neshamah*). The creative power in itself is conceived as 'thought', which in the process of creation becomes 'light' or 'illumination'. The primal light is utterly beyond human (or even angelic) comprehension. But as the grades descend, the 'lights' (which form, as it were, a vestment to one another) swim into human ken, until between the lowest grade and the conscious soul of man a close communion is established.

The main purpose of the Zoharic exposition of the first chapter of Genesis, in so far as it is contained in the pages mentioned, seems to be to derive this doctrine from (or read it into) the text of the Scripture. The way in which the Scripture is made to yield the desired meaning is more or less as follows.

The first grade—the 'Most Mysterious and Recondite'—indistinguishable from the *En-Sof* (limitless, uncharacterisable), and corresponding to absolute nothingness in the work of creation—is not directly mentioned in the Scripture, unless it is alluded to by the letter *beth* (=in) of the word *bereshith*, implying that it went, so to speak, into itself, and so made a start. This start consists in a 'flash' (*zohar*), which thus releases the creative powers of the 'limitless'.

From this 'inwardness" resulted a point or focus capable of infinite development and expansion; this is called in the Scripture *Reshith* (beginning), and it is identified by the *Zohar* with *Ḥokmah* (Wisdom), the architect of the creation. This is the second grade.

The next word, 'created', according to the *Zohar*, denotes in this place the expansion of *Reshith*, which produced a 'palace' or 'house' containing in itself the germ of creation. This place is called in the Scripture *Elohim*, and it constitutes the third grade, the artificer of the creation. By the

Zohar it is called more specifically *Elohim Hayyim* (living God), the word *Elohim* being a generic name for all the grades. Its creative powers or faculties are pictured as 'letters' or 'seed', and are divided into an active and a passive principle. The active principle is called in the Scripture 'heaven', and is identified by the *Zohar* with the 'Voice'. The passive principle is called in the Scripture 'earth', and in v. 2 it is identified with the primordial elements of the terrestrial, the celestial, and the spiritual worlds (*v.* page 39*b*).

Up to this point there has been no clear differentiation between creator and created: the creation has not yet emerged from the realm of potentiality. From this point, however, the two are distinguished, the creator using and the created obeying the Voice. This is indicated in the Scriptural words, 'And God said'. The Voice henceforth issues in a series of *maamaroth* (creative utterances) which shape the material universe, or, in the language of the *Zohar*, 'imprint and inscribe letters'. With the new developments of the creation there issue new grades of the Godhead, which are called by the Scripture 'days' (*v.* page 39*b*).

The first *maamar*, according to the *Zohar*, produced light in three grades, one called light, the second firmament, and the third darkness. The first seems to be regarded as the light of mind, the second as that of light proper, and the third as that of fire. The first is called by the *Zohar* right, the second centre, and the third left. The first vanished as soon as it appeared, so that the second became the right. This is apparently derived from the verse: 'And God saw the light (i.e. the centre) that it was good, and God divided between the light (i.e. the right) and the darkness.' The centre was thereupon given continued existence in a category of time called day, and the darkness in a category of time called night. To produce these is the function of the next grade, called in the Scripture 'one day', and by the *Zohar* Right, or sometimes *Ḥesed* (Kindness).

In some way not specified in the *Zohar*, the 'light' and the 'darkness' of the first day became 'upper waters' containing, in solution as it were, 'lower waters'. The second *maamar* created an instrument for separating or liberating the lower waters from the upper. This instrument is called 'firmament' or 'expansion' (a different firmament from that mentioned in connection with the first day). The upper waters are characterised after separation as 'male', and the lower as 'female'. To effect this separation is the function of the next grade, called in Scripture 'third day', and by the *Zohar* Left or *Geburah* (Force).

The next *maamar* gave a certain flow or direction to the upper and lower waters, so that they should meet in ' one place' in a kind of sexual union, the result of which is to enable the 'earth' or 'dry land' to appear. This means that, as a result of the meeting of the upper and lower waters, the existence of the earth is rendered possible. To confirm this possibility a new *maamar* produced the 'Throne of Glory' with its attendant angels, figuratively referred to in the Scripture as 'the earth putting forth verdure and fruit trees' (pages 18a, 19b). To effect the union between the waters and to guide the 'Throne of Glory' is the function of the grade called in the Scripture 'third day', and by the *Zohar* Ḥé 'Olmin (Life of Worlds).

The next *maamar* produced a 'membrane for the brain' in the shape of a lower firmament containing heavenly luminaries which reflected the upper light, and served as a kind of screen to the 'Throne of Glory'. These luminaries are, properly speaking, not those which are visible to the human eye, but sentient beings which stand to these in the same relation as the human soul to the body. The chief of them are the sun and the moon, which were originally equal in status. They are charged 'to give light upon the earth', i.e. to determine the forms and characters of all beings on the earth. To procure for these luminaries their light and energy is the function of the grade called in Scripture 'fourth day'.

Having pursued the development of the grades up to this point, the *Zohar*, on page 22a, goes off on to quite a different tack, nor does it anywhere complete the exposition of the first chapter of Genesis on these lines. In later passages, however, we find frequent references to a grade called *Zaddik Yesod 'Olam* (the Righteous One, the Foundation of the World), which upholds God's covenant with the earth and procures sustenance for the living beings upon it. As it is also called 'ninth', we may without hesitation identify it with the 'sixth day' of the Scripture.

On page 29a the *Zohar* reverts to the beginning of the first chapter in order to define the position of what it calls the 'Female'. If this part of the *Zohar* is to be brought into harmony with the preceding part, then this 'Female' can only be the tenth grade, corresponding to the 'seventh day' in the Biblical account. The function of the 'Female', according to the *Zohar*, is to reproduce in a new medium the work of the original creative force. This medium is called 'the lower heaven and earth', and the work itself 'the lower world'. What exactly is meant by these terms is not specified, but we may surmise that in reality the medium of the 'Female' is the human consciousness, and the 'lower world' stands to the 'upper world' in this connection in the relation of phenomenon to noumenon; or, in Kantian language, that the 'upper world' is the *Ding an sich* and the 'lower world' the human idea of it.

II. The development of the grades, according to the *Zohar*, corresponds not only to the development of the created universe, but also to the emergence of a certain name, which is their unifying element. It is a postulate of the *Zohar* that the Biblical name *YHVH*—the so-called tetragrammaton—has an intimate, if unspecified, connection with the primordial Thought. It is the chosen instrument for rendering the Thought intelligible or realisable to the human mind. It is regarded as having been 'in' the Thought from the first, and its emergence into external or objective existence is stated to have been one of the purposes of the creation (page 29a). According to the *Zohar*, it emerged in various stages, each of which is symbolised by one or more of its constituent letters and is associated with the emergence of one or other of the grades. Thus with the grade *Reshith* emerged the letter *Yod;* with the next grade, *Elohim Hayyim*, the letter *Hé*, called the first or upper *Hé;* with the heavens, the letter *Vau;* with the earth, the second, or lower *Hé;* with the first day the combination of the letters *Yod, Hé;* with the second day, the combination of the letters *Vau, Hé;* while with the third day all the four letters were combined. The resultant Name is the absolute One or unit of being, representing on the one side the first integration of the Thought, and on the other the ultimate discoverable cause of existence (v. page 18b).

The above explanation, while leaving much obscure, will perhaps suffice to give a general idea of what the *Zohar* has in mind in this exposition of the first chapter of Genesis, to bring the whole, as it were, into focus, and exhibit the purpose which runs through it. It remains to complete the picture of the grades by bringing them into connection with the *Sefiroth* of the Cabbalah and with the names of the Deity used in the Scripture.

It is worthy of note that the *Zohar* rarely uses either the term *Sefirah* or the names of the *Sefiroth* current in the Cabbalistic literature. Where these names do occur, it is usually in passages which on other grounds may be suspected of belonging properly not to the *Zohar* but to one or other of the allied works (e.g. page 21b). Nevertheless, there is an exact correspondence between the Zoharic grades and the Cabbalistic *Sefiroth*, and they could be interchanged with one another (as indeed they are by most of the Zoharic commentators) without causing any confusion. Similarly there is, according to the *Zohar*, a correspondence between the designations of the grades found in the first chapter of Genesis and the names of the Deity scattered throughout the Scripture. This fourfold correspondence may be conveniently exhibited in the form of a table giving (*a*) the designation of each grade in the first chapter of Genesis; (*b*) the special Zoharic names of each grade; (*c*) the corresponding name of the Deity in the Scripture; (*d*) the corresponding *Sefirah*.

M. S.

APPENDIX I

TABLE SHOWING THE CORRESPONDENCE OF THE GRADES WITH THE SEFIROTH, ETC.

Designation in Genesis I	Zoharic Appellatives	Names of Deity	Sefiroth
B' (In)	Most Mysterious and Recondite; King	Ehyeh	Kether (Crown)
Reshith (Beginning)	First Point; Wisdom; Father	Asher (or Asher Ehyeh)	Hokmah (Wisdom)
Elohim (God) (Heaven and Earth)	Palace; Elohim Hayyim; Mother	YHVH	Binah (Understanding)
One Day	Right; Kindness	El Gadol	Hesed (Kindness)
Second Day	Left; Force	Elohim	Geburah (Force)
Third Day	Life of Worlds; Central Column	Jehovah	Tifereth (Beauty)
Fourth Day		Zebaoth (?)	Nezah (Victory)
Fifth Day		Shaddai (?)	Hod (Majesty)
Sixth Day	Righteous One, Foundation of the World	El (?)	Yesod (Foundation)
Seventh Day	Female	Adonay	Malkuth (Kingship)

APPENDIX II

HEBREW ALPHABET

Sign	Name	Transliteration	Numerical Value
א	Aleph	ʼ	1
ב	Beth	B	2
ג	Gimel	G	3
ד	Daleth	D	4
ה	Hé	H	5
ו	Vau	V	6
ז	Zayin	Z	7
ח	Heth	Ḥ	8
ט	Teth	T	9
י	Yod	Y	10
כ	Kaph	K	20
ל	Lamed	L	30
מ	Mim	M	40
נ	Nun	N	50
ס	Samekh	S	60
ע	Ayin	ʻ	70
פ	Pé	P	80
צ	Tzaddi	Ẓ	90
ק	Kuf	Q	100
ר	Resh	R	200
ש	Shin	Sh	300
ת	Tau	Th	400

GLOSSARY

HEBREW AND TECHNICAL TERMS IN VOL. I

ADAM (lit. man). The ten *Sefiroth* represented as a man, e.g. *Kether* as the centre of the brain, *Hokmah* as the right side, *Hesed* as the right arm, etc.

BEASTS OF THE FIELD. The higher angels.

CENTRAL COLUMN. The connecting-link between the Right and the Left, the source of day.

CHIEFTAINS. The celestial chiefs and guardians attached to the various nations of the earth.

COLOURS. The divine attributes, mercy, rigour, etc.

CROWNS. Proper names of the Deity formed by combinations of letters.

CURTAIN. The partition between the divine and other intelligences.

DALETH (lit. poor). The fourth letter of the Hebrew alphabet, symbolising the earth without the Shekinah.

EARTH. The passive principle of the third grade, the original material of Creation.

ELOHIM (lit. Power). The generic name for all the grades; applied specially to *Geburah*.

EN-SOF (lit. without limit). That of which nothing can be predicated and which yet must be postulated.

ETH (sign of accusative case). An indication that something has to be understood in addition to what is expressed; a name of the Shekinah.

FATHER. The Zoharic name for the second grade; the 'begetter' of the Creation.

FEMALE. The last of the grades (*v.* Appendix, p. 383).

FIRMAMENT. A reservoir of light or illumination.

FORM. The type or ideal form of a thing.

FRINGES. *v.* Numbers XV, 37 *sqq.*

GAN-EDEN (lit. Garden of Delight). The abode of souls before union with and after departure from the body.

GEBURAH (lit. 'force', 'might'). The grade associated with darkness, the source of rigour and chastisement.

GEHINNOM. Hell, the fire of the primordial darkness when separated from light.

GRADE. The creative power of the Deity functioning in a particular sphere (*v.* Appendix).

GREEN. The symbol of the divine attribute of mercy (*raḥamim*).

GUPH (lit. body). The totality of bodies qualified to receive souls.

HABDALAH. The benediction recited on the departure of the Sabbath.

ḤAYAH (plu. ḤAYOTH, lit. 'animal', 'living'). One of the higher ranks of angels.

HÉ (FIRST or UPPER). The second letter of the sacred Name, symbolising the grade called 'Mother' (*q.v.*).

HÉ (SECOND or LOWER). The fourth letter of the sacred Name, symbolising the grade called 'earth' (*q.v.*).

HEAVENS. The totality of the letters (*q.v.*), constituting the active faculty of the third grade (*v.* Appendix).

ḤESED (lit. kindness). The grade associated with light, the source of blessing.

ḤEY OLMIN (lit. Life of Worlds). The grade emanating from the Central Column, the source of being.

ḤOKMAH (lit. Wisdom). The second grade, the architect of Creation.

LAD. A synonym for Metatron (*q.v.*).

LANDS OF THE LIVING. The Future World.

LEBANON (TREES or CEDARS OF). The Six Days of the Creation.

LEFT. (a) The third degree of light, called 'darkness', the source of evil and suffering. (b) A synonym for *Geburah* (q.v.).

LETTERS. The primordial forms of all beings, contained in the original heaven and earth (v. Appendix).

LIGHT. The source of illumination, mental and physical.

LILITH. Female night-demon.

LIMBS. The constituent letters of the sacred Name.

MAAMAR. A creative utterance, the embodiment of the Voice (q.v.).

METATRON. The chief of the Chieftains (q.v.), charged with the sustenance of mankind.

MIRROR. The prophetic faculty.

MOTHER. The Zoharic name for the third grade, containing the Creation *in posse*.

NESHAMAH. The highest or spiritual soul of man, emanating from the Tree of Life.

ORAL LAW. The Mishnah, the Rabbinic code.

ORLAH (lit. foreskin). The condition of being unreceptive of or inaccessible to the Shekinah (q.v.).

PRINCE OF THE WORLD. A synonym for Metatron (q.v.).

RED. The symbol of the divine attribute of severity (*din*).

RESIDUE (lit. 'squeezings', 'drippings'). What is left of the divine blessings after Israel have had their portion.

RIGHT. (a) The first or second degree of light, the source of day. (b) Another name for the grade of *Ḥesed* (q.v.).

SACRED LAMP. R. Simeon b. Yohai.

SEFIRAH. The Cabbalistic name for the divine grades (v. Introduction, p. xvii).

SERPENT. The principle of evil inherent in the primordial darkness.

SHEKINAH (lit. 'neighbourhood', 'abiding'). The Divine Presence, UPPER as associated with the higher grades, and LOWER as associated with the Female.

SHEOL. The under world.

SHOFAR (lit. trumpet). The instrument of the Voice (*q.v.*).

STREAM. The flow of existence produced by the union of the upper and the lower waters.

TETRAGRAMMATON. The sacred Name, composed of the four letters *Yod, Hé, Vau, Hé* (*v.* Appendix, p. 383).

TORAH. The Mosaic teaching (used especially of the esoteric doctrine of the grades); the archetype of the Creation.

TREE OF LIFE. The point from which the stream of existence commences to diverge into separate souls.

UNCOVERING. The drawing-back of the flesh after the operation of circumcision.

VAU. The third letter of the sacred Name, symbolising the original heavens.

VOICE. The instrument of Creation, identified with the original heavens, the totality of the letters.

WATERS. The primordial form of the created universe.

WHITE. The symbol of the divine attribute of kindness (*ḥesed*).

WISDOM. (*a*) *v.* ḤOKMAH. (*b*) Like Torah, the esoteric doctrine of the grades.

WORLD, LOWER. The created universe.

WORLD, UPPER. The grades of the Deity, regarded as separate creative forces.

YOD. The first letter of the sacred Name, symbolising the grade called *Reshith* (beginning), or *Ḥokmah* (wisdom).

ẒADDIK (lit. righteous one). The ninth grade, associated with the Covenant.

www.ingramcontent.com/pod-product-compliance
Lightning Source LLC
Chambersburg PA
CBHW020329240426
43665CB00043B/152